THE ESSENTIAL GUIDE TO PSYCHIC SELF DEFENCE

by

Tylluan Penry

THE WOLFENHOWLE PRESS

ISBN 978-1-912231-46-1

Cover Image from Shutterstock, No. 206101726
Cover Design by The Wolfenhowle Press ©
Pen and ink and pencil drawings by Tylluan Penry
Fonts licensed by Scriptorium Fonts

Published by: The Wolfenhowle Press,
Redcroft, Nile Road,
Trealaw, Tonypandy, CF40 2 UY

https://thewolfenhowlepress.com

Printed by: Book Printing UK, Remus House, Coltsfoot Drive,
Woodston, Peterborough PE2 9BF

Many thanks to **https://cyberfreakz.com/** *for their unstinting computer and website support.*

Other Books by Tylluan Penry

A Witch for All Seasons published by The Wolfenhowle Press, 2019

The Magical Properties of Plants and how to find them published by Capall Bann 2009, republished by The Wolfenhowle Press, in 2017

Seeking the Green, published by Capall Bann 2008. Republished by The Wolfenhowle Press, in 2017

Working with the Anglo-Saxon Runes published by The Wolfenhowle Press, 2016

An Introduction to Anglo-Saxon Magic and Witchcraft (Booklet in the Seeking the Green Pathways series) published by The Wolfenhowle Press, 2015

Knot Magic published by The Wolfenhowle Press, 2015

A Little Book of Inspirations, (Booklet in the Seeking the Green Pathways series) published by The Wolfenhowle Press, 2014

Magical Nature Walks, (Booklet in the Seeking the Green Pathways series) published by The Wolfenhowle Press, 2014

Sacred Shadows: Ice Age Spirituality, published by The Wolfenhowle Press, 2013

The Magical World of the Anglo-Saxons, published by The Wolfenhowle Press, 2012

Staying on the Old Track, published by The Wolfenhowle Press, 2012

Magic on the Breath, published by The Wolfenhowle Press, 2011

The Essential Guide to Psychic Self Defence, first published by Capall Bann, 2010

Also the essay, *'Eating With the Dead: Funeral Meal Practices'* in the anthology ***Memento Mori*** (ed. Kim Huggens) Avalonia Books 2012

Pagan-themed fiction for children/young adults, writing as **T. P. Penry** (available only as Kindle downloads) all published by The Wolfenhowle Press:

The Dolly Run
Stalker's Moon
Silent Night, Deadliest Night
The Dead Sleep Better
The Girl in the Tartan Skirt

Children's fiction as **Tylluan Penry** published in paperback by The Wolfenhowle Press:

Guardian of the Gateway 2018

A Note on References

I have tried to keep references to a minimum, but nevertheless they are sometimes necessary. Understanding them is simple: in this book they appear as numbered footnotes at the foot of the page, so that they don't interfere with the flow of the text, and we don't need to look for them at the end of the chapter or book.

A footnote such as: (Jones 2016:21) means the work was written by someone whose surname was Jones, it was published in 2016 and the page the information originally appeared on was page 21.

You can then look up the author and the work in the Bibliography at the end of this book.

Ibid means that the reference is exactly the same as its immediate predecessor; *ibid:*15 means that the work is the same as the previous reference although the page number is different.

About Tylluan Penry

Tylluan Penry is a solitary pagan witch, independent scholar and the author of numerous books and magazine articles dealing with many aspects of magic and folklore. She has also been a popular and regular speaker at various events including Witchfest International, The Artemis Gathering, Witchfest England, Witchfest Wales, together with talks for local groups and the Pagan Federation, and at independent, private events.

Her articles have appeared in a variety of publications including *Witchcraft & Wicca, Myddle Earth* and *The Faerie Times.* She is regularly consulted by the media for advice in accurately portraying witchcraft and paganism and has featured on BBC Radio 2 and various other stations.

Tylluan believes in trying to help other solitaries and those just beginning on their spiritual paths. To this end she set up The Wolfenhowle Press in 2011, with the intention of making beautiful, informative and inspiring books about paganism widely available and affordable.

On her website at www.thewolfenhowlepress.com you can access both of Tylluan's blogs with many useful and informative posts dating back ten years.

In 2014, she set up her own YouTube Channel, *Tylluan Penry at the Wolfenhowle Press* which you can find here:
https://www.youtube.com/channel/UC48MN8sa7_lFsBX9v2ZAeAg/featured

In keeping with the ethos of The Wolfenhowle Press, there is no advertising on these videos, just sensible advice and information, freely available to everyone.

Tylluan is married, has a large family, grandchildren, many pets, an overgrown garden and a gloriously ramshackle house where she lives and dreams with Mr Penry, her love of many lifetimes, in the South Wales Rhondda Valley.

Lammas 2019

CONTENTS

PREFACE

The purpose of this book is very simple:

- To identify psychic attacks and distinguish them from simple hauntings and other psychic phenomena such as vampires, werewolves and the Night Mare. If we know the type of attack, we then know what to expect and how best to deal with it.
- To identify the source of the attack.
- To learn techniques and strategies to deal with psychic attacks so we can defend ourselves
- To learn how to prevent psychic attacks

Bullies always pick their victims, and psychic bullies (of which there are many) are no different. However, most will leave us alone if they see we can defend ourselves and even the most persistent attacker soon learns to have a healthy respect for us.

This book is intended to give the reader the tools they need to become confident and capable of dealing with a wide range of psychic attacks. It's designed to reassure, not terrorise! It's not an exhaustive list of every possible attack but does set out the thinking behind psychic self defence, thus enabling us to feel confident in almost any situation that comes our way.

In the first part of the book, Chapters 1-8, there are descriptions of the many different types of attack. A number of these have come from my own records compiled over the years. These will help us to recognise what we're dealing with and act accordingly.

The second part of the book, Chapters 9-18 sets out various tried and tested methods of dealing with psychic attacks. The introduction to Part Two explains the principles behind the different methods so it is easy to choose whatever seems most appropriate. It's important to be flexible and adapt when necessary.

Rest assured, however, that contrary to what some films and books claim, the world is *not* full of demons and devils all waiting to leap out at us. Most psychic attackers are motivated by the very basic human emotions of jealousy and spite. They may seem all powerful and overwhelming, but nevertheless *can* be defeated using a handful of defensive techniques.

This book will show you how.

PART ONE

Psychic attacks: what they are, what they do. How do we know we're under attack? How does a psychic attack work? What sort of person becomes a psychic attacker?

CHAPTER ONE

Basically a psychic attack is an event (sometimes a series of events) conveyed by psychic means and intended to cause physical, emotional or mental harm to the victim. The attack can either build up very gradually or can come right out of the blue like a bolt of lightning. For example:

> *'I was on the floor retching by the time it had finished. It was so sudden it flattened me. People just don't understand… there are people out there doing all kinds of horrible things.'*[1]

The sort of harm caused by psychic attacks varies. Most attackers try to terrify the victim or drain her energy. Unexpected and dramatic psychic attacks can cause accidents or sudden illnesses (sometimes quite severe). With a more prolonged, stealthy attack however, the victim becomes progressively more tired and prone to chronic illness over a long period of time as the attacker quite literally steals their energy as a means of empowering themselves. This type of attack is sometimes known as psychic vampirism.

One of the biggest problems with any psychic attack is not what the attacker does, but the victim's response. This is not victim-blaming, but I know that many become so terrified that their fear turns inwards, and they end up attacking themselves. Then we

---

[1] Author's personal notes.

need to deal not only with the original attack, but also with the fall-out from the victim's own attack upon herself.

Throughout this book I always stress the importance of looking for other causes before leaping to the conclusion that we are under psychic attack. If we feel tired and drained, for example, we should visit the doctor and find out whether there are any physical reasons such as fibromyalgia, ME, CFS, anaemia etc. causing the fatigue and/or pain.

Pre-existing ill health sometimes makes us more vulnerable to psychic attacks, since psychic attackers always try to exploit our weaknesses. Even if we are convinced we are under psychic attack, we must always treat any underlying physical conditions in addition to disarming the attack itself.

How do we Know we're under Attack?

Firstly, it goes without saying we must investigate what's happening. Keep written notes because often psychic attacks can last some time and it's easy to forget exactly what happened a few weeks earlier. Keeping a record also helps us spot patterns. What we are looking for is a combination of psychic activity and some evidence of attack (or at least hostility). Both need to be present for there to be an actual psychic attack. For the time being, however, just write down anything that seems a little unusual, together with the date, time and, if possible, the moon phase and even the weather or the tide (especially if we live near the sea or a river).

Sometimes people feel a sense of unease a few days before the attack. This is difficult to describe exactly, but it's rather like the feeling we get just before a storm. The air feels and sometimes even smells different, and we might even pick up on a vague, buzzing energy. If we notice this, then begin with some of the basic defensive measures set out in Chapters Nine and Ten. Done early enough these often stop an attack in its tracks.

There are many misconceptions about psychic attacks and it's tempting to over-react. Feeling uneasy in another person's company is not proof of psychic attack although it *might* be our subconscious trying to send a warning about something. Seeing a ghost, or an orb of light may suggest psychic activity, but it doesn't mean we're under psychic attack, and although a run of bad luck can feel very personal at times, there are often other, mundane explanations. For example, I once had a case once where someone was convinced she was being hexed when her washing machine, car and central heating all broke down in the same week. If that sort of thing happened to me, I know I would probably feel it was personal too – but we should still avoid leaping to conclusions.

In this particular example, closer investigation revealed that the washing machine became blocked when a pair of old curtains disintegrated in the wash, while the car and central heater boiler were both ancient and hadn't been serviced for years. This is cause and effect, not psychic attack.

We are also sometimes told that if we think we're under psychic attack then we probably are. Not only is this nonsense, it's also dangerous, for too much thinking along these lines will have us chewing the carpet. Remember: panic makes things worse. No matter what is going on, we *can* deal with it. Just stay calm.

Luckily for us, very few psychic attacks, even those launched by skilled occultists, are ever as dramatic as those depicted in horror films. In fact, most attacks build up gradually, like the remorseless dripping of a tap. And therein lays the problem, because by the time we realise something is wrong, the attack is already well under way and may be more difficult to deal with.

On the other hand, we must avoid paranoia. Not every paranormal event is a psychic attack. For example, some people claim that if we live in a haunted house, then we must be under psychic attack. Not so. Very little ordinary psychic phenomena have any hostile intention. Hearing ghostly footsteps in the middle of the night can be unnerving but it's not necessarily a psychic attack. Often a haunting is simply an echo of former inhabitants, no more a threat to anyone than a scene from a DVD being replayed from time to time.

Some hauntings *do* appear to be trying to contact the living, but again, if there's nothing hostile in this, we should not rush to banish it. Sometimes entities 'on the other side' simply need a little help and once they have it, will stop bothering us.

Personally, I will always help if I can, although we should never promise help if we have no intention of following it through. Rather than break our word, it's better to suggest the spirit contacts someone else.

Occasionally our problems are caused by house brownies, fairies or poltergeists with too much time on their hands. These are rather like small children demanding attention. Instead of rushing in to banish them (and I'm not entirely convinced that it's either wise or desirable to even try) it's better to treat them kindly. Leave out small offerings, and if they do something helpful, remember to thank them. If they are mischievous, avoid letting them see our fear or annoyance as they tend to play on this.

Prevention is always better than cure, so keeping our home, car, bicycle, workplace etc., psychically clean, perhaps with the aid of amulets and charms is easier than dealing with an attack once it gets out of hand. (Details of suggested amulets are in Chapter Nineteen).

How do Psychic Attacks happen?

Normally, in order to acquire a new skill we need to undergo a certain amount of training, either from a suitable teacher, by reading a book or even watching a video on YouTube. Years ago however, information about magic or psychic self-defence was scarce and it wasn't easy to find a teacher unless we came from a family that practised the Craft. Even then, we had to persuade them that we were mature enough to handle such information. If they believed we were irresponsible or reckless the lessons simply stopped, and no amount of pleading would get them to start again.

Not all witches behaved responsibly, either. My mother and her family grew up in an era when magical knowledge was usually passed on by word of mouth; they had an almost pathological hatred of books. Worse, virtually all they ever did was hex. I don't know why, but there must have been some point back in dim and distant past when their whole ethos became twisted.

Instead of carefully considering all the options available, they developed an 'I can do it therefore I shall,' mentality. Their Craft motto, 'Wishes and curses are like old hens, they always come home to roost,' was basically wise and sensible, stressing that whatever we do for good or evil has the potential to rebound on us. In practice, however, they mostly ignored it. A classic example of cognitive dissonance if ever there was one.

At first, being around such people is exciting. We know we are witnessing something on the borders of illegality, and that in itself can make it seem thrilling. But ultimately it becomes dreary, just one spiteful spell after another, all with only one intention, to cause misery. In the end, having watched my family in action down the years, I began to wonder why, if they had all that power, they couldn't do some good with it.

One thing I did learn from them, however, was how hexing worked. From a practical point of view much of their hexing was spontaneous and improvised, suggesting they had an advanced knowledge of the mechanics of spell-casting. There were no candles, incense or potions although sometimes they used images, including drawings, photographs and dolls made of old-fashioned wooden clothes pegs dressed in left over scraps from the sewing basket, which they inaccurately referred to as a wax effigy. Of course, dolls have been used in magic all over the world for thousands of years, and were bound, buried, burned or mutilated when used in cursing rituals and erotic magic.[2]

I was never admitted to the family's innermost circle, partly because I left them when I was still quite young, and partly because they considered my main interests of herbs, healing and divination were a bit feeble. I often saw them use drawings, but only once saw a doll being made from start to finish although such practice was often hinted at.

Back when I was young, girls still knitted, sewed and even made the odd doll, either by sewing, knitting or using clothes pegs or wooden spoons. I discovered I had a real talent for doll making using clothes pegs, although back then I never made any with magical intention. As far as I was concerned, they were just for fun and I gave most of them away as gifts.

---

[2] Faraone (1993)

I do remember one strange incident, however. Years ago, when I was in my late teens, a friend asked me to make a pair of dolls to represent her and her fiancé. I made the first doll to look like my friend and then my mother offered to make the male doll. She had the most peculiarly intense expression on her face while she worked at it, glancing at me every so often to make sure she had my attention. When it was finished, it was a remarkable likeness of my friend's fiancé. I always used pipe cleaners to make the arms and hands and set about shaping them so that the two figures were romantically linked and holding hands.

'No,' said my mother, when she realised what I was doing, and swept them apart with her hand. 'Now see what happens.'

I was so in awe of her, I think I half expected the dolls to start walking and take on a life of their own. But of course, the magic was more subtle than that. A few days later I had a phone call from my friend, in floods of tears. She and her fiancé had broken up very suddenly.

I mentioned it to my mother and she just stared at me for a few moments. 'I'm not in the least surprised,' she said.

And looking back on it, neither was I.

Nowadays of course, we don't need to come from a family of witches or know a local wise woman in order to get our information. There are plenty of books and websites available. In many ways, this is good, but unfortunately sound information and utter rubbish jostle side by side and it can sometimes be difficult to tell them apart.

The abundance of information - good and bad - also means that many more people can access basic magical techniques, which can be used both to launch and repel psychic attacks. Remember though that the abundance of graphic online images depicting violence, cruelty and pornography often do our visualising for us, providing powerful aids to creating some truly revolting psychic attacks.

The internet has taken magic into a new phase, speeding up the availability of information that used to take a long time to find. Yet this delay years ago had its uses, since it gave us time to cool off!

Hexing is easiest when we are incandescent with rage. It takes sense and maturity to realise that power and being in control are not one and the same thing, and with proper magical training we will hopefully learn the difference. When there is unchecked power at our fingertips on the internet, however, it's like putting a machine gun in a child's hands.

The internet gives us other magical opportunities our ancestors lacked. The amount of personal information available online makes it easy to find a target's weakest spots. Large groups of 'friends' on social networking sites can be used to gang up on the victims. For those who are unscrupulous or malevolent, the internet offers endless opportunities for mounting psychic attacks.

Who becomes a Psychic Attacker?

The sort of person who launches psychic attacks is not unlike those who actively go around doing physical and mental harm to others. They may not have the courage (or the strength) to go up to someone and punch them on the nose, but magically that is exactly what they are doing. Yet whereas someone who launches a physical attack may be identified by witnesses or caught on CCTV, psychic attackers – like internet trolls – often work unnoticed and are not accountable to anyone.

It's hardly surprising that for some people, hexing and casting the Evil Eye has become a way of life. We don't even need an active interest in the occult provided we have a certain type of disposition, for example an explosive temper or the ability to fume endlessly about every slight, real or imagined.

Of course, not all attackers realise what they're doing, initially at least. They may indeed be resentful, jealous and downright spiteful, but many believe in their heart that simply thinking mean and spiteful thoughts won't do any *real* harm. Unfortunately, this isn't always true. Magic – for good and ill – depends largely upon the force of one's will. And people who are jealous and spiteful by nature are usually extremely strong willed and can produce some very powerful results without even realising it.

It's rather like setting off a firework in a crowd of people. The person who lights the blue touch-paper may not know any of the people standing nearby, but this won't lessen the extent of their injuries if the firework explodes.

A deliberate psychic attack is usually termed a direct or conscious attack, while an unintentional attack is an indirect or unconscious one. The difference between them is usually that a direct psychic attack throws energy at a target while an indirect attack takes energy away.[3] However, this is not a hard and fast rule and there are always exceptions. Left unchecked, both can be equally damaging.

The following is a good example of an unconscious attack that most certainly blasted the victim with a bolt of energy, even though the perpetrator (now a middle-aged man) knew nothing whatsoever about magic at the time.

> *'Years ago, when I was about fifteen, a couple of other boys, older than me, set on me as I was walking home one night. I was pretty strong and fit and thought I might be able to fight them off, but there were too many of them. One started to throttle me, and I found myself 'seeing red'. It was weird. People call it 'the red mist' and that's just what it was like. I was so angry at them, furious, because I knew they wanted to kill me and I didn't want to die. It was like a blazing hot rage building up inside me.*
>
> *'When I tried to push my attacker away I felt as though fire was rushing through my hands. Suddenly he seemed to spring backwards, almost as though someone had pulled him away. And there were two great burn marks on his shirt, like handprints, just where my hands had been. His friends stood there, staring but not doing anything, and I got up quickly and ran off. Nobody followed me.'*[4]

---

[3] Belanger (2000) Psychic Vampire Codex, a Manual of Magick and Energy Work (see Sacred Texts website in Bibliography)

[4] Author's personal notes.

In this particular case, the attack was propelled by a combination of the victim's willpower and rage, and for many months afterwards he suffered from terrible headaches and nosebleeds. But was it a psychic attack? Well, there was certainly a physical assault, and since the mere touch of our hands doesn't usually result in burn marks, I think we must accept it *was* a psychic attack. Although not typical, it's by no means unique.

I generally use the term 'hexing' to cover spells designed to harm others, but the term could also include the ability to impose one's will on someone else, i.e. coercive control in the magical world. Another name for hexing is the Evil Eye, while in the ancient world the Romans referred to it as *maleficium,* and the Greeks called it *katabaskainein.* They believed it could be performed with the breath, a single word or a look; this is why people used to be discouraged from looking at their own reflection in a mirror, because it's so easy to hex ourselves!

The Roman author Horace[5] described the 'sidelong glance' that could blight love affairs and magic, while Pliny the Elder[6] claimed that many women possessed the Evil Eye, and that those who did could not be drowned. Clearly this is a forerunner of the medieval ordeal of Trial by Water, or 'Swimming the Witch', yet the belief was old even in Pliny's time (the 1st century CE) because he cites an earlier writer, Cicero, to back up his claim.

I've been on the receiving end of the odd psychic attack at various times in my life, some stealthy, others dramatic. All were deliberate, direct attacks, making it easier for me to identify the culprit, since deliberate attacks always leave some sort of trail.

Some of my worst experiences were in the early days when I had less experience, and one attack actually put me in hospital. But I learned from it, determined that as soon as I was recovered, I would never allow anyone to ever do that to me again. Psychic attacks *can* be prevented. They can also be stopped. Even if we never intend casting a spell, we should all know how to defend ourselves.

---

[5] Horace, *Epistles,* 1.14.37-8

[6] Pliny, *Natural History* 7.16-8, 28.39

How Do Psychic Attacks Work?

Although psychic attacks manifest in many different ways, the methods of actually launching an attack are fairly limited. It's rather like a car – just as cars come in all shapes, colours and sizes, their actual method of propulsion usually relies upon a diesel, petrol or electric engine. Most gearboxes are either manual, automatic or occasionally a combination. The way the hex manifests is like the car's appearance (i.e. varied), while the method of sending it is limited in much the same way as the workings under the bonnet.

Looking back to my childhood, one thing I remember about my family's hexing is that usually it was very low-key and unobtrusive. The whole thing comprised almost entirely of mental focus, i.e. the Evil Eye. Deep down, I believe that most hexes and psychic attacks still operate in this way. The attacker, fuelled by envy, rage, malice, spite – or any combination thereof – visualises exactly what he wishes to happen to his victim. The power of the emotions he invokes help propel the hex along. Although sudden rage sometimes causes psychic attacks, they are normally very brief and intense, rather like the mood of their creator.

Naturally, we all lose our tempers from time to time. And if something unpleasant happens to the subject of our anger, it's easy to believe we must somehow have 'caused' it. However, a true psychic attacker is not someone who feels a sudden flash of rage and then calms down and apologises. *He (or she) never feels guilt.* They believe they are fully entitled and justified in their actions.

In the early days, they inwardly seethe, for weeks, months, even years about the wrongs – real or imagined – that have been done to them. Nothing brings them respite, not even sleep. Indeed, sleep doesn't come easily to such people; they often lie awake into the small hours planning their revenge. With such a personality, is it any wonder that *some* psychic attacks will cause accidents and illness?

Hexing also seems to attract people with drink and drug problems, perhaps because these things lower our inhibitions. Personally, I don't think it's a good idea to embark on any magical work when under the influence of alcohol or drugs. I know some people believe they enhance the magical experience, increase visualisation skills, and claim that various types of hallucinogens have been used in magic for thousands of years, but this was always only after proper training.

Just as the drunk driver believes his reactions are unimpaired by half a bottle of whiskey, so some people believe their magic remains unaffected. It doesn't. Drink and drugs often give only the *illusion* of control, which is what makes them dangerous in the hands of people who are magically irresponsible and whose training has never progressed any further than '*The Idiot's Guide to Sorcery*'.

We should also avoid alcohol if we feel we are under psychic attack, partly because we need a clear head but also because attackers often visualise an image of 'spinning' in order to confuse their victims. Drinking alcohol does the attacker's work for him.

From the psychic attacker's point of view, alcohol, drugs and hexing have something in common: they are all potentially addictive. If we use either alcohol or drugs to empower our spell, our addictions are likely to get considerably worse. The same can be said for spells requiring sexual climaxes. Used with care, it can be a useful technique. If it becomes the end rather than the means however, it will defeat the object of the exercise.

Unfortunately, hexing can quickly move so far beyond the pale that hexers will try and justify just about anything they use to empower their spells. A responsible spell caster understands the need for caution and self-discipline. A reckless hexer however, claims that the end *always* justifies the means.

If we are under psychic attack, we need to be brave. There is nothing wrong with being afraid or anxious provided it doesn't prevent us from reacting to events. The ancient Greeks believed that terror was beneficial as it induced *katharsis* which could purify the entire nervous system. I can vouch for this; when I was young, I was very afraid of the dark. Then one night, after a particularly frightening experience, I suddenly realised I wasn't afraid anymore; instead of being reduced to a quivering jelly, the experience had somehow cleansed me.

Unless we use our fears in a positive way, by learning the basic techniques of cleansing and grounding, our inner demons will do more damage to us than any psychic attack. Before we can defeat others, we must face up to our innermost fears and defeat them. Our own imagination is capable of causing us more harm than any psychic attacker.

CHAPTER TWO

The warning signs of a psychic attack. Certain types of Smells, noises, materialisations, blood, slime, scratches, certain animals that seem to cluster around us, smoke alarms going off without reason. How much is it reasonable to put up with? What about Poltergeists and ghosts?

No two psychic attacks are identical. Some begin suddenly while others build up gradually, a series of small things that pass unnoticed until we suddenly realise that they form part of a bigger pattern. For example, we may become aware of a feeling of dread, as though something has chilled the very heart of us. When we know what to look for, such things act as a warning, but until then they can have the opposite effect, by weakening us psychologically and emotionally.

It can often be difficult to decide whether we are under psychic attack or simply going through a run of bad luck. What we are looking for is a combination of patterns that shows harm or hostility combined with some sort of psychic phenomena, i.e., evidence of psychic activity *and* evidence of an attack.

For example, if someone heaves a brick through our window that's an attack, but probably not a psychic one. On the other hand, although poltergeists are fond of throwing things, they rarely break anything. If our window breaks, the sensible thing is to try and identify the culprit. A small boy with a stone is unlikely to be waging a psychic attack against us.

However, sometimes it's not so clear cut. For example, we may have a neighbour who is making our lives a misery by physical means, and then notice there is a sudden increase in psychic activity. Is it an attack or not? Well, perhaps. Sometimes psychic attackers try to cause discord just to throw us off their trail. They will even encourage others (in this case, the small boy with a stone) to do their work for them.

Although most deliberate direct attacks leave some sort of trail back to the attacker, others are more difficult to identify. But even if we never identify our attacker, we can still follow the guidelines in Part Two of this book to protect ourselves and prevent any further attacks.

Ideas about exactly what constitutes a psychic attack or curse and how to treat it have varied through the ages. The Anglo-Saxons believed that elves caused hiccups and heart burn (Old English *ælf-sogoða*) and treated it with a type of exorcism. Later, when people feared witches more than elves, they blamed the Evil Eye for hiccups and heartburn instead.

Accounts of old witch trials often mention the victim's heart being pinched, (which was just another term for indigestion!) Wishing indigestion on someone was a popular method of hexing; in 1608 in Cambridgeshire, Alice Skilling confessed that she hoped that '…the food and drink they ate may go up and down their bellies as men go to harrow.'[7] An envious person could hex his victim so they lost their appetite or choked on their food, so if one was sitting at the table when someone began choking, the traditional response was, 'Well, *I* don't begrudge you your food.'

The 'hug' (in Anglo-Saxon *hyge)* was another way to convey a hex. Far from a gentle cuddle, the hug was a strong force of the human will that caused people and animals to sicken and pine away, and even made buckets of milk leak! The word appears in several dialects, showing that the belief was widespread. In the North of England 'hig' meant a fit of temper or passion, and 'taking the hig' meant taking offence.

The hug could also cause a variety of trivial but annoying ailments, such as sudden noises in the ears, tingles, and itches attributed to other people's thoughts. This may explain the old belief that if our right ear itches it mean that someone was praising us, whereas an itchy left ear meant we were being slandered!

In Norway, people would slap their hand on any part of the body that was itching and say, 'I have your hug now.'[8] In some places a special type of hug known as the rehug or 'riding hug' was blamed for the Night Mare (see Chapter Seven). The hug could also be visible, appearing as a living person, animal or even as a thick mist.

---

[7] Oates (2003): 220

[8] *Ibid*

Psychic attacks often cause sudden insomnia. Many centuries ago, erotic curses tortured their victim (usually female) with sleeplessness until she agreed to have sex with the spell caster or his client. Other things associated with psychic attacks are high levels of unease, restlessness, and psychic experiences - especially when we're either about to go to sleep or just waking, sometimes called the 'threshold of sleep'. But don't forget to look for physical causes too. For instance, some people wake up gasping for breath because they suffer from sleep apnoea or even acid reflux.

Other common symptoms of psychic attack are vivid nightmares (not necessarily the Night Mare), bite or scratch marks on the body, foul smells, noises, materialisations, blood, slime, the feeling of being throttled during the night, certain animals that seem to cluster around us, smoke alarms going off without reason (though do check for a physical cause such as a worn out battery), indigestion, heartburn and wasting diseases.

Traditionally, whips and sticks - either visualised or real - were used in hexing, so when red welts appear (usually noticed on waking) this is because the attacker is trying to drive or goad us to do his will. However, if these marks only appear on our wrists or ankles it is more likely that someone has used a binding spell against us, perhaps tying the ankles and wrists of a doll or effigy. The mistreatment of the doll is then projected onto the living victim. However, do look for physical explanations since red welts can sometimes be caused by ringworm or even allergies and these must be ruled out first!

It's quite possible for psychic phenomena to occur in the absence of a psychic attack, but although some of these can be very frightening, they are just evidence of a presence and not an attack. Children report many such experiences, although they seem to become less vivid and frequent as they grow up.

Sometimes however, although the psychic activity may be relatively mild, there is a clearly malevolent intention behind it. For example, seeing a ghost may not be proof of psychic attack. Even seeing a ghost hanging at the end of the rope may not be remarkable if someone had hanged themselves at that spot in the past. We could simply explain it away as a ghostly 'replay' of a highly charged moment. However, what if we see a ghost apparently hanging from the end of the rope in a house with no history of suicides - but perhaps we have known someone who *did* kill himself using this method? This takes the ghostly apparition to a different level altogether, suggesting the victim is being deliberately targeted *with something intended to cause maximum distress and fear.* And that could certainly be classed as a psychic attack.

I mentioned smoke alarms earlier. If they repeatedly go off without cause and are not faulty, one explanation is that they are being set off by fairies or house brownies. If we suspect the Little People are the cause, we should try calling out, 'Thank you, that's enough now!' (I've witnessed this being done successfully.) For safety's sake, however, do get the alarms checked to see they are working properly. If they are, then let the culprits know we are aware what they're doing, and they soon seem to tire of it.

Often symptoms of psychic attack are worse at night. Victims sometimes wake feeling that something pressing down hard on their chest, trying to suffocate or strangle them. They may even become afraid to fall asleep which is precisely the intention behind such an attack, since sleep deprivation quickly weakens us. A variety of attacks peculiar to the night are explored more fully in Chapter Seven.

If we suspect we are under psychic attack we must record what is happening to help build up an accurate picture, since it's easy to forget events or even exaggerate or confuse them later. If any witnesses are present, ask them to write their own account too.

Psychic attacks are often directed at a single individual who then ends up being the only witness and can end up doubting her own sanity. With each event record the time, date and moon phase. It's surprising how many psychic events occur at the full moon! Sometimes even when the evidence suggests nothing much is happening, our gut instincts insist otherwise:

> *'Something in the last house we lived in was very hostile to us. We were all ill in that place. We all argued and rowed with each other.*

We'd even all have the same nightmares on the same night – how weird is that?'[9]

In this type of situation, the best thing to do is to use some of the cleansing rituals in the second half of this book rather than wait for something big to happen. The rituals are also useful if we find ourselves suddenly under attack. I've known of places with very unpleasant psychic activity where blankets were pulled off the beds, furniture moved about, and witnesses reported seeing strange shadowy figures; nevertheless things calmed down considerably once some simple cleansing rituals had been performed.

Once the home or workplace is properly cleansed, we can also perform a small blessing ceremony to replace the negativity with something beneficial and positive. Examples and suggestions for blessing ceremonies are given in Chapter Fourteen.

Conditional Curses

Very occasionally a hex was set in motion years ago. This is sometimes called a conditional curse, and it operates when the victim does something – even unwittingly – that sets the curse in motion. Usually such curses are set upon a place or object, especially something of value although they are fairly rare.

One ancient example is, *'I am the jug of Tataie. Whoever steals me will go blind.'*[10] Another famous example is the curse allegedly set upon the tomb of Tutankhamun (although no written curse has ever been discovered.)

The unfortunate victim may not know the person who laid the original curse, and indeed, sometimes the originator may have long since died. Although it can be useful to know that such things exist, rest assured that very few of us are likely to encounter a conditional curse. If we do however, then thorough cleansing, using methods given in the second half of this book are the best

[9] Author's personal notes

[10] Faraone (1996) :81

defence. Also we should seal our Aura regularly until the attack is past. (See Chapter Nine)

Unpleasant Smells

Unpleasant smells, such as drains, excrement or rotting flesh often manifest in the early stages of a psychic attack and are always intended to frighten the victim. Before jumping to conclusions, however, always check first for a physical explanation. This includes pulling up drain covers, since occasionally a 'psychic attack' will turn out to be a dead rat or blocked sewer, while mice have been known to die behind cupboards or cavity walls.

Blocked sinks and drains can produce a terrible stench. So can cat's excrement. Even if we don't own a cat, a neighbour's pet may have got into the house and left his calling card. Nine times out of ten there will be a physical reason for psychic smells particularly if they are constantly present. A pungent smell that comes and goes is more likely to be supernatural in origin.

However, even then it pays to be cautious. I once investigated a large walk-in pantry where the occasional smell of flowers had been noticed. Pleasant smells don't usually occur in a psychic attack, so I was intrigued, and sure enough, when I opened the door and stepped inside the smell really hit me. I stepped back, left the door open and the smell disappeared after a few moments. Some serious rummaging at the back of the cupboard finally revealed the culprit - an old bottle of sweet-smelling disinfectant was slowly leaking on the floor under a pile of bags and junk. When the door opened, the smell was at its strongest, when it was left open it dissipated into the air!

Unlike the smell of drains, excrement, and rotting flesh, the smell of smoke does not always signify a psychic attack. Obviously check first whether anything is burning, especially electric cables that may be slowly smouldering. If only one person smells smoke however, they should get a check-up with their doctor as soon as possible since it may be a physical warning of an impending stroke, migraine or sinus problem.

Even if the smell has a psychic origin, it still may not be part of a psychic attack. I once knew someone whose spirit guide smoked a pipe, and the smell of smoke always preceded his approach. Unfortunately, she was frightened of fire and immediately assumed she was under psychic attack. Instead, as she later discovered, the burning smell meant that her spirit guide was warning her to be on her guard because she was at *physical* risk in some way. She still checks for a physical cause for the smokey smell just to be on the safe side, but it no longer terrifies her in the way it once did.

Yet suppose we've investigated the drains, changed the dog's diet, cleaned out the cat litter, disinfected the bin and still this smell persists, what then? The traditional method of dealing with a bad psychic smell was to counter it with a good one, i.e. incense or strong-smelling plants such as thyme, rosemary, sage and lavender which are all considered protective and anti-demonic. Chapter Twelve gives methods of using incense to counter a psychic attack.

Seeing smoke as opposed to smelling it is rather different and may be a manifestation of something called ectoplasm which manifests as a white, gauzy mass. Unlike tobacco smoke (which is slightly blue), ectoplasm is nearly always pure white. In the nineteenth and early twentieth centuries, 'materialising mediums' specialised in producing ectoplasm from various orifices in the body, although ectoplasm can also appear spontaneously.

It can be very disconcerting to see a white, smoky-looking substance suddenly appear and begin to move around the room before disappearing again. Sometimes it manages to assume a recognisable shape but often it will just disappear after a few moments.

There can be other causes too. Driving home one cold winter's night I saw a white, horse-shaped 'mist' standing in the middle of the road. There was no mist anywhere else and visibility was good. My headlights shone through the figure with some difficulty. Later research revealed that appearances of the Ceffyl Dŵr, the mythical Welsh water horse, were often reported in that area. Of course, both ectoplasm and water horses are only signs of psychic *activity* and we shouldn't jump to the conclusion they are part of a psychic *attack* without further evidence.

Slime and Blood

Slime is another symptom of psychic attacks although most instances will have a physical explanation: it's surprising how many homes possess small colonies of slugs and snails that slither around at night! However, on rare occasions we may encounter slime that has no apparent physical cause and this needs clearing, cleansing and purification. (See Chapters Ten, Twelve and Thirteen).

The sudden appearance of specks of blood that have no obvious explanation is always alarming. Bear in mind however, that many things look like blood – ink, paint, rust and even stains from some fruit and vegetables. The presence of blood is almost always a sign of psychic attack *provided we have first ruled out any physical explanation.*

We must therefore check for wounds, using a magnifying glass on our skin if need be, looking for small puncture marks, scratches or even bite marks. We may have scratched ourselves accidentally with a broken fingernail or knocked against furniture the previous day and only now the bruise is noticeable. We need to check whether our fingernails are jagged or whether there are any sharp edges on the bed. Could a hairpin have fallen into the bedclothes unnoticed? If we have pets then check for fleas, even the cleanest cats and dogs can pick them up!

I once had a case where a woman who had recently moved into a new flat became convinced that she was under psychic attack, from a vampire after waking up a few times with tiny bite marks on her legs. Then one day she spotted a flea in the bedroom carpet – an unpleasant reminder that the previous tenants had not regularly de-loused their pets. Once the house was treated appropriately the 'psychic attack' vanished.

Even in a psychic attack, blood rarely appears in the context or amounts shown in horror films! Making things materialise takes a great deal of energy, and energy expended on producing gallons of gunge that oozes through the walls is a waste of the attacker's psychic force.

Cold Patches and Things that Drain Energy

Cold patches often accompany both hauntings and psychic attacks, affecting an entire house, single room or just a small area. The cold is dense and bone chilling; even on a warm summer's evening it can feel like a slap in the face. The reason for the drop in the temperature is that the energy from heat is being drained in order to help something materialise.

Occasionally cold patches also occur at portals, places where entities cross into our world and then return to their own. In the absence of strong evidence to the contrary, noticing a cold patch does not prove we are under psychic attack. Indeed, there is a portal in our home at the foot of our stairs.

Since we don't fully understand how – or why – portals exist, it is much better to try and negotiate a compromise than to try and banish it. Basic cleansing (see Chapters Ten, Twelve and Thirteen) will improve most cold patches and clear away any negativity attached to the area. We should also explain to any entities we suspect are present that although they are perfectly welcome to continue using the portal, they should respect our space too.

Other symptoms of energy being drained include high levels of static, batteries suddenly dying in torches or toothbrushes, and unusually high electricity bills. Again, don't jump to conclusions. In cold weather batteries do 'die' suddenly. As electricity prices have risen in recent years, do check the actual usage not just the amount when comparing with earlier bills.

Some people notice their clocks stop whenever there's a sudden bout of psychic electricity. Quartz clocks run on batteries, which might explain why this happens, although it can happen with mechanical clocks too. Occasionally these symptoms occur just before something manifests, e.g. batteries suddenly die and a moment later an orb of light starts bouncing round the room. Of course, none of this 'proves' we are under psychic attack, simply that our surroundings are particularly active.

The biggest risk when energy is drained - even if no obvious attack is present - is that entities may begin by draining batteries and electricity before moving on to drain human energies. This can make us very unwell indeed, so we must be prepared to keep up with the psychic cleansing. Be persistent, it's the only way to prevent an attacker from having easy access to our energy and eventually persuade them to leave us in peace.

Another thing I have noticed is that damp houses attract more psychic activity than dry ones. Although many people believe that water helps to cleanse, it is best if it is consecrated to that specific purpose first. (See Chapter Twelve). Left in its natural state, water is more likely to be utilised to conduct psychic attacks particularly via underground streams or springs of whose existence we may be quite unaware.

Even condensation (which is particularly problematic in stone-built homes) can increase psychic activity noticeably. I've found the best remedy for this is a dehumidifier; although it uses electricity, it does save money on the damage done by mould. On fine days, opening the windows will also air the house and help to dry it out, which in turn reduces unpleasant psychic phenomena.

Aural Disturbances

One of the commonest early signs of a psychic attack is the sound of a bell. Even if we keep a bell in the house for cleansing purposes, an aural disturbance usually has its own sound source, and rarely sets a physical bell ringing (although it can happen.) We can check this by ringing our own bell and seeing whether it sounds the same. Don't take anything for granted. I once was convinced I'd heard a bell ring out at dead of night, only to find out that one of my daughters had gone downstairs that night – something she never normally did – and blundered into a bell that hung on the stairs!

Other sounds we may hear are clicking, tapping and knocking, again without any apparent physical cause although these can also accompany ordinary haunting. We must not let them unsettle us; it's unlikely that any aural disturbance *on its own* will launch a psychic attack. It *may* be a warning sign that a psychic attack is on its way, but the sound itself is probably quite harmless.

Aural disturbances are often more common during the months of May and November, when the veil between worlds is stretched to its thinnest. Common symptoms include restlessness: dogs will bark at nothing and cats will find it difficult to settle and sleep. Chiming clocks sometimes go haywire during these times of the year. We once had an otherwise sober grandfather clock chiming constantly through the night one November! We may also notice our home and workplace etc., crackling with energy, some of it quite unpleasant. Very similar energies are present to a lesser extent at the New and Full Moon, and around the Winter and Summer Solstices.

Another aural disturbance that sometimes occurs in conjunction with psychic attacks is whispering or disembodied voices. Because they sound human, these can be more frightening than bells and footsteps, and are usually sent to intimidate the victim. If there is no obvious physical cause (such as the TV or radio being left on, or real voices in the street) then start working through the defensive measures in Chapters Nine, Ten and Twelve and check whether there are any psychic cords attached to our solar plexus (Chapter Eleven).

Priming the Victim

Often a psychic attacker wants us to realise that we are under attack. They might even go out of their way to warn that 'trouble is coming', or that we have been cursed. Some will send hexes through the post, anything from a paper covered in strange symbols to a doll with a pin in its heart. Or they will place these objects somewhere they know we are likely to see them.

Even people with little occult knowledge play this game in the hope of intimidating their target since psychic attacks tend to work better (from the attacker's point of view) if the victim is already 'primed.' Although it's not true to say that if we believe that we are under attack then we are, it is true that anyone who believes they are under attack tends to be more anxious thus making the attacker's job that much easier.

I had one particularly malevolent aunt who *always* made sure that her victims knew she had cursed them. The effects could often be devastating, as I witnessed at first hand. The correct response to this sort of thing is to send the hex straight back at them. If someone says, 'I curse you,' just reply, 'Back at you,' or 'May it return to you tenfold.'

Unfortunately, people were too terrified to think of doing this to my aunt – and she knew it. Remember that most psychic attackers are bullies, picking on victims they know will not retaliate.

Some people believe that even sending back a hex is as wrong as the original attack and can never be justified. Yet very few psychic attackers play by any rules. If we simply allow someone to curse us, then we are letting them go on and attack others who may be more vulnerable. Remember, our reaction can increase or decrease severity of *any* psychic attack.

The best methods of dealing with psychic attack always involve cleansing, sealing, and protection; but there are times when a bully simply deserves a psychic slap in the mouth (which is what happens when we return their hex to them). Anyone arrogant enough to stand there and declare that they have cursed us deserves to receive the same thing back in return.

Missing Objects

When things go missing on a regular basis without any real explanation, it's easy to feel that this must be due to a psychic attack especially if it happens often or involves objects of sentimental value. It can be difficult not to feel that it's personal and we are somehow being 'attacked.' However, this sort of activity is most often the work of mischievous entities playing with us, rather than attacking us deliberately. There *is* a difference – although admittedly sometimes the line between the two is very thin indeed!

The most common explanation for this sort of activity is that we have a house brownie. These are surprisingly common and live alongside humans and although they are rarely seen they can certainly make their presence felt. Traditionally they do household chores, but the one that lives with us prefers to find and fix things! This is a very typical account:

> *'Something has been bothering me for a couple of years. I think there are several of them, like the Little People. They play pranks, sometimes they're just mischievous, they take things and then bring them back. Sometimes, though, they don't bring things back. They've taken my keys, money… I thought they might be house brownies so I tried leaving a saucer of milk out for them. I'm not frightened of them, I'd like to be friends with them, but it's getting out of hand.'*[11]

Clearly in this case there was evidence of psychic phenomena (since objects do not normally disappear), and a strong element of mischief rather than hostility. Eventually, a combination of leaving out milk and talking to them helped quieten things down, and if anything was taken it was always promptly returned.

Although some people believe that anything and everything should automatically be banished, I believe it's more effective and well-mannered to first speak to house brownies, fairies, ghosts etc., and try to come to some sort of arrangement. There are many worlds beside our own and it is sheer arrogance to suppose that we must always take precedence.

Traditionally there were two types of household spirits: the brownies who lived alone in the house (or sometimes in an outbuilding) while the Good Neighbours lived in small groups away from the house and protected the land. By the Middle Ages attitudes towards these helpful spirits had hardened and people were told that the Good Neighbours only brought luck at the expense of one's neighbours.[12] Fairies can also cause psychic

[11] Author's personal notes
[12] Briggs (1978): 54

phenomena including strange noises such as music, ringing bells, and practical jokes. Although originally regarded as mostly harmless, in his *Daemonologie* King James I claimed that brownies were devils that haunted the house.[13]

Nobody is quite certain exactly who or what fairies, brownies, hobgoblins etc., are. They may be as yet unknown races, operating solely within our own world, or they may occupy one of the Other Worlds, occasionally crossing over to ours. Some traditions claim they are the children of Adam and his first wife Lilith. Folk names, such as the Good Neighbours, the People of Peace and the Gentle Folk suggest that at some time in the distant past, they were friendly towards mankind. An alternative explanation is that people gave them favourable names for fear of causing offence.

Fairies etc., could also be a folk memory of entities such as the Roman *Lares* and *penates,* who were domestic gods attached to each household.[14] The *penates* had their own household altars and people offered them sacrifices and libations. This sounds very similar to the tradition of leaving out food for the fairies. There were always two *penates* in each household, and their images were set out on the table at mealtimes, when they were offered the first helping of food. In return they protected the home, and the fertility of its crops and animals. Unlike other household deities, they were known as *dii* or *divi,* meaning 'god.'

By contrast, the *lar familiaris* was solitary and like the northern House Brownie he lived alone either in the house or in an outbuilding. He was regarded as the luck of the house and its land. The name *lar* may be Etruscan, meaning 'Lord,' and he is sometimes depicted as a young boy dancing with a horn of plenty or cornucopia held above his head. His altar was set up in the hearth alongside the *penates,* the *genius* and Vesta, goddess of the hearth. The *lar* was honoured with sacrifices on all important occasions, but especially after funerals and weddings. Later traditions, however, portrayed the *lares* as unpleasant entities that troubled houses.

---

[13] King James VI (Scotland) I (England), (1591) :65

[14] Ritson (1831) :16

A common sign that we are sharing our home or garden with fairies is the presence of small stones - often marked in some way - turning up unexpectedly. I have a small altar in my garden in a sheltered spot, and every so often a small white pebble (sometimes several) will appear there. Other things we may notice are plants (especially those that grow from bulbs rather than seeds) suddenly growing in new places. We may also see plants moving as though something is swinging on them on a clear day when there is no wind. At such times, just greet offer a polite greeting, respect their space, and we will usually all co-exist quite comfortably.

Normally, fairies, house brownies etc., make their presence felt soon after we move into a new home. If we have lived somewhere for a while and the activity has only suddenly begun, it is more likely to be a spirit entity returning for a visit. Keeping a record enables us to see whether there is some sort of pattern occurring at certain days, months, seasons or moon-phases. Possibly certain times are somehow easier for them to cross over to our world and many simply choose to revisit a place where they were once happy.

Some hauntings occur only on anniversaries and are little more than a re-run of a specific event, like replaying a scene on a DVD. They are sometimes referred to as place-imprints and lack any intelligence. They may even appear if nobody is there to see them! Possibly certain types of stone and building materials 'store' these memories better than others. They are not psychic attacks and there is no point in trying to banish such ghostly visitors unless they are particularly disturbing.

Occasionally we encounter an entity that seems to be trying to make contact. It is not only aware of our presence but will also react to it. The best solution is to talk to it, asking what it wants and, if appropriate, offering to help. However, never make promises we cannot be certain of keeping. If we are asked to help and cannot, we should just say so and suggest they contact someone else. Never allow an entity to make us feel guilty. Just be firm and polite and most will move on. After all, if they want something badly, they are not going to bother haunting someone who cannot or will not help them, nor will they waste precious energy trying to punish us! On the other hand, if we help them, they have no reason to linger. This type of entity is rarely connected with a psychic attack, and any phenomena associated with it are simply intended to attract our attention.

Other categories of spirits/ghosts include those who do not realise they are dead, often because their death was sudden. Unable to move on, they may be lost or confused, sometimes regarding us as some sort of interloper in their old home. Again, be patient but firm. If they are aware of our presence, then in time we can make them understand that it's time for them to move on. (Instructions for this are given in Chapter Eighteen).

Often our own reactions are more of a problem than the ghost itself. Some people believe that every shadow, apparition and ghostly figure should be banished because they will at some point try and attack us. This is nonsense. Ghosts very rarely initiate a psychic attack; these usually come from humans. I have always felt that we can, within reason, share our home with these 'others' and if so, then that's fine. It's neither wrong nor dangerous.

When we start believing that every ghost is a potential source of harm, we risk attracting all sorts of psychic mischief, and what begins as a simple manifestation can quickly turn into a psychic *infestation.* I do appreciate, however, that sometimes we cannot bear to live with certain ghosts any longer. Some suggestions for dealing with them are given in Chapter Eleven along with some methods for co-existing with any house brownies or fairies that share our lives.

Peripheral Sightings

Children (and some adults) often 'see things' out of the corner of their eye, a phenomenon known as 'peripheral vision.'

> *'When I was about twelve, I began seeing a dark figure, just at the edge of my vision. If I looked at it straight on it would disappear, yet I could see it quite clearly from the corner of my eye. It seemed to be wearing long robes and would appear at any time of day and*

night. It would even appear when other people were present although nobody else seemed to notice it.' [15]

Some believe that sightings on the periphery of our vision are less 'real' that a sighting where we can observe clearly. In my experience however, not all entities manifest in the same way or to the same extent, and perhaps our peripheral vision is more equipped to pierce the veil into one of the Otherworlds. Our psychic powers are particularly strong in childhood, but as we get older, we tend to accept only things we can see when we are staring straight ahead, disregarding those very interesting images that appear fleetingly, right on the edge of our vision.

Ghostly figures, even if benign, frighten many people. Yet many children calmly report their experiences without any apparent fear, so it's important not to over-react if they confide in us. Listen carefully and, if necessary, ask questions.

'When I was a child, I used to like to lie on the floor to do my homework and read. Often I would hear someone come into the room and stand behind me. Sometimes it was one person, sometimes two. I was never frightened... they'd stay a while, almost as though they were checking up on me, seeing what I was doing, and then they'd leave again. My grandparents were all alive and to this day I still don't know who these figures were.' [16]

The important thing to note in this account is that the child was never afraid. These entities might have been ghosts revisiting a former home or guardian spirits interested in the child's welfare. This type of experience is not unusual and we certainly shouldn't jump to the conclusion it must be a psychic attack, however uncomfortable we might feel with the idea of spirits visiting our offspring.

If our child says they have had an encounter with something supernatural, just stay calm and *listen.* It's the only way we'll find out what's happening. Don't make fun of them or insist they were

---

[15] Author's personal notes

[16] Author's personal notes

mistaken. Ask questions rather than trying to put our own spin on things. There is a world of difference between saying 'Tell me what you saw,' and 'You didn't see a ghost, did you?'

Most importantly, avoid making the child feel that anything evil or dangerous is happening (even if we suspect it might be.) All too often, adults transfer their own fears to the child until eventually the psychic energy in the home is positively crackling! When an adult over-reacts, children feel confused, guilty and reluctant to confide further. Many try to blot out their own psychic experiences and abilities. The important thing is that we, as adults, remain calm and sensible. Running around like headless chickens does far more harm than good.

If any entity or presence makes us feel uneasy, then we must tell it that we're not comfortable with whatever it's doing and we'd like it to stop. People are often surprised to find that spirit entities can be quite amenable to such an approach.

Poltergeists

The entity most closely associated with children and young people is the poltergeist. Although sometimes frightening, it's important to remember that most poltergeist activity is probably caused by a surge in psychokinetic energy rather than a psychic attack. Children - especially those entering puberty - have particularly strong untapped psychic energies and sometimes a little extra stress will trigger off a series of dramatic psychic events.

Poltergeist activity may just be the psychic equivalent of shaking a bottle of lemonade and then unscrewing the stopper - the 'fizz' is the uncontrollable energy that veers off in all directions. Whether the poltergeist is a separate entity attracted by such energies, or whether it is an offshoot of the child's own energy is still widely debated.

The commonest symptom of a poltergeist attack is the throwing of objects such as toys, fruit, cushions, plates etc. although they are rarely broken. Another common symptom is bed shaking, which can range the odd nudge against the mattress to having the whole bed thrashing about wildly. The causes of bed shaking are still not fully understood. One theory is that it is caused by a hypnic jerk, which occurs when our muscles start twitching just as we fall off to sleep. However, this does not explain why some people are actually woken by the shaking, suggesting it can happen when one is fully asleep and is quite independent of anything the subject does.

Bed shaking is more common in childhood and puberty than at any other time of life, although some people continue to experience it for many years afterwards. What is rare however, is for someone to experience bed shaking for the first time in adulthood and if this occurs, it suggests a psychic attack rather than poltergeist activity.

One's religious outlook can also affect how we view poltergeists. For example, at a farm in Illinois, US, back in 1949 a Roman Catholic priest was invited to investigate an outbreak of poltergeist activity that centred around a young boy.[17] After several experiments, including communicating with the poltergeist by placing a pencil and paper between the child's bed and the wall, the priest became convinced that the entity had once been a living person and also a Catholic.

Eventually he changed his mind, concluding that the disturbance had been caused by the child's guardian angel. Interestingly the disturbances, which included knocking on the boy's bed, began on May 1st and lasted for a month before ceasing abruptly. A pagan might have considered this date significant, since May 1st is Beltane, a time when the veil between worlds thins out, just as it does around Samhain /November 1st).

Although poltergeists can be very frightening, it is important to remain calm no matter what they throw at us. Fear breeds fear. The more we scream and cower, the more daring it will become. If there are no children in the house but we still have poltergeist phenomena, then it might be due to a child's ghost. These, like poltergeists, can be mischievous, but will always behave more like a child than anything else. Usually all they need is a little understanding and patience to persuade them to leave.

---

[17] Anonymous (1949): 377

Sometimes child spirits become friends with human children although rarely with the dramatic outcomes so popular in horror films. We do not need to do anything about a child ghost unless we are convinced that the entity is having a harmful effect upon us or our family. The mere fact that the entity exists is not a good enough reason to banish it.

Animals: Ghosts or Thought Forms?

Poltergeists are not the only type of psychic phenomena that are attracted to people. Another frequently reported experience is repeatedly seeing a specific creature, symbol or person. Animals seem to be the most common, and wherever we happen to be we may notice a dog, cat, kestrel or even sometimes a symbol such as a rune, nearby. Mr Penry was once dogged by Victorian china comforter dogs. It was curious, but not a psychic attack.

The animals may not be identical, but they will often be eerily similar, for example a black cat, or a small dog etc. These experiences usually start in childhood and tail off by the early twenties, although with some people they persist throughout life. There seems to be a strong protective element in these experiences, and some people report their belief that seeing their 'special' creature is often a warning of danger or difficulties ahead.

The following account seems more like a guardian spirit of some sort and certainly doesn't appear to be hostile or unlucky.

> *When I was young I had this kitten that followed me everywhere. It wasn't real, because it would appear and disappear at will. But other people saw it too. And I still see it sometimes.*[18]

Seeing the same sort of animal wherever we go is unlikely to be a psychic attack unless it begins to threaten us. Likewise seeing the *occasional* ghostly animal is usually quite benign. Pets often return to visit their owners; I still see many of my old pets from time to time and regard them as welcome visitors, certainly not something to be banished. Sometimes the pet will appear as it

---

[18] Author's personal notes

looked towards the end of its life but often it appears much younger than it when it died, suggesting the afterlife restores them to their prime. Although some people feel uncomfortable with such experiences, they are quite common and there is nothing normally threatening about them.

Very occasionally, a ghostly animal will attach itself to us even though we did not know it in its lifetime. If it is a spirit entity it will often look solid but slightly shadowy, making it difficult to be precise about its markings. These cases are quite intriguing but unfortunately can rarely be fully explained.

If this happens to us, we should first look for any physical signs that the animal was present. These include paw-prints or hair so try pressing Sellotape on bedding, cushions, sofas etc., to see if this will pick up anything. Finding physical signs usually – but not always – suggests that a real animal has somehow got into our home. (Very occasionally a spirit animal can even trigger an attack of sneezing or itching in people with pre-existing allergies.)

Also check for open windows, doors, anywhere the creature could have entered earlier in the day and ask neighbours whether they've noticed any animal answering its description in the area. One of the best tests is to put out a tasty titbit and see if we can tempt the animal to come out so we can get a closer look at it. If it eats the food then it's a real animal, not a spirit one!

Even if it turns out to be a spirit creature, unless there is evidence of an actual psychic attack, I would recommend leaving it well alone. A little research – asking the neighbours, for example – might reveal that such an animal once lived in our home, in which case it's probably simply returning as a spirit visitor. It may even be a guardian animal, sent to watch over us. If we feel comfortable doing so, try speaking to it and asking what it wants.

However, if we also are experiencing some of the other phenomena listed in this chapter, such as smells, noises, slime etc., then the animal may be a thought form. These are often used in psychic attacks, either to frighten or spy on the victim. Basically, if the animal tries to menace us in any way, then it's part of the attack; if not, then it may have been sent as a spy. This is not as scary as it sounds since a thought form *is only as powerful as the mind of the person who created it.* It has been created by thought and we can destroy it in the same way. (See Chapter Five for more details)

Psychic Infestations

Seeing a single animal on a regular basis is one thing; dealing with a psychic infestation of cats, rats, snakes, ants, cockroaches, birds and/or flies is quite another. These regularly accompany psychic attacks and have been noted since ancient times. In Persian mythology, demons sometimes turned into flies after being exorcised while Beelzebub, the Philistine god of Accaron near Jerusalem, translates literally into English as 'Lord of the Flies'.[19]

Some of the animals seen or heard in a psychic infestation will be real, summoned or sent from their normal haunts. Others are not. For example, we may indeed see some real spiders, but others will be sent by our attacker who knows that because of our arachnophobia we will start seeing them everywhere. Even when they're not there, we are afraid they *might* be.

Some will be thought forms. Sometimes just a few will appear on an almost daily basis, other days we may confronted with dozens or even hundreds, often disappearing as quickly and mysteriously as they arrived.

Animals that form part of a psychic attack are often those we particularly dislike or fear, simply because psychic attackers try to turn our own phobias and fears against us. So if we are scared of spiders, and suddenly our home seems to be invaded by them, we should ask ourselves who knew about our fear and whether they would be likely (or capable) of conducting such an attack.

The usual method of dealing with these infestations is by cleansing and exorcism. The technique for exorcism is given in Chapter Eighteen and should be repeated as often as necessary until they depart. Since there will almost certainly be some *real* creatures amongst the group, we may also need physical deterrents as well, such as fly sprays, mouse traps, etc.

---

[19] Seligman 1997: 47

'Watchers'

This is a name given to thought forms that have been sent to spy on us and discover our weaknesses, or even just to check on the progress of a psychic attack. They are less common than they used to be, mainly because the victim has already told all and sundry (usually through social media) everything an attacker needs to know. Hopes, fears, dreams, phobias... the list is endless. Attackers don't even need to get to know us well in order to access this sort of information online. My family had a saying:

If you have a friend, keep her as such,
And do not tell her your secrets much;
For if that friend becomes your foe,
Out into the world your secrets go.

Although we shouldn't be paranoid, it's foolish to share information that can one day come back and cause us harm. Just be aware, more circumspect about privacy and more cautious.

Is it my fault?

It is often suggested that 'dabbling' with the occult makes us more open to psychic attack; for example, when something happens, some claim it must have been caused by having a pack of Tarot cards in the house. Then we worry that they have somehow invited 'the Devil' into their lives, and some clergy (who really should know better) encourage this view, although it's not true.[20]

Evil almost always originates with human beings, not spirits, and a truly 'evil spirit' is a rare beast indeed. Obviously, anyone who performs spells or does divination becomes more aware of other worlds and the entities that inhabit them, but such activities

---

[20] http://www.independent.co.uk/life-style/firsthand-i-dont-spend-all-my-time-with-poltergeists-casting-out-demons-and-laying-ghosts-to-rest-is-routine-for-dominic-walker-church-of-england-vicar-and-exorcist-1445788.html

don't act as a magnet for psychic attacks since people who have never done a spell in their lives can still be victims.

It's even possible to hex ourselves, which is often what happens when we become convinced that we must have done something to invite evil into our lives. It's easy to become so neurotic we end up viewing every shadow in the night as an evil spirit out to get us. What might have started off as a relatively minor psychic attack or even just a stray psychic phenomenon, can end up being a very unpleasant psychic attack against ourselves.

However, the most common cause of a self-hex is when we fail to act against those who torment us and end up despising ourselves instead. We know we should stand up for ourselves, but for a variety of reasons we don't. Perhaps it's a friendship, relationship or a complicated family situation, or we're scared we'll lose our job; meanwhile the bullies chip away at our self-esteem until we end up hating ourselves. Once that happens, we damage ourselves (especially our Aura) so badly that we become vulnerable to all sorts of things. For more information about the Aura see Chapter Five. For information on repairing the Aura see Chapter Nine.

Self-hexes are often the most difficult attack to deal with because they are hard to recognise, and we have work against some aspect of our self. Methods for dealing with a self-hex are in Chapter Seventeen.

Still not sure whether it's a Psychic Attack?

It is up to us to decide whether we *really* feel threatened. Sometimes it can be difficult to know whether something is mischievous or malicious. For example, if we hear footsteps one month, something pulls our hair the following month, and we hear disembodied voices the month after that, these are psychic experiences, but not necessarily psychic attacks.

I always stress that if we keep records right from the start, it will help us find the cause of the problem. It should also identify whether certain dates, times, weather, tides or moon phases play a part in these events. Keep a clear head and an open mind. Above all, avoid being superstitious: being born on Friday the 13th is *not* proof we will be psychically attacked for the rest of our lives, or that we are destined to become psychic attackers!

How much activity is it reasonable to put up with? It depends whether we are talking about ordinary psychic activity or outright psychic attack. In a haunting for example, it's up to us how much we will tolerate since it's unlikely to make us ill unless we happen to be of exceptionally nervous disposition. I've lived in several haunted houses, and some are decidedly easier than others.

We may experience various things, from cold patches, smells, lights to aural disturbances, yet still feel that the atmosphere generally is quite acceptable. Often haunted homes are just a bit 'quirky'; provided we don't feel menaced we may decide to simply co-exist with whatever is there. Even so, we should still regularly cleanse the place since negativity and psychic debris are not conducive to a bright and happy home.

That said, if we *do* feel threatened and our enquiries convince us that we are under psychic attack, then we should take steps to protect ourselves immediately. Remember – a real psychic attack is intended to harm and manipulate the victim, but we don't have to put up with this. Instead we keep cleansing and protecting ourselves, our family, our home and personal effects etc. Never allow the attacker even the tiniest foothold. A whole range of remedies are given in Chapters Nine – Eighteen depending on the type of attack.

CHAPTER THREE

Defending ourselves and others against psychic attack – what's the difference? The genuine and not-so-genuine. How geography and earth energies can affect us. Psychic vampires.

We should never be afraid to defend ourselves against psychic attacks. No matter how skilful the attacker may be (and rest assured that most are simply spiteful individuals with too much time on their hands), we are not powerless. There is plenty we can do to help ourselves and the second half of this book sets out a wide range of techniques for putting even the most persistent attacker in his place. Also, remember that nobody, not even the most experienced psychic, will do half as good a job of defending us as we can do for ourselves.

However, there are times when we may have to act on behalf of others. This is usually when the victim is too young, too elderly or perhaps too ill to do much for themselves, or perhaps the victim simply doesn't know where to turn and asks for help. There are also a few occasions where the victim doesn't understand or refuses to admit the danger he is in. We may be a concerned friend or relative, watching helplessly as the victim walks blindly into danger. Perhaps their friends or relatives have asked for our help and advice.

In situations like this, what do we do? Shake our heads and refuse to do anything because it would mean interfering with another person's free will? Or do we try to help, having first established that the victim is indeed under psychic attack? If we are still uncertain, then we should ask ourselves, 'What would I do if the victim was *physically* at risk? Would I pull someone out of the water first and ask questions later, or would I insist they signed a written consent form before I offered them a helping hand?' The old saying 'As above, so below' still holds good; the physical world is a mirror of the psychic one, and what applies in one should also apply in the other.

Investigating someone else's claim to be under attack is not the same as investigating our own situation and we should understand the potential pitfalls before agreeing to help. Firstly, we don't know the full story. People exaggerate or even miss out important information because they are unaware of its significance. Secondly, it's not uncommon to find oneself suddenly become the subject of a psychic attack during the course of trying to help someone else. There are several possible explanations for this: it may be that the attack has somehow bounced off the original victim and hit us instead (or as well.) Or – and this is more common – the person who claims to be under attack is, in fact, an attacker. I have come across several such cases, where the alleged victim waits until he has our attention and sympathy, and then goes on to attack *us*.

A variation on this is when someone asks for help but really wants to drain our energy (sometimes in order to help them attack a third party). Both types of attacker are forms of psychic vampire. If we are asked for help by someone we don't know very well (the 'friend of a friend' is a typical example) we should be particularly on our guard against this. The subject of vampires – psychic and otherwise – is dealt with in Chapter Eight.

However, let us suppose we have agreed to help – what can we do? Firstly, we should encourage the victim to carry out some basic cleansing and purification rituals (See Chapter Nine). Unless they are extremely young, very elderly or infirm, they should at least be able to perform these rituals for themselves.

Always be wary of people who claim to be so hopeless, frightened or otherwise helpless that they will do nothing at all to help themselves. Our job at this stage is to help, explain, and keep our own set of notes about what is happening. In particular, we are looking for patterns to indicate whether the attack is deliberate or accidental, or even a self-attack by the victim. Although prolonged psychic attacks are enough to make anyone paranoid, some accounts do ring a few warning bells right from the start. For example, look at this request for help:

I'm being pschicly (sic) stalked; someone has the power to observe my movements, read my mind, and knows everything about me. I don't know who's doing it. This has been going on for twenty years. Please advise me.' [21]

The first question to ask is: how can something continue for twenty years and yet this person still doesn't have a clue who's behind it? How many people even remain in our lives for so long? And if he doesn't know who's behind the attack, how on earth can he 'know' that this attacker knows everything about him and reads his mind? While the man clearly needs some help, I don't think his problems are due to psychic attack.

So how can we distinguish the genuine victims of psychic attack from frauds who are only trying to get our attention so they can drain us? Fortunately, there are often 'tells' we can look for, such as the way a person writes or speaks. Some will simply tell a story; others – the fakes – demand that we must believe them.

Their accounts are endless sagas of cruelty, abusive childhoods, violent relationships, and/or children and family who do not value them. Although many people have indeed had difficult lives, few experience *all* these things. Even if they do, genuine victims rarely confide in graphic detail to a virtual stranger.

Also, beware the breathless, one-attack-after-another story. In reality, psychic attacks tend to start very low key, inching their way forward as the attacker decides how much he can reasonably get away with. Unfortunately, there are people who crave attention so much that they will relate wild stories straight out of films. Look out for those who exaggerate and play the 'Pity me' card once too often. They don't want our help; they want our attention and energy. They are not victims but attackers.

Another clue that we are dealing with a psychic vampire is the use of over-dramatic language. People who talk about 'the hell of my existence' or 'the unspeakable game of destiny' are rarely genuine. Nor are those who appear to have fallen out with every neighbour, boss, colleague and family member they have ever known. Any of these situations, taken singly, deserves sympathy

---

[21] Author's personal notes

and understanding, but when they are lumped together, one drama on top of another, we are right to be cautious.

Also be very wary of people who do not like it if we ask them to look for a physical cause for the events they describe. It's a reasonable request. Yet I've known any number of people who stubbornly insist on believing they're under attack even when we can prove that the 'psychic smell' is caused by an overflowing drain! Again, this suggests it's not help they want, it's attention. While we are occupied with their problems and doing their cleansing for them, they will quietly start siphoning off our energies which will be raised higher than usual precisely because we are trying to help them.

Another thing to remember is that just because someone has asked for our help does not mean they will allow us to help them. Often we find that our suggestions are repeatedly rejected until in the end we wonder why they asked for our help in the first place. It's simply not true to claim that a psychic attacker has such a hold over their victim that they dare not break it. If they have enough free will to ask for help, then they surely have enough to allow themselves to be helped? Even in those rare cases of obsessing entities, it's more a case of the victim enjoying the entity's attentions rather than being totally powerless in its grip.

One of the greatest differences between defending ourselves against psychic attack and defending someone else is that when we defend ourselves, we have made up our mind to deal with the situation. When someone turns to us for help, it is just possible that they are using us as a crutch to avoid having to do anything for themselves.

It used to baffle me when victims refused to sever all contact with their attackers since normally breaking contact will halt a psychic attack in its tracks, or at least give us some breathing space while we decide what to do. It's a simple remedy: no visits, no letters, phone calls, emails, don't even visit the attacker's social media pages. Yet I'm constantly amazed how many people who have described themselves as the victims of the most horrific attacks will refuse point blank to cut contact with the very person who is harming them.

Admittedly, breaking contact can be difficult if our attacker is someone we must see on a daily basis, such as our teacher, work colleague or a family member. But even then, we can construct psychic shields and armour to minimise the damage (See Chapter Nine). When someone refuses to sever contact or do anything whatsoever to help themselves, it begs the question: what exactly do they expect *us* to do? We cannot help people unless they allow themselves to be helped.

Likewise, we sometimes encounter people who protest that our methods are somehow against *their* religious beliefs. In such cases just point them gently in the direction of the psalms or a local minister and leave them get on with things.

The Serial Victim

Serial victims are, in my experience, another type of psychic vampire although the damage they do is largely circumstantial. They engineer a crisis (or several) and then beg for help, all the while refusing to take even the simplest steps unless we stand by their side all the time. Be very wary of this. Most genuine victims are so unhappy and frightened they will gladly try our suggestions. But those who only want attention are often offended unless we leap to their defence with rituals, ceremonies, and endless 'chats' about what is going on in their lives, while never lifting a finger for themselves.

A few years ago, I received a fairly typical letter from such a person, and it gives a good idea what we should be looking out for. After a page and a half of barely coherent rambling about her own powers and the problems she was having with a psychic attack, the writer added '*Any ideas other than the usual?*'

This for me was a dead giveaway, showing that she had already asked the same questions elsewhere. Her demand is clear, barely hidden beneath the surface, that I should somehow dig deeper and find something new for her. Towards the end of the letter she added, '*...had spells in bottles done for us but still no good.*' Again this shows that the writer had asked for – and received – help from many others before me. Whatever the problem, she didn't want to solve it. What she craved was attention and access to someone else's energy. She may not intend to attack you, me or anyone else for that matter. But she won't do us much good, either.

Some people *always* seem to be under psychic attack. Obviously, psychic attacks do happen, sometimes several times in the course of a lifetime. But never constantly. Be very careful of those who experience the slightest glitch in their lives and interpret it as magical malevolence. Psychic vampires are very good at picking their victims and will often have already managed to convince someone else to back their story of psychic stalking and endless attacks. We must not be taken in by this – particularly if the only contact we have with such a person is via the internet. Remember that we're only getting a small part of the picture, the part they wish us to see.

Traditionally the Evil Eye was cast while the attacker praised a person, animal or object. It was a case of deflecting the victim's suspicions, appearing kind while doing harm. The same holds good for psychic vampires who will try and flatter our insight or knowledge, all the while trying to work out the best way to rob us of these very same things. They will pretend to be terminally helpless and hopeless, insisting that were it not for us they would be unable to cope.

Don't believe a word of it. These people know what exactly they're doing and are very good at making us feel guilty if we attempt to ration the time and attention we give them. Make no mistake, they will suck us dry if we let them. We must not be around them a moment longer than necessary, at least not if we value our spiritual and physical health.

The Spiritual Guru

This type of menace usually claims to possess amazing powers. He doesn't of course, but he is very good at hiding his shortcomings. Such people will often ask us to demonstrate the sort of things we can do in order to decide whether we are worth draining. Remember, people who brag are almost always fakes while those who are powerful rarely need to boast. There is no need. *They know what they can do, and they can do it whether or not anyone else believes in them.* They are content to earn the respect of those they care about. Genuinely gifted psychics tend to be rather reticent. Sometimes they view their gifts as a very mixed blessing.

Unfortunately, those with no talent (other than being able to suck the life force from us) have no such qualms. They generate tremendous nervous energy with their attention seeking, endless brinkmanship, feuds, love triangles and the like. Just a short time in their company is tiring. Much more than that and we can feel exhausted and irritable because they are hell-bent on sucking the life energy or *dynamis* out of anyone unlucky enough to come within their orbit.

Finally, when we have nothing left to give, they move on to their next victim, although they may well return now and then, just as we are starting to recover in order to drain us a little more. Unless we ignore them and steer well clear we will end up feeling about as powerful as an old AAA battery.

Geography and Psychic Attacks

The role of the landscape is often overlooked in psychic attacks. Although it is highly unlikely that any area will take such a dislike to our presence that it will launch a psychic attack of its own, landscape can certainly have a bearing on the type of phenomena we experience. It's as though certain features in the landscape -for example, the presence of water or certain types of stone - facilitate the production of certain types of paranormal event.

Sometimes the land seems to absorb something from the uses to which it has been put in the past, and the *genius loci* of a place can be extremely powerful even if it has not been used for its original purpose for several centuries. The most obvious examples are ancient sites such as megaliths, standing stones or yew groves, although I've also noticed that converted chapels and church houses which have reverted to secular use often generate more than their fair share of psychic phenomena.

The Anglo-Saxons believed that magic was not as effective on people out of doors as it was when they were in their homes[22] yet the earth does sometimes generate very powerful psychic effects. For example, energy springs sometimes rise vertically from the earth, usually as spiral or pillar. These are pure energy and nothing to do with water, and while some are beneficial and healing, others (for example, where an energy line crosses an underground stream) may be harmful. The old saying, that witches (and sometimes also demons and vampires) cannot cross water is probably a folk memory of earlier knowledge about the harmful effects of underground water and energy channels on humans, animals and plants. However not everyone reacts in the same way to this energy; what is harmful to one group for example, may be beneficial to another.

If the paranormal activity is earth related, we may notice light anomalies such as small dancing 'fairy lights' or spirit orbs. We may also feel light-headed, faint, heavy, drowsy, nauseous or hear humming or buzzing sounds (although obviously we should check with our doctor first in case these have a physical cause.)

Quartz watches and clocks are sometimes affected both by magnetism and psychic attacks that drain their batteries. Interference in mechanical (i.e. wind-up or chain driven) timepieces however can also be due to an individual's magnetic field. For example, if I try to wear any type of watch on a regular basis it will always stop working with no apparent cause!

The geology of our local area may also encourage certain phenomena, for example, basalt is significantly magnetic. Many living organisms sense variations in geomagnetic field activity and humans probably do this too, albeit unknowingly. For example, in the Scilly Isles, flower bulbs planted near large granite boulders flower earlier than those planted in other fields in the same area where there are no boulders present.[23] Granite is thought to emit radon gas which may contribute to the mystic atmosphere of many

[22] Turner (1840) :196

[23] Devereux (1990) :187

ancient sites; it may be no coincidence that granite-rich areas, such as Cornwall and Brittany contain many megaliths. The solstices and the winter full moonrise may also increase radiation in certain ancient sites.[24]

Hauntings are not confined to old dwellings; many newly built homes also report paranormal activity. I once investigated a house where the owners repeatedly heard the sound of a steam engine rushing through their home, even though there had never been a train station in the village, steam trains were long obsolete and the house was barely a year old.

Eventually, by checking old maps and asking around, we discovered the house had been built on a drained marsh and the entire village had a reputation for being extremely damp. As we've already noted, psychic phenomena are very common in and around water. As for the noise of the train – there had once been a station a few miles away that had closed in the 1960's. It seems that the sound was somehow imprinted into the landscape and then carried further afield by the water.

Nobody had noticed it before because the area was then uninhabited marshland. Although the land had been drained, the 'imprint' of the sound remained; there may even have been a blind spring still present nearby. Water, especially in underground streams, can also carry small amounts of radioactivity. Water from a well, however, seems to have power only at its original location.

If we suspect that our home is affected by earth energies, look for marker stones, large mounds of earth (sometimes called *tumuli*) and clumps of trees, especially yew which is able to regenerate from within; old specimens may be thousands of years old. Check old Ordinance Survey maps in local libraries, since these often mark boundaries, standing stones, *tumuli* etc that have since vanished. If there is evidence of human activity – even centuries ago – this may be linked to what is happening in the home.

Often in summer, for example, I notice the sound of many footsteps walking up our street even when there's nobody there. A mid-nineteenth century map of the area showed that at the top

---

[24] Devereux (1990): 167

of the street, where the road peters out into the mountain, there were several 'ancient sheep folds' marked on the map. These don't usually appear on modern Ordinance Survey maps, but further research showed that these sheep folds were in fact *hafodtai* or summer dwellings where people lived when they took their animals up to the high mountain pastures many centuries ago. What I had heard therefore was almost certainly an echo of an earlier annual summer journey up into the mountains.

Earth energies sometimes trap certain phenomena so they are later experienced by people who had nothing to do with the original event. For example, it is possible for certain houses to exert a baneful influence on virtually everyone who lives in them. Or certain people find they are constantly at loggerheads with everyone who moves into a certain house. We may be able to trace this back to a specific family or events, but usually these things are hard to uncover. It's always worth checking, however, with people who have lived in the district for a long time and may remember old feuds or stories about an area.

Sometimes earth energies have a man-made source, such as electricity pylons, underground cables or watercourses. These can cause lethargy and dizziness. Aerial photographs and Ordinance Survey maps are often helpful in locating them. The energies given off by these power sources can affect our own health. Likewise, rooms that contain electrical appliances (especially computers) benefit from regular cleansing. If we feel the atmosphere becoming stale and heavy, keep a dish of consecrated salt there for a few days; change it regularly until the situation improves.

We've already seen that some psychic attacks can result in people feeling tired and drained for no obvious reason. The same goes for certain spirit entities that obtain the power they need by draining batteries or even people. Indeed, it's not uncommon for contact with the spirit world to leave us feeling tired and washed out, although some are more affected by this than others.

A home that is severely affected by earth energies can take some getting used to, although it may be reassuring that at least they are not personally hostile to us. Try moving the furniture around since some parts of a room may be less affected than others. If a good night's sleep eludes us due to the presence of earth energies, it may be worth moving the bed to the other side of the room to see if things improve. We often notice that children and animals will instinctively avoid sleeping in certain areas. If this happens, then move the bed so it is well clear of the places they already avoid. It's worth remembering too that natural earth energies (as opposed to electricity pylons etc.,) are not constant but fluctuate, particularly at certain times of the year, for example at the solstices and equinoxes.

Phenomena caused by chthonic (or earth) entities such as fairies, house brownies, elves, black dogs, water horses etc. are often difficult to distinguish from an ordinary haunting, although the former also involves 'practical jokes' such as moving and hiding things. If we don't overreact to this, they will often return what they've taken and if they do, remember to thank them.

The idea that fairy folk need to be banished seems to be relatively recent. If, as some suggest, they were once the *lars*, *genii* or *penates* of the ancient Classical world, then they were originally honoured as valued members of the household. Christianity however, taught that all chthonic entities, including fairies, were damned.[25] Personally I don't like the idea of banishing any of these entities, who belong to the earth, were here long before we arrived and will still be here long after we leave.

Treat them with respect, talk to them politely and we will almost always get along well together.

---

[25] Evans-Wentz (2004 edition): 62

CHAPTER FOUR

Types of attack and attacker. The various ways attacks are conducted. Using the elements to convey psychic attacks. Pictures, signatures, tattoos and hidden objects. The cursing psalms. Cursing stones. Magnetism and charging. Hair and nail clippings.

It would be a mistake to think that just because we have never attacked or hurt anyone, we cannot become the victim of a psychic attack, although I have met many people who believe just that. The truth is that psychic attackers do not always need to have a good reason for their actions.

Sometimes we are just in the wrong place at the wrong time and part of a random attack comes our way. Sometimes hexes that have nothing to do with us 'bounce' and catch us in their crossfire. Sometimes we must accept that we may never discover the culprit or know why we are being picked up on, although with a prolonged attack there is usually a very good chance of finding whoever is behind it. With any sudden, one-off attack however, our main concern must be to protect ourselves and those we love.

Some psychic attackers don't realise what they are doing. Hexing can be very easy for people with a certain type of character: anyone who erupts in fury can do a great deal of damage before finally calming down, as can the person who sits brooding, night after night over some real or imagined slight. Another problem is that hexing is very, very addictive. Often people begin to hex just to see whether they can do it. When they discover they can, it becomes difficult to stop since it gives them a wonderful sense of power and control. Eventually – if they don't take steps to put a stop to it – they hex because they must, not necessarily because they want to. Before they know it, they're addicted.

Some people combine magical attacks with physical ones. I once had a case where the psychic attacker not only hexed her neighbours but also went around surreptitiously poisoning their plants. This was her way of intimidating them, making them feel that everything they owned or loved was cursed. So even when we find a physical explanation for strange phenomena, we may still have to deal with a few underlying psychic matters.

I have already suggested making a note of the times and dates of any psychic phenomena. Unintentional attacks often happen unexpectedly whereas most intentional attacks happen within a month or two of an argument or quarrel. Very few hexers have the patience to wait for years before seeking their revenge; most, if they know they have the power, tend to strike quickly. If we suspect our attacker's identity, then we need to investigate their character and consider whether they are the type of person who believes that revenge is a dish best eaten cold. Also, try to discover whether they have ever harboured long-standing grudges in the past. What we are looking for is a pattern of hexing.

With deliberate attacks there is a good chance we will be able to discover exactly who is responsible. Sometimes hexers will actually announce their intention to attack us, probably hoping we'll be so terrified that we'll do their work for them and end up hexing ourselves!

In the ancient world, curses were usually hidden so they could do their work in secret; they were buried in the ground, in graves or wells etc. However sometimes they were set up in public places such as temples to intimidate the victim. Really skilled psychic attackers – as opposed to psychic bullies – rarely give any warning but operate like snipers. Half the battle with learning to defend oneself against them is to recognise who is doing the attacking and how they are doing it. Most psychic attackers belong to one of four main groups:

Attacker Type 1

This, the rarest type, is an experienced and powerful magician. Many people claim to belong to this group, but in reality they belong in the second group below. This first group do not normally hex all that often, having their minds on greater things than sending out the odd hex or two. Also, they tend to reserve their skills for dealing with rivals rather than people who simply cross their path. If we do happen to get on the wrong side of someone in this group then we will soon know about it.

In Brief: Usually attacks by this group are sudden and devastating, although a really spiteful Type 1 attacker can sometimes mount a prolonged attack. They will rarely if ever, admit what they are doing, nor will they openly advertise any interest in the occult.

There are exceptions of course, where a skilled occultist adores the limelight to the extent that someone needs to shove him off the stage, but these are few and far between. In my experience, the show-offs are generally more interested in magical fireworks than psychic attacks!

Attacker Type 2

The second group is slightly larger, but still not that common. They have some knowledge and skill, not enough to be considered powerful, but enough to frighten. Often, they like to intimidate others by claiming to belong to Type 1 above or by fixing us with a steely glare while muttering threateningly. Usually this is complete and utter gibberish. I once knew a woman who claimed she could kill with a single 'word of power.' In fact, the only words of power she had ever had any contact with were 'on' and 'off' on the TV remote control!

Members of this group tend to court publicity. During World War II, Life Magazine reported on 'hexing parties' set up to curse Hitler.[26] These featured a life-sized model of Hitler (made from the sort of mannequin displayed in clothes shops) that was tortured, stuck with pins and nails and finally buried in a pine forest to be 'food for worms.' (Similar activities have been reported recently – 2018 – with dolls and pin cushions representing Donald Trump).

Quite apart from the fact that the model of Hitler mentioned above was made of material that would not decay and which no right-thinking worms would be tempted to eat, the whole tone of the article was frivolous and flippant. We shall never know how

---

[26] *Life Magazine* 10th February 1941

skilled the participants were, although the fact they were prepared to pose for Life Magazine suggests it was more about publicity than anything else. To paraphrase George Bernard Shaw: *Them as can do, them as can't simply threaten.*

If anyone in this group does try to hex us, it is rarely as bad as they would like us to believe. We are perfectly capable of dealing with it – and them. We should get into the habit of saying 'Back at you!' to any nasty comments they send our way. I guarantee they will not like it.

In Brief: Type 2's try to intimidate by claiming to be powerful witches and/or magicians. They will boast about their past 'successes' which they cannot prove. Some even claim the credit for causing accidents and disasters that had nothing to do with them.

Far from being masters of the dark arts, this group are mostly play-acting. They cause more harm through intimidation and fear than through any magical ability.

Attacker Type 3

The third group is much larger. These attackers have little real knowledge but an abundance of spite and malice; their attacks can be very unpleasant. Many people wrongly believe that we must dabble in the occult in order to launch a psychic attack. This is not true. Psychic attacks are almost always the product of a spiteful and brooding nature and we should never underestimate spite or jealousy. Poets may claim that love makes the world go round but it's spite and jealousy that cause the firework displays!

We can easily be hexed by someone constantly directing spiteful, malicious thoughts towards us. They may not have the knowledge to hex us properly, but their attacks are nonetheless effective because of the sheer amount of time and energy they devote to ill-wishing.

While most people will have the odd nasty thought or send out a sudden burst of unkind energy (which they often regret soon afterwards), a Type 3 hexer devotes an incredible amount of time to ill-will and often attacks at night. It's as though they cannot sleep for inwardly raging about the real or imagined slights they believe they have suffered.

Spite can manifest in many ways including unpleasant 'digs' and snide comments. If challenged, they may try and justify it, with comments such as, 'She's got a better home/job/car than I have.' 'She flaunts her money at me.' 'His wife loves him more than mine does…' 'Why should they have XYZ and I don't?' Or they may pass it off as harmless banter, 'What's the matter? Can't you take a joke?' They will try anything to deflect attention once there's a chance they've been rumbled.

And so it goes on; the resentment builds and the rage is suppressed like a simmering volcano until one day it erupts. We may not be there to see it happen, but if we're the target, we'll soon know.

There are unintentional attackers in this group, too. Often they are lonely and become fixated on another individual either because they find them sexually attractive or because they envy their life and would like to be part of it. While not initially wishing their victim harm, this type of attacker eventually becomes so frustrated and angry that their psychic malice and negativity sprays out right, left and centre, so that the victim (and often her family) become the focus of the attack.

These attackers may be initially unaware of what they are doing, but the effects of their activities can still be devastating. People who launch accidental or unintentional psychic attacks are often difficult to identify. Their anger and lack of magical skill makes the whole thing a bit like firing a blunderbuss - they could hit anyone, not just the original target.

Attacks by groups of people can also fall into the Type 3. Group attacks are always deliberate and often use thought forms. They can also be extremely powerful whether they have any real occult knowledge or not, simply because group energies are stronger than that of an individual.

Dealing with attacks by a group can be difficult since we must often have to break off all contact with quite a wide circle of people which can be difficult. However, although their energies can be strong initially, they often tail off as members lose interest – which they will eventually. In the early stages though, group attacks can feel overwhelming. The methods for dealing with attacks by groups and individuals is essentially the same, however.

In Brief: Type 3 individuals may attack accidentally or deliberately. They usually manifest as a slow build up of small incidents, but it's also possible to have the odd violent burst of activity. Usually it's someone we know who harbours a grudge. Very occasionally we can be hit by a ricochet and may never know who was responsible. Type 3 *Group* attackers are always deliberate, however.

Attacker Type 4

The fourth type of hexer is... us. Self-attacks seem to come from nowhere although many victims of these have noticed certain tell-tale signs beforehand. These can include being touched when nobody's there, especially at night. Low level poltergeist-type activity is another symptom such as bed covers being moved slightly. I once experienced the corner of the duvet being whipped back very sharply and a cold breath blowing on my face.

Occasionally we may hear quiet murmuring or chattering, loud enough to notice but too low to identify more than the occasional word. (However, murmuring sometimes occurs when we are attacked by a third party.) Mechanical items, such as clocks, often go a bit wild or stop altogether when their owners are stressed or under intense pressure. It can be very disconcerting.

Women sometimes notice that this sort of phenomena peaks around their menstrual periods. These aren't so much attacks as warning signals, although they are difficult to get to grips with because most of us would rather believe that any attack must come from a third party rather than ourselves. It's always easier to blame someone else for our problems.

In Brief: It's always worth considering a type 4 attack, if only to rule it out. We must be honest with ourselves, though: are we particularly stressed or angry at the moment? Are we unable to sleep for worrying? Try taking a simple anti-stress remedy such as Dr Bach's Rescue Remedy for a few days and see if things quieten down. If they do, then carry out some thorough cleansing and try to honestly assess what we might be doing to encourage them. Remember, in the early days at least, these are more likely to be warning signals than actual attacks. There are suggestions for dealing with them in Chapter Seventeen.

The Basic Types of Attack

Having identified the basic types of attacker, we can now look at the two most common methods in use. The first uses mental focus while the second sends out a thought form or other entity. These two methods account for 99% of all psychic attacks and can manifest in a wide variety of phenomena. Sometimes attacks are a combination of both methods - mental focus and thought forms.

Each of the first three groups of attackers above can have a variety of intentions when they hex. Some want to harm their victim physically, perhaps by inducing sudden acute ill health (such as a heart attack) or an accident. Psychic phenomena are often minimal in this type of attack as the hexer concentrates his efforts on the victim's health and well-being.

Another type of attack aims to harm mentally and emotionally, by terrorising the victim until she becomes a nervous wreck and unable to function normally. These attacks often involve objects and the fabric of the home rather than the victim's health although experiencing a high level of frightening psychic phenomena will eventually take its toll on our physical well-being.

Finally, there are those who prefer the long, drawn-out process of draining the victim, often with a series of non-specific illnesses and mishaps that gradually mount up over time causing chronic poor health, minor accidents and misery all round. Sometimes the attacker does this in order to empower himself, although often that is just an added bonus to the main intention of causing harm to others.

What all types of attack have in common is the desire to control and harm the victim. Now we shall look at them in more detail.

Type of Attack 1 : Mental Focus

Mental focus is where the attacker focuses on the victim, or on some aspect of the victim, and wishes him ill. We might sense this type of attack at first as a growing sense of unease followed by a stream of inexplicable psychic phenomena. The Evil Eye requires mental focus. So does *maleficium.* The attack can be carried out at close quarters or over a distance of many miles and methods vary. Some people use full-blown ritual while others just seem to be able to stare at the victim and achieve their intentions via mental focus.

If we're dealing with such an attacker face to face, they usually try to imprint their will on us through the third eye - that invisible area in the forehead, just above the nose. Observing them carefully, we notice they either stare at us (in order to set up a connection from them to us, so they can get inside our head) or they close their eyes when speaking (this can often be disguised as rubbing the eyes). Closing the eyes prevents us setting up any kind of connection to them, which is just another way of dominating us, since it makes all conversation a one-way process. (See Chapter Eleven for methods for dealing with this type of attack.)

Sometimes the attacker may not have personal access to us, but has managed to get hold of something personal of ours, for example a lock of hair, nail parings, clothing, bandages, used hankies and tissues, chamber lye (the greyish brown matter from the bottom of a used chamber pot) and anything stained with semen, menstrual blood, urine, ear wax, or faeces. By mistreating something the victim has had contact with, the attacker can magically transfer this harm to the victim herself.

Another - very old - method of using such material is to incorporate it into a doll made to represent the victim. Whatever is done to the doll is then magically transferred to the victim. Thus a pin stuck in the head, for example, causes a headache. If the attacker cannot get hold of nail parings, hair etc., they will sometimes make (or buy) a doll that physically resembles the victim. It may have the same colour hair or wear the same sort of clothes. What is important is that in the attacker's eyes, *this is his victim*. Some hexers formally name the dolls after their victims, and a few even go so far as to baptise them!

Using dolls for magical purposes (especially erotic curses) can be traced back into ancient Greece and Egypt. The traditional method of harming a doll is to pierce its body with a pin, although I have occasionally heard of other methods – tying string tightly around the neck, or even ritually breaking a limb. Other methods could include making a miniature handbag and purse for a doll meant to represent a victim who values money above all else. Piercing the bag and purse would result in the woman suffering heavy financial losses. The remedies for dealing with an attack conveyed by a doll are given in Chapter Fifteen.

Sometimes a curse tablet (often of metal but occasionally of paper) is tied to a doll, along with locks of hair, scraps of the victim's clothing and even to lengths of thread. Threads occur surprisingly often in curses, possibly because many such spells demand that the victim be twisted and spun around until they lose their senses.[27]

Type of Attack 2 - Using Thought Forms

Another popular method of conveying a hex is to use some other entity, such as a thought form, as a courier. Anyone can create a thought form (children do it all the time) and they are not intrinsically harmful. Some are conjured deliberately, others accidentally. One of the most common problems with thought forms is that they can sometimes become rather wayward if not properly set up and controlled, which often happens when someone has created it accidentally or carelessly.

Some thought forms can be very frightening and play an important role in a psychic attack. Others may be sent out as spies (as we saw in Chapter Two), either gathering information on a victim's habits and routine or finding out whether the attack is having the desired effect. If we suspect that we are dealing with a

[27] Mees (2009) :60

thought form 'spy' then we are almost certainly being attacked by someone with a reasonable amount of occult knowledge.

How can we be sure it's a thought form? If we *suddenly* begin seeing or hearing entities who were not present before, then we are either experiencing a ghost returning for a 'visit' or dealing with a thought form. However, whereas visiting ghosts were once human, and will appear and behave as they did in life, a thought form may be a little more fantastic in appearance and behaviour. Also, a visiting ghost rarely threatens, whereas a thought form sent as part of a psychic attack may be quite menacing. Since a ghost was once alive it may be possible to identify it by talking to people who have lived in the area for a long time and might remember that person when they were alive. There is more information on thought forms in Chapter Five.

How Hexes are Conveyed

Even if someone works a hex by mental focus alone, they often find it very helpful to physically convey an attack to the victim. There are two basic methods, both requiring an item that is in some way charged, empowered or magnetised.

The first method uses something belonging to the victim which falls into the hands of the attacker. This can include hair, nail parings etc., that have been magnetised by their close contact with the victim. The attacker then works on the object, usually by mistreating it, and the abuse is magically transferred to the victim.

The second method conveys the hex by allowing something belonging to the attacker to fall into the unsuspecting hands of the victim. It may be given as a gift or even deliberately hidden in cushions, books (especially if it has been written on parchment or paper), slipped into a pocket or otherwise concealed amongst something similar where it will not be noticed.

For example, an empowered or hexed photo will be hidden in a photo album, a hexed crystal will be hidden in a box of crystals and so on. Once magnetised or charged by the attacker it can transfers itself to the victim *provided it is accepted willingly.* That's the reason why so many hexes are disguised as something else;

while we're busy looking out for a cursed talisman made of a planetary metal and incised with strange glyphs, the real hex will arrive disguised as gifts or greeting cards that we would not dream of refusing unless we understood their true nature!

Although a hex works best when it has been readily accepted, there are still people who will try and hide something in our home without our knowing, so we should check thoroughly, under rugs and carpets and even in the hems of curtains! The first time I ever found a hex, it had been concealed within a row of books, having been offered (and refused) as a gift.

Also look for pictures which can conceal several complex visual messages. In the case of hexes, a picture quite literally can paint a thousand words! Nor is it necessarily in a frame – I once found a very decorative tea towel that was being used to convey a hex! If we find something, then we need to ritually destroy it. I prefer burning whenever possible or burying in salt (and sometimes a combination of both.) Further suggestions are in Chapter Fifteen.

Signatures can also be used in hexing since they are unique to each individual and contain something of our essential self. We don't have to be famous in order to possess a powerful signature. I once knew a witch who constantly wrote her name over every scrap of paper that came her way: old envelopes, newspapers - you name it and she had written her name on it! This was a method of marking out her territory, in effect she was magically 'claiming' everything as hers. If we notice anyone doing this in our own personal space, we should keep cleansing it until things settle down. (See Chapters Ten and Twelve).

Unlike hair and nail clippings, it is all too easy for our signature to fall into the wrong hands. Think of the number of times we sign letters or cards! We should therefore, whenever possible, avoid allowing anyone hostile to us to have free access to our signature. Likewise, if we have *their* signature we should try and get rid of it, preferably by burning as soon as reasonably possible.

If this is not possible, perhaps because it happens to be on an important deed or document, sprinkle it with very dry salt, then brush it away and cleanse the page using a suitable cleansing method from Chapter Fifteen.

Something else that can be used to manipulate unwitting victims is a tattoo, especially those featuring names. Remember that when we name something, we exert power over it. That's one reason why the sacrament of baptism was so important in the early Christian church. Naming is an aspect of *claiming*. With a tattoo, the wearer has literally assimilated the person named into his or her own flesh.

A less permanent version of the tattoo – although it works on exactly the same principle - is the love-struck teenager who writes a boyfriend's/girlfriend's name on their hand in biro or felt pen. Although this isn't a permanent name-claim, remember that teenagers can be magically very powerful, yet have no idea how to control it. With both tattoos and biro marks the person who is being named has no say in the matter, they are, in effect, possessed by a third party, *whether they like it or not*. It is still a form of magic, and in the wrong hands, can be extremely potent. (For dealing with these see Chapter Fifteen).

Hexes can be conveyed in various other ways: on metal, silk, linen, cut glass, dolls, screwed up pieces of paper and even signet rings. Stones can sometimes be used to convey a hex – they are usually larger than the ones the fairies bring (see Chapter Two) and are almost always marked.

I once moved into a place where the former occupant had left several curse stones marked with black electrical tape in the shape of a sun wheel. They looked for all the world like very sinister hot cross buns, but the magnetism in them was quite appalling. To neutralise these, I removed the black tape and burned it, then ritually cleansed the stones before burying them in salt. Another possibility would be to throw them into a fast running river.

If we suspect the identity of the person who is attacking us, then we should look for anything they may have given us. In particular, look out for objects made of leather, fur, grasses, straw or linen. Perhaps because these are all 'natural' they seem to accept a magnetising charge more easily than synthetic materials such as plastic or nylon. They may also be conveyed on metal, such as tin and lead which are relatively easy to inscribe with sigils and texts.

Usually these were buried in the ground (especially in cemeteries, where the victim was unlikely to find them).

The act of burying can also be an integral part of the spell, and an ancient Celtic curse from Gaul states, '*Just as this lead cannot be seen and is buried, so may the youth, skin, life, ox grain and wellbeing of the ones who have done me wrong be buried.*'[28] Nasty stuff indeed.

This type of 'Just as... so may...' inscription is known as the *similia similibus curantur* technique. It is very popular in hexing because the action (in this case burying) physically supports the magical intention of the curse.

Curses were often cast into water. In the ancient world, public baths were particularly popular for casting various types of spells, although only certain locations, such as the healing spring and baths at Aquae Sulis, in Bath were used for hexes. This may reflect the belief that the healing deities present in such places could both give health and take it away. Healing springs were particularly popular for binding spells, and also for cursing those who had broken vows. Sometimes a hex may be a self-imprecation, where a group of people with a common interest, vow that anyone who breaks their rules is automatically cursed.

There's a psychological advantage in displaying the curse where the victim can see it. In the ancient world curses were sometimes displayed at the local temple for all to see, because this not only intimidated the victim but also forced him to make some sort of reparation for whatever he had done.

What sort of things were written on hexes? Often the spell is constructed in the form of '*Just as.... so you too...*' for example, '*Just as this plate is broken, so may* [Name's] *heart be broken too.*' Hexes have worked this way for thousands of years. Traditional words and phrases such as *rogamus* meaning 'we asked' or '*et deprecamus*' meaning 'and we curse' may be written either back to front or as anagrams with the words jumbled up so they're not immediately recognisable.

Another reason for jumbling the words is to show the twisting and confusion intended to be visited upon the victim. Sometimes

---

[28] Mees (2009): 71

the letters of a name may be concealed within the hex. This almost always belongs to the victim; a skilled hexer rarely writes their own name on a hex.[29] Occasionally, just to complicate things still further, random letters (or even a complete alphabet from A-Z) may be added to the written curse.

Sometimes we encounter objects that have such an unpleasant feeling to them that we cannot bear them any longer. For example, I once bought a piece of furniture that made me very uneasy. It was an innocuous-looking blanket box, and although I couldn't quite put my finger on it, I felt as though it was watching me. One of its previous owners *had* been interested in occult matters, but we barely knew each other and certainly not at the time she had owned or disposed of the box. She had no special grievance towards me, as far as I knew.

In the end, convinced I was being rather foolish (not to mention paranoid), I decided to strip the paint off, varnish it, thoroughly cleanse it and then give it away. It was then I discovered that the previous owner had painted eyes (rather like the ones seen on ancient Egyptian coffins) all over the wood and *then* painted over it. I don't know what sort of paint she used for the eyes, but it resisted both paint stripper and a heat gun. Eventually we had to sand the wood right down and get rid of them that way! I then blessed and cleansed the piece and there were never any more problems.

Interestingly, an old word for a psychic attack or hex was to 'overlook' someone. One of the most common places to feel 'overlooked' is on the internet. It's easy to sneak around behind the anonymity of our computer screen, watching, waiting, gathering information. We must be very careful what we allow others to see and know. Before putting any information on the internet always consider whether it could be useful to a potential attacker. Try and avoid handing anyone information that will enable them to dominate us.

Remember we can all be who or what we wish on the internet, a fact that makes magical visualisation far too easy. Those who are

---

29 Mees (2009): 57

timid in the everyday world may find an energy online that is normally lacking. It is precisely because their everyday lives are relatively lonely, that they *stay* online, in this new *persona,* gradually building up their strength and learning how to dominate others. Meanwhile their bewildered victims find themselves growing progressively weaker.

Using Elements to Convey a Psychic Attack

When the four elements - fire, air, earth or water - are used to convey a psychic attack, they usually manifest as follows:

- Attacks using the element of Air tend to produce foul smells without physical cause, ghostly entities (or thought forms), and swarms of flies or birds. This element can also be responsible for aural disturbances such as whispering and knocking.

- Attacks using the element of Fire can be extremely frightening, often manifesting as poltergeist-type phenomena. Victims may experience itching, thirst and insomnia. Since deliberate psychic attacks often involve making a burnt offering of some sort, they are best countered using water and salt. Regular showers or baths (especially if we add a little salt to the latter) will go a long way to countering this type of attack. We should also keep our body temperature as cool as is comfortable and do everything possible to ensure a good night's sleep.

- Attacks using the element of Earth tend to involve moving objects and thought forms.

- Water is probably the most versatile conveyer of psychic attacks and may be used in just about any type of attack.

The Cursing Psalms

Whenever people work themselves into a state worrying about being attacked by demons, ghosts etc., they miss an important fact: the vast majority of psychic attacks – 99.9% - are caused by *living human beings*. And since only a very few of these are going to be practising witches or pagans, it stands to reason that many of the people who launch psychic attacks may in fact be members of other faiths, including Christianity.

Many people are very surprised to learn that there are curses in the Bible, particularly those known as the 'Cursing Psalms.' It is worth knowing about these in some detail since what can start off as a benign, even beautiful, psalm can end up wishing all sorts of hellish misfortune upon others. It we hear someone apparently reciting an innocuous piece of scripture at us, it pays to remember that the end of the quote (which might not be spoken aloud or within earshot) could in fact be a curse. It was a favourite method when I was young, perhaps because people were more likely to learn and quote the scriptures in those days.

The words that are omitted are often more important than those that are spoken, and the speaker is hoping we don't know the psalms as well as he does. Interestingly, most people who use the psalms to curse tend to use the rather elegant language of the King James translation. It's sad, but the outwardly devout are often among the worst culprits for using Biblical texts for hexing.

A good example is Psalm 143. It is one of the Seven Penitential Psalms and at first sight seems to be a statement of confidence in God despite all the trials and tribulations of life. The early verses (5 – 6) include the apparently harmless, *'I remember the days of old; I meditate on all thy works; I muse on the work of thy hands. I stretch forth my hands unto thee: my soul thirsteth after thee, as a thirsty land.'*

Read on, however, and in the final verse the Psalm takes a much darker turn: *'And of thy mercy cut off mine enemies, and destroy all them that afflict my soul: for I am thy servant.'*

No wonder that many clergy avoid reciting that particular Psalm nowadays!

One of the most famous cursing psalms is Psalm 109. Again, the first few verses are unremarkable, such as verse 3: *'In return for my love they set themselves against me, even though I had prayed for them…'* Within a few short verses, however, we find:

- *Let his days be few; and let another take his office;* (verse 8)
- *May his sons be orphans, and his wife a widow;* (verse 9)
- *Let his sons always beg and wander, and seek food out of their ruins;* (verse 10)
- *Let the moneylender lay a snare for all that is his; and let strangers plunder his labour;* (verse 11)
- *Let there be none giving mercy to him; nor any to have pity on his orphans;* (verse 12)
- *Let his posterity be cut off; let their name be blotted out in the following generation;* (verse 13)

Any one of these imprecations would be quite at home in the magical papyri of Graeco-Roman Egypt! Psalm 69 was a particular favourite when I was young; people would mutter, *'Lord (or God), thou knowest,'*[30] rather self-righteously, while mentally adding the rest of the Psalm which included: *'Let their table become a snare before them: and that which should have been for their welfare, let it become a trap. Let their eyes be darkened, that they see not; and make their loins continually to shake. Pour out thine indignation upon them, and let thy wrathful anger take hold of them. Let their habitation be desolate; and let none dwell in their tents'.*

Perhaps most sinister of all, they would have been muttering verse 28 which reads: *'Let them be blotted out of the book of the living.'* Strong stuff indeed.

Since the Cursing Psalms can be found in the Old Testament, they may have originated with ancient pagan tribes such as the Hittites. For example, Esarhaddon, king of Assyria included a list of curses as a precaution in his treaty with his vassal king Ramataia of Urakazabann: *'As rain does not fall from a heaven of brass, so may*

---

[30] This quote turns up surprisingly often on gravestones! Indeed my eldest aunt's grave bears this line.

dew and rain not come upon your fields and lowlands; in place of dew may it rain coals upon your land.' [31]

This is repeated almost word for word in the Old Testament, Deuteronomy (Ch. 28 v. 23): *'And the heavens over your head will be brass, and the earth under you shall be iron. The Lord will make the rain of your land powder and dust; from heaven it shall come down upon you until you are destroyed.'*

Of course, the Old Testament with its 'eye for an eye' mentality, might be considered a more suitable vehicle for curses and revenge than the New Testament with its 'turn the other cheek' approach. However, in the Acts of the Apostles, Peter's rebuke kills both Ananias and his wife Sapphira, while the apostle Paul, never one to mince his words, declared *'But though we, or an angel from Heaven, preach any other gospel unto you than that which we have preached unto you, let him be accursed'.* (Galatians Ch.1 v.8) During the last two thousand years, those who were excommunicated by the Catholic Church were declared *anathema,* which is an ancient Greek word meaning a curse.

In order to psychically defend ourselves, we must understand the nature of hexing. All too often people simply shy away from it, hoping it will go away if they ignore it. This rarely happens, partly because hexing is highly addictive. Normally, the better someone becomes at magic, the less she needs to do it. But for people with a certain temperament, hexing becomes an obsession.

One reason for this is that it gives people a power they otherwise lack. If we go out into the street and punch a passer-by, we run a high risk of either being arrested or receiving a black eye in return. It's perfectly possible however – and I've seen it done – to sit at the window and make people fall flat on their face without them ever realising that it was not an accident.

Hexing's great attraction is that it appears to remove the risk of retaliation, punishment or even detection, although morally I believe it is just as culpable as anything else designed to harm a third party. Hexers often attack people not because they wish to,

---

[31] Greehy (1978)

or even because they feel justified in exacting some sort of revenge, but because they *can*. And once they start, it's very hard to stop.

However attractive hexing may seem, it comes at a price. For a start, it encourages some very bad magical habits. Hexers are often wildly reckless. For example, we should never hex someone when we are in a rage. Although it can be a powerful impetus for our spell, uncontrolled emotional turmoil drives all sensible magical practice right out of the window.

Yet I know from experience that one witch within my family often hexed when she was in a temper, never giving herself chance to calm down; she certainly never looked for any kind of compromise. No, she got down to magic while the smoke was still streaming out of her nostrils. As a result, her spells, although intended to hurt her victim, often turned into a psychic scattergun. Sometimes she even unintentionally injured those closest to her.

Luckily for us, the world is basically a good place, and most people are not out to do us harm, psychically or otherwise. However, most of us, if we are honest, will admit there are times when we are tempted to hex, just as there are times when we say something rash and five minutes later wish we hadn't. By the same token, most people can set a hex in motion and then regret it.

Those who *regularly* resort to hexing however, don't usually bother with much hand-wringing or soul-searching either before or after. They just do it again and again. And they never, *ever* feel guilty about it.

CHAPTER FIVE

How attacks using Direct Thought will manifest. How attacks that send out thought forms manifest. Thought forms, elemental essence, and the Artificial Elemental. The Aura. Setting up a guardian thought form.

As we saw in the previous chapter, using a thought form is a popular method of sending psychic attacks and has been used magically through the ages in many different traditions. The basic method remains the same: the attacker creates an entity using the power of thought and this is then sent to intimidate (and sometimes spy on) the victim. Thought forms can be created unintentionally too, since they require no special occult skills or knowledge. Children often create them as imaginary friends.

Thought forms can look surprisingly solid and realistic, capable of impressing themselves on any of our five senses. Unlike ghosts, which replicate the appearance of a once-living person or animal, a thought form's appearance is only limited by the imagination of its creator. This is helpful when we need to establish whether something is a ghostly entity or a thought form. If the figure differs in any way from what could be expected of its real life equivalent, then it is almost certainly a thought form.

Symptoms of a Thought Form Attack

Whereas an attack sent by the power of thought alone (i.e. without it manifesting as an entity) usually manifests as sudden illness, accidents, telekinesis (things moving without apparent cause) and poltergeist type activity, an attack by thought form is rather different. We may see things such as shadowy figures or experience illnesses that slowly drain all our vitality.

We may even notice the sudden appearance of certain types of animals, insects or birds. Some may be thought forms, while others are real creatures attracted by the thought forms in their own image. Attacks by thought form usually happen at night, when the victim is tired and vulnerable, and the attacker is lying awake, brooding.

Thought forms can be very frightening, almost as though their creators know our weak spots and how to exploit them - which is often true, since many victims hand this information out to all and sundry on a plate, blogging and posting on social networking sites about their terror of snakes and spiders etc. If we do find ourselves confronted with a thought form that seems to have stepped right out of our worst nightmares, bear in mind that we probably confided our fears - directly or indirectly - to our attacker.

How Thought Forms are Created

Whenever we use our minds, we create thoughts, the seeds from which thought forms grow. However, seeds won't normally grow if we just throw them in a bucket of sand and forget about them; they need proper soil, the correct temperature and regular watering. The same applies to thoughts, which only turn into thought forms when certain conditions are present.

As we can see from the diagram on page 72, our physical bodies are enveloped in a number of layers sometimes referred to as our Aura or the Auric Field. Although invisible to most people, psychics and clairvoyants see the Aura as layers of colour and shapes or even as vibrations.[32] The Aura is three-dimensional covering, surrounding us like a shell or bubble.

Closest to our physical body is the etheric body, which influences nutrition, growth and reproduction. Next is the astral body, the seat of all emotions and feelings. There are other bodies, as shown on the diagram, but it is the astral and etheric bodies that concern us for the purposes of thought forms.

---

[32] Not all psychics and clairvoyants agree what the Auric Fields look like. Some have a very precise definition made up of a spectrum of colours like a rainbow, beginning with red nearest the body and violet furthest away. Some people just see one or two colours, others prefer the term 'field of light.' Nor is there complete consensus about the number of divisions in the Auric Field; some claim there are seven, others say there are twelve.

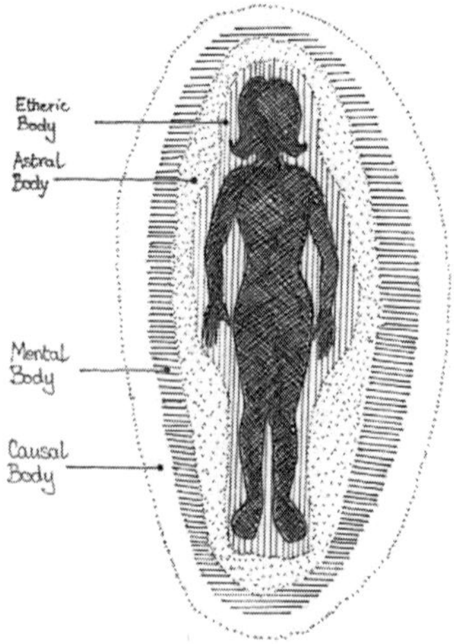

Whenever we create thoughts, they are projected through our Auric Field and out into the world beyond. Most don't get very far, dying for lack of support and nourishment, just like the seed in the bucket of sand. For our thoughts to become thought forms, they need to meet up with something known as 'elemental essence'. This is sometimes described as a half-intelligent life form, which simply follows its basic instinct to 'take shape' and become an animated form.

In order to achieve this, the elemental essence searches for discarded thoughts (usually human but occasionally animal). When it finds something suitable, it nourishes the thoughts which in turn give the elemental essence its character or shape. Once this happens, it becomes an entity in its own right with an independent physical existence.

However, it is not yet a fully-fledged thought form. Something else is required: emotion. This is where the victim and the hexer come into the picture. Although most of us find it impossible to think without becoming a little emotionally involved, these emotions usually fade after a short time.

Usually what happens is that we create a thought, give it the necessary attention and sometimes return to it again later. But a psychic attack isn't like that because the thoughts have been produced using extreme emotions such as jealousy and rage which have a much longer shelf life than the average thought. We all have our emotional weak spots and some are quite surprising. I know one elderly gentleman who turns purple and starts ranting if anyone mentions caravans! Thus any thoughts produced when someone has brooded on something for hours – sometimes even days or weeks – already have some strong reserves of emotional fuel. These can be unwittingly topped up by the victim's own fear and mental anguish. The stronger the emotion, the clearer the thought form it will produce.

Another thing to bear in mind is that a perfect Auric Field is unlikely to be damaged by a third party, no matter how skilled he is. Unfortunately, most of us have damaged our own Auric Field in some way, long before a thought form comes along. Our own character traits start the damage - the odd pinprick here, a little tear there. Gradually they either repair or heal, or they grow bigger. We each have within us the means of our own defence – and the means of our own destruction. It is therefore essential to take care and look after our Aura, because it's the equivalent of a psychic suit of armour.

Unfortunately, there is no single way of looking after our Aura. It's not just a matter of burning a certain incense or saying a specific magical formula. We are each unique and require a care plan that is tailored to our individual needs. Obviously, it's important to look after our health since illness can certainly damage our Aura, as can too much stress and anxiety. However, a certain amount of stress is quite healthy, and we would lead very bland, quiet lives without it; it's when things regularly get to screaming pitch that we need to try and pull back a little.

Sometimes we are 'drawn' towards people and situations that are damaging for us. The cause may lie in our early lives, or in abusive relationships but on a practical level, even silently counting to ten can be a positive way of taking charge and giving us time to step back. A few minutes a day set aside regularly for reflection and contemplation can do wonders for a tired, damaged Aura.

How Thought Forms Work

Although thoughts forms are relatively easy to create, they can require considerable effort to maintain. We often hear people claim that once we stop thinking about something it ceases to exist in the psychic world. This is not always true. Thought forms cease to exist *once the originating thought has lost its energy.* There is always the possibility that it will have been picked up by someone else's mental energy in the meantime.

This is one of the biggest problems we face whenever we are dealing with an attack by a thought form: it not only gathers strength from both the original attacker and the original victim, but also from the thoughts of total strangers in the area who happen to have similar emotional surges. If there's nobody suitable at hand for the thought form to feed on, it will sometimes turn around and latch back onto its creator so the whole situation goes around in circles! Although a prolonged thought form attack is usually the work of a skilled occultist, even beginners can create thought forms that have taken on a life of their own by picking up other peoples' thoughts and emotions along the way.

People are often surprised to discover that strong thoughts and emotions can travel incredibly long distances in the right circumstances, rather like sound waves. When this happens, the *character* of the thought can be conveyed to a totally independent third party. This is the reason we can sometimes find ourselves overwhelmed with a feeling of, for example, utter despair, yet never discover where it originated.

This rather disturbing phenomenon is made worse when thought forms begin to cluster either in certain places or around certain people. Although they have long since detached themselves from their original creator, they still manage to find enough energy to propel themselves around, often following water courses. Given a sudden burst of just the right emotion, they can return to full power in a very short time.

Thought forms require constant nourishment in the form of emotion fuelled thoughts. In the right circumstances they can linger for many years, often attaching themselves to one specific place they know they will be regularly visited by people with the 'right' type of thoughts. This explains why some places have such a dreadful atmosphere. It can also go some way to explaining 'copycat events' and 'suicide hotspots.'

Like often (though not always) attracts like, so anger may attract yet more anger, jealousy attracts yet more jealous thoughts etc. A person's own character may therefore act as a magnet for certain types of thought form who will be attracted, however briefly, to feed off their new host. Also, if our own Auric Field is in any way damaged, perhaps through injury (emotional or physical) or ill health, nearby thought forms can take advantage of our weakness and latch on to us, causing even more damage.

It's a bit like blood attracting all the sharks in the area. They are just homing in on something that is already weakened. Depending on how they were created in the first place, and to what extent they have been nurtured by others since then, such thought forms can do considerable harm.

Thought forms can be used agonistically – which means both for and against something. Just as we can use them to launch a psychic attack, they can also be used protect ourselves either by setting up a defensive thought form as a guardian or by instructing it to weaken the negative forces around us. Understanding how thought forms are created is therefore an essential aspect of psychic self defence.

'Spy' Thought Forms

As we saw earlier in this book, experienced hexers with occult knowledge may send a thought form as a spy, either to check on the victim's routine or to make sure the attack is having the desired effect. Whereas most people can summon enough extreme emotion to enable them to conjure up a thought form to terrify the victim, it requires substantial occult knowledge to conjure up a 'spy.'

Unlike some thought forms, spies are rarely frightening since attackers prefer not to alert us to their presence. They will therefore either assume a form that fits in with our surroundings, perhaps as one of a crowd, or we may just catch sight of them on the periphery of our vision. Spy forms usually appear as ordinary animals or people, sometimes just a little paler than the rest of their surroundings. A sudden change of light, either a sunbeam or cloud passing overhead, will usually pinpoint them since they do not seem to react to light changes as easily as the rest of us.

However, not all thought forms - even terrifying ones - are proof of psychic attack. I once knew someone who created a thought form, complete with horns and a trident and sent it to watch over a friend who was home ill in bed. It was all done with the best and kindest of intentions because my friend believed that a fierce looking thought form would scare the flu away and drive back any negativity. But her sick friend, who happened to be very superstitious, thought she was seeing the Devil and had hysterics!

Group Thought Forms

Dealing with a thought form created by an individual is one thing; dealing with something that has been created by a group is something else entirely. The group mind of any community is enormously powerful in creating attacks and psychic phenomena.

To understand how this works, imagine that we have a problem and decide to enlist our friends' help in dealing with it. First, we sit around together while we tell our side of things, then our friends join in and suddenly we find we're talking about nothing else. Obviously, we have already given the problem some thought before calling our friends, meaning we may have already generated a thought form or two, and now when we all sit together discussing things, even more thought forms will be produced. Although there is a saying that a problem shared is a problem halved, where thought forms are concerned, a problem shared is often a thought form doubled!

Even if we realise that we're overreacting a bit, we will have begun feeding off each other, and just when we stop talking somebody else starts up again. It's like a snowball going downhill, gathering speed and getting bigger. The energy builds up – a bit like a coven or a group working – the thoughts multiply, and any elemental essence in the vicinity has a field day. No wonder group thought forms are so powerful and difficult to banish!

One place where group thought form attacks are particularly common is on the internet where increasing use of social media has made attacks by thought forms more common than they were even ten or twelve years ago. The reason is not hard to find: it's easy for extremely large numbers of people to band together, often without even knowing each other. Information exchange is virtually instantaneous, and the internet grants an anonymity that enables people to say and threaten some very mean and spiteful things. Just look at the comments posted beneath articles in online newspapers. Very few people would have the nerve to come out with some of this stuff on a face-to-face basis.

In addition, news reporting can create and encourage certain types of thought forms. Look at what happens, for example, when a gunman opens fire on a group of shoppers or schoolchildren. Reports focus on the 'loner' gunman, his face looking out at us from every front page, every website. His background is analysed, we are told that he hated certain types of people. The events of the fateful day are analysed endlessly. There are also reports about the victims, the survivors, even stories from people who heard the shots, or who might have heard the shots if they had been where they were supposed to be. Mostly though, the emphasis is on the culprit.

What happens next is predictable. People reading and listening to these reports soon find themselves visualising the gunman, trying to imagine his motives, and sometimes, if there is already some comparable damage to their own Auric Field, they might take on board his motives and even his anger. From a magical point of view, this sort of reporting creates a disturbing response in the minds of some of the people who read and hear about it, simply because it's impossible to read about something so terrible without feeling a surge of emotion. Unfortunately, it's this very combination of intense emotion, thought and the elemental essence that is all around us that helps to create a thought form.

Luckily most thought forms are relatively short lived. Their creators, the journalists and reporters, move on to other stories within a few days. However, once a thought form has been created it wants to prolong its existence, so it starts looking for opportunities to attach itself to someone else, preferably someone with the same thoughts and emotions. If it succeeds, it will grow larger and more demanding, attaching itself to more individuals and groups, feeding on their sense of isolation and paranoia.

Fuelled by the media with its endless news stories, articles and broadcasts, the thought form soon becomes a force in its own right. It can even begin directing others, becoming a group Oversoul, or Artificial Elemental. The creation of an Artificial Elemental has sometimes been blamed for outbreaks of unexplained aggression either towards others or oneself.

The difference between an Artificial Elemental and a thought form created by an individual is largely a matter of scale. It's important not to underestimate scale. I once had an elderly neighbour who successfully fought off a mugger with a dog lead. But if there had been a group of robbers, all intent on attacking her, then no single dog lead would be able to stop them. There is the same sort of distinction between an individually created thought form that can be controlled and an Artificial Elemental which cannot. It takes a great deal of effort and courage to break away from a group which has become dominated by one of these beings, let alone challenge it.

It's nothing new, either. I remember hearing about someone from the UK who had heard Hitler speaking at Munich in the 1930's. Although not understanding much of what was said, she was astonished to find herself carried along on the same waves of emotion as the rest of the crowd. The Third Reich certainly used the occult to further their aims, and the creation of thought forms was probably a major part of their work.

The Etheric Double

Usually the purpose of a thought form is to terrify and weaken the victim; thought forms used in psychic attacks are basically warped mirrors, reflecting all their creators' traits of anger, rage, jealousy and spite, so it's easy to see why they're so frightening. Luckily, they are unlikely to launch a physical attack although they could influence a third party to do so.

However, the Etheric Double - which is often confused with a thought form - *can* physically attack in some circumstances. All humans and animals have an etheric body which, as we can see on the diagram on page 73, lies next to the physical body. The two 'bodies' are joined by long ties, rather like a series of umbilical cords. However, because the physical and etheric bodies are not firmly joined all over, there are tiny spaces between them, and this is where we will find something called First Matter or ectoplasm.

Victorian and Edwardian mediums often claimed to produce this substance, and some early photographs (many, but by no means all have been revealed as fakes) look as though they are trying to vomit a pair of net curtains.

An Etheric Double is created when ectoplasm is moulded using the power of thought into the shape of its living owner, whether person or animal. In comparison, a thought form uses elemental essence which exists outside of and separate from us. Obviously, malevolent thoughts create malevolent Etheric Doubles that are quite capable of launching a psychical attack.

However, whereas a thought form is always quite separate from its creator and can be banished (or attacked) without harming him, if the Etheric Double is attacked, its creator will *also* be harmed. This risk alone is usually enough to dissuade many would-be occultists from trying use their Etheric Double in a psychic attack. Thought forms, however, can be destroyed without harming whoever made it.

Not all Etheric Doubles are created for the purposes of psychic attack, however. It has been known for someone on the point of death to send their Etheric Double to visit their next of kin. There are many reports of these manifestations happening during wartime or disasters such as the sinking of the Titanic. These are not, strictly speaking, ghosts since the person is at the point of death and not actually dead. They are at the moment of crossing over, and it is this combination of anguish, pain, fear and anxiety for a loved one that combines to produce a spontaneous Etheric Double without the need for any special occult skills.

When I first saw an Etheric Double, it fooled me. The only thing that seemed slightly different was the lighting. It was an overcast day in January, yet what I was seeing looked slightly brighter than everything around it. The Etheric double may be where traditions such as the *doppelganger* or 'fetch' originated.

Although thought forms can appear in the semblance of monsters, an Etheric double can *only* be the exact copy of its creator. Of course, from the attacker's point of view this means he can no longer remain anonymous, since his victim will recognise him, which is another reason why Etheric Doubles remain a comparatively rare phenomenon.

Prevention and Cure

One of the most difficult aspects of dealing with any psychic attack is the feeling of powerlessness. A thought form, being generated by somebody else's mind, offers us little control over what it does or where it goes – at least, that's what we're supposed to feel. One of the most effective defences is to show as little reaction as possible. Remember that any thought form requires three things in order to manifest properly: thought, emotion and elemental essence. Fear generates extreme emotion, which is just what it needs in order to function.

But how do we avoid showing our fear when we're terrified? The secret is in preparation. Psychic attacks rarely happen out of the blue. Often there are warning signs, such as foul smells, odd sounds, or the sudden appearance of large numbers of animals such as cats, flies or rats. We can use these warnings to prepare, for no matter how frightened we feel, must not to show it.

There are a variety of coping strategies for this. Whistling has always been popular, so is laughter, and I even knew someone who used to taunt a thought form that bothered her by chanting her times-tables at it! After a few renderings of 'Twice one is two, twice two is four, etc.,' the thought form beat a hasty retreat and never returned.

Why do these simple remedies work? It's because thought forms are only as strong as the mind of the person who created them, and we are confronting them with something they don't expect. Psychic attackers often take it for granted that their targets will simply roll over and let them do what they please. It never seems to occur to them that the 'victim' might instead laugh it off, fight back, or do anything to disrupt their plans. When confronted by the unexpected, attackers are often dumbfounded.

At first their reaction is, 'How dare they fight back/laugh at me?' Perhaps for a very short time the attack *might* intensify, although this doesn't last because creating a thought form is exhausting, and the attacker was depending on it feeding off the victim's fear. If she wants to keep it going now, she will have to feed the thought form herself, which is going to drain her own energies. That makes the thought form a far less attractive proposition to the average psychic attacker. Indeed, some are so surprised to have their plans thwarted that they pull back straight away and go after an easier target.

Setting up a Guardian Thought Form

One of the simplest preventative measures is to set up our own guardian thought form to protect us. First, however, we must decide what we want the thought form to do. It's not enough to say that we want it to be a guardian – who or what do we want it to guard? Our home? Our room? Our car? Do we want a bodyguard for us or for someone else? A thought form is our servant, so we must tell it exactly what to do and when to do it. We should not expect it to anticipate our wishes; it won't.

The easiest way to create a thought form is to start thinking about it – but how? I often draw a picture and focus on that; alternatives would be a picture from a magazine or the internet. A head and shoulders will not do, it needs to have a complete form for best results. For a few days we should carry the picture around with us and look at it often, as this is all part of the process for thinking it into existence.

One mistake people often make in creating a thought form is to think of it purely in visual terms. If something exists, we don't just see it, we can hear, touch, smell and sometimes even taste it. We must engage all our five senses. However, these are not all equally strong in each of us. For example, I have a poor sense of smell, but my hearing is better. So although I may not be able to reconstruct what my thought form smells like, I can reconstruct in my head the sound of its footsteps, or its voice. In this way I can make up for the fact that most of the time I can't tell whether something smells of lavender water or manure! What is important is that our thought form should be real, three dimensional. Try mentally walking around it, looking up to it and even looking down on it.

The next thing is to name it. This gives it individuality, a sort of psychic soul. It can be an everyday name like 'Fred' or something more unusual, that's up to us, but don't give it the name of a deity or demonic entity and resist the urge to be sarcastic or jokey – these things have a habit of backfiring when we least expect it. It *is* possible for thought forms - even benign ones - to take on a life of their own, especially if we do not pay proper attention to what we are doing at these early stages of creation.

Now think of the attributes or character we want it to display. Obvious possibilities include loyalty, energy, strength, etc. But we should always bear in mind what we want it to do. There's no sense in endowing a thought form with nothing but energy if all we want it to do is guard our parked car. In that case we might be better off stressing watchfulness, patience and/or steadfastness.

At this stage, people sometimes complain that creating a thought form is very slow and tedious. It is, yet there's no sense in creating a thought form that disappears into the wild blue yonder because we forgot to tell it exactly where we wanted it to stay and what we wanted it to do. Nor is it any good if we brainstorm a thought form into existence only to find it has somehow joined forces with whatever is attacking us.

I find that creating a thought form using a garden ornament is often a good way to keep it in one place and helps us visualise it as a real entity (which of course it is, although it may not feel that way to begin with.) Placed near entrances and exits, we should remember to greet these guardians whenever we pass. Remember though, that thought forms must always serve us and not *vice versa*.

Although it can be tempting to set up a guardian thought form and leave it permanently on guard, this can have its drawbacks. If it's too protective it might prevent good things reaching us as well as bad. An alternative is to create a temporary guardian, which can be dismantled or de-activated when the threat is past.

To do this, we need to create a symbol at the same time we create our thought form – a drawing on a piece of paper is fine – to encapsulate everything the thought form represents to us. Some people look no further than a sign of the zodiac or a rune symbol for their inspiration, which is a pity because the more effort we put into creating this pictogram, the greater power it will have.

We can also, if we wish, set a cut-off date for the thought form, but this is difficult to predict in cases of psychic self defence. Keep the symbol safe for the period when the guardian thought form is active, but when it is over and we wish to disperse it, we should burn the paper together with any pictures and notes we used when creating the thought form while saying something like:

> *'Just as I burn this paper and turn it into ashes and dust, so I destroy these images of my guardian thought form. I thank you for your service, but your time here is over. Now you must leave. Be gone. You have no existence anymore.'*

Then cast the ashes to the four winds or into running water. This brief ritual can also be adapted if the guardian thought form shows any signs getting out of hand and needs to be stopped.

An alternative to creating a temporary thought form is to only put it 'on guard' for short periods at a time. I have had several that have been set up in this way for many years, and whenever I want them to be particularly vigilant against a specific threat, I simply tell them to wake up and be on guard. This is useful for example, when we must be out at work or go on holiday.

Creating a guardian thought form takes time, and we may need to fall back on a few other defences until it is ready. If we are ever confronted by a hostile thought form, make the sign of the pentagram immediately, beginning at the bottom left hand point, saying 'Go away' (or whatever variation we prefer) as forcefully as possible. If there are several entities (which is extremely rare) then repeat the sign for each of them.

It's important to react quickly and firmly, because when a thought form is sent to terrorise us, we need to be seen to do something. If we are reduced to a gibbering wreck the attacks will quickly intensify, whereas if we react calmly, looking as though we know what we are about, the attacker may begin to wonder whether he has underestimated us. His own self-doubt then works against him, making it harder to attack us. Dealing with psychic attacks is rather like playing poker – a good player can often beat the person who holds the best cards!

After making the sign of the pentagram, and commanding it to leave, we may then feel confident enough to visualise either disabling or destroying it. We can visualise it disintegrating or fading into nothingness, alternatively we can chop it up using one of the psychic weapons in Chapter Nine. This is perfectly legitimate practice even if normally we prefer to 'harm none.' A thought form is not a real creature but – in this instance – the product of someone's malevolent imagination. There has never been any Witches' Law (or any other magical law for that matter) that says we cannot defend ourselves against psychic attack.

The story of the Welsh children in Chapter Twelve – who defeated a poltergeist by making an even greater noise with sticks – also holds good for thought forms and other psychic phenomena. In this case, the entity was defeated because the children showed no fear and treated it with contempt.

We can learn from this: we must never allow anything to feed off us by making it a gift of our terror. Fear is meat and drink to these entities, and if allowed free rein they will drain us to the point of exhaustion. Even if we don't feel brave, we must act as though we do.

Dealing with the Etheric Double

Dealing with a threatening Etheric Double follows much the same procedure as dealing with a thought form. (Crisis-type apparitions of the Etheric Double mentioned above are quite harmless.) As soon as we feel menaced, we should speak and make it clear that we know what - and who - it is. Often this is enough to make it back off because of the risk that we may harm it and thereby its creator. Very few attackers are willing to take that chance.

Also visualise taking up one of the psychic offensive weapons - preferably a sword (see Chapter Nine) - and adopt a suitably threatening pose with our weight balanced equally on both feet, and both hands gripping the hilt. Then tell the Etheric Double that it must leave and never return otherwise we will counter-attack.

This may all sound very aggressive but do remember that if an Etheric Double has been sent as part of a psychic attack then it means business. By all means try to send it away first, but in the last resort, we must be prepared to carry out our threat. If we hesitate it will quickly take advantage of our weakness. Besides, anyone who deliberately conjures up their Etheric Double *for the purpose of a psychic attack* has put himself beyond the pale. We have nothing to lose by fighting back and everything to gain.

Few victims ever turn on their psychic attackers, but when we do we have the benefit of surprise. Always imagine our psychic weapons sheathed in fire and mentally lash out at it, hacking and slicing until it is driven back. Later, when it's over, thoroughly cleanse all areas where we saw the Etheric Double (See Chapters Twelve and Thirteen).

Afterwards, a short blessing ceremony (see Chapter Fourteen) can help calm the atmosphere. If we still feel badly shaken by the experience, then perform the grounding exercise in Chapter Nine to help recover from the sudden surge in our own psychic energies.

Although I have gone into defences against the Etheric Double in some detail, please remember that most people will never meet one. It is as well to be prepared, however.

Dealing with Artificial Elementals

Whereas we should not hesitate to engage an Etheric Double, with an Artificial Elemental the key word is avoidance. This is because an Artificial Elemental has gained its strength from many people's thoughts and may be much stronger than we expect. The best way to deal with it is to flatly refuse to engage. Refuse to play. Any contact with those involved with it – people whose thoughts are making it stronger – should be avoided or at least kept to an absolute minimum.

Decline to discuss the matter with anyone. This is often easier said than done, because when something is troubling us it's natural to want to share our hopes and fears. But when we suspect an Artificial Elemental has been created, then talking, thinking, reading or hearing about it is just adding fuel to the fire. Instead we must do whatever we can to dilute its power by refusing to make it a gift of our own thoughts.

It goes without saying that it's best to avoid alcohol and drugs while any threat from an Artificial Elemental is active. We need to keep our wits about us because such attacks tend to come suddenly, often in the form of a sudden urge to self-harm. If we start to feel this, then we *must* seek professional help straight away. Also avoid being alone, or in any place where we might be tempted to act on impulse.

Artificial Elementals are powerful, but not invincible. If we refuse to engage with them then eventually they will leave us alone. However, if we dwell on them, or on the people who have been involved in their creation or in any way affected by them, then we will, in effect, be inviting them into our life. Shut them out mentally and emotionally and wait while they pass us by. Although it sounds extremely simplistic, we really do need to busy ourselves with other things. There is no quick fix solution; we must just keep working through the cleansing, grounding and general protective measures in Part II of this book.

Finally...there is no point trying to talk or reason with any thought form or Etheric Double that has been sent as part of a psychic attack. We must not, under any circumstances try and 'turn' it against its attacker, or we may get more than we bargained for. Remember – the purpose of this book is to teach us to defend ourselves and prevent further attacks, not to equip us to start a full-scale magical conflict.

CHAPTER SIX

Unintentional and intentional psychic attacks. Self-attacks. Attacks by chthonic entities. Attacks caused by constant negativity. Obsessing Entities. The ethical challenge of acting on someone else's behalf.

Unintentional psychic attacks create their own, unique problems. They are difficult to anticipate, the culprit may not be easily identified, and often they aren't very focussed. Therefore, even if they hit their original target, they can also strike anyone unlucky enough to be within range. Problems can also be caused by lack of magical skill or even recklessness, for example when spells are cast under the influence of drink or drugs. The best defence against any type of attack is always to start with thorough cleansing and grounding exercises etc., which can be found in the second half of this book. This is particularly helpful in cases of unintentional psychic attacks where there is often little else to go on and we don't know the cause.

Unintentional psychic attackers often don't intend to harm their victims, although this does not minimise the damage they do. Most are simply people who cannot or will not let go of a grudge. During the day they do nothing but talk and think about slights and injuries that most people would consider trivial. At night they lie awake at night seething, endlessly reliving all the things that have upset them. The malice and resentment build up like a volcano until eventually it's released as a psychic attack.

Yet although an attacker may harbour great bitterness and might be pleased to think of his victim experiencing all sorts of problems, it doesn't automatically follow that he really intended to hurt that person. Unfortunately, the combination of their own peculiar personality and their well-developed sense of injustice makes it all too easy for some people to launch their attacks, intentionally or otherwise. Also, even though some are horrified when they realise that they have hexed someone, many still refuse to accept any responsibility for it, far less express remorse.

Intentional psychic attacks are different; we almost always know the culprit, who usually knows exactly what he is doing and fully intends to cause as much harm as possible. Like the unintentional attacker, he may be motivated by a complex combination of revenge, jealousy, desire or spite. Sometimes intentional attackers will also attack physically, for example, slashing tyres or poisoning plants, just to make sure that their victims are thoroughly demoralised and intimidated.

Since a deliberate attack is more focussed, it has a better chance of hitting the intended victim and avoiding incidental damage to others. Intentional hexes are also more likely to physically harm us. The amount of damage depends on the skill of the hexer but be warned – it can be considerable.

Intentional attacks sometimes use physical methods to convey a hex such as a doll or written curse, but these are quite clear in their intentions. The victims are named and occasionally the reason for the attack is stated, together with what form the curse will take. Good examples are found in cursing tablets (known as *defixiones* in ancient Rome, and *katadesmoi* in ancient Greece). Even today these curses make chilling reading. For example, one lead tablet stated:

> *'May each one rot, may each cry out for help because of their dishonesty towards their masters, those (slaves) whose names are here dutifully recorded, so that [although having escaped] from a beating or with their property, the things they have said [and] done [may be consigned] to the gods of the underworld.'*[33]

Many of these inscribed curses were hidden, buried deep in the ground or cast into wells, pits and even graves. The victim is never meant to see or know about them, only to feel their effects. This means the attacker must rely entirely on his own powers to activate the curse, and not everyone has the power to do this; some prefer to intimidate the victim by openly proclaiming their curse. This method relies as much on psychology as it does on true magical power! Even so, it should not be underestimated. For some

---

[33] Jentoft-Nilson 1980: 199-201

people, being told that that they are under a curse can have a truly devastating, self-fulfilling effect.

There is another, less obvious type of attack that occurs when people constantly criticise others. This type of attack is almost always deliberate, and often comes from family members, work colleagues and other people whom we must see regularly. They know our weak spots, and because we cannot easily avoid their company, they can attack whenever they feel like it.

At first glance it might seem as though there is nothing psychic involved in this sort of attack, and initially, at least, that may be true. However, if we are on the receiving end of enough constant negativity and criticism it can *turn* into a psychic attack. There's a world of difference between constructive criticism and the type that chips away at a person's self-confidence and shatters it.

If we're not careful we turn into a sponge, mopping it up even as it eats into us like acid, and it is difficult to claim that such criticism in not intentional. In cases of psychic attack, the old saying, 'Sticks and stones may hurt my bones but words will never hurt me,' simply isn't true. Words can – and do – cause great harm.

Whenever we are subjected to endless criticism, where someone forces their own negativity onto us for any length of time, our psychic energy is drained. Our Auric Field is damaged until we no longer have the willpower or strength to fight back. This also makes us vulnerable to attack by any passing thought forms that have been attracted to our damaged Auric Field. Things that would normally have passed us by or bounced off us, suddenly latch on and drain whatever is left of our energies.

Remedies for such attacks include using the psychic armour explained in Chapter Nine, together with the cord cutting exercises in Chapter Eleven. Do remember though that our greatest defence is that such attackers are rarely very skilled at what they do; they don't have many tricks up their sleeves and rarely respond effectively if the victim finally stands up to them.

Sometimes however, the constant negativity comes not from outsiders but from within ourselves. This can happen when we are constantly pessimistic, always looking for the worst life has to offer rather than the best, never expecting anything good to happen. Again, if this continues for long enough, we will damage our Auric Field just as surely as if we were being criticised by a third party. In other words, we end up attacking ourselves. Never underestimate the damage we can do in a psychic self-attack. In fact, self-attacks are often more difficult to identify and deal with than any other, partly because people find it difficult to believe that they are the authors of their own misfortune! There are remedies for dealing with this type of attack in Chapter Seventeen.

Finally, there is the possibility that entities attached to certain places are hostile to us although in fairness this is *extremely* uncommon. Another name for them is chthonic entities which just means entities of the earth, and as their name suggests they usually linger in places to which they are particularly attached.

Like demons, chthonic entities are neither intrinsically good nor evil although they can be used for either purpose. As with all types of magic, much depends on intention. It's true that chthonic entities are often attracted to the energies of places where some accident or crime has occurred, but they can just as easily attach themselves to areas of great natural beauty. When this happens people often experience feelings of great peace and calm.

Sometimes we encounter problems with entities such as grounded spirits who are unable or unwilling to move on and who have attached themselves to certain places. This sort of attack often happens near water or in damp houses because water conducts psychic activity. It often (though not always) accounts for the negative atmosphere we sense in some places. Such attacks don't usually involve a physical attack, although over time they can wear us down with a range of unpleasant but unspecified aches and pains, chronic illness and a feeling of being oppressed. Simple self-protection remedies (given in the second half of this book) will help cleanse the atmosphere.

If we must deal with any area or space that 'feels' wrong, our first response should be to cleanse it, since psychic attackers can make use of any pre-existing negativity and chthonic entities to strengthen their attacks. Sometimes it is difficult to differentiate between straightforward psychic attacks and those attached to particular places. Typically, in situations where a chthonic entity is involved, people such as neighbours may remark that 'something' has been going on in the area for a long time and have noted that the atmosphere is less than pleasant:

> *My sister has had 'something' in her house for years, ever since she moved in. She has tried to co-exist with it, but it just isn't interested. It makes the place feel very threatening and we've all felt it. We've noticed our cat seems aware of something in the cellar. She often sits at the top of the steps and stares down there and sometimes goes into a very defensive pose, with her tail up like a bottle brush.'*[34]

The cat's reaction is interesting, since animals are usually much better at sensing a chthonic presence than humans although traditionally only neutered animals can actively *hunt* ghosts and spirits. I have often come across reports of dogs growling and cats hissing at something their owners cannot see. Some pets refuse to enter certain rooms or will hurry out as soon as possible. Although we shouldn't regard an animal's reaction as cast-iron proof, we should certainly pay attention to it. Bear in mind that chthonic entities can exist for a long period of time, building up their strength gradually; they rarely, if ever, suddenly manifest.

Of course, the presence of a chthonic entity does not necessarily indicate that we are under psychic attack. Always check for other phenomena such as foul smells, noises etc., and investigate to see whether the unpleasant atmosphere is worse in one part of the house than another. It's a good place to start.

In the case given above, the most likely explanations were either that an entity had become trapped in the house and was unable to leave or that it had arrived there by choice. Further enquiries revealed no evidence of smells, sounds or any other paranormal phenomena, just an awful atmosphere, especially in the cellar. People who went down there would literally run back up again, convinced they were being chased. Some had even felt invisible hands trying to catch hold of them. Women, in particular felt menaced by it. Gradually I became convinced we weren't

---

[34] Author's personal notes

dealing with a psychic attack and that it was more likely to be some sort of chthonic entity or thought form. My main reasons for coming to this conclusion were that the entity seemed to have been around for some time, had remained in one place and targeted a certain type of person.

I was later told that some years earlier, a psychic had held a séance in the house and reported sensing something, 'very simple but voracious.' The psychic also sensed the entity's need to pursue women rather than men, possibly because it felt it could intimidate them more easily, or because they were physically weaker. It had no need to break out of the cellar in order to feed on others' thoughts, because sooner or later someone would go down there taking their fear and dread with them. The entity - whatever it was - fed on this and over the years a great deal of negativity had attached to it, helping it grow stronger.

I worked with the family on several cleansing and protective rituals, such as those outlined in Chapters Nine to Thirteen. Once the negativity was dispersed the entity weakened considerably, and as it did so, people no longer feared going down the cellar. With nothing left to feed upon, it eventually withered away. A house blessing (see Chapter Fourteen) completed the cleansing process, and nowadays the cellar is used regularly without any incidents.

Obsessing Entities

Very occasionally I come across cases involving something called an 'obsessing entity.' Fortunately, these are so rare that most people will only ever read about them in books and never actually have to deal with them. Even so, it is wise to be prepared since they can be a serious psychic threat that should not be ignored.

An attack by an obsessing entity is sometimes mistakenly referred to as demonic possession. Both are completely focused on an individual with the intention of taking over his (or her) life. However, there is a difference, due to the nature of the force we are dealing with. An obsessing entity is - or has been - human, never demonic. It is *always* sexually fixated on the victim, although the victim may not admit this even to themselves. Sometimes the entity has passed on, but usually it is an aspect of a living person who is known to the victim. With careful investigation therefore, the culprit can usually be identified, making it easier to deal with. Demonic possession on the other hand, involves an entity that was never human, and the sexual element may not always be present.

One of the main problems in dealing with an obsessing entity is that the victim is often flattered by its attentions. He (the victim is often male although the attacker may be either gender) may begin to lead something of a double life at first, with one foot in the everyday world and the other in the world created by the obsessing entity. It takes great effort and willpower to give up and get rid of an obsessing entity, but there are no half measures with these things, and we cannot learn to live with it because of its nature. Obsessing entities are extremely jealous and represent a threat not only to the victim but also to his partner and children.

As already mentioned, a living person is almost always behind these attacks, using some form of astral travel to reach and drain the victim. Obsessing entities are created when someone becomes sexually fixated on the victim, the motives for the attacks being sexual gratification and power.

Attacks by obsessing entities are not sudden (unlike those of the Incubus, Succubus or Night Mare), but build up over a period of time, like a spider weaving its web. They can continue for years without burning themselves out, are ferociously intense and utterly destructive because the entity is so possessive that nobody else is allowed to compete with it for the victim's attention. As a result, the victim becomes estranged from everyone who cares about him.

Sometimes the attack starts off as a thought form, created when the victim fantasises about a fictional lover and masturbates while thinking of them. Now obviously, many people do this at some point in their lives, and usually such thought forms are short lived and never become a problem. However, occasionally a person becomes obsessive about this, while at the same time feeling guilty, perhaps because of their religious or social background. This mixture of sexual frustration, desire and guilt can be a potent combination. Bearing in mind that sex provides a very powerful magical climax, some of these thought forms can linger for years. Even then, however, most do no harm at all. But very, *very* occasionally they seem to take on a life of their own.

In fact, what happens is this: the original thought form was created and kept alive with fantasies and sexual climaxes. If its creator finds a suitable real-life partner, then the thought form gradually becomes less important and fades. However, if no real-life partner is found, or if for some reason the thought form is still being regularly summoned, there is a chance it will grow progressively stronger and that other, similar entities will start to attach themselves to it, together with chunks of elemental essence. Even then, the thought form is not yet an obsessing entity. That only happens when an attacker with a working knowledge of thought forms manages to successfully hijack it.

A particularly worrying characteristic of these attacks is their sheer ruthlessness. The victim's partner is not only wretched but physically at risk, because the attacker wants to isolate their victim and will stop at nothing to achieve this. At first it may try and destroy trust and normal relations between the couple; eventually it will try and oust the unfortunate partner altogether.

If friends and family do not lose patience with the victim and become estranged, they too may become ill with persistent, chronic illnesses that sap their energy and strength. This is the obsessing entity operating as a psychic vampire on the victim's next of kin. Meanwhile the entity appears totally benign to its victim, who will insist there is nothing wrong and that others are jealous of such a 'special', and 'beautiful' relationship. They sometimes even claim that there is a sexual relationship.

Meanwhile, the obsessing entity persuades its victim that he will be safe for as long as they are together, and it is a marked characteristic of this type of attack that the victim welcomes the entity's attentions and is not afraid (although he should be!) Attacks – which the victim might describe as an 'encounter' – usually occur at night when the victim's guard is down and he is at his weakest.

Attacks by obsessing entities are often accompanied by persistent but low-level paranormal activity around the victim's home. Lights, noises (knocks and taps), someone breathing on our face, things moving, even orbs of light. These are not in themselves threatening, although they can be unpleasant, especially for anyone of a nervous disposition. Sometimes the air fairly crackles with psychic energy. This is not surprising given the amount of tension the obsessing entity can cause in the household.

Another feature of this type of attack is that the victim becomes convinced that he and the entity have shared past lives together. Even if we believe in reincarnation (and I do) the fact remains that each lifetime is precious, and we are supposed to embrace the present and learn from it rather than remaining fixated on the past.

However, the victim of an obsessing entity is so infatuated, he is deaf to all reasonable argument and blind to what is going on under his nose. He becomes convinced his relationship with the entity is not only a rare and beautiful relationship, but also a telepathic meeting of souls. The victim may use words such as 'guardian angel,' 'true empathy', 'meeting of minds' and 'soul mates' when referring to it. It is difficult to convince him that the entity is insanely jealous and interfering in everyday relationships; he prefers to view their liaison as the single most important relationship of his life.

Often the victim will cite examples of times when he has been saved from certain death or injury, exaggerating wildly in the process. We can argue with them until we're blue in the face, we can even present people who actually witnessed first-hand the events he describes, but he will still stick doggedly to his version of events. Friends and family become exasperated as everything good in the victim's life is constantly attributed to the entity. There are only so many times that concerned relatives can tolerate being told by a loved one that only the entity truly understands him.

Unsurprisingly, such victims steadfastly refuse to help themselves or to allow others to help them, at least for as long as they enjoy the entity's attentions which make them feel special, important and/or different. Victims often seem to lose track of the real world, resisting all offers of help even when it's clear that their health and relationships are suffering; they refuse to recognise the danger they are in. Usually it is friends and family who realise that something is wrong long before the victim does and seek help on his behalf. This is a stark contrast to the victims of most other types of psychic attack who will seek help for themselves willingly.

Whereas the typical obsessing entity emanates from a still-living person, occasionally it can be totally spirit-based, for example, a former family member or friend who has died but feels unable to move on and instead latches onto a living person in order to enjoy some sort of 'life.'

There are several important differences between this type of attack and the true obsessing entity. Firstly, there is less obvious jealousy and hostility towards the victim's partner, since the entity is only concerned with maintaining its own existence by 'taking over' its living victim and trying to live vicariously through him.

Secondly, there is rarely a sexual motive, and the victim is just as likely to be male as female. Also, the victim is more likely to view the entity as a problem than a blessing and can usually be persuaded to protect himself and seek help. Unlike the true obsessing entity whose attacks linger for years, a spirit-type obsession tends to be quite short lived.

This spirit-based type of obsessing entity often attaches itself to the victim near the upper back and shoulder. Although they are not always malevolent in their intention, if they begin to cause the victim problems and there is a change in his personality (such as increased anger, changed habits, etc.) we should take steps to deal with the entity using a combination of the techniques in Chapters Eleven – Fourteen. We should also keep telling the entity that it does not belong here and must move on to the spirit world. Another possibility is to hold up a mirror so the entity can see a different image reflected back at them. There is no single correct way to deal with any psychic attack, so we should not be afraid to try many different methods until we find what works for us.

Dealing with a true obsessing entity (where the culprit is still alive) is slightly different. Most types of psychic attack manifest within a specific space, for example a home, or even a room. These are relatively easy to cleanse using a variety of techniques in the second part of this book. Getting rid of an obsessing entity is more difficult because (a) it has attached itself to a person and (b) its victim doesn't want it to leave. This means that others must try and get rid of the entity on someone else's behalf. The sexual element in these attacks often makes victims very secretive so by the time anyone else realises what's happening, the attack may already have been going on for some time.

Although concerned partners and family can take some preventative measures to lessen the entity's grip, they must be prepared for the victim to reject and in some cases even resent such efforts. Worse, the entity will redouble its own efforts to isolate its victim from friends and family by insinuating that everyone is conspiring against their 'special relationship.'

This type of paranoia is dangerous and if things reach this stage we should always seek medical help for the victim. Despite our concern for him, our own health and safety are paramount at all times. We must not place ourselves in any situation where we could be at physically risk and we should also protect ourselves against psychic vampirism (see Chapter Eleven).

If we are trying to help a family in this situation, do remember that much of the information about a specific obsessing entity will come from third parties: the victim's partner, family or friends. Write everything down no matter how trivial, because there will be some glaring inconsistencies, particularly in the victim's version of things. If so, these must be exposed in order to encourage him to take the threat seriously.

In the beginning at least, appear interested but not judgemental, otherwise he will stop talking and it will be more difficult to help him. Although it's annoying, these victims rarely welcome advice and often alternate between unreasonable secrecy and demands for information. The latter can involve visits to psychics and clairvoyants, although if any of them suggest he is in any sort of danger from the entity he will become very defensive.

Other useful remedies include physical and magical cleansing to deal with the increased psychic activity around the home, together with sealing the victim's Aura, that of family members and our own. (See Chapter Nine) The longer an attack has been happening, the harder it will be to deal with it, and the victim is unlikely to give up the entity without a fight. Even if we succeed in banishing the obsessing entity, victims often go looking for it, months or even years later. Because of the risk of a relapse in this type of attack it is important to keep up the cleansing and purification rituals for some time afterwards. Teach the family and friends to do this for themselves if possible, since we cannot be with the victim all the time.

It is essential to try and identify the obsessing entity. No matter what the victim thinks, it *is* someone he knows - or at least someone who knows him. Ignore his tales of previous existences. They may well be true, but it is *this* life that concerns us for the moment.

Think back to when the entity first made itself known and work out who was in the victim's life at this time. Victims are often little help with this, convincing themselves instead that they have known the entity forever.

Remember too: *The gender adopted by the obsessing entity may not be a true reflection of the gender of its creator.*

Because the attacker will require huge amount of energy in order to project such an entity over such a long period of time, obsessing entities will also operate as psychic vampires. Apart from draining the victim's nearest and dearest, the entity's creator is likely to have an ailing spouse or family member. This can also help us identify the culprit.

Once the entity's creator is identified, it is essential that the victim should cut all physical ties with that person immediately. Since the victim does not believe the entity is a real person anyway, this may be easier than we expect. But of course, the attacker will be furious, and there may be a sudden increase of paranormal phenomena as a result. The effects of its psychic vampirism may also become more noticeable, usually targeting the next of kin or anyone it believes has 'interfered'.

Fortunately, these 'secondary victims' are easier to help. It's probably best not to alarm them by saying that we think an obsessing entity is the cause of their problems, instead ensure that they get proper medical advice if necessary. Also we must encourage magical cleansing, protection rituals and sealing the Aura. If they are too weak to do this for themselves then we can do it on their behalf until they are well enough to take over.

Other practical measures are equally important. Refuse to see, speak to or communicate with the attacker in any shape or form even if this means breaking off contact with the victim's friends too. Otherwise there is a risk they will act as a go-between, telling the attacker what's happening. Also get rid of anything belonging to the attacker that they may have given us (or the victim) preferably burning it and casting the ashes into fast flowing water. If for some reason an item cannot be destroyed, then cleanse it regularly until the attacks abate. Any of the techniques in the second part of this book will be useful, and the introduction to Part II will explain how to choose the most appropriate method.

Also bear in mind that because the victim has become unwilling, unable or incapable of acting on their own behalf, others will have to make most of the decisions. This raises some challenging ethical questions. Some people believe that we should always have the victim's permission before stepping in and that without it we cannot do anything under any circumstances.

Personally, I would argue that if someone was wandering into the path of a speeding car, I would not wait and ask their permission before pushing them out of the way. I would (I hope) act instinctively, hoping they would understand that I was only trying to keep them safe. It is the same with psychic self defence, and the '*As above, so below*' maxim of Hermes Trismegistus can sensibly be applied in such situations.

Another reason I recommend others acting on the victim's behalf against the obsessing entity is that this type of attack often has several victims. Firstly, there is the victim himself, whose life is being turned upside down; secondly there are his friends and family who are bewildered to find themselves not only pushed aside in favour of the entity, but also the victims of its secondary attacks. It can be infuriating when the victim clearly regards his psychic relationship as sacred and refuse point-black to relinquish it. In that sense the entity is also attacking everyone close to its principal victim.

Remember: *Never ask the victim of an obsessive entity to choose between you and it; the chances are that you will be the loser, at least in the early days.*

Finally, remember that no matter what we do, we will not successfully banish an obsessing entity unless the victim himself really wishes to be free of it. We may, however, manage to weaken the attack enough for the victim comes to his senses. This is done by determined and regular cleansing, sealing the Aura etc.

Do note however, that if the victim only pretends to be getting rid of the entity while secretly hoping that it stays, then sooner or later it *will* return, sometimes stronger than before. Once the victim is determined to be free of his obsessor however, then things change completely. By severing all ties, enlisting the help of others, performing magical cleansing rituals both around the home and on himself he will finally force the entity to recognise that it is no longer welcome.

An obsessing entity is a challenging foe, certainly, but it is not invincible.

CHAPTER SEVEN

Night-time attacks – Night Mare, Hag, Incubus, Succubus. The Night Mare as a cat and other animals. The Origins of the Night Mare, Incubus and Succubus. Why does the Night Mare attack? Sexual undercurrents in night-time attacks. The theory of sleep paralysis. How dangerous is the Night Mare? Preventative measures against night-time attacks.

Many people notice that psychic attacks are worse at night. This could be partly due to our fear of the darkness since unlike most animals (who use all five senses), human beings tend to rely more on their sense of sight than any other. Remove that and we feel helpless, our imaginations running wild even if nothing is there! We are even afraid to fall asleep because then we are no longer in control.

Dreams can sometimes be terrifying, and the more we worry about them the worse they seem to become. Yet usually dreams are only manifestations of our subconscious mind and will do us no harm. Looked at in the sensible light of day they can even help us make sense of issues that are worrying us.

Occasionally however, our dreams make us feel we have ventured to the boundary between our world and other magical realms. Although frightening, it's normally safe since there seems to be a built-in safety mechanism that prevents us straying too far or staying too long while we're asleep.

If we are troubled with extremely disturbing dreams and believe these form part of a psychic attack, however, then this is likely to be the work of someone with some occult or magical knowledge. The best method to deal with it is to cleanse our sleeping quarters using any of the basic methods in Chapters Ten – Thirteen and seal our Aura before we go to sleep.

Other things we may notice around the time of falling asleep are visions and dreams, often clairvoyant in nature and known as hypnopompic events. There are also hypnagogic events, which usually occur just as we're on the verge of waking, and these *can* include a wide range of paranormal phenomena and the occasional psychic attack.

The Commonest Types of Night Attack

Night-time psychic attacks are quite distinct from just having a bad dream. They can include Night Terrors and attacks by various entities including the Mare, the Hag, The Night Mare, Incubus or Succubus. Often these are all lumped together as a 'night attack' but each has its own distinct features. For example, a nightmare is quite distinct from the Night Mare. A nightmare is just a bad dream, and although the memory of it may be vivid, once the sleeper is fully awake he realises it was just a dream.

The Night Mare, on the other hand, can generate a deep terror that spills over into the following day and is never really forgotten. Confusing the two is a bit like calling a migraine a headache or mistaking the common cold for the flu. Some people wake with scratches and bruises, while others are so psychologically scarred they become afraid to go to sleep.

For example, In the seventeenth century, a Puritan named Richard Norwood was so terrified by his experience of the Night Mare that he took, '...a naked knife in my hand when I went to sleep, thinking to strike at it.'[35] Others have taken even more drastic action in their attempts to rid themselves of the problem.

For example, in Somerset in 1876, a twenty-six year-old Somerset labourer was prosecuted for threatening his elderly neighbour, whom he accused of 'hag-riding' him at night in the form of a cat (hag-riding is another name for the Night Mare.) He had already killed both his own and a neighbour's cat in the mistaken belief that this would get rid of the nightly visitations.[36]

It's tempting to dismiss this type of case as the action of an uneducated, superstitious man. However John Bond, who wrote the first English medical study of the Night Mare in 1753, suffered so badly from these attacks that he confessed, '*I have been so much afraid of its intolerable insults, that I have slept in a chair all night, rather than give it an opportunity of attacking me in a horizontal position.*'[37]

---

[35] Oldridge (2000): 44

[36] Davies (1999): 132

[37] Bond (1753): 71

The Night Mare is often (but not always) sent with a malevolent intention as part of a full-blown psychic attack. In the past, some magicians even claimed they sent the Night Mare to kill people, presumably by frightening them to death. The Night Mare is often confused with Night Terrors or *pavor nocturnes*, although these are quite separate types of attacks. Usually occurring in childhood, Night Terrors often culminate in a high-pitched scream that usually succeeds in waking the victim (and everyone else in the house). Up until that moment however, the dreamer is fast asleep and although she may be very upset on waking, little of the dream can be recalled the following morning.

This is quite unlike the Night Mare where the sleeper is aware what is happening and wants to cry for help but cannot. Also, Night Mare induced terror is vividly recalled months and even years after the event. In some cases, Night Terrors recur regularly, in which case the condition becomes known as Sleep Terror Disorder.

Another type of night-time disturbance is sleep apnoea, where the sleeper wakes very suddenly feeling she needs to take a deep breath because she has stopped breathing - which in some cases is true. Sometimes the sleeper wakes spontaneously, gasping for breath, sometimes her partner becomes alarmed that she appears to have stopped breathing and will wake her up. It is very distressing especially since it can happen several times a night.

However, sleep apnoea is quite distinct from the Night Mare, as it lacks the same feeling of being paralysed, crushed, throttled or suffocated. Sleep apnoea is *not* a psychic attack but can be a warning of a serious health condition so we must seek medical advice immediately if we believe we are affected by it. Acid reflux can also cause similar symptoms to sleep apnoea.

The Night Mare

The Night Mare, (also known as The Mare or The Hag) is one of the most common types of night-time attack. Those who have never experienced it can find it difficult to appreciate the sheer level of fear it generates. Even battle-hardened veterans have described it as more terrifying than anything they have ever known. It can be caused by a deliberate psychic attack and while some people only experience it once, others may experience it more often, even several times in one night. It's believed to occur when people undergo periods of intense stress in their lives, although this could simply be a reaction to the stress of a psychic attack.

The Night Mare is also said to occur more often when the victim is tired and stressed. We might therefore expect that women with young children, whose sleep is often disturbed for months - even years - on end, would be prime candidates for sleep paralysis. Yet this doesn't seem to be the case, although women *are* more likely to experience the Night Mare during pregnancy than at any other time in their lives. A sizeable number of witch-trial records suggest that the victims of these Mare attacks were either pregnant or had recently given birth.

For example, in 1666, a pregnant woman named Anna Cramer alleged that a witch visited her at night and lay down on her. A few years later, in 1685, Georg Schmetzer testified that his pregnant wife was attacked by a presence that lay on her body in the night and pressed her down. [38]

Most attacks by the Night Mare have certain similarities. They almost always happen at night, often when the victim is wide awake, but feels unable to move. He may then become aware of ghostly footsteps, sensing something or someone in the room which then climbs on top of him and kneels on his chest before trying to suffocate or strangle him. Sometimes however, he will not wake until the attack has started.

Although many reports suggest the Night Mare is more likely to attack when the victim is sleeping on his back, there have been many cases where people sleeping on their sides, their stomachs and even sitting up in chairs have been attacked. Some have reported being pushed down into the pillow and mattress so hard they were afraid they were going to suffocate. Often victims report

---

[38] Davies (2003): 186

hearing the Mare speak to them; the words vary but popular phrases include, '*Be pressed down,*' and the rather sinister, '*You knew I would come.*'[39]

Although the attacking entity is often referred to as 'the Hag' or 'the Mare' its appearance varies. Some describe it as a beautiful young woman, others report being attacked by an animal (wolves and cats are common), or a witch, demon, bird, dark shadows, masked men, elves, dwarfs and even faceless figures. Attacks are sometimes described as being ridden by the Mare (or the Hag), witch-ridden, hag-ridden, and a number of similar variants.

Because belief in the Mare persisted so late into the historical period, we have numerous written accounts, all surprisingly similar in many details. As late as the eighteenth century, a paragraph in the London coffee-house journal, the *Athenean Mercury,*[40] described feeling, '*...perfectly awake, and with such a vehemency that they are not able to stir either hand or foot, or move the least member of their bodies, nor can utter one word distinctly, but make a kind of grumbling noise...*'

The response to that statement came from none other than Samuel Wesley, the father of John Wesley, founder of the Methodist Church, who was at that time on the journal's editorial board. Samuel Wesley replied that although the same symptoms could be caused by excessive drinking, '*...sometimes 'tis really effected by witches, which first gave the name to the common oppression in sleep called the night-mare.*'

Wesley was also able to give an example of a personal acquaintance who had witnessed the effects of such attacks on a young boy who was '*...worn out even to consumption, by the common load and oppression of a witch.*' Eventually, an elderly local woman confessed that she had spirited herself through the boy's bedroom window, lying on him and tormenting him.

Occasionally the Night Mare is believed to ride the victim around the countryside, like a horse. Folk tales such as '*The Blacksmith's Wife of Yarrowfoot*' and '*The Two Fellows*'[41] usually

---

[39] The Author - Personal notes

[40] *Athenian Oracle* (1728): 292-3.

[41] Oates (2003): 211

follow a similar pattern: A young man confides in his friend that their master's wife comes to him every night, puts a bridle on him which turns him into a horse, and then rides him all night so that by the next morning he is exhausted. People have already started noticing he is pale and always tired. The helpful friend offers to swap places.

That night, the mistress arrives as usual, throws a magic bridle over the friend and transforms him into a horse which she then rides to a witches' meeting. Knowing in advance what to expect, the friend is ready for her when she comes back and slips out of the bridle which he then throws over the woman's head, changing *her* into a horse instead. With the tables now turned, he rides her home and ties her up in the stable (or, in some versions, takes her to the blacksmith for shoeing) before removing the bridle.

Next morning, the master finds his wife in the stable, or in some versions, in bed with a horseshoe on her foot! The first youth is never troubled by the Mare again, and to help him recover from his ordeal is given butter from the milk of cows fed on churchyard grass, which was a regarded as the best remedy for '*consumption brought on through being witch-ridden.*'

Transformation by a magic bridle also features in witness statements given at witch trials in England and Europe. Anne Armstrong, whose testimony was responsible for the execution of several women in Northumbria in the early 1670's, claimed to have been transformed into a horse on various occasions and ridden to a witches' meeting by means of a magic bridle.[42] When it was removed she then changed back into a human being. However, she was unable to speak until she ate a piece of cheese which she discovered beside her when she woke and found herself in a field.

Faced with such a fantastic tale, it's easy to overlook the small details that are so important - in this case, the piece of cheese. At first sight it seems rather surreal, but ever since Anglo-Saxon times, eating bread and cheese (known as the 'holy morsel') had been used as part of a trial by ordeal, to discover whether someone was telling the truth. Only the innocent or truthful could swallow it,

---

[42] *Ibid:* 213

whereas the guilty would choke. This might even be where the saying 'hard cheese' meaning 'bad luck' originated!

The tradition persisted long after the Anglo-Saxons, and in the Jacobean play, *The Witch of Edmonton* (Act 4 scene 1), written barely fifty years before Anne Armstrong's accusations, a falsely accused witch demands, '*Let 'em eat cheese and choke.*' Possibly either Anne (or the prosecutors) included cheese in her testimony to convince the court that she was telling the truth.

Although the Night Mare sometimes changed its victims into horses, other accounts show that sometimes the Night Mare attacked horses. The following morning, they would be bathed in sweat, their manes tangled so tightly that sometimes the only solution was to cut the knots off. Even today, hairdressers sometimes describe customers' hair as 'cobby' if there are knots near the nape of the neck (and of course, a cob is a type of horse). Like horses, human victims of the Night Mare often described waking with palpitations and soaked with perspiration. The Night Mare is also believed to attack cattle in a similar way.

The Night Mare as a Cat and Other Animals

One of the most common manifestations of the Night Mare is as a cat, a creature long associated with witches. In particular, cats were said to kill babies and young children by 'sucking out their breath.' (Witches were also sometimes accused of doing this). In 1810 *The Lincoln and Hull Chronicle*[43] reported how a cat and its kitten almost suffocated a fourteen-month-old baby in its cot. The article stated that if the mother had not noticed in time, the cat '*...would by its weight upon the child's stomach, have speedily deprived it of life.*' Barely twenty years earlier, at an inquest into the death of an eighteen month-old child in Plymouth, the verdict stated that '*...the child died in consequence of a cat sucking its breath, thereby occasioning strangulation.*'[44]

Even when I was having my own babies, I heard the same stories from older female relatives. Of course, such tales ensured

[43] 4 May 1810, *The Lincoln and Hull Chronicle*

[44] 25 January 1791, *Annual Register*

that cats had a sinister reputation, although many were probably seeking the warmth of the child's bed – it's easy to forget in these days of central heating just how cold winter could be years ago.

The idea of the Night Mare manifesting as a cat is widespread. At the Salem witch trials of 1692 Susanna Martin was accused of changing herself into a cat which attacked her victim, '*...flew upon him, took fast hold of his throat, lay on him a considerable while, and almost killed him.*'[45] In Norwegian folklore, the *mara* or Night Mare often took the shape of a black cat or *marekatt*. In Hungary, the strong underlying link between nocturnal cat visions, witchcraft, and the Night Mare (*mora*) was referred to as the 'Mora Trinity'.

Obviously, we cannot take everything said at witch trials as fact. Some accounts begin by sounding like the Night Mare and end up sounding like an obsessing entity. For example, at a witch trial at the Suffolk Assizes in 1599, Olive Barthram was accused of sending a shape-changing spirit to torment her victim at night.[46]

The spirit manifested as a toad, a cat and '*...a thick dark substance about a foot high, like to a sugar loaf, white on top,*' (amongst other things). The creature then lay '*...on her breast he pressed her so sore that she could not speak, at other times he held her hands that she could not stir and restrained her voice that she could not answer.*' This certainly has many of the hallmarks of the Night Mare. However, the victim went on to claim that the entity identified itself as 'Gyles' and claimed that Olive had sent him. If true – and we have no way of knowing for certain – this suggests an obsessing entity rather than the Night Mare.

Sometimes Night Mare attacks have been witnessed by others. In 1601, for example, Jacotte Simon testified that she was in bed alone one morning when she felt something pressing down on her. Eventually she managed to raise her head and saw someone she recognised at the foot of her bed; her husband then came into the room and reported seeing two '*marvellously big and ugly*' cats running off.[47]

---

[45] Davies (2003): 185
[46] Ewen (1933): 188
[47] Briggs (1998): 74

Cultural conditioning is often suggested as an explanation for the Night Mare. In other words, we see whatever we expect to see. For example, perhaps people only saw cats because of their association with witches who were believed to cause the Night Mare. However, this is not entirely true since witches were also traditionally associated with other animals such as hares, which have a number of similarities with cats: both have fur, move quickly, and are approximately the same size, with the average cat reaching 5kg and a full grown adult hare reaching 6.5kg.[48]

As long ago as the early seventeenth century, people were warned that eating hare's meat was risky since it was *'…hard of digestion; it breeds Incubus, often eaten, and causeth fearful dreams.'*[49] Yet there are no accounts that I know of that specifically mention a Night Mare in the form of a hare. Also, there are no accounts of any of the many other creatures that regularly inspire fear in us in the everyday world, such as spiders or snakes manifesting as the Night Mare (apart from a reference to the '*spiderwight*' in an Anglo-Saxon charm.)

The Night Mare sometimes takes the form of a bird, though these are rarely feared as much as snakes and spiders. In Ireland, a large fierce bird often settled on the victim's legs before moving up the whole body and pressing down on it, while in the Balkans, the Night Mare manifested as chickens, hens and cockerels, all popularly thought to be witches' familiars in that region.

The biggest obstacle to the explanation of cultural conditioning is when we start dealing with creatures that are not recognisable as specific animals or birds. These are more likely to be chthonic entities. In Cornwall, for example, the Night Mare often appeared as the *hilla*, described as, *'a great hairy thing which lay on them with a dead weight that almost stopped their breathing.'*[50] It was sometimes believed to be a malevolent form of a Cornish Piskey. The Anglo-Saxons believed that elves caused the Night Mare, while at

---

48 http://www.bbc.co.uk/nature/species/European_Hare
49 Oates (2003): 217
50 Davies (2003): 194

Neuchatel in Switzerland, people believed it was caused by a *tchutch-muton*, a type of fairy that appeared as a black sheep.[51]

It's curious that in folklore and legends both elves and fairies usually appear vaguely human, give or take the wings and pointed ears. When they manifest in the Night Mare however, they are truly monstrous. Yet if cultural conditioning can explain the Night Mare, then surely fairies and elves should look as they do in folk stories - otherwise how would we recognise them? Why call a monster an elf if it appears in the Night Mare but not if it turns up in a fairy-tale? I have even heard people claim it is easier to visualise an animal form because most people have more contact with these on a daily basis than with fairies and elves! Yet surely it would be easier to visualise elves and fairies in the way we usually think of them rather than suddenly change them into cats and wolves?

The Origins of the Night Mare

Nobody really knows how old the legends of the Night Mare are, nor where they first originated. As early as 400BCE, a Chinese book on dreams describes something very similar,[52] although the English word 'Mare' probably shares the same root as the Germanic *mahr* and Old Norse *mara* which meant a supernatural being who lay on people's chests at night, making them feel smothered or suffocated. In Anglo-Saxon, '*mare*' means Night Mare although originally it described a white female elf of the air; there are various charms against the influence of elves.

The concept of the Mare is present in many languages right across Europe, from the Polish *zmora*, to the Croatian *morica*, the Serbian *mbre*, the Czech *muera* and the Russian *kikimora*. The words for Night Mare are also very similar to each other: *nachtmahr* in German, *nachtmerrie* in Dutch, and *cauchemar* in French. Given so many similarities, there is a strong likelihood that the words probably originated in the prehistoric Indo-European culture, suggesting a primordial phenomenon rooted in the mists of time.

---

51 Davies (2003): 195

52 *Ibid:* 182

Many of the above words have an underlying meaning of pressure or pressing, and most Night Mare accounts mention the sensation of terrible pressure on the chest. The French *cauchemar,* derives from *caucher* which means 'to tread on,' while in medieval French the Night Mare was *appesart,* deriving from *peser,* a verb that means 'to press down upon,' similar to the Italian *pesuarole,* Spanish *pesadilla,* and Portuguese *pesadela.* In German, '*alpdruck*' means 'elf pressure', *alptraum* means 'elf dream' (i.e. Night Mare) while *hexendriicken* means 'witch-pressing'. The Polish *zmora* not only referred to the Night Mare, but also to living beings that disturbed their neighbour's sleep by making them feel a great weight pressing down on their body.[53]

This shift from blaming non-human agents such as elves, to blaming real people, i.e. witches, is noticeable all over Europe by the Middle Ages. And of course, unlike elves and fairies, human beings could be - and were - arrested, tried and executed.

Incubus and Succubus

The Night Mare is often confused with the Incubus and Succubus, but although there are some similarities there are also a number of important differences. The Latin word *incubus* derives from the verb *incubare* meaning 'to lie down upon' while *ephialtes,* the ancient Greek term for this sort of entity, means 'to leap upon.' Both refer to an entity that gets on top of its victim, whereas the Succubus is an entity that usually gets *beneath* its victim. This might even explain why some argue that the Incubus, which took the upper position during intercourse, was male, while the Succubus was female, although it is perfectly possible for them to be either gender. Themison of Laodicea, a physician in the first century CE, coined the name *pnigalion* meaning 'strangler' or 'throttler', which is much closer to the traditional Night Mare that tries to strangle or suffocate its victim.[54]

Another important difference between an Incubus/Succubus attack and the Night Mare is the sensation of temperature. Women

---

53 All from Davies (2003): 184

54 Stewart (2002): 285

who claimed to have been sexually assaulted by the Incubus, demons or Satan (and sometimes also by animals) often remarked that both the penis and semen were icy cold, whereas few accounts of attacks by the Mare (or sleep paralysis for that matter) ever mention temperature. Likewise, very few of the Incubus/Succubus reports mention the victim's inability to move, the sensation of being suffocated or the impending feeling of dread that accompanies a visit by the Mare.

It is possible therefore that many of the accounts of the Incubus/Succubus are simply erotic nightmares rather than a true Night Mare. Another theory is that a repressed sexual imagination can sometimes create - or attract - an Artificial Elemental. This may be created either by the victim or sent by a psychic attacker.[55]

Remember too, that people do occasionally create thought forms which they later find difficult to get rid of. Usually this is because they cannot stop thinking about it, although in the ancient world, the medical author Soranus claimed that the Incubus/ Ephialtes was not a demon but a contagious disease that spread like plague!

Investigating the Night Mare

Not all unpleasant night-time experiences - even those involving the Night Mare - are caused by psychic attacks. It really depends on the circumstances, which is why it's so important to keep notes of what is happening to avoid jumping to hasty conclusions. Knowing what to ask is half the battle. For example, at first sight this appears to be a typical Night Mare experience:

> *'I often wake up feeling I cannot move. One day this happened and I could see a shadowy figure in the corner of the room. It looked human but I couldn't make out the details of the face although I was certain it was looking at me. I had to really struggle to try and move and eventually I managed to sit up but by then it had disappeared.'*[56]

---

[55] Fortune (1970): 146

[56] Author's personal notes

How can we be certain what happened in this instance? Without more evidence it's difficult to say for certain whether it was sleep paralysis, the Night Mare or some sort of paranormal visitation. It was a hypnagogic event, certainly, as it happened on the verge of waking, and the faceless figure in the corner of the room is typical both of sleep paralysis and attacks by the Mare. But the account (scribbled down hastily in my youth) is woefully incomplete. What I should have asked was firstly whether there was anything else unusual going on (try and avoid using the phrase 'psychic attack' initially), and secondly whether the victim had felt pressure on the chest or a feeling of suffocation.

It can also be helpful to read accounts of old witch-trials and think about the sort of questions that should have been asked at the time. For example, in 1650, at Ann Wagg's trial on a charge of witchcraft at Ilkeston, Derbyshire, Ann Ancoke testified that her sick daughter must be 'witch-ridden' since she could not speak.[57] But what did that prove? Being unable to cry out is certainly a symptom of the Night Mare, but normally speech returns as soon as the Night Mare ends. Was the daughter suffering from a physical illness? Was she unable to speak *as the result* of a night-time attack or did she become ill first?

Even when witnesses were present, we should ask ourselves much they really saw and how much they imagined. Other witnesses at Ann Wagg's trial claimed to have seen one of their serving girls being attacked by a cat that sat on her chest. This certainly sounds like an attack by the Night Mare, but what makes it so unusual (though not impossible) is that it was witnessed by third parties.

Some thirty years later, Elizabeth Fenwick of Longwitton in Northumberland, was accused by Nicolas Raynes of continually threatening and tormenting his wife, claiming she '*...rides on her, and attempts to pull her on to the floor.*'[58] But did he *see* Elizabeth in his bedroom or was he simply describing how his wife struggled during the attacks? There may well have been some sort of manifestation, but perhaps it had nothing to do with the woman

57 Davies (2003): 186

58 Ewen (1933): 320, 406

he accused. We just don't know. However, these are exactly the sort of questions that should be asked whenever we need to investigate possible attacks by the Mare.

Sometimes eyewitnesses add to the confusion. At the first Salem witch trial in Massachusetts, a witness named Richard Coman stated that eight years earlier (when he was about twenty four), he had been in bed with his wife, when a woman named Bridget Bishop had *'oppressed him so, that he could neither stir himself, nor wake anyone else, and that he was the night after, molested again in the like manner.'*[59] Terrified, Coman then slept with a sword at hand to protect himself, and a friend who was staying with him claimed to have seen Coman struggling with the sword although nobody else appeared to have been present.

What makes this account so interesting is that if Coman was indeed struggling with the sword then he wasn't paralysed (paralysis being a feature of both the Night Mare and sleep paralysis.) Although the first attack could have been a visit by the Night Mare, the episode with the sword, which the friend claimed to have witnessed, sounds as though it was staged for maximum effect.

The basic rule of thumb whenever we are investigating a psychic attack is:

Always keep an open mind, ask plenty of questions and don't alarm the victim. It's our job to calm things down, not crank up the tension!

Why does the Night Mare attack?

Leaving aside the witch trials, there are several theories about who or what is behind Night Mare attacks. Sometimes ghosts were blamed, especially those of children. Night Mare attacks were also believed to be caused by vampires, the 'living dead' and werewolves, although the evidence for this is slight. Even wearing the humble onyx, a semi-precious stone, was sometimes said to cause the Night Mare because it was believed to contain a demon

---

[59] Davies (2003): 185

that woke at midnight, and then caused terror and disturbance to the wearer as she slept.

In the case of psychic attacks however, the Night Mare is more likely to be sent by someone living and motivated by jealousy, spite and anger. In a survey taken in the Netherlands in 1937, it was noticed that Night Mare attacks often followed a broken engagement; the jilted partner then haunted the former lover, by turning herself (in this survey it was usually a female) into the Night Mare or sending the Night Mare as a separate entity [60]

This suggests that the Mare could attack by means of a thought form or even shape-shifting. Whereas a thought form is distinct from its creator, someone who shape-shifts remains essentially the same but changes their outward appearance, either into a different person or even a completely different species.

Curiously, traditional methods for invoking the Night Mare as a thought form often involved Christian prayers. Sometimes people cursed the victim by reciting the Lord's Prayer backwards in the name of the Devil. This summoned the Night Mare as a distinct, separate, supernatural entity which was then sent to harass the victim. In the shape shifting method, the attacker actually transformed into the Mare, before travelling in spirit form to the victim. Again, this often involved saying the Lord's Prayer backwards, with the additional ritual of driving a knife into a piece of wood three times.

The most commonly accused culprit of course, was the Devil, and since this figure occurs so often in psychic self defence, it is worth taking a closer look. Where did the Devil come from? Pagan religions such as the Greek, Roman and North European certainly had their share of trickster deities and unpleasant entities, but never anything that came anywhere near the all-encompassing evil of the Christian concept of the Devil.

What seems to have happened is that the early Christian Church amalgamated several aspects of popular pagan deities, including Pan and Cernunnos with the Old Testament concept of Satan or Lucifer. Rolled together, these became the Devil,

[60] de Blécourt (2003): 240

demonising the old pagan gods to discourage people from worshipping them, and creating a great Bogey-Man figure. Yet this also created a problem: for how could an all-powerful Christian God allow evil and the Devil to go unchecked?

One solution - still popular nowadays - blamed the victim, accusing him of inviting the Devil into his life by 'dabbling' with the occult. Now it's quite true that some things just aren't suitable for dabbling with; for example, we wouldn't, I hope, experiment with rewiring our home without first ensuring we had a good working knowledge of electricity.

However, the range of activities usually lumped together under the 'occult' can include virtually any 'New Age' interest, including fortune telling, the paranormal and even working with herbs and oils. This is absolute nonsense, because if it were true then people such as clergymen (who presumably never invite the Devil into their lives), would surely be exempt from psychic attacks. Yet they are not.

For example, we read of an eighteenth century clergyman who '*...imagin'd the Devil came to his bedside, seiz'd him by the Throat, and endeavour'd to choak him. Next day he observ'd the black impressions of his fingers on his neck. After being at a wedding or christening, he never escap'd it; and his servant is oblig'd to watch him all the next night, and rescue him from the paws of Satan ...*'[61]

Another example, from the sixteenth century author, Reginald Scot, recorded a priest's experience thus: '*There cometh unto mee, almost everie night, a certeine woman, unknowne to me, and lieth so heavie upon my brest, that I cannot fetch my breath, neither have anie power to crie, neither doo my hands serve me to shoove hir awaie, nor my feete to go from hir.*'[62]

Other Explanations for The Mare

Although not all Night Mares are psychic attacks, those that are will always have a human creator. However more recently,

---

[61] Bond (1753): 55

[62] Quoted in Oates (2003): 205

physicians, psychologists and others have sought to present other explanations which we shall now look at more closely.

One old explanation is that we have eaten something to trigger the attack. As long ago as the second century AD, the famous physician Galen claimed that the Night Mare or *ephialtes* was caused by gastric and digestive problems. This view that went unchallenged for many centuries. Even now, many people swear that eating cheese before going to sleep causes bad dreams and visits from the Night Mare, while others claim the same for eating food containing MSG (Monosodium Glutamate). Although much of the evidence is anecdotal, it is still worth considering.

Other explanations for the Night Mare (and other types of night attack) are that they are somehow linked with epilepsy. Alternatively, some claim that sleeping in an awkward position causes poor circulation which in turn leads to the sensation of being suffocated. The medieval Abbess, Hildegard of Bingen (AD 1098-1179) believed the Night Mare was caused by the blood drying out, and demons exploiting the '*trace of sin*' that was left in people from the sexual act had that formed them at conception.

In 1584, the Elizabethan sceptic Reginald Scot wrote a book called *The Discoverie of Witchcraft*, describing the Incubus as, '*a bodilie disease ... although it extend unto the trouble of the mind: which of some is called the mare, oppressing manie in their sleepe so sore, as they are not able to call for helpe, or stir themselves under the burthen of that heavie humor, which is ingendred of a thicke vapor proceeding from the cruditie and rawnesse in the stomach: which ascending up into the head oppreseth the braine, in so much as manie are much infeebled thereby, as being nightlie haunted therewith. They are most troubled with this disease, that being subject thereunto, lie right upward: so as, to turne and lie on the one side, is present remedie.*'[63]

Even King James I, who was no fan of Reginald Scot and burned his books when he became king, joined in offering an explanation. He believed the Incubus was caused by '*a thick phlegm falling into our breast upon the heart while we are sleeping... [which] takes all power*

---

[63] Scot (1972): 49

from us, as makes us think that there were some unnatural burden or spirit lying upon us and holding us down.'[64]

Down the centuries, doctors and scholars struggled to explain the Night Mare and between 1650 and 1850 no less than twenty-five works were written on the subject.[65] In the early twentieth century, even Freud and followers of his psycho-analytical approach sought new explanations for the Night Mare, suggesting it was triggered by mental conflict. In particular, they put forward the theory that the attacking animal, demon or pressure represented the parent in an incestuous wish, and that the Night Mare, '*...occurs only in persons with a considerable masochistic element in their constitution.*'[66]

I cannot even begin to image the damage such views did to people already terrified by their experiences of the Night Mare. It's barely one step removed from the medieval church's prurient obsession with nocturnal emissions, traces of sin and erotic dreams. For example, the monk, John Cassian in his works *Institutions* (6.20) and *Conferences* (2.23) claimed that nocturnal emissions could only be excused if one had gone to bed on a full stomach, but even then, not if they occurred more than once every two months. Three times a year was the maximum acceptable! The medieval churches, both east and west, concerned themselves with the minutiae of this 'problem' for many years.

Amongst other remedies, it was recommended that sufferers should fight such sensations with the '*knife of the will*' which may explain the old remedy of sleeping with a knife under the pillow to protect against the Night Mare.[67] In my view, both the religious and psychoanalytical approaches to the Night Mare are somewhat skewed and should really be ignored, or at least treated with a bucket of salt!

---

64 Davies (2003): 87

65 Stewart (2002): 294

66 Jones 1974 [1932]: 113

67 Stewart (2002): 290

Sexual Undercurrents in Incubus, Succubus, and the Night Mare

Many are embarrassed by the way sex features in many accounts of night-time attacks, something noticed back in the seventh century CE, when the Greek medical encyclopaedist, Paulus Ægineta remarked that '*...some imagine often that they even hear the person who is going to press them down, that he offers lustful violence to them.*' Here the attacker is clearly male, although by the Middle Ages the Night Mare and the Succubus were usually considered female.

The indefatigable sixteenth century author, Reginald Scot,[68] in his *Discoverie of Witchcraft* was openly sceptical of the Incubus phenomenon, claiming, '*Thus are lecheries covered with the cloke of Incubus and witchcraft ... speciallie to excuse and mainteine the knaveries and lecheries of idle priests and bawdie monkes'.*

The attacker's gender is interesting, since men who claim to have been attacked by a Night Mare in human form usually describe it as female (only a few have reported attacks by another male), yet women report attacks by either gender.

Often these entities, whatever the attacker's apparent gender, are referred to as Incubus or Succubus. There is much confusion over these terms. When I was young, I was taught that the Succubus was female and drew the semen out of her male victims before turning into a male Incubus and impregnating a female victim. In some versions, however, the Incubus and Succubus were distinct, separate entities, while in others the Succubus simply morphed into the Incubus. Nowadays, many people believe that the Incubus attacks women, while the Succubus attacks men. However, circa the first century CE, the term *Incubus* may have been used as the Latin equivalent of the Greek *ephialtes,* and used only to refer to a demon that lies or sleeps on top of the dreamer.

Over time, the term *Incubus* acquired much stronger sexual connotations, perhaps because of its similarity to *concubinus*

[68] Quoted in Davies (2003): 191

meaning concubine. A few centuries later, the term *Succubus* appeared, used to describe any demon that lay beneath the sleeper,[69] and initially at least, it was perfectly possible in the ancient world for a female Incubus to attack a man.

By the fourteenth century, a manuscript describing a 'night-mare' that lay on top of people at night shows that by the Middle Ages, the terms Incubus, Succubus and Night Mare were used interchangeably, while a document written at the University of Tübingen in 1666 related how the victim of the Night Mare '*...gets pressed, squeezed, twisted, excited or forced to sexual relation.*'[70]

Gradually, the term 'Night Mare' was used to describe any sexual dream, or, '*...when you dream something dirty and when you wake up you're still stiff because of it,*' or, '*When you sinned without wanting to.*'[71] Since so many accounts of night-time attacks describe them only in sexual terms, never mentioning paralysis or the sensation of suffocation, it seems likely that a true Incubus/Succubus manifestation is something quite separate from the Mare.

Unfortunately, the terms have become so muddled down the centuries that it is now difficult to differentiate between them. Both the Hag and the Mare are described as riding their victim, which is a popular euphemism for sexual intercourse. In fact, one folklorist surveyor noted that not only was '*being ridden by the mare*' another term for sexual intercourse, but was also used to denote '*impure*' love and even sometimes used to denote a whore.[72] It is therefore easy to become convinced that every Night Mare must somehow have some sexual content, although this is not true. Some attacks by the Night Mare have no sexual content whatsoever.

One of the best ways to identify the Night Mare is to ask ourselves – or the victim – what the attack was intended to achieve. Whether or not a sexual element is present, *all* Night Mares have one thing in common: the intention to instil terror in the victim.

---

69 Stewart (2002): 286

70 Davies (2003): 190

71 de Blécourt (2003): 241

72 *Ibid:* 240

The Theory of Sleep Paralysis

Nowadays the most popular explanation for attacks by the Night Mare is Sleep Paralysis, a condition that has only been properly categorised in the past fifty years. Basically, there are said to be five stages of sleep - during the first four stages the brain and heart rates slow, but during the fifth stage, known as REM (Rapid Eye Movement) sleep, the brain becomes more active, there is intense central nervous system activity but muscle activity remains inhibited. In other words, the brain has woken up, but the body remains asleep.

Nobody is sure why this happens. Some claim that the body is unable to act out its dreams; sleep walking only occurs during non-REM phases of sleep. Yet REM sleep does not always inhibit physical activity, and in REM Sleep Behaviour Disorder – where people punch the bed, jump out of bed, or even injure their partner sleeping beside them – the subjects are very energetic and uninhibited.[73]

Nowadays sleep paralysis is used to explain a wide range of frightening experiences, including nightmares, the Night Mare, night terrors, feelings of violation or assault, and even alien abductions. Indeed, I have heard it suggested that sleep apnoea (which can have several physical causes) is caused by sleep paralysis which is highly unlikely!

Therefore, before accepting sleep paralysis as an explanation for every episode of the Night Mare, do bear in mind that although people's dreams, sleep disorders and REM patterns can be wildly diverse, experiences of the Night Mare remain steadfastly similar. This suggests there is something that connects this particular type of experience together.

Surveys around the world suggest that between 20 - 45% of people experience at least one episode of sleep paralysis episode in their lifetimes usually in the early hours of the morning or when on the point of waking.[74] Most 'attacks' last barely ten minutes,

---

[73]http://www.abc.net.au/science/news/health/HealthRepublish_535895.htm

[74] Davies (2003): 182

although up to half an hour and more has been reported. At this point, it's worth setting out the precise criteria that are usually met in the Night Mare:

1. The victim feels she is awake. Often she can see, hear and even smell.
2. The victim cannot move – either because something is preventing her, or because she feels paralysed. A typical description is, '*I felt as though someone was holding me down. And I couldn't do anything, I couldn't even scream properly.*'[75] In REM sleep behaviour disorder and sleep walking, the sleeper does not feel paralysed.
3. The victim knows where she is, for example, she will know she is in her bedroom. In an ordinary dream she could imagine she was somewhere else.
4. She is terrified.[76] Victims usually report something – or someone – trying to press down on their chest making it difficult to breathe. They often believe they will die if they are not awakened. In fact, there is some evidence that some people *do* die as a result of these attacks.[77]

Other symptoms which are sometimes – but not always present – include the sense of a physical presence in the room. Sometimes the attack is preceded by the sound of ghostly footsteps, or by the entity speaking to the victim.

As we can see, the Night Mare has a precise set of symptoms. The feeling of weight or pressure is always an essential component of the Night Mare, but is *not* always present in sleep paralysis. Some people researching sleep paralysis note that a sense of pressure on the chest was mentioned by only 35% of those experiencing sleep paralysis; others have reported 40% and 50%.[78] This still leaves at least half of all those reporting a 'Night Mare' who do not experience the one essential aspect of it!

---

[75] Author's Personal notes

[76] Hufford, (1982): 25

[77] Adler (1991): 54

[78] Davis (2003): 197

I once came across a case where someone was fully awake for an hour, turned over in bed only to see a creature beside the bed, yet was still told that this was sleep paralysis. When it was pointed out that the sleeper was clearly not paralysed, the answer was, 'Paralysis isn't always present in sleep paralysis,' which is mind boggling to say the least.

Stranger still, sleep paralysis as a diagnosis can also include people who feel they are floating above their beds, flying, accelerating, rising, lifting, spinning, swirling, or being thrown at great speed through a tunnel. Far from feeling terrified, these 'victims' often report feeling pleasantly lightheaded or dizzy. Yet many people still believe they all come within the remit of sleep paralysis.[79] Certainly anyone with an interest in magic and the occult would regard 'floating above the bed' as an out of body experience and nothing like a psychic attack.

Of course, knowing what has happened doesn't always explain *why* it has happened, at least, not without further investigation. Think about when we cough. We have a good idea how coughs happen, that they are a reflex action caused by the nerves in the lining of our respiratory passages or airways. But coughing can be *caused* by a number of things including colds, chest infections, heart failure or lung diseases, smoking, having heartburn, snoring, poor air quality, damage to the vocal chords or even swallowing a fish bone!

Therefore we can see that simply knowing *how* coughs happen is not the same as knowing *why* they happen. What caused the damage to the vocal chords? What sort of virus is it? Why did nobody remove the fish bone? And in the same way, knowing that sleep paralysis may affect some individuals is not the same as saying that every night attack is actually due to sleep paralysis. We don't, for example, know why these attacks affect people when they do, or exactly what triggers them. Why do they happen some days and not others? And why to some people and never others?

For instance, if lack of sleep is a major reason for these attacks we might expect sleep paralysis to affect almost all new parents. I

---

[79] Davies (2003): 198

know I got very little sleep for years when my children were small, but I never had an attack of the Mare. Nor did I when I lived in an inner city and used to keep getting up during the night in response to every small sound out in the street. So clearly, sleep paralysis doesn't affect all people equally, and there is a great deal more research that needs to be done.

How Dangerous is the Night Mare?

People often claim that sleep paralysis, although unpleasant, is basically harmless apart from the obvious risks in driving or operating machinery if we do not get a good night's sleep. However, medical science is well aware that some very strange things can happen during an episode of the Night Mare. For example, in 1980, a medical examiner in Portland, Oregon, US, noticed what seemed to be a pattern of unexplained deaths among South East Asian immigrants.[80]

In the fourteen years after the first death was reported in 1977, more than a hundred apparently healthy individuals died in their sleep with no known cause. All but one of the victims was male, they were all healthy and their average age was thirty-three. Many were Hmong refugees, especially from Laos, although other nationalities included Filipino, Thai, Khmu and Cambodian.

This disorder became known as 'Sudden Unexpected Nocturnal Death Syndrome' or SUNDS. Although various causes have been considered, including toxicology, heart disease, sleep apnoea, genetics, metabolism, and nutrition, the exact cause is still a mystery. Autopsies revealed nothing useful and most death certificates for SUNDS victims gave the cause of death as unknown. These were otherwise healthy people who just died in their sleep.

What is interesting however, is that Hmong traditions include a belief in a nocturnal spirit called the *dab tsog* which is associated with pressing its victims, something that sounds very like the Night Mare. More intriguingly, when researchers interviewed the

[80] Adler (1991): 54

families of twenty-nine SUNDS victims (all Hmong males) they concluded that '*the only clue to emerge from our discussions . . . was a dream, forewarning death.*'[81] Unfortunately, the researchers do not seem to have taken their questioning any further, and lost a valuable opportunity to delve deeper into the nature of these prophetic dreams.

The researchers did however investigate the case of another Hmong refugee, Vang Xiong, who suffered a series of Night Mares back in 1978[82]. His account certainly sounds very typical of what we would call the Night Mare, with first a cat, then a dog and finally a white skinned female taking turns to sit on his chest and prevent him from breathing properly.

Unfortunately, the researchers dismissed his account as symptoms of '*anxiety, depression, and paranoia that threaten all victims of trauma and extreme stress*' and even suggested it was a case of '*spirit possession*'. It's a great pity that such researchers never seem to see the need to question a little more thoroughly in these cases. One thing that was recorded however was that although the *dab tsog* was quite common amongst the Hmong people, deaths from SUNDS were apparently unknown in Laos, which is where most of the victims originated.[83] It seemed that it was only once people emigrated, often as refugees, that the Night Mare proved fatal.

Preventing Night Attacks

As with all cases of psychic attack, remember that attackers always go after our weakest point. For example, if we are prone to dizzy spells, an attacker will make us fall. If we already fear our home is haunted, a psychic attack will make it suddenly seem more active and menacing. And if we are prone to these night attacks, then an attacker will send a particularly horrifying type of attack at dead of night. Remember that all attacks have two main purposes: to

---

81 Tobin, Friedman (1983): 9

82 *ibid*: 440

83 Organista *et al*, (1978): 269

cause harm and to cause fear. Sometimes they do one or the other, sometimes both.

Knowing how these attacks operate is important. Basically, the more frightened, tired and stressed we are, the more likely it is that we will be successfully attacked. The people most likely to suffer from the Night Mare and other night-time attacks were those who didn't - or couldn't - go to bed until they were exhausted.

For example, in sixteenth century Breslau in Silesia, a local shoemaker who had recently committed suicide made ghostly night-time visits to his neighbours, lying on them, smothering and squeezing them. At the time, it was remarked that those who were most affected by the shoemaker's attacks '*...were those who wanted to rest after heavy work.*'[84]

However, although this case looks like a typical Night Mare, closer examination suggests it may have been some sort of vampire attack since when the shoemaker's corpse was exhumed, his body was found perfectly preserved. In fact, some witnesses claimed he now looked plumper! The link between vampires and the Night Mare will be explored more fully in Chapter Eight.

In nineteenth century Scotland it was noticed that women who were stressed with a heavy workload of spinning and missed their supper were particularly susceptible to attacks by the Mare. Another theory suggests that children suffer from the Night Mare because of the pressure put upon them by their parents to do well in exams,[85] although historical records show that even young people who never went to school still suffered from these attacks. As a precaution it seems sensible, however, to ensure we get as much rest as possible and try to avoid sleeping on our back as this seems to be the most common position for attacks to occur.

Remedies for dealing with night attacks of various sorts are given in Chapter Sixteen, although we should also cleanse and purify our sleeping area as a precaution. This is particularly useful if we are in the habit of keeping an altar in our bedroom, since these can act as gateways that sometimes pick up magical flotsam and jetsam.

---

[84] Davies (2003): 188

[85] *Ibid:* 192

As we have already seen earlier in this Chapter, sometimes a woman's sleep becomes disturbed during the later stages of pregnancy. One explanation is that as pregnancy progresses, she is more comfortable sleeping on her back, the position when these attacks (and also sleep paralysis) often occur. Also, pressure on the bladder in late pregnancy causes her to wake more often needing the toilet, which in turn disturbs her sleep pattern.

This link between pregnancy and the Night Mare was remarked upon as early as the sixteenth century, when Paracelsus, in his work *The Supreme Mysteries*, remarked that '*...some people, especially women in child-bed, have been so oppressed in the night in their sleepe, that they have thought themselves to be as it were strangled, neither could they possibly cry out, or call any helpe, but in the morning have reported that they were ridden by a hag.*'[86] Interestingly, a recent survey in Finland[87] found that most sleep disorders (such as sleep walking, sleep talking and night terrors) actually *decrease* during pregnancy.

Of course, there will always be people who say that an encounter with the Mare is simply a bad dream. But to the victims, it is much more than that. The memory of it doesn't fade easily, unlike the average nightmare. People can remember attacks many years after they happened and although some insist that such attacks are caused by sleep paralysis, those who have these terrifying experiences are rarely hooked up to any electrodes that might record exactly what was going on. Conversely, medical experts who put everything down to sleep paralysis rarely have any knowledge of what psychic attacks and thought forms can do.

Perhaps this haunting quote from a labourer in Anzegem in the Belgian province of West Flanders best sums it up, '*Yes, they say they are all superstitions... but you still feel it.*'[88]

---

86 Paracelsus (1656): 58-9

87 Davies (2003): 188

88 de Blécourt (2003): 233

CHAPTER EIGHT

Psychic and soul vampires. Interesting connections between the Incubus, Succubus, Night Mare, Werewolves and Vampires. Satanic rituals and Black Masses.

Belief in vampires or *revenants* has existed all over the world since ancient times. The Polynesians believed that vampires left their graves and crept into houses where they would kill a sleeping man by eating his heart and entrails. In Hebrew folklore, Lilith was Adam's first wife but refused to be obedient to him and flew away, later becoming a vampire who preyed on new-born babies. She also sometimes assumes the form of a giant black cat called El Broosha.[89] In the King James translation of the Bible, (Isaiah Chapter 34, v.14) her name was translated as 'Screech owl' which, like the cat, is closely associated with vampirism. The Revised Standard Version translates the word as 'Night monster'.

In ancient Greece, it was believed that dried out dead bodies or *nekroi* could transform into *alibantes,* a particularly horrifying category of the dead. In his work, *The Republic,* Plato claimed that just mentioning the *alibantes* made people shudder.

In the ancient Greek story of Orestes[90], the Furies threaten to suck his life-blood until he is dessicated *before* he dies, so that '*...leprous blains that shall leap upon his flesh, and with savage jaws eat out its erstwhile vigour.*' This threat to leave Orestes withered and dried out is very significant since dessication still plays a significant role in some hexing traditions. Any threats to cause the victim to rot or dry out should always be taken very seriously - whether or not vampirism is suspected.

The early eighteenth century author Calmet[91] believed there were four different categories of vampire:

---

[89] Howie (1989): 173

[90] Aeschylus *Choephori* lines 280-281

[91] Stetson (1896): 4

- **The first category** included people who had been buried alive yet somehow managed to leave their tombs. However, Calmet did not attempt to explain why someone who had managed to escape from the grave would then willingly return to it.

- **The second category** included dead people who had God's permission to return to their bodies for a time. This, according to Calmet, explained why corpses were sometimes exhumed and found to be uncorrupted, their blood still red and fluid with no trace of *rigor mortis.* He did not, however, explain why God would allow people to live the wretched life of a vampire in the first place.

- **The third category** contained those whom the Devil ordered to become vampires order to harm people and animals. This is an old theory, and the twelfth century author, William of Malmsbury claimed, '*In England they believed that the wicked came back after death by the will of the devil.*' It was also thought that anyone who was the victim of this type of vampire would in turn became a vampire when he died.

- **The fourth category** contained mortals who turned into vampires as a result of being excommunicated. These sucked blood from people, often announcing their arrival by rattling the doors and windows. This type of vampire was also likely to visit the Church while out of its grave.

Of course, vampires were not the only creatures with a liking for human blood. In some parts of Scotland, kelpies and even mermaids were also supposed to suck their victim's blood. This is quite at odds with the popular modern, romantic view of mermaids that seem to adorn everything from pillow cases to tea cups!

A sudden death or murder - especially when the body is not properly buried - was also thought to turn people into vampires. Suicides were denied a proper burial right up until the nineteenth century and were considered prime candidates for turning into vampires after death. A popular remedy was to either pin the corpse in its grave by means of a wooden stake or behead it. Plague victims were also a group that was improperly buried since they were often hastily thrown into a mass grave or burned. Interestingly, vampires were also believed to *cause* outbreaks of plague, particularly if the individual had been unpopular before their death.[92]

In some areas, the undead turned up at parties or family gatherings, where they sat down amongst the other guests. Some vampires were mute while others walked and talked quite normally amongst the living although if they nodded to someone, that indicated the person would soon die. In Germany it was believed that vampires still needed to eat, even gnawing their own flesh and shrouds while in their graves. Some people claimed to be stalked by a vampire disguised as a white spectre that followed them everywhere.

Another popular belief was that vampires targeted their surviving relatives, sometimes for many years, continuing to attack until the entire line had died out. Centuries ago, in New England, it was believed that if a person died of consumption he would turn into an obsessing astral entity. Although nowadays, thanks to many books and films, we think of a vampire biting his victim and drinking her blood, in the past it was the presence of consumption that was regarded as 'proof' of a vampire attack.

A more mundane explanation is that consumption was highly contagious and untreatable, therefore it would indeed strike down entire families and sometimes even their neighbours. The disease might then seem as though a vampire (i.e. the first victim to die of consumption) was pursuing his next of kin.

Although the New England tradition doesn't use the term vampire, the underlying principle is similar to vampire myths all over Europe: for as long as the corpse still has blood in its heart it will drain the blood from all living relatives.

---

[92] Barber (1897)

Exhuming a Vampire

Given that vampires often pursued living members of their families, survivors (almost into the twentieth century) sometimes chose to exhume their relatives and destroy his body. A New York journal reported '*At Peukuhl, a small village in Prussia, a farmer died last March. Since then one of his sons has been sickly, and believing that the dead man would not rest until he had drawn to himself the nine surviving members of the family, the sickly son, armed with a spade, exhumed his father and cut off his head.*'[93]

There are also several accounts of vampires being dissected by surgeons in the seventeenth and even eighteenth centuries. The pattern of phenomena that was observed in many of these cases suggests that the folklore surrounding vampires was rooted in observation. Doctors were apparently astonished to discover that corpses had not decayed.

Obviously, there could be practical reasons for this; for example, certain types of poison inhibit decay, while bodies buried in cold weather decay more slowly than those interred in the summer. Yet surely doctors – who dealt with disease and death on an almost daily basis – must have known how decomposition affects bodies. The alternative explanation is that in some cases, there really was something a little uncanny at work.

The tradition of exhuming and destroying a vampire still grips the imagination, fired by horror films and books, but it often surprises people to learn just how recently people went hunting vampires in cemeteries. For example, Highgate Cemetery in London became a focal point for vampire hunters in the late 1960's and 70's, leaving many graves desecrated and bones scattered.

Apart from the cultural disgust most people feel at the thought of disturbing the dead, the idea of a vampire being reduced to a skeleton is very much at odds with European folklore. Traditionally, vampires never decayed and even after many years would be found in their graves looking 'fresh.' The skin was believed to have a pink, rosy hue, the hair and fingernails would

[93] Stetson (1896):10

have grown since death, and there would be blood (stolen from the vampire's victims) present in the veins.

The idea of trawling through Highgate Cemetery hoping to spot a lurking vampire would have been far too haphazard for the methodical Hungarians and Russians. Their method was to have a young boy ride on a black horse that had never stumbled and make him ride over all the graves in the cemetery. Any grave that the horse refused to cross was declared a vampire's grave, and the corpse would then be exhumed and disposed of accordingly.

But what are we supposed to do if we encounter a vampire? In countries such as Hungary and the Balkans it was traditional to exhume the corpse, drive a stake - ash or aspen were favoured woods - through the heart, then decapitate the body and burn everything. In Normandy, only the priest and sexton were allowed to dig up suspected vampires, although this may have been an early attempt to prevent the sort of excesses that eventually happened in Highgate. After exhuming the body, the sexton's used his shovel to cut off the head and throw it into the nearest running water.

There was a general consensus that vampire's heads were so heavy that they sank straight to the bottom, through the river bed and on down to hell.[94] Alternatively, the severed head was sometimes be placed beneath the corpse's arm, while in Wallachia (part of modern Romania) people drove a long nail through the skull. The most common method to dispose of a vampire's corpse was simply to burn it and scatter the ashes, although in New England only the heart was burned.

Voltaire[95] described how in the Levant (the lands around the eastern Mediterranean including present-day Israel, Lebanon, western Jordan, Sinai and parts of Syria) the heart was torn out and burned while the rest of the body was cut into pieces and boiled in wine.

---

[94] Kittredge (1885): 166 Footnote 5

[95] Voltaire, *The Works of Voltaire, Vol. VII (Philosophical Dictionary Part 5)* 1764 can be read online - see Bibliography

Preventative Methods

Even if we are convinced we are dealing with a vampire, most of the above methods are likely to get us into trouble, so it is better to prevent the vampire from walking in the first place, or at least from attacking anyone. One method was to secretly draw a little blood from the corpse of someone likely to turn into a vampire, such as a murder victim or suicide. This was then added to bread dough that was cooked, and anyone who ate the bread would be protected from future vampire attacks. Disgusting as this sounds, it was more considerably more palatable than eating earth from the vampire's grave or drinking his blood before burial.[96]

Other methods to prevent vampires troubling the living were intended to distract them, rather like the traditional methods of distracting ghosts and evil entities. Scattering poppy, millet or mustard seeds into the grave would cause the vampire to stop and gather them up one by one. Another remedy was to place a fishing net or sock into the grave, so the vampire would be kept busy unravelling the knots at the rate of one a year; again, a never-ending task.

Iron objects placed on a body were believed to prevent it turning into a vampire, as did placing a clove of garlic into each of the body's orifices before burial. As a precaution people carried garlic whenever they were in the presence of a corpse and would also eat the plant and even rub it onto door frames and windows.

Sometimes objects buried with the corpse were intended to harm the vampire. Sickles, for example, were hung around the corpse's neck in the belief that they would cut the vampire's throat if it attempted to leave its grave. This practice seems closely related to the tradition of death as a skeleton carrying a scythe or sickle, one of the oldest agricultural tools. One of the Slavic words for vampire *pri-kosac* may derive from an early word for scythe.[97]

Some Roma people believed that a simple curse could destroy a troublesome vampire. In one such tale from Romania, for example, a vampire is quickly destroyed simply by saying to him,

---

96 Barber (1987) :16

97 *Ibid*

'*God send you burst.*' On hearing this, the vampire became so angry that he exploded leaving nothing but a large pool of blood where he had been standing.[98]

It's rare indeed that we encounter a full-blown vampire attack but it does happen occasionally, so it is just as well to be prepared. Unlike horror films, where the puncture wounds usually appear on the neck, in real life a vampire attack may manifest as a series of small pinpricks, we may even need a magnifying glass to identify them.

Other attacks leave scratches, particularly on the face or neck. I once knew someone who had recently moved into a flat and became convinced that she was the victim of a vampire because she kept waking up covered in what appeared to be small bite marks. Within a month her legs were covered in them. We soon realised, however, that the problem lay in the carpet, which had been colonised by fleas from the previous tenant's cat. Cat fleas will often bite people's legs and feet rather than any other part of the body. The remedy was simply to treat the carpet with proprietary sprays and powders and the problem soon went away.

Psychic Vampires and Soul Vampires

The most common type of vampire most people encounter is the psychic or soul vampire although there is some controversy surrounding these terms. Some people deny the existence of this class of vampire altogether, preferring instead to see them as manipulative individuals who generate chaos, confusion and often feign helplessness in order to drain others. While it is true that many people do this occasionally, a true psychic vampire will attack regularly. Like all forms of psychic attack, vampirism, whatever form it takes, is very addictive.

While a true vampire drains blood from the victim making them anaemic and fatigued, the psychic and soul vampires drain so much energy they also cause noticeable ill health. However, whereas a psychic vampire makes the victim physically ill, a soul

---

[98] *Ibid* : 11

vampire leaves her emotionally drained and depressed which in turn makes her susceptible to wide range of physical illnesses.

That said, it's important not to overreact and see vampires (even psychic ones) where none exist. If we feel drained in someone's company, it may just be they are hyperactive and exhausting, while others drain us with their constant moaning and complaining. However, none of these things prove that such people are vampires.

Usually the best way to check whether someone is a psychic vampire is to see whether things not only worsen when they're around but also improve when they're not. If this happens then try and avoid their company as much as possible, but certainly whenever we feel tired or unwell, since our defences will then be lowered, and an attacker will be able to drain us more easily.

When someone *accidentally* drains our energy, they rarely feel energised as a result and we usually recover quite quickly. With a true psychic or soul vampire, however, they are not only aware of receiving the victim's energy, but will continue doing so, keeping the attack simmering and thus making it more difficult for the victim to make a full recovery.

One of the most important things to consider about any vampire attack is its intention. They may never admit it to others, but true vampires – traditional, psychic and soul – know what exactly they're doing. They *know* that if they behave in a certain way, they will be able to gain energy from another person. And at some point, if they are a true vampire and not just a particularly demanding individual, they make the conscious decision to act the way they do.

There is a clear distinction between this type of person and anxious or obsessive individuals who simply leave us feeling stressed after listening to hours of their complaining. Yes, these people may leave us drained, but that's simply a reflection of their type of personality; they haven't set out to drain us, it's just the way they are. Sometimes these 'accidental' vampires realise what they are doing and stop. Others may realise what they are doing, decide they like it, and turn into true psychic and soul vampires.

One of the most common ways for a soul or psychic vampire to manifest is in repeated requests for healing energy, something that has greatly increased with the advent of the internet and social media. In the main, there is absolutely nothing wrong with asking for help or healing – in moderation. But with some people, the slightest cold, the tiniest difficulty and there they are, asking for help. Lots and lots of help.

Most people mean no harm at all, nevertheless this can be typical psychic/soul vampire behaviour because it is such an easy way to gain access to another person's energy. We should take care not to spread ourselves too thinly in response to such requests and unless it is a real emergency with someone we know well, we should never send healing to others when we feel ill.

Even with intentional vampires, some are more of a threat than others. The commonest type drains energy through a combination of curiosity and laziness. She will continually ask questions without really listening to the answers, and worse, sometimes tries to pass off any answers she does receive as her own. She never comes up with an original thought yet is happy to milk other people's minds. For as long as she remains a low-grade vampire, she is more a nuisance than a real threat.

Of course, some people are not content to leave it at that. The extra energy they drain from their victims can make them ambitious, and this is when an unintentional vampire may morph into something more sinister. She may decide, having drained us of all the information we possess on a given subject, that *she* is now a greater authority on the topic. A psychic vampire may drain all sorts of things – even cookery recipes and plant cuttings – from their victims! Trivial though it sounds, we're not talking about one or two recipes or the odd lavender cutting – psychic vampires may start small, but that doesn't last for long. Eventually they will claim to know as much – or more – than we do.

For a psychic vampire, the attraction of becoming an authority in her own right is that she can then attract her own followers and begin draining them of *their* energy. This time she isn't interested in draining knowledge (she has already gained most of what she needs) but pure energy. Since vampires normally prefer an easy victim, such people will often claim to be able to heal others. This gives them plenty of access to people who are already too weak to resist.

Always remember that psychic vampires are only concerned with their own ambitions. People rarely become psychic vampires in order to pass on energy to a third party, such as a sick child; they almost always drain energy *for themselves alone.* The cost to the victim is never even considered. Worse, when things go wrong for the vampire – which tends to happen often because their ambitions are so demanding and unrealistic – they will take out all their anger and frustration on a weak target who cannot fight back.

Sometimes, when we are around such people, we notice a shift in the way we feel straight away. At other times we may feel the air is positively buzzing, but later realise we feel washed out and tired. Then we recognise that the reason the other person's energy was crackling was because they were making use of *our* energy.

Another way that psychic vampires latch on is by being constantly negative, draining us with their criticism and forcing us to defend or justify everything we do. Internet trolls often drain their victims in this way too. In particular they thrive in situations where we are forced to tolerate their behaviour, perhaps for fear of upsetting a third party or losing our job.

Luckily, there are a number of 'tells' that can alert us when we are in the presence of a psychic or soul vampire. Try and notice how he looks our way, for often they either fix us with a stare, close their eyes or shield them when speaking to us. When they stare, they are trying to set up a link (sometimes called a red cord) from their third eye to ours. (The third eye is sometimes called the *anja* chakra, or third eye or Brow Chakra. It is located approximately above the bridge of the nose.)

These prolonged stares are a way of allowing the attacker to impose their will on ours and invade our mental space. When they close their eyes, they are trying to ensure that we cannot dominate them in any way. We often notice this sort of behaviour with professionals such as doctors and lawyers who will sometimes shield their eyes (it may appear as though they are tired or sensitive to bright light) or rub them.

The old tradition of shaking hands when people meet could also be a useful guide as to their true nature although I would never suggest that simply feeling uneasy when we're in someone's company is proof of a psychic attack! Sometimes however, we do pick up on hints that someone is untrustworthy or dangerous. Possibly it's an animal instinct that most of us normally do not need to use in the modern world.

If we ever feel physically sick just from shaking someone's hand, or feel ourselves cringing if they touch us, then we should pay attention, and consider that perhaps our subconscious is sending us a warning. The other person might be trying to pierce our Auric Field.

Before leaping to the conclusion that we are under any sort of attack, however, it is important to get our general health checked first. Sometimes, symptoms such as lethargy may have a physical cause. Even if we have a clean bill of health, we should pay attention to our diet, sleep and exercise. Too much junk food or stress, too little fresh air or exercise can quickly make us feel washed out. Even if we don't have any physical problems, remember that too much stress can – initially at least – also produce very similar symptoms to a psychic attack.

If we notice such symptoms, or believe we are being drained by a psychic or soul vampire, then we must avoid contact - physical, mental and emotional - with them as much as possible. Apart from avoiding physical contact, stop visiting their websites, blogs, social networking sites and refuse to even read their emails or text messages.

Unlike some psychic attackers who can operate from a distance, psychic and soul vampires need to be physically quite close to their victims in order to harm them. If the psychic vampire happens to be a work colleague, close friend or family member, it may not be practical to shun them completely, but we should at least protect ourselves with careful shielding, visualising psychic weapons, sealing doors and exits and other protective work (see Chapters Nine through to Twelve). The magical reflection techniques in Chapter Fourteen are also helpful against this type of attack. Protective psychic weapons are particularly useful if we suspect we are dealing with a 'real' vampire, i.e. one of the undead. We must also pay attention to sealing the Aura (Chapter Nine) in all cases where any sort of vampiric activity is suspected. This will help limit and eventually reverse any damage that has been done.

Sometimes people feel that it is wrong to take the same preventative measures against an unintentional attack as we would for a deliberate one. However, the damage caused by unintentional attacks can be just as severe, and we do have a duty to protect ourselves. It is virtually impossible to 'help' a psychic vampire because they already believe they can control everything. and if we don't take steps to stop them, they'll be right.

Another important remedy for this type of attack is sleep, which allows the body and mind to repair themselves. Night-time attacks are more common with traditional vampires, but even so are less common with psychic and soul vampires, so there is no reason to fear going to bed. We just need to ensure that we cleanse our sleeping quarters regularly, using one of the methods suggested in Chapter Twelve.

Psychic vampires can be found in all walks of life. They may attach themselves to individuals or to groups, according to whatever suits their particular talents. Some enjoy the challenge of manipulating a large group of people and outwitting them. Others prefer to pick off the weak and isolated because they make such easy targets. We cannot generalise about the type of person who will turn out to be a psychic vampire, but the results of their handiwork are usually very similar.

It rarely takes much effort to discover the culprit behind such attacks because intentional psychic vampires tend to be so arrogant that they don't bother to cover their tracks. And why should they? They have little or nothing to fear. They are doing nothing illegal and there is no court in the land that will convict them.

However, that doesn't mean we are powerless. The biggest problem for most victims of this type of attack is that they have been made to feel worthless or too drained to fight back. And some psychic vampires (along with psychic attackers generally) take great delight in telling us how powerful they are and describing the various curses they have laid against others. Some will even send wax effigies and poppets to their victims to further frighten them. On the internet especially, people often claim amazing psychic powers, much of it nothing more than the result of cutting and pasting from a variety of online articles.

In fact, most of them have the psychic ability of a peanut. What they do usually possess however is a good grasp of human psychology. Most victims are so intimidated that in their weakened state they begin to finish what the psychic vampire has started, i.e. they start to attack themselves. Once we understand how psychic vampirism works, we can put a stop to it.

Black Masses and Satanic Ritual

People are sometimes convinced that if they are under psychic attack then someone must be using Satanic rituals or Black Masses against them. Often would-be attackers enjoy hinting darkly that they have 'special powers' in order to intimidate others, but just because someone claims to be a powerful 'black' magician with 'super-powers' doesn't make it true. It is perfectly possible for *anyone* to curse, hex or psychically attack another; we don't need any special occult knowledge. Mostly it's down to a combination of resentment, spite or jealousy fired up with plenty of energy. A person with the right temperament and a well-developed sense of injustice can launch a psychic attack that would do credit to the most experienced occultist.

Much of what is written and said about Satanic rituals and Black Masses is little more than a muddle of lies, half-truths, speculation, opinion, boasting and wishful thinking and does a great deal of damage, even in the modern world. In the 1980's and 90's, many parents were wrongfully accused of involving their children in Satanic rituals and sacrificing babies. Although not a single allegation was ever proved, children were taken from their parents, often for many months as a result of these hysterical allegations. As I am very fond of saying – hysteria has no place in psychic investigations. Either keep calm or keep out. Later generations will probably look back in amazement at the Satanic Ritual Abuse (SRA) scandal it in much the same way as we look at the activities of the Witchfinder General Matthew Hopkins in the seventeenth century.

Of course, allegations of child sacrifice are nothing new. In the Roman Empire, Christians were accused of killing children as part of their rituals; by the mid nineteenth century it was the Freemasons who were being blamed. By the mid twentieth century, Satanism and Black Masses became regular themes in popular fiction by authors such as Dennis Wheatley and even C. S. Lewis, and many people, even those in authority, happily accepted them as fact.

It is difficult to underestimate the effect all this had on public consciousness, especially since terms such as spiritualism, the Devil, witchcraft, Satanism, the Black Mass, and 'black magic' were all lumped together and often used interchangeably. Dennis Wheatley wrote eight books based on 'black magic' each of which sold over 80,000 copies per annum throughout the 1960's and early 70's.[99] Certainly there was a renewed interest in the occult during this period, both by those who wanted to learn about it and those who feared it. Following the repeal of the Witchcraft Act in 1951, and the publication of Gerald Gardner's book *Witchcraft Today* in 1954, more information gradually became available.

Throughout the 1950's and 60's, tabloid newspapers published regular exposés of Satan worship in suburbia, while former Chief Inspector Robert Fabian of Scotland Yard (one-time Head of their Vice Squad) published his memoirs and made vivid claims about orgies in 'secret temples' as though he had witnessed them personally. When asked to explain why no arrests had ever been made, his excuse was that all the witnesses had been 'hypnotised.' In one case, Fabian claimed that a twenty-one year old girl had been driven out of her mind by exposure to 'occult obscenities' but that the police were unable to arrest anyone 'because there was no evidence' and the girl had been 'willed' to forget how it had happened.[100]

By the late 1950's therefore, one allegation of witchcraft or Devil worship came fast on the heels of another, which seemed to

---

99 http://www.denniswheatley.info/denniswheatley.htm

100 Ellis (1993): 16

support Fabian's claim that there were Satanists around every corner. On 16th March 1958, *The Sunday Empire News* ran a story about a London priest who had begged for police protection because he was being threatened by a 'Satanic cult' in Chelsea.

Later that year, the same newspaper published the alleged confession of a former cult leader who claimed to have indulged in blood-drinking and orgies, where members were blackmailed to prevent them leaving, and some had even been driven to commit suicide. Before long, the newspapers were full of stories about 'witches' celebrating Black Masses and worshipping the Devil.

Anyone who knows anything at all about modern Witchcraft and Wicca will already realise that their members do not celebrate the Black Mass, nor do they believe in the Devil. In fact, the 'Black Mass' is a parody of the Catholic Mass, and to be properly performed was supposed to be celebrated by a defrocked priest and a former nun.

However, during the 1960's the British film company, Hammer Studios produced a series of very popular horror films that featured occult themes. Following the success of *The Devil Rides Out* in 1967, (based on a Dennis Wheatley novel of the same title) the studio quickly produced a number of other occult films.

It's difficult for anyone who didn't live through that period to understand how deeply ingrained the idea of black magic cults was at that time. An article in the *Tonbridge Free Press* of 29th November 1963, described a number of ghostly manifestations in the area. One witness reported an *'eerie bat-like figure,'* while another saw *'this red light, like a red ball of fire'* which morphed into a figure with *'webbed feet and no head ... carrying a red lantern.'* What you or I might interpret as a haunting or manifestation of earth energies was swiftly denounced as black magic cult, purely on the grounds that, *'This is the evil sort of thing they would do.'*

Part of the problem of course is that it is all too easy for people to attribute things they do not understand to black magic, Satanism – or witchcraft. Both clergy and psychologists have been too eager to make sweeping statements with little regard for the truth. They were more concerned to push their own agendas without really bothering to properly investigate.

For example, when a bell ringer in Westham, Sussex discovered four men lighting candles in the chapel, the vicar quickly told a reporter from *The Times* (9th December, 1963) '*I have no doubt this was a black magic game. They have been practising in Somerset and are known often to set fire to churches,*' without providing a shred of evidence to support his claims.

However, such stories sell newspapers, which began sending out undercover reporters to approach Wiccans and request to be initiated. *The News of the World* was still running regular exposés of 'Witchcraft' early in 1969, hinting darkly that teenagers and even children were being 'lured' by occultists into orgies of ritual nakedness and flagellation. (In fact, reputable covens do not normally accept anyone under the age of eighteen, and then only if a parent is a member already.)

It's also very easy for people to perpetrate hoaxes, scribbling mysterious symbols which are promptly interpreted as Satanic. Even the pentagram is occasionally referred to as a Satanic symbol.[101] Sometimes people persist in believing there has been Satanic activity even *after* it has been revealed to be an elaborate hoax. Unfortunately, many of these sensationalised stories feature self-proclaimed 'authorities' who clearly know very little.

For example, I once watched a programme that discussed whether Hitler was an occultist. Plenty of historical experts gave their views, but not a single occultist. It would be like making a gardening programme with people who had never seen a real garden or flower.

Unfortunately, once the roller-coaster of rumour and allegations starts, it becomes very difficult to stop. The claim that a baby was sacrificed near Brighton in 1958 seems to have begun with a talk that Leslie Roberts gave to the Brighton Forum Society. He claimed there were many covens in the area and offered to show police where a baby had been sacrificed during a Black Mass. Police investigators found nothing, but Roberts was undeterred by

---

101 Ross (1995): 114

the lack of evidence, claiming instead that police were deliberately shielding the cults.[102]

Things took a more sinister turn by the late 1980's/early 1990's. On October 3rd 1990, the Channel Four programme *Dispatches* solemnly claimed that in Nottingham babies were cooked in microwaves, sheep were killed in order to drink their blood and sexual abuse was conducted in tunnels underneath cemeteries.

The programme also featured a visit by torchlight to the alcoves and tunnels of a dilapidated graveyard in Nottingham called the Rock Cemetery. Here viewers were shown half-burned candles, graffiti, and 'something that looks like a little altar,'[103] which is hardly proof of very much at all. It was however a good example of how a little information could be twisted to make it stretch a long way. The local police were already aware the tunnels were being used for sex, drinking, and even drug use, but had never uncovered any evidence of underground rituals or Satanism, let alone SRA (Satanic Ritual Abuse).

Unfortunately, the reports whipped up so much hysteria that many UK children were removed from their families. Nowadays, most of the theories of SRA have been discredited, along with the whole idea of recovering such memories through hypnosis, but the damage that was done to innocent people cannot be undone, and it remains a shameful episode in our history.

Remedies Against 'Black Magic'

Although magic is all about intention, there is still confusion about the difference between black magic and any other colour magic. Even if we have good reason to believe that we are the victim of a psychic attack launched by a defrocked priest who celebrates a Black Mass, that person is no more powerful than someone with a grievance and a particular type of personality. The methods of psychic self defence remain the same: avoiding all contact, then

---

102 The story can be followed in the *Evening News* [18 December 1958]; *Brighton and Hove Herald* [20 December 1958]; *Brighton and Hove Gazette* [20 December 1958]

103 Ellis (1993): 13

cleansing, clearing, strengthening and general protection. These are all listed in Chapters Nine through to Eighteen and can easily be adapted to virtually any situation.

Psychic attacks are much the same as physical ones; even if our opponent is larger and stronger than us, or is trained in the martial arts, we can fight back. The important thing is not to be intimidated. Often attackers claim superior knowledge to frighten and terrorise their victims when in truth they have little more knowledge than the average man in the street.

We must always remember that if we *believe* we are vulnerable then we will be, whereas if we *know* we can defend ourselves, we shall succeed.

Werewolves

The term 'werewolf' derives from the Anglo-Saxon *werewulf* which literally translates as 'man wolf,' and the tradition of a human being changing into an animal (not necessarily a wolf) is widespread, from Asia to Northern Europe, and beyond. In Africa for example, people changed into hyenas, while in parts of Northern Europe they turned into bears, cats and wolves.

There is a strong belief in central Europe, the Balkans and Greece, that the wolf is the natural enemy of the vampire and will destroy him whenever possible. A contradictory belief states that when a werewolf dies, it turns into a vampire! In some parts of central Europe, villagers welcomed the presence of white wolves in local cemeteries believing they would keep down the vampire population.

Elsewhere in Europe, people claimed that vampires and werewolves were at their most active in winter, while in Poland werewolves were considered particularly dangerous at Christmas and the Midsummer Solstice. In many European traditions, werewolves were at their most active at Christmas, New Year's Day and Easter.[104] According to the late second century author, Marcellus Sidetes, February was the month when people first

104 Senn (1982): 206

changed into werewolves and were at their fiercest. They hid at night in cemeteries, living like real dogs and wolves.

There was also a connection between werewolves and the Night Mare. In Rome, the deities Pan, Inuus, Faunus and Silvanus – all closely associated with sexual energy – were also connected with the *Lupercalia* festival celebrated on the 15th February, at the Lupercal, a great cave at the foot of the Palatine Hill. This was the place where the she-wolf suckled Romulus and Remus, the founders of Rome. Two relatively minor entities, Incubus and Ephialtes were also associated with the festival. As we have already seen in Chapter Seven, the word Incubus is Latin for *'he who lies on you,'* while Ephialtes comes from the Greek *'he who jumps on you.'* As minor deities, both Incubus and Ephialtes were associated with the *pilosi,* 'the hairy ones,'[105] who were young men in costume who ran around Rome during the festival, striking young women to make them fertile or ensure an easy childbirth.

With the coming of Christianity, such a festival did not survive for long, and it was taken over and changed to Candlemas, the purification of the Virgin Mary and the presentation of the infant Christ in the Temple, on February 2nd each year in the Catholic Church. The word February comes from the Latin *februare,* meaning to purify. In the Eastern Orthodox Church however, the festival is celebrated on the 15th February, the same day as the pagan *Lupercalia.* The Ancient Greeks also held a wolf festival, known as the *Lycaea.*

Perhaps surprisingly, the nearest thing we have to the Lupercalia in modern times is Shrove Tuesday or Pancake Day which is held just before the penitential period of Lent (which begins the following day on Ash Wednesday). Making pancakes allowed people to use up the eggs and flour that were forbidden during Lent. In some parts of Europe, the days before Lent were celebrated with a Carnival. The word comes from the Latin *carnivale* and basically means 'farewell to meat.'

However, the Carnival and Shrove Tuesday celebrations were not just about eating up meat and pancakes before the strict weeks

---

105 Wiseman (1995): 8

of Lenten fasting. In 1481, the Carmelite friar Baptista Spagnuoli of Mantua, wrote a poem *De sacris diebus* describing '*the evil custom of Shrove Tuesday*' as a revived Lupercalia.[106] He complained that young men ran about the town in masks, manhandling young married women whom they whipped, very much as they had once done during the pagan Lupercalia. Similar celebrations persisted well into the seventeenth century in Saxony. Modern Shrove Tuesdays are nothing like the earlier boisterous celebrations, although I suspect that the round-shaped pancakes are possibly a faint memory of its close association with the moon.

How do People become Werewolves?

From the Middle Ages onwards, people believed that illegitimate children, especially boys, automatically turned into werewolves, although this may just have been a way of trying to discourage sexual activity outside marriage. This may also explain why in some areas, the Church taught that children conceived at Christmas, Pentecost or Easter were destined to become werewolves, since these were days when the Church laws forbade any sexual relations even between husband and wife.

In Italy and Sicily, even children conceived at the time of a new moon were thought to be pre-destined to become werewolves. Elsewhere, children born deformed or displaying animal characteristics were thought to turn into werewolves from the eve of St Andrew's Day (30th November) until Epiphany (January 6th).

Mothers were sometimes blamed for creating werewolves by 'dabbling in magic' before the child's birth. Given that there was so little medical help available during labour, sympathetic magic, such as placing a knife beneath the bed to 'cut' the pain, was very popular although these magical protections were not normally connected with werewolves.

It was the more ritualistic methods that attracted criticism. For example, sometimes a woman stretched the membrane that had once enveloped a foal at birth between four sticks. She would then

---

106 *Ibid*: 22

creep through it naked, at midnight. Regardless whether such remedies worked or not, the Church taught that all the woman's sons would be werewolves and all her daughters would turned into the Mare. However, in many European traditions both men and women could turn into werewolves.

The most popular image of a werewolf is that of a living person who either transforms voluntarily, or is forced to do so by circumstances, perhaps after being bitten by another werewolf. Others seem to have been changed by some outside force, such as the moon phase. In Norway, people who can change into a wolf (or, indeed a bear) were said to either be Trolls or to have been given the gift by the Trollmen.

Strange as it may seem, some people willingly changed into werewolves. According to the fifth century BCE Greek author Herodotus,[107] the Neuri people all changed into wolves once a year, remaining that way for a few days before changing back again. This might have been based on the observation of shamanic practices, although we cannot know for certain.

In Russia, anyone wishing to become a werewolf first had to enter the forest, find a fallen tree and then stab the trunk with a small copper knife. He then walked around the fallen tree repeating the following incantation:

On the sea, on the ocean, on the island, on Bujan,
On the empty pasture gleans the moon, on an ashstock lying
In a green wood, in a gloomy vale.
Toward the stock wandereth a shaggy Wolf,
Horned cattle seeking for his sharp white fangs;
But the wolf enters not the forest,
But the wolf dives not into the shadowy vale,
Moon, moon, gold-horned moon,
Check the flight of bullets, blunt the hunters' knives,
Break the shepherds' cudgels,
Cast wild fear upon all cattle,
On men, on all creeping things,
That they may not catch the grey wolf,

[107] Herodotus, *The Histories,* (Book iv c.104)

That they may not rend his warm skin!
My word is binding, more binding and sleep,
More binding than the promise of a hero! [108]

He then leapt over the tree trunk three times and ran off into the forest, by which time the transformation into a werewolf was complete.

In parts of Wales, the transformation was only temporary and for a specified period, after which the werewolf would revert to human form for good. This is curiously similar to the ancient Greek tradition that the Arcadians could change themselves into werewolves at will by stripping off, hanging their clothes on an oak-tree and swimming across a marsh in a remote area. By the time the swimmer reached the other side, he had turned into a werewolf and would then live with others of his kind for the next nine years. Provided he had never eaten human flesh, he could return after that time, swim back across the marsh, return to his human shape and even collect his abandoned clothes![109]

In most parts of Europe, a werewolf could only be disenchanted if he had never tasted human flesh, while in other areas the affliction was for life no matter what he had eaten. In France, a werewolf could live as a man but would change back into a wolf at certain times such as a full moon. In Serbia, Bulgaria, Slovenia and the Czech Republic werewolves were able to swallow both the sun and moon, while in Romania the werewolf ate only the moon.

The process of magically changing into a wolf is called lycanthropy. Not all werewolves changed their form before they killed animals or humans, although many did. Some would first strip naked while others put on an entire wolf skin or a wolf skin girdle (which was a special belt sometimes made of human skin) or applied a magical salve. Another method of changing into a werewolf was to plunge into a spring or fountain. By the time he emerged again, he would be covered in dense fur and walking on all fours. To change back into human form the werewolf had to be

108 Baring Gould (1973 edition): 117
109 Brown (1973): 545

back at the spring by dawn and plunge into the water which would restore him to his former self.

Although people apparently changed very convincingly into werewolves it was said that their eyes never become wolf-life but remained the same as their human counterpart. This was often how the creature was later identified, and werewolves who were captured were often charged with witchcraft and executed (usually by burning). In this respect, the medieval werewolf was quite different from those of ancient Greece and Rome.

Dealing with a Werewolf attack

Just in case we ever find ourselves dealing with a werewolf, it may be useful to know the traditional methods of dealing with it and making it change back into a human being. One traditional method is to wound it and shed three drops of its blood, although how anyone in the clutches of a homicidal werewolf could be that precise is anybody's guess. In Normandy, an alternative method was to stab a werewolf three times in the head which would disenchant it, as would the kinder option of persuading the creature to roll over in the dewy grass.

For most of us however, our first reaction when confronted by a werewolf would be to flee: the best place to head for is a field of rye, since werewolves dislike this crop intensely and will avoid it at all costs. In the absence of a nearby rye field, however, another method was to throw an item of clothing such as an apron or a hat at the creature which will distract it, so it will start tearing the garment to pieces while we can make our escape. Some traditions claim that throwing the clothing releases the werewolf from its enchantment, as does finding and destroying any magic girdle that he had used to transform himself.

Another method, which only worked provided we recognised the creature's human identity, (presumably because his eyes still looked the same) was to address him by his baptismal name three times. Despite their bloodthirsty reputation, it was often claimed that some werewolves only attacked if they were first harmed.

And Finally...

Before dismissing the werewolf back to the realms of myth and legend, it's worth noting that several studies, including one as recent as 2009 in the *Medical Journal of Australia,*[110] have shown that violent and acute behavioural disturbances are more common during the full moon. It was noticed, for example, that twice as many people required sedation and physical restraint in A & E compared to other moon phases. Some were described as attacking staff like animals, biting, spitting and scratching. It was also noticed that people with behavioural problems seem to indulge in alcohol and drugs - possibly the modern equivalent of the werewolf ointment noted earlier in the chapter - more often when the moon is full.

Although some may feel that werewolves are nothing more than folklore and legend, there are still people walking among us who honestly believe they are werewolves and that they can shape-shift. They report a heightened sense of smell and hearing during these episodes, a feeling of being more alert and able to 'read' the landscape around them, even in the dark. Some claim to be overwhelmed by a need to hunt, although this doesn't always mean that they go on a murderous rampage; some report that it is enough just to stalk their prey.

Witnesses sometimes report noticing such people sniffing the air, rather like a dog, and that they have unusually long, thick fingernails. Other characteristics include their bodies being very hairy and that when they hurt themselves their cuts and bruises heal more easily, sometimes in less than a day.

Although for most of us there is little likelihood of being attacked by a true werewolf (or even someone just pretending to be one) as with anything paranormal, it still pays to keep an open mind. Just in case.

---

110 13th December 2009, http://www.ama.com.au/node/5233

PART TWO

Techniques of Psychic Self Defence

Although no two psychic attacks are ever identical, all we really need in order to defend ourselves are a handful of techniques that can be easily adapted to deal with just about everything and anything that it likely to come our way. The four main methods of psychic self defence are:

- Grounding - This helps the victim stay calm and in control of the situation, something that is essential if we want to avoid running around like a headless chicken. Fear breeds yet more fear.

- Cleansing and purifying - This gets rid of the 'stain' of a psychic attack. Just as we would clean a rug if we had spilled something on it, so psychic cleansing gets rid of harmful energies and replaces them with good ones.

- Creating and using psychic weapons - We use these to defend ourselves, much as we might pick up a stick or a rolling pin if we were physically threatened.

- Taking protective measures/precautions - If we knew, for example, that someone had stolen our keys, we would change the locks on our home. In the same way, if we suspect we are under psychic attack, we must use protective measures to prevent the attacker gaining access to us.

The Ethics of Banishing

There will always be those who will try and tell us that we must never harm anyone or anything, and that banishing or counter-attacking is somehow 'wrong.' This is nonsense. A psychic attacker has no right to invade our space or threaten us, and if he does, we have every right to defend ourselves, our home and those we love.

The Romans had a saying: *Si vis pacem, para bellum* which means, '*If you want peace, prepare for war.*' Even if we're not in the habit of doing much magic, I'd strongly advise familiarising ourselves with the main techniques of psychic self defence - just in case. With luck we may never need to use these skills, but we may be able to prevent a vaguely threatening situation from developing into something more serious. The more prepared we are, the less likely we are to be attacked.

When dealing with psychic attacks it's best to start with a very basic plan and stick to that, at least until we feel more confident. There are only a few things we need to attend to, and these are all quite straightforward.

The following chapters will show exactly how to do all these things and more....

CHAPTER NINE

Planning how to defend ourselves. 'To know to dare to will – to keep silent' – the importance of maintaining secrecy when under attack. The basic techniques of visualisation and how to visualise. Grounding exercises.

Most responsible books about ordinary, practical self defence advise us to walk as though we know where we are going, and to avoid looking lost or vulnerable (which literally means 'able to be wounded'). The same principles apply in psychic self defence, too. We need to appear capable of looking after ourselves and the best way to do this is to learn a small repertoire of magical responses such as cleansing, grounding and dispersing negativity. Quite often this is all it takes to stop a psychic attack in its tracks.

However, some people are afraid to attempt any sort of psychic self defence because they fear they are up against something they cannot handle. In fact, this rarely happens. Most of what we come up against in a psychic attack is pretty much the same as we find in everyday life: angry, spiteful, mean-minded bullies. If we can deal with them in work, school or our family, then we can also deal with them on the magical planes.

It is important not to allow ourselves to be intimidated. No matter what physical effects are produced, such as things that go bump in the night or the odd visit by the Night Mare, what the psychic attacker is really working on is our minds. To have any hope of defeating him, we must fight back using our own mental and psychic powers.

Some of the exercises in this book may seem very simple – too simple perhaps, if we were expecting complex Latin formulae and magic wands. But everything I suggest here is based in solid magical foundations, and more importantly *it will work.* A simple exercise done well is much more effective than a complex one performed without real understanding. All we need is a handful of methods that we can keep adapting to suit any given situation.

So far in this book we have looked at the most common types of psychic attack and the various ways to gather evidence to discover whether we really are the victim of such an attack. If we are, then we must discover who is behind it because it's easier to defend ourselves when we know what - and who - we're facing.

Although deliberate attacks usually come from someone we know, sometimes we find ourselves the victim of an accidental attack, a hex that has simply rebounded on us even though we have no links with the attacker. We were just unlucky, in the wrong place at the wrong time. Remember though, that paranoia is the enemy of good sense. So even if we are convinced that we are being hexed, it is vital to resist the temptation to blame every bit of bad luck or ill health on a psychic attack.

If we know the identity of our attacker, then we should, if possible, sever all links with that person. Obviously, this won't be easy if our attacker is a family member or work colleague but even so, we can usually minimise contact. Another useful strategy is to avoid discussing our plans, hopes, dreams etc., with anyone who may not wish us well.

We should always be careful what we tell others, especially on the internet, which is becoming a very popular means of conveying psychic attacks nowadays. If we are in the habit of posting regular updates about what we're doing, then we should be careful who can read them. If privacy settings are available we should use them, since often we don't have a clue who might be tracking us on the internet, so we should never post anything we would not want an enemy to know. (If we must post, then we should at least make sure we know exactly who can read it.)

Of course, computers didn't exist when I was young, but nowadays many psychic attackers seem to be using this as yet another weapon in their armoury. Sites such as Facebook, which gather large groups of people together at the click of a button are particularly easy to manipulate. We often read of online bullying in the newspapers; online psychic attacks are also regrettably common. I've even seen people using a blog to curse their enemies! So be careful - the internet is, to all effects and purposes, one of the Other Worlds. Treat it with respect.

Obviously, we shouldn't become too fearful, but it always amazes me how careless some people are with very personal information that could do them great harm if it fell into the wrong hands. If we frequently tell the whole world and his dog what sort of things annoy us or make us miserable then we shouldn't be surprised if these are used against us. It is amazing how much psychic trouble can be prevented by exercising a little discretion and caution! When I was young, I was taught a very useful verse:

If you have a friend, keep her as such
But do not tell her your secrets much,
For if that friend becomes your foe,
Out into the world your secrets go.

We do well always to remember that we should not share our innermost thoughts indiscriminately. By the same token, we should never let an attacker know - even indirectly - if their activities are having any bad effect on us. Just smile and pretend nothing is wrong, otherwise the attacker will sense victory and redouble their efforts.

In his work, *Transcendental Magic,* Eliphas Levi[111] described the 'Four words of the Magus' that were inscribed on the four symbolical forms of the Sphinx. These were: '*To know, to dare, to will, to keep silence.*' They can be applied equally well in matters of psychic self defence: we need to know what's happening and have some plan how to deal with it. We must also be daring, otherwise we'll just sit back passively and allow ourselves (and others) to be attacked. Unless we use our will - the power of the mind - anything we say will just be poetry and lack real authority. We should also keep silent, never advertising where we are or what we're doing to anyone who might wish us ill.

No matter how the psychic attack manifests, there are certain basic measures we should take as soon as possible. These will buy us some time and hopefully prevent the attack from getting any worse. We don't need specialist magical knowledge or equipment to do this, just determination and a refusal to be intimidated.

---

[111] Levi (1976 edition)

As mentioned before, if we know our attacker's identity, we must cut off as much contact as possible and destroy anything that may have conveyed the hex to us. The most popular methods for doing this are via skin, fur, leather, dried plants and basically anything that has once had life. The items are easily disguised as something innocuous, such as a picture and may even have been hidden somewhere in our home without our knowing. The best thing to do is burn such things and cast the ashes into fast running water if possible.

Another popular method of conveying a hex is using stones, especially quartz crystals. Again, these are easy to conceal, and some are incorporated into magical tools such as wands or jewellery. Obviously, we cannot burn stones and crystals, so we should bury them in salt, somewhere they are unlikely to be disturbed again. We can say a suitable incantation as we bury them, it doesn't have to be anything elaborate, we just need to speak from the heart and make it plain what we are doing. Something like this is perfectly suitable, *'I bury you, and all the ill wishing that attaches to you in this earth and salt. Be still. Be at peace. Do not trouble me or mine again.'*

Basic Steps – Cleaning and Polishing

There are certain techniques that are useful no matter how the attack manifests. If we feel that the hex is directed at our personal space, such as our home, car or office then begin by cleansing that first. If it seems to be directed at us (or our loved ones) personally then we need to get in the habit of washing our hands with a small pinch of ordinary kitchen salt added to the water. Since salt has a drying effect on the skin, make sure to use hand cream regularly too. Other preventative measures, such as sealing all exits and entrances (salt is good for this) gives us chance to deal with the existing psychic attack before anything else can move in.

Whenever we begin to cleanse anything - whether it's our personal space or our body - we should always be practical. Clutter and dust provide good hiding places for unpleasant magical influences that are often the precursor to a full-blown attack, so we must deny them the chance of gaining a foothold. Even if normally we don't mind tolerating a bit of mess, when we feel under attack, we should physically clean and tidy the affected area. Sweep, polish, dust and tidy those areas where we live, sleep, work or even travel as soon as we suspect we might be under attack.

Also, we should ensure that our clothes – especially our shoes – are clean. Sort out old garments we no longer wear. Cleansing is also a good preventative measure even when there's no active attack in progress. We can start cleaning and tidying while we're still gathering information to decide whether we are really under attack; it will do no harm and might even disperse the problem before it can grow any stronger.

Although these methods may sound ridiculously simple, remember that whatever we do in the everyday world reflects in the magical one. This means that even ordinary spring cleaning will clear away any magical debris provided it is done with the correct intention. So the next question of course, is, 'What is an intention?'

Basically, an intention is our will, our desire. Whatever we want to happen next. We must use our will to support our physical actions: if we are sweeping the floor as part of our psychic self defence work, we should at the same time imagine that we are sweeping out the particles or negativity from the attack. Never mind that we can't actually see or photograph them. We know they are there. Getting rid of them is our intention.

With a little effort we can even envision them: grey dust, black specks, strands of cotton etc. This is a simple but effective form of visualisation, and in magic there is not all that much difference between imagining something and visualising it. Other examples of uniting physical cleansing with magical visualisation are:

- Polishing the window while imagining/visualising that we are preventing ill-wishers from looking in on us.
- Polishing a mirror while imagining/visualising that we are reflecting the hex back at its source.

What gives this work its strength is our willpower and mental effort. The more focussed we are, the better. If we are trying to do these exercises while feeding the dog or changing the baby's nappy, we are just making life hard for ourselves. This type of visualisation, where we enforce what we are thinking with physical actions, need only take a few minutes. It is silent - even our commands can be thought rather than spoken aloud. If we can, we should pick a time when we can work undisturbed, however briefly.

Remember that almost all magic takes place in the mind. Words and rituals are important but rarely powerful enough by themselves unless the mind is working too. Even if an attack has made us so ill that we are lying flat on our back in bed, our mind is still the strongest weapon we possess. Whatever cleansing methods we choose, we must ensure we focus our thoughts on driving back our attacker. Obviously, it isn't possible to visualise for hours on end, so the best solution is to get on with the physical cleaning while imagining/visualising the magical work. When we need a break from the physical work, don't forget to have a mental break too!

There is no single 'correct' technique for magical cleansing. Everyone does it slightly differently. We just need to remember that we are trying to clear away something we can feel but cannot see. Also consider what exactly our attacker is expecting to gain by initiating his attack; what's in it for him? What does *anyone* expect to gain from attacking another person? There's no simple answer to this but, generally speaking, there are four main possibilities:

- Some attackers don't try to gain anything; they just lash out in anger to hurt. In the same way, some psychic attackers simply seethe until they create an attack either intentionally or accidentally. The most they gain is a sense of having got their own back but little else.

- Some people, such as muggers, attack in order to rob others and there are psychic attackers who are just like this. They want something their victims have, in this case usually energy, strength or health.

- Some people attack others because they like to see them suffer. They enjoy it. Some psychic attackers, particularly those for whom hexing has become a way of life, do this. They don't even need a particularly good reason to attack.

- There is a fourth, much rarer group, in which the hexer is acting to prevent a greater harm or to redress a wrong that might otherwise go unchallenged. This was common practice in ancient times, and although it is definitely a form of psychic attack, it is motivated by a sense of acting for the greater good. The ethics of this type of attack are hotly debated; some say we should never act in this way while others claim that in certain specific circumstances it is justified. If we feel we are on the receiving end of this type of attack, the best defence is (a) to try and make amends for whatever we did in the first place or (b) to try and prove that we were not involved. Even so, keep up with the cleansing and protective work.

If a psychic attack is intentional then the attacker will be watching to see how we respond. Generally, he will expect either of the following:

- Firstly, that we will be too terrified to do anything. Panic and fear are an absolute gift to psychic attackers, they can feed off them, making them even more confident and daring.

- Secondly, the attacker hopes that even if we are told how to defend ourselves, we will lack the confidence to try. Psychic attacks are a form of bullying, and bullies always pick their victims.

Always remember that we have power too. Even though we may not be an experienced occultist we can still repel a psychic attack, even a strong one. We are not aiming to get into a full-blown magical war, just defending ourselves, and those close to us. We are all capable of good defensive work when necessary.

Even if we still feel too frightened to fight back, we should nevertheless keep up with the cleaning, tidying and polishing around our personal space especially in those places where we feel the attack most strongly. Grab a duster, a rubbish sack and a tin of polish and get started. Whether we can see it or not, there is certain to be some psychic debris in that area and we can get rid of at least some of it with a good, old-fashioned clear-out. By the time we've finished, we can physically feel that the atmosphere has lightened. Not only that, but the physical cleaning makes the subsequent magical cleansing easier.

Once the place feels a little less threatening, we can move on to the *magical* cleansing work. Don't stress over this, just remember that the main difference between ordinary cleaning and magical cleansing is that ordinary cleaning deals with dust and grime that we can see and wash away, while magical cleansing gets rid of the (often invisible) negativity and magical dirt that have accumulated in the course of the psychic attack.

It is always advisable to perform some magical cleansing, however brief, when we move into a new home or workplace to make sure we aren't troubled by any negativity or psychic disturbances left behind by the previous occupants.

Getting to Grips with Visualisation

We have already seen that our imagination is closely linked to the way we visualise things. Some people find visualising an easy skill to learn, while others struggle. Much depends on how motivated we are. If we want something badly enough, our minds can be very good at helping us visualise. In fact, most of us probably visualise things such as winning the lottery, going on holiday etc., more than we would like our friends and family to know. Magically speaking therefore, if we can visualise what we are trying to do in psychic self defence, we are well on the way to defeating the attack.

Of course, some will disagree, claiming that those lacking imagination cope better when under psychic attack because an unimaginative person will be less frightened than someone who can imagine what might happen next. This is nonsense. A true psychic attack can operate quite independently of the victim's imagination. Indeed, someone who remains stubbornly unaware of danger is often more likely to be harmed because they persist in ignoring the early warning signs until the psychic attack is well under way. Visualisation is a key skill that helps us protect ourselves. It doesn't make things worse!

So, what exactly must we visualise for psychic self defence? It's simple – we need to visualise driving back the attack by whatever means we have to hand. We could, for example, imagine ourselves armed with all sorts of wonderful magical weapons, hurling thunderbolts and holding our own against the attack.

Luckily, since all this is going on in our minds, we don't need to feel remotely self-conscious and nobody else needs to know about it. Visualisation is a great skill to have if, like most people, we don't have much privacy at home or work. It enables us to perform powerful magical cleansings that don't involve any obvious ritual or ceremony, in the privacy of our own minds.

Of course, when we are in the middle of a psychic attack – even a mild one – it can be difficult to concentrate and focus on visualising. I find the best thing to do is to write a few prompts. Keep asking, 'What do I need to do/think/say next?' and then write a brief note as a reminder. Something like, 'Cleanse... sweep... polish the mirror... tell attacker to leave' is quite adequate.

Prompts are also useful for creating chants, repeating them as often as we need, either aloud or mentally. Chanting is useful (though not essential) because it is repetitive, and one of the main reasons why psychic self defence can fail is because we give up too quickly. Do persevere. We could say, 'I cleanse this space, I make it clean,' while mentally focusing on physically cleaning up our personal space. Then move on to, 'I sweep away all negativity and psychic debris. I make it clean,' etc. Just keep going!

A word of advice here – it is always good magical practice to put these commands into the present tense. Say, 'I drive you back, you have no power over me,' not, 'I *will* drive you back' because using the future tense allows a gap between what is happening in the here and now and what *will* happen, and a skilled psychic attacker can make use of that gap to launch a further attack on us.

Other useful phrases to use at this stage include, 'I clean this room. Harmful thoughts, words and deeds are not welcome here. Go away. I do not want you here. This room is clean.' These are all clear phrases that are not open to interpretation. When we say them either aloud or mentally, we must imagine/visualise that we are literally cleansing the room, sending the harmful thoughts etc., away, making them leave.

Visualisation is probably easiest when combined with physical action. One of my favourite methods is to imagine literally sweeping the attacker away, rolling him over and over in the dust and down the path or stairs, out of our home for good. We can use a real sweeping brush to help us visualise this, but avoid vacuum cleaners, since these only suck the debris into the machine and then blow a lot of it back out again! The best brush to use is a traditional besom-shaped one, because it will sweep in any direction whereas an ordinary sweeping brush basically sweeps forwards and back.

It is important to gather up the sweepings and dispose of them properly, not simply sweep everything into a corner and forget about it. As we sweep, we need to imagine our attacker collapsing down into the dust, buffeted here and there. Be prepared to put some mental and physical effort into this, and then visualise him dissolving into a very fine powder that is swept up and either put into the household refuse or better still, burned with sage, salt and some incense. The final ashes should be dispersed into running water or buried in salt in the ground.

Alternatively, visualise sweeping the magical detritus right out of the home and then sprinkle the doorstep with salt or salt and water to ensure they cannot get back. Salt has been a powerful purifier and barrier since ancient times. We can either use a packet of cheap table salt and scatter this on the doorstep or imagine opening the packet and scattering the salt as a barrier. We can even physically scatter table salt while at the same time visualising that we are scattering *magical* salt if we wish. As always, our words – spoken or visualised – should be simple and clear. For example,

'You cannot cross this barrier of salt. I forbid you to return,' or even, 'Go away. I drive you back. Do not come here again.'

These small cleansing and banishing rituals are simple but surprisingly effective, with one important proviso: *they won't work if we don't do them.* It's surprising how many people claim that a certain ritual did not work only to later admit they had never actually tried it! Either they were too nervous, lacked confidence, or believed that trying to protect themselves would make the situation worse.

The latter is a common misconception. I've often been asked whether a 'really powerful occultist' might take exception to his victim fighting back and harm them even more. In truth, these things happen more often in Hollywood than in real life. Most 'really powerful occultists' have much better things to do with their time, while most psychic bullies (who are the driving force behind almost all psychic attacks) are completely bewildered once we turn on them. We must never, ever be afraid to stand our ground against a psychic attack.

Of course, there are other reasons why people don't try and defend themselves. Sometimes they are just too lazy to try, or 'waiting for the crows to feed them' as my grandmother used to say. But nobody else will ever psychically defend us in the way that we can defend ourselves, because the victim always has the most at stake, so it is up to us – and nobody else – to ensure we succeed. We have nothing to lose by fighting back.

Even if we must repeat the exercises a couple of times, what does that matter? Every time we fight back, the attacker will sense our resistance. He may persevere for a short time, but eventually – provided we don't lose our nerve – we *will* succeed. The most determined attacker is nothing compared to a courageous underdog.

Dealing with Nerves: Grounding and Breathing

Some psychic attacks are enough to make anyone feel nervous and of course, that's often their intention. The problem is that when we're frightened, we don't always defend ourselves as well as we should, so we need to deal with any potential anxiety right from the start. One of the best ways to do this is with an exercise known as grounding, which uses earth, the most solid of the four elements, to steady us. Its effect is rather like recharging our batteries: first we allow pent up tensions, stress, fatigue etc to drain away into the ground, and then we draw up some of the earth's power into ourselves.

At its simplest, a grounding exercise can consist of lying on the bare earth and feeling at one with it. Some people like to imagine putting down roots into the soil, so they become anchored like a tree that not even the strongest storm can uproot. Others find they can visualise something similar just by standing on the earth (or even the sand) in their bare feet. If we need to ground ourselves in the depths of winter and find this type of visualisation difficult without some sort of practical prompt, then I often find it helpful to stand barefoot on a soft towel. There are no magical rules to say we cannot make use of anything and everything to help ourselves.

Some swear by 'grounding stones', such as obsidian, jet or black onyx, although we can just as easily use an ordinary smooth pebble that happens to be pleasant to touch. If we use a grounding stone, however, remember that anything capable of absorbing a lot of energy needs regular cleansing and recharging.

To do this, either leave it outside under a full moon or place it on the bare earth for a day or two before using it again. If we use grounding stones regularly, it's a good idea to have several so that one can be cleansing while the others are in use.

My own favourite method of dealing with the anxiety and fear that accompanies a psychic attack, is to treat it as a form of stage fright and concentrate on steady breathing. This is based on sound ancient magical practice, for the ancients Greeks believed the breath had its own *dynamis* or magical power, rather like the Polynesian word, *mana*. Not only does the magus or magician possess *dynamis*, but so do plants, stones and man-made objects.[112] It's a simple method, easily adapted to suit the occasion; all we

112 Luck (2006): 497

need is to be able to tell the difference between breathing in and out, and to be able to count at a steady pace.

Begin by breathing in through the nose to the count of two and then out through the mouth to the count of four. We can gradually increase the length of each breath but remember to keep the ratio the same, so the out breath is twice as long as the inhaled breath. For steadying ourselves, breathing in for a count of six and out for twelve is usually best but we shouldn't worry if we can't manage this. Just use whatever is easiest. As with many things, the more we practice, the easier it becomes, and being able to control our breathing calms us down.

The next task is for us to cleanse any spaces we feel are affected by the psychic attack. For cleansing a room, for example, we need to move around the four corners, pausing in each to declare, 'I cleanse this room. I drive away all negative energies, all harmful thoughts, all ill wishing. I drive away all unwelcome entities. I break them up and make them harmless.'

If we can't remember the words, write them down as prompts on small slips of paper. Take a steadying breath and breathe out steadily before moving on to the next corner. Think of the breath blowing the attacker away, pushing him back beyond the walls of the room.

Some people find that basic cleansing works for them straight away, but if it doesn't, just repeat the basic breathing exercise (e.g. breathe in for a count of two, and out for a count of four or whatever we can manage.) As soon as we feel calm again, repeat the same words, and then exhale strongly to drive the attack away from our own personal space.

Some people like to combine this simple ritual with scattering a little salt in each corner, although be careful since salt can become very wet and ruin carpets and furnishings. Another possibility is carrying a joss stick, candle or some solid incense in a thurible (a specially designed censer or container on a chain), being careful to observe sensible fire and safety precautions.

Using our breathing is a tried and tested method to fight off that awful feeling that we have strayed out of our depth. No matter what's going on around us, even if the room is crackling with energy, we should just keep on with the exercise until we've completed it. If the atmosphere is still unpleasant when we've finished, just go around the four corners once more, until it feels better. Persistence is vital; just as some stains take more effort than others, so does clearing some types of psychic oppression.

It is important not to confuse cleansing our personal space with trying to banish a ghost or spirit entity. The two things are quite different and although ghosts etc., can be frightening and unpleasant, they rarely initiate psychic attacks and most of the time we do not need to banish them. I certainly don't recommend casting something out just because it happens to be there. If it's causing problems that's different, but most of the time we can live with it. There are several worlds and dimensions that seem to run parallel to our own, so certain entities will annoy us and vice versa. There is usually room for compromise.

Visualising Psychic Weapons

Once we know how to put our imagination to work for us, there are many other things we can do with it. Think about how the attacker uses visualisation. He must rely totally on his mind and willpower. Even if he decides to summon a thought form or chthonic entity to come after us and give us a fright, it always began with a tiny seed of thought.

Therefore, in order to defeat him we need to use our own thoughts to visualise some sort of appropriate defence. If our attacker creates a terrifying thought form then we should visualise some sort of bodyguard, preferably something bigger, nastier and more menacing, that will not be easily intimidated.

One of the most useful things to visualise is a set of psychic armour. We will need at least two pieces, one offensive and one defensive. The offensive weapon is ideally a sword or dagger, something we can keep in our hand at all times, neither too heavy nor too small. (Spears are not suitable because once thrown we are unarmed.) Even if we are terrified at the thought of brandishing a sword, we must look convincing. The defensive weapon should always be some sort of shield.

Since we don't encounter swords and shields on a daily basis, we must do a little preparatory work. Look at pictures of swords and shields in books and films; get to understand how they work. How do we hold a shield on our arm? How heavy is it? It must be sturdy enough to withstand a fight, but light enough that it won't tire us when we need to hold onto it for any length of time.

Because we are visualising a physical item rather than a situation, we need to be able to see our weapon from all angles. We need to know what it looks like, sounds like (think how the sword will sound if it strikes metal or stone, for example), feels like etc. Learn everything about it. Practise – mentally – how to hold the shield, how to raise it to block whatever is heading in our direction. Also learn to raise the sword in a threatening manner, feet slightly apart so our weight is balanced.

Sometimes it helps, at least in the early days, to carry a picture of the sword and shield with us, so we can keep referring to it whenever we have a few spare moments. Another alternative is to set up pictures of the weapons on our computer desktop. I find it helpful while visualising to use one hand to rub the back of the other. I'm not sure exactly why this works, but it does!

Of course, some people dislike the idea of carrying psychic weapons. They believe that since *all* weapons have the capacity to harm others, it is therefore unacceptable for us to have them. While it is true that psychic weapons can be just as harmful as ordinary ones, there is an important difference – in the real world, people do not normally carry weapons without knowing about it.

In the magical world, however, it is quite possible for someone to carry - and use - a veritable arsenal of weapons without much knowledge or understanding. This is because psychic attacks sometimes occur unintentionally, brought about by a potent combination of rage, jealousy, spite etc., of which the attacker may only be very superficially aware. Even if it's pointed out to them that they are responsible for a psychic attack, they still may not know how to stop themselves. Unless we want to allow all and sundry to attack us at their leisure, we need to know how to defend ourselves. Just in case.

Next, we need to look at methods of using these weapons. A psychic shield for example, is useful for blocking unpleasant and hurtful remarks and preventing negativity from turning into a full-blown psychic attack. If someone regularly makes snide and spiteful comments, just visualise raising our shield the moment he opens his mouth so that his comments hit the shield instead of us. Some people even visualise unkind words striking the shield and sending showers of sparks up into the air.

If we know our attacker's identity it's a good precaution to visualise our sword and shield as soon as we see him approaching, especially while the attack is active. Keep the shield raised whenever he is about. We should also visualise raising our sword if an attacker attempts to summon a thought form. This not only protects us against the thought form but also threatens the attacker.

At one time when I was having to deal with psychic attacks on an almost daily basis, I visualised a huge Scottish broadsword that required all my strength to raise with both hands. The downside was that I could not also carry a shield, but since my attackers were using thought forms I felt the sword would be more effective than a sword and shield combined. Luckily, once it was clear I meant business, the attacks fizzled out pretty quickly, but I still polished my psychic broadsword for many years afterwards, as a precaution.

One of the most fascinating things about visualising a psychic shield is that most attackers are instantly aware of it. Some will physically back away and avoid confrontation, even though previously they have gone out of their way to provoke the victim. Once an attacker realises that their victim is fighting back, they will often try to avoid or at least reduce all future contact.

I once knew a woman who lived under cover of her shield for several days until her psychic attacker finally stopped what he was doing. She said afterwards that it was amazing how much better she felt, knowing that his hurtful comments were being constantly deflected. She also remarked how puzzled her attacker looked when he realised his comments were no longer having their desired effect!

A Variety of Protective Barriers

If we face regular, persistent attacks that do not involve thought forms, it can sometimes be helpful to set up protective psychic barriers such as circles, psychic bubbles and walls. These not only prevent attacks from reaching us but are also be useful when we need to protect those unable to protect themselves, such as young children, the elderly or the sick.

Protective Circles

The easiest way for a novice to construct a protective circle is with salt, scattering ordinary table salt around the area, item or person we wish to protect. As we create the circle, we should also visualise it protecting whoever or whatever is within. It can be helpful to state our intention as we work, for example, 'May this circle bless and protect all those within it.'

This method is particularly useful for protecting animals kept outside the house (rabbits in hutches, livestock etc.) who are often vulnerable because they tend to be overlooked when the home and its occupants are being attacked. It can also be useful to set up a protective circle around our bed at night before going to sleep.

Another method is to construct the circle using our psychic sword to trace a line of visualised fire around whatever we want to protect. Be swift and decisive in this sort of work since it can be difficult to maintain the visualisation for longer than a few seconds, especially for beginners.

Luckily, this doesn't matter very much since no psychic attacker is going to lurk all night on the edges of our protective circle. The very fact we have created any sort of barrier warns that we are on the alert and are a force to be reckoned with. For protective purposes we do not need to set up a full magic circle complete with the four elements and calling the quarters etc. All we need is a barrier to keep us (or the rabbits etc.) safe. If we stand *within* the circle however, we should aim to stay there until we are done. Although some claim we can visualise cutting a hole in the circle whenever we wish to exit or re-enter, it's best avoided unless there's some sort of emergency. Using doorways, even magical ones that have been repaired, risk weakening our defences.

Protective Bubbles

A protective bubble is useful whenever we need to separate ourselves from an unpleasant or threatening atmosphere. Unlike a circle which is fixed in a specific place, a bubble is three dimensional and encloses us completely. It also allows us to move around if we want, rather like a giant hamster ball.

We can visualise any type of ball we wish but it is important to be able to see out of it – the bubble may be visualised, but in other respects it conforms to the physical world. A clear bubble is ideal because it allows us to see out of it while moving around. I would also recommend visualising the bubble made of clear plastic rather than glass, which (in the real, everyday world) is brittle and shatters easily.

Unlike a circle which we can easily visualise and inscribe on the floor, three dimensional bubbles can be more challenging. One of my favourite methods is to visualise it inflating, rather like a hot air balloon. Don't just rely on *watching* the bubble inflate, either; mentally try and hear the great 'Whoosh!' as it encircles us. As with most types of visualisation, it's a good idea to practice this exercise long before we need to do it in an emergency.

If an attack is imminent but we don't need to move around much, we can visualise being wrapped in a protective cocoon. This is a good technique whenever we just want to sit quietly, read or sleep. Made of white (or at least very pale) light, it should cover us from head to toe, and if the attack is particularly severe we can even visualise a shower of tiny mirrors all facing outwards. These will bounce the attack back to its source, but this method should only be used when we are certain we are beset *on all sides* by an attack. This is because mirrors – both real and magical – are hard to control and can bounce hexes all over the place! If we use a mirror, we must visualise exactly where the energy is supposed to go (i.e. back to the attacker) otherwise it could hit some innocent soul who just happens to be in the wrong place at the wrong time.

Make no mistake, mirrors are powerful things and should not be taken lightly. They can be used agonistically, that is both for and against something, for example, to protect and to attack. When I was a girl, we had literally dozens of mirrors dotted around the house. I counted them once and there were over sixty. When I asked my mother why, she claimed they were for dressmaking even though some had been placed in areas where I needed to stand on a chair or perch on a cupboard just to see my reflection!

I later discovered their purpose was not only to reflect incoming psychic attacks, but also for 'bouncing' outgoing ones (my family seemed to do very little but hex) making it almost impossible for their victim to trace his attacker.

A similar magical principal applies to the tiny mirrors sewn into clothing, particularly in countries such as India. Sequins serve the same purpose since they reflect, which makes them protective. Even horse brasses worked on the same lines; the brightly polished brass would flash in the sunlight (tiny bells and reflective moon discs were often fixed to the horse's headpiece too).

If we are attracted to the idea of visualising a protective mirror it might be better to build it into our psychic shield. That way, at least we will be consciously projecting the psychic attack back at the sender, with less risk of it bouncing off and hitting an innocent party.

The Psychic Hand

Another useful visualisation technique is something called the Psychic Hand. This is very useful for pushing away attacks and negativity before they can settle down in our personal space. Basically, we imagine that our hand (left or right, it doesn't matter which, just choose whichever is more comfortable - most people choose the hand they write with) has grown in size. It is now so large and powerful that we can push back anything that threatens.

At first, we might try physically gesturing with our hand, with the palm facing outwards towards whatever threatens. As we do so we should say (either aloud or mentally) *'I drive you back.' 'Get away from me'. 'Get away from those I love.' 'Leave this place'* or any other statement that seems appropriate.

The important thing is to really believe in what we're saying; this is not an empty gesture. Think of it as a policeman directing the traffic – his hand is no more powerful than anyone else's, it is the authority of his uniform and badge that gives him the power to tell the traffic where to go.

Cleansing People

So far we've looked at cleansing the home, but occasionally we need to cleanse a person, particularly if he has been physically affected by an attack and his health or emotional well-being is suffering. Be tactful about this. Sometimes simply cleansing someone's personal space using any of the methods suggested in this chapter will be enough.

Alternatively, place a few drops of lavender oil on the pillow, at the same time visualising the sleeping area being magically cleansed to ensure a good night's sleep for them. Yes, it sounds simple, but remember it is our skill at visualising that gives it power. Otherwise we are just making the pillow smell pleasant, whereas visualisation endows the whole act with magical power. More extreme afflictions requiring remedies such as exorcism are dealt with in Chapter Seventeen).

Another option is to encourage the victim to prepare a bath (or even do it for him), adding some salt and blessing the water (instructions for this are in Chapter Twelve). Adding salt to bathwater can also be used for dealing with self-attacks and to prevent further damage to our Auric Field. We can also add aromatic herbs such as rosemary, lavender or mint.

To create a helpful gift for someone unlikely or unable to make their own bath mix, try mixing sea salt with the finely chopped herbs and put in a pretty container, perhaps including a bar of pure olive oil soap which has wonderful magical cleansing properties (a *small* drop of ordinary olive oil in the bathwater is a good substitute). Remember to bless the soap and the salt and herb mix.

If the victim is feeling particularly fragile, performing a short simple blessing for them can work wonders, provided they feel comfortable with this, so we do need to ask them first. People often worry how to give a blessing, but all we need do is wish them good things. For example, in this situation we might say, *'Be blessed and protected by the waters, herbs and oil in this bath.'*

It's very important that blessings should calm and not frighten its recipient. If we say something like, *'May this blessed water, these herbs and oil cleanse and protect you from all who wish you ill,'* we may only frighten someone who is already anxious and that will do no good at all. It's different when we do it for ourselves.

A clear head and steady hands are essential in psychic self defence. There is no place - and no need - for high drama. In *extreme* cases where the victim is a nervous wreck, we may have to offer our blessing without asking their permission. Say something like, *'You'll feel better after you've had a bath,'* and then mentally give the blessing. Some may feel this is unethical, but personally I feel there are times - admittedly few and far between - when we need to help first and ask permission later.

Remedies for Self-Attacks

As we have seen in Chapter Six, we can sometimes psychically attack ourselves. Just as others can unwittingly hex us by simply fuming and raging for hours on end, so we do the same to ourselves when we refuse to let go of certain incidents, particularly those in our past. Magically this attracts our tormentors back to us again and again, until we end up feeling trapped with no means of escape.

If we suspect we may be attacking ourselves, then begin by thoroughly cleansing our home, personal space and self. We should also spend time sitting quietly, concentrating on listening to our breath flowing in through the nose and out through the mouth (just several breaths will suffice, we don't have to stick at it for hours.) Once we feel our breathing has become calm and steady, visualise blowing our negativity away like dead leaves.

Finding the right type of breath can be tricky so experiment: place a few small items on the table, e.g. lengths of wool, small screwed up balls of paper, etc. Now blow on them gently so that they move out of the way without flying off in all directions. While doing this, we imagine these are all the negative elements that are attacking us. This method of psychic self defence requires regular practice to break up the negativity, but soon we will be able to visualise the whole process without any need for balls of paper!

Another simple but effective method of self-cleansing is to ritually wash our hands. To turn a simple everyday task into a ritual, all we do is add more care and thought to our actions and intentions. For example, we might set aside a small bar of pure olive oil or lavender soap especially for the purpose. Before using it for the first time we need to consecrate it; this means blessing it and afterwards using it for one purpose only, i.e. to drive away the negativity that our own hex has caused. When we consecrate anything, we make it special towards a specific purpose, so don't be tempted to use it later for everyday washing!

The best way to consecrate a bar of soap is to unwrap it and hold it in both hands. Don't attempt this when feeling angry or sad otherwise these emotions will simply rub off onto the soap and produce more of the same whenever we use it. Aim to feel as calm as possible. Even if we are psychically attacking ourselves, there will be times when the attack is dormant. Pick one of these quiet times for the consecration and breathe on the soap gently. Our breath contains *dynamis,* which is the essence of a person's power. It can be passed into other people, animals and even inanimate objects.

When we breathe on the bar of soap with magical intention we imbue it with some of our own power. This is sometimes also known as charging with power or magnetising. In this case we empower the soap for the purpose of cleansing ourselves from the psychic self-attack.

As we hold the soap in our hands, breathe gently on it and say (either mentally or aloud) '*I consecrate this soap so that it washes away and cleanses all negative and harmful thoughts, deeds and words.*' Afterwards, whenever we wash with the soap, we can visualise washing away those aspects of our character that are making us self-attack.

Any type of soap can be used, although olive oil has been used for ritual cleansing and protection for thousands of years. Lavender is another, in fact its name comes from the Latin *lavare* meaning to wash. Rose was also traditionally used for cleansing, so was pine. We should be guided by our noses: if it smells fresh and clean, then it will do the job!

The Aura

The importance of having a well-protected Aura cannot be over-stressed. An unhealthy Aura, especially one pierced by jealousy and spite cannot protect a healthy body or mind. The three things, Aura, body and mind are so closely interlinked that if one is damaged then the other two will also be affected. As we have already seen in Chapters Five and Six, a damaged Auric Field can leave us open to all sorts of psychic problems, and if someone is attacking us, a damaged Aura makes it easy for them to move in and finish the job! If we get into the habit of regularly sealing our Aura and it will keep any damage to a minimum.

Sealing the Aura

This is sometimes referred to as the Openings of the Body Ritual and the version I give here is very simple, but effective. There are more complicated versions but I'm a great believer that we are more likely to perform simple rituals. What matters is that we perform the ritual as and when it's required, without having to hunt down exotic ingredients or wait for the right moon-phase.

This ritual is necessary sometimes because the Aura – that invisible shell that protects our physical body – has a number of weak points that can make us vulnerable to psychic attack especially when we are tired, stressed or physically unwell. These include any wounds or scars, together with the ears, eyes, nostrils, mouth, nipples, navel, anus and the tip of the penis in the male or the urethra and vagina in the female. We can seal the Aura at these points either physically, using consecrated salt and blessed water, or visualise the entire procedure.

One method for sealing the Aura is to dip our first and second fingers into a solution of consecrated salt and blessed water (See Chapter Twelve). Then touch each of the points of the body listed above (in the previous paragraph) in turn. I usually begin with the eyes but there's no hard and fast rule. Each time we touch an opening, we just say, '*I seal you against all evil,*' and before touching another opening dip our fingers in the salt water again.

To perform the ritual mentally, simply visualise the entire procedure. Don't be afraid to prompt yourself if necessary, for example, '*I now dip my fingers in the salt water and anoint your right eye, I seal you against all evil.*' Some people like to imagine using a white light for the sealing process. Don't be afraid to experiment until you find a method that works best for you and always work quickly and decisively. A ritual doesn't normally suffer for being swift, but it may well suffer if we allow our concentration to wander. Also, remember that doing something swiftly is not the same as doing it in a rush. If we are quick and decisive that's fine; however when we hurry it is all too easy to forget things or do them badly.

Sealing the Aura can be performed equally well either for ourselves or for someone else. I have sometimes been asked whether it is all right to seal someone's Aura without their permission. It really depends on the circumstances. If we must protect someone who is too young, too sick, or otherwise unable to protect herself then maybe the questions to ask are:

- Would I help this person up if someone pushed them over or would I insist on asking their permission first?
- What if that person had been knocked unconscious? Would I wait until they came around before I would help them?'

In many cases we just tend to act on instinct and hope for the best. And usually this is exactly the right thing to do. Remember that with psychic attacks we are not dealing with forces that recognise any moral compass. By sealing the Aura, all we are doing is the equivalent of applying a sticking plaster, providing the Aura with a layer of protection and giving it chance to heal before anything else comes along and damages it further.

Banishing Spells and Moon Phases

Traditionally banishing spells are best done on a waning moon, the idea being that as the moon diminishes, so does the strength of the attack. Personally, I feel that when we are under psychic attack, banishing and protection are best done as soon as the need arises. In an emergency we don't have time to wait for the moon!

It can be useful to spend some time – preferably when we're not under any sort of attack - watching the moon and identifying the moods of the various moon-phases. Write down anything that occurs to us at certain times of the moon's cycle throughout the year. Do we personally find a full moon happy or threatening? What about dark or new moons (when the moon is so faint it cannot be seen), or waxing moons?

Sometimes working with the moon can be a luxury. If a psychic attack crops up during a waxing moon, do we really have to wait until it starts to wane? Of course not. But if we are in the habit of writing things down in our notebook, it's much easier to find something about each moon phase that we can use. For example, if I had to banish during a waxing moon, I would draw on the strength of the moon to enhance and strengthen my spell rather than worry about waiting for the waning moon to help diminish the attack. Again, this can be simply visualised. Just imagine standing out under a waxing moon, allowing its light and power to flood us with strength and insight.

Remember: What empowers our psychic self defence is the link we set up between the physical world, our mind, our intention and will.

Nobody else can do this for us; it must come from within. With a little creative thinking, almost anything - including moon phases - can be made to work for us as and when we need them!

CHAPTER TEN

A set of basic rituals for cleansing, sealing exits and entrances. The protective power of the pentagram and how to use it. Using Plants as a protective barrier. Protective stones and crystals. Mirrors and incense.

Once we've physically and magically cleansed our personal space, our next task is to protect ourselves against further attacks. The easiest methods are to set up some sort of boundary or seal all exits and entrances. We can either make use of physical boundaries in the real world, or visualise them entirely, depending on our circumstances at the time. If we don't have much privacy for any sort of magical work then it's much better to visualise our boundary from start to finish.

Visualising boundaries is not difficult. Just imagine there is some sort of barrier between us and our attacker. The type of barrier is entirely up to us, but it's easiest to visualise something we are already familiar with, such as a fence, hedge or brick wall, often with something sharp or spiky (broken glass, barbed wire, thorny plants) along the top. Alternatively, visualise a clear, Perspex wall (so we can see out, but nothing can get in), or a two-way mirror that stops anyone seeing us while we can still see them. Another possibility is a boundary of fire.

The simplest physical boundary however is salt, which is easy to use and relatively cheap. We don't need expensive sea or rock salt from the delicatessen, a packet of ordinary table salt will do the job just as well if not better because we can afford to use it generously. Do remember though that it can damage furnishings and carpets so be careful if using it indoors.

The first time I ever created a salt boundary, the psychic attack had been lingering for a while before suddenly gathering momentum. I didn't have much time to think about what I was going to do and acted more by instinct than anything else. I took a bag of ordinary kitchen salt (nowadays I always keep a bagful handy – if nothing else if helps to clear icy steps in the winter) and walked around the outside of my home.

Scattering the salt as I walked, I kept repeating, '*Bless this house; let no evil enter in; bless the people I love; let no evil enter in...*' I didn't feel particularly confident but tried to look as though I did! All I knew was that I had to get a solid rhythm going that matched my steps, to 'drive' the spell. It's the same sort of principle as armies marching into battle accompanied by drums and bagpipes; as we see time and again, many old practices have some underlying magical basis!

If we decide to mark out a physical barrier, we need to choose an area that we can surround completely. This is no problem if we're protecting a car or bicycle, or lucky enough to live in a detached house where we can walk right around the property. If this isn't possible, then we should just put down a barrier for those areas we *can* access and visualise the rest or combine a physical barrier with sealing exits and entrances. Another traditional method is to scatter salt on doorsteps, windowsills and the hearth.

Whatever we choose, the barrier should be unbroken around the space we are trying to protect and of course if it's completely visualised there will be no problems about shared boundary walls or paths. If we are protecting a large space such as a house, we will need to cross the boundary sometimes, so when we first create our barrier we need to state, '*Nothing that intends us harm may enter,*' or words to that effect. This gives us free access while keeping our attacker at a distance.

If it impossible to do any sort of ritual out of doors, then walk through each room in your home, scattering just a *little* salt in the corners of the room, and laying a small trail across windows sills and the hearth. As already mentioned, salt can damage carpets, curtains or paintwork, so a useful alternative is to wipe the windowsill and/or doorsteps with a cloth wrung out in weak solution of salt water. A teaspoonful to a bowl will do the trick. Another method uses a paintbrush dipped in salt water to paint a line either right around the vertical edges of the window or door or just across the windowsill or doorstep.

When I was young, the traditional method of dealing with psychic attacks was to throw salt on the open fire in the kitchen and burn a shoe! The wonderful thing about some of these old-fashioned methods was that they were very instinctive, and people did them without stopping to worry about whether they would work; they had complete faith in them. This is an important aspect of all psychic self defence - we must have confidence in it. If we set up a boundary and go through the motions while secretly feeling like a complete idiot, we are undermining our efforts right from the start. It's essential in psychic self defence (just as in all types of magical work) to believe in what we're doing.

While setting up any boundary, we should remember to bless our home, family, friends and ourselves. We aren't trying to imprison them within a sterile space, just wishing good things upon them while keeping the unpleasant things, i.e. the psychic attack, beyond the barrier. We can choose whatever words seem most appropriate but some of the simplest and most effective are:

- *Bless this room, bless this door, bless this window, bless this hearth*
- *Bless the people I love*
- *Bless the people who live here*
- *Let no evil enter in*
- *Nothing that wishes us ill is welcome*

Remember that we are only trying to get a good rhythm going; the words don't have to rhyme!

Likewise, when we are sealing just the doors, windows and chimneys, we keep prompting ourselves with words that describe what we're trying to do. We need not speak aloud, repeating them mentally will work just as well. Suitable phrases include, '*Let no evil enter in, let nothing that wishes me/us harm enter in... go back... you are not welcome here...*'

When we feel that a psychic attack is focussed entirely on our home, it's easy to forget that anyone and anything close to us is also at risk. Remember when sealing that we need to protect everything, including pets, the garden, car, bicycle and workspace, etc. It's obviously better to seal everything at once, but sometimes it's not possible and has to be done in stages, beginning at the centre with our home and working outwards since this allows us to drive the attack further away as we work.

Combining a salt barrier with a visualised one is useful if we must we share walls and living space with others. We can use the same words as for a physical barrier, but as we stop strewing the salt we instead focus our thoughts on creating a visualised barrier instead until we can start the salt again. For example, if we cannot seal the outside of a boundary wall because our home or room is joined to next door, then just seal it on the *inside,* visualising the ritual sealing our side of the bricks and mortar as we work.

Don't be too fanatical in trying to get this just right; we don't need to know precisely how thick the walls are, for example. What matters is that we do *something,* that we do it sooner rather than later, and with complete confidence that it will work.

When we want to seal doors and windows etc., we can make the sign of the pentagram. This is the five-pointed star that symbolises the four physical elements of fire, earth, water and air, together with the fifth which is spirit or ether. Although some people still regard it as an 'evil' symbol, the pentagram has been used since ancient times to symbolise (amongst other things) medicine.[113] For protective purposes, begin drawing at the bottom left hand point so the single point of the star shape points upwards, and there are two points at the bottom.

I usually draw a pentagram in the air with my finger a few inches away from the windows and doors or even on the window glass if I can reach. Some people always use the hand they write with, others deliberately choose the other hand, feeling this is somehow more sacred for magical purposes. It doesn't matter whether we use one finger or our whole hand; I usually use my outstretched index finger, simply because I feel it concentrates my will/intention/power into a single small area. However, when a more controlled and subtle approach seems called for, I often use

[113] Dölger (1929)

the first two fingers of my right hand, either closing the third and fourth fingers against the palm or resting them on top of the thumb.

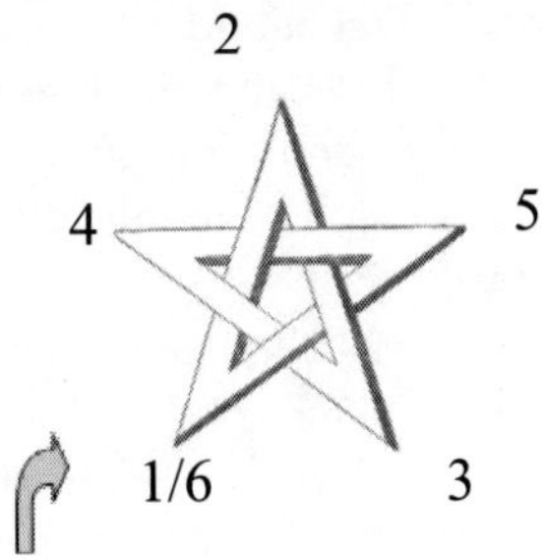

Start drawing here:

I like to make the pentagram as large as possible when I'm sealing doors and windows. However, if this isn't possible, perhaps due to lack of privacy, then just trace a small pentagram onto a windowsill or doorstep. Even though it's invisible to the naked eye, we should still be able to feel its power. A slightly more visible but still temporary measure is to paint a pentagram using blessed water and a paintbrush. Once it dries it will be completely invisible but still potent.

Don't panic, even if faced with an emergency. Stay focused. There is a job to be done, so get on with it and don't dither. Just stick to a single, simple, well-practised ritual. If the attack seems worse at night, then we simply seal our bedroom door and windows with a pentagram.

On flat surfaces, the general rule of thumb is to make the single point face wherever we feel the threat is strongest. The two points face whatever we wish to protect.

At the end of the day if we make a mistake there is no need to panic. *We* know what we're trying to do, and if we accidentally draw our pentagram the wrong way up it will NOT cause psychic chaos. The Universe has better things to do than hide in the bushes waiting to leap out and shout '*Gotcha*!' whenever we make a genuine mistake.

Drawing a pentagram in the air is also useful if something suddenly manifests and threatens us. As before, begin at the bottom left hand point, drawing swiftly and decisively in order to concentrate our energies more effectively. As we draw, we should tell whatever is bothering us to leave immediately. And yes, we *can* swear if it makes us feel better!

It is always important for us to look as though we know what we're doing while at the same time sounding suitably stern. *'Go away!'* and *'Stay back!'* are quite suitable, but *'Leave me alone!'* is not. This is because most of us do not actually *want* to be left completely, irrevocably on our own. We should never ask for something unless we're certain we want it.

The pentagram, cross and crucifix are some of the most commonly used symbols in the western world for dealing with psychic attacks although there are others. For example, since ancient times, the horseshoe with its lunar crescent shape has protected homes, stables and cow sheds. Horseshoes are traditionally displayed so that the gap between the two 'arms' is at the top and not the bottom although some prefer to hang them the other way around. In my own experience I have found the former method more effective. Both horseshoes and pentacles (a pentagram in a circle) can be placed anywhere there is a particularly strong psychic presence that we wish to contain.

Groups of protective symbols can also be a powerful defence. Years ago, people used a hazel twig to draw the following symbols in newly dug earth to protect the garden:

x ♡ x / + ♡ +

The methods I have suggested for use with the pentagram can also be used whenever we need to cleanse and purify places and people after psychic attacks. Repeat them regularly until they become second nature.

Using Plants as a Protective Barrier

There is a wide range of easily available plants and herbs such as lavender, chervil, dill, celery, parsley, caraway, and fennel that can be used to form a protective barrier. We can grow them from seed or buy them as pot-herbs in the local supermarket. Methods range from planting them near doorways, placing potted plants on the windowsill to dried lavender bags in the linen cupboard. We can also display items such as corn dollies, the 'palms' that people brought into the home on Palm Sunday (and kept until the following year), and even wreaths on the door or vases of flowers on the windowsill. These were all originally intended to magically protect the home and its occupants.

One of the most popular times of the year for using plants protectively was the 30th April, also known as Walpurgis Night, May Eve, or the Eve of Beltane. Plants were hung in bunches above the doorways, windows and fireplaces before being taken down and burned on the Beltane bonfires the following day. The magical thinking behind this was that the flowers absorbed any harmful influences which were then destroyed by burning. All plants should be removed before they start to droop since then their protective properties decline sharply.

Roses - with their protective fragrance and sharp thorns - make particularly effective natural barriers, either placed in a vase as cut flowers or planted outside the front door. Like all prickly plants, their thorns ward off evil and negativity. In some traditions, brambles were deliberately planted on graves to prevent the dead from walking, while the spiky hawthorn drove out demons, vampires and ghosts.

The rose's strong fragrance is also very protective, countering the foul smells that often accompany a psychic attack. Other strong-smelling plants used for magical protection include the not-so-sweet smelling shallots, leeks, garlic, chives, onions and wormwood. These can be cut, sliced and left in a room to absorb unpleasant energies, or cut up and rubbed on doors or windows (although that method leaves a lot of messy streaks). Whatever we choose we should replace it regularly while an attack is ongoing.

Potted plants can also protect the home. Since ancient times, sweet bay (*laurus nobilis*) has been planted in pots near exits and entrances. Its strong, clean fragrance immediately alerts us to its magical cleansing properties and in ancient Greece and Rome it was sacred to Apollo, a deity famous for his insistence on proper cleansing. Although bays grow slowly, they can reach several feet given a medium sized pot, but even small specimens can still work their protective magic while sitting on a kitchen windowsill.

Hyssop is another good cleansing herb; it grows easily in the UK and is even mentioned in Psalm 51, v7 in the Bible, '*Purge me with hyssop and I shall be clean.*' It can be used alone or combined with Mugwort if we feel that the psychic attack is making us physically ill. Hyssop can also be combined with cedar bark and the protective colour red. The belief in red as a protective colour is very ancient, and also applies to plants with bright red berries. A single hip from the dog rose was considered so powerful (probably due to the combination of thorns and its bright red colour) that people buried it under the floors of outbuildings such as stables or dairies to protect the entire area against enchantments and hexes.

Wreaths are another form of protective magic. Although we usually think of these hanging on the front door around Yule or Christmas, they are effective at any time of year. Kitchen wreaths are ideal for incorporating herbs, such as bay, rosemary, sage and lavender which are all strongly protective and anti-demonic. Also, since these herbs all dry out rather than shrivelling as soon as they are picked, the wreath will look fresh for some time.

Whole corms of garlic are both protective and anti-demonic; they look very attractive dotted among a kitchen wreath of herbs, especially against a background of red ribbons. In ancient Rome, garlic was said to protect not only against demons, but also against the restless dead or *lemures* and in some traditions also against vampires. An alternative is to simply place a pot of living, strong-smelling herbs such as mint on the windowsill or in the hallway.

Other protective decorations include combining red ribbons and blue beads; these were hung up at windows and considered a powerful remedy against the Evil Eye. Because they are attractive but not obviously associated with anything occult, they are useful if we live in a household unsympathetic to other methods of magical protection. Apart from making small displays of ribbons and beads, they can also be incorporated into a kitchen wreath.

While creating these, empower them by mentally reciting a few simple blessings such as, '*Bless and protect* [Name]; *bless and protect this home,*' etc. This helps our mental focus to rub off and empower the ribbons, beads, plants etc.

Plants can also be used to make a powerful potion for sealing rituals. One traditional method was to paint around doors and windows using water in which red rowan berries had been soaked. Although these are only available at certain times of the year, if we have access to a rowan tree we can experiment with drying some of its berries. These can be soaked in boiling water to release their protective properties when needed.

Oak salve was another popular remedy against psychic attacks. It was usually made by heating oak leaves in either lard or olive oil to release their magical properties, while stirring the mixture with a leafy oak twig. Alternatively, a small piece of oak was used to draw a protective circle around one's bed at night. By the same token, an oak walking stick offered general protection, and it's no coincidence that many traditional walking sticks were made from woods such as blackthorn, hawthorn, rowan and ash, trees that were all well-known for their protective properties.

Sticks made from elder wood protect against enchantment and werewolves, although most people preferred to avoid cutting the elder if they could as it was said to bleed if it was cut. It was even known to launch the occasional magical attack without any human help. Most people avoided using it for firewood, preferring to shiver rather than burn its wood and risk the anger of Mother Elder.

Incense

Just as fragrant and strong-smelling plants protect against psychic attacks, so does incense. Not only does it break up strong pockets of negativity and generally lighten the atmosphere, it also counters the unpleasant smells often associated with psychic attacks. It is useful if we find ourselves suddenly under attack and need to repel psychic phenomena and harmful influences.

Although joss sticks are probably the easiest type of incense to use, burning incense on charcoal blocks allows us to create our own unique mixtures for each situation. This utilises the magical properties of the plant matter and resin we use. It produces a thicker, more fragrant smoke, useful for censing an entire house in one sitting. It will certainly set off our smoke alarms, so if this will cause problems it is better to hang up suitable plants or place them in pots around the home and forget about burning incense.

True incense is usually a resin such as frankincense, myrrh, amber or the cheaper benzoin, although we can add herbs, barks (larch wood and oak are particularly effective) and flowers for variety and enhanced magical protection. Rosemary leaves or juniper berries make a good substitute for some of the resins and will burn on a charcoal block. Both are aromatic and have sharp needle-like leaves, characteristics which immediately suggest their use in psychic self defence. Some people also collect the small blobs of resin that collect on pine trunks and burn those although be warned – they can produce billows of smoke!

Mixing our own incense gives more control over the potential combinations of herbs and resins. Some of the best anti-demonic plants include ferns, lavender, betony, burnet-saxifrage, fir, cypress and hornbeam. Abbess Hildegard of Bingen recommended these as long ago as the twelfth century. Mugwort and vervain are protective, along with herbs such as dill, fennel and caraway, which are all readily available in supermarkets and delicatessens.

Herbs can be used fresh or dried on the incense blocks, but succulent leaves such as basil should be used sparingly because they do not burn easily and have a tendency to 'spit.' Dried herbs usually burn very well. Basically, when mixing our own incense we should be guided by our nose. If something smells clean – for example, pine, rosemary or bay - then it's suitable for magical cleansing. Because of its slightly narcotic and sedative properties, bay is particularly useful for calming any space troubled by active psychic phenomena. As a precaution, though, I would only burn it in a well-ventilated room.

Whenever we burn incense for the purposes of psychic self defence, it is important to remain focused. This can be difficult with block charcoal since it can burn for as long as 30-60 minutes with proper tending. To keep our minds alert, write out some prompts to use whenever we add more resin or herbs to the charcoal. Any of the following would be appropriate:

- *Drive back the power of those who wish me harm*
- *As this smoke rises, so may it heal all hurt and pain caused by this attack*
- *As this incense burns, so may all hatred, spite and ill wishing shrivel to ashes*
- *Cleanse this place, take away all negativity and ill wishing, make this place a safe haven for me and for those I love*
- *May the power of this incense drive out all powers that wish me harm*

As we speak, we visualise our intention and see our prompt coming to pass. So when we say, '*Drive back the power of those who wish me harm,*' we visualise driving the attack back to its source, forcing it out of our life and personal space. There is no ethical concern here: all we're doing is sending back to the attacker what he has tried to send to us; we have the right to fight back in order to protect ourselves and those we love. This is not the same as launching our own attack on a third party out of the blue.

Incense is also useful if we feel our attacker is harnessing his attack to any of the elements. For example, psychic attackers often use the element of water; psychic phenomena are much more common in damp houses than dry ones, and attacks often follow underground watercourses and streams to their intended targets. This type of attack has a powerful effect on the emotions, perhaps because water is closely associated with tears.

Using incense to counter this type of attack calls upon the power of the other three elements: fire, air and earth. Fire is the flame used to light the incense and keep it burning; air is the smoke given off by the incense, while the earth is the charcoal block, herbs and bark etc.

The element of fire makes us courageous and creative, while the element of air traditionally governs intelligence, thus helping us fight back against our attacker's mind games with rational thought and refusal to panic. Finally, the element of earth helps to keep us grounded, prevents panic and overreaction to whatever is going on around us. As we go through the ritual of lighting our incense and feeding it with resins and plant material, imagine each element coming to our assistance. Again, written prompts can be useful if we don't feel confident:

- *As this charcoal/incense burns, so may the element of fire protect me and those I love.*

- *As the smoke rises, so may the element of air drive out all ill wishing and harm.*

- *As the charcoal and the incense burn, so may the element of earth keep me grounded and unafraid. May it keep me and those I lose safe from harm.*

The '*As the... so may...*' formula in these prompts is very ancient. It also appears sometimes as '*Just as… so may…*' Both examples link the physical world (in this case the burning charcoal) to the magical one (banishing the psychic attack.)

Using incense is a good way to finalise a magical cleansing, making the room smell and feel much lighter and less oppressive. Although carrying a joss stick from room to room is probably more practical, if we can possibly remain in the room for the hour or so it takes to burn the charcoal block, it is well worth it.

If we need to use incense over a larger area, such as a garden, then burning plant material and resin on a small, controlled bonfire is probably the best method. Again this is rooted in tradition, since it was customary to cast herbs and plants into the flames at certain festivals (especially the Summer Solstice, Halloween/Samhain and Beltane/May Day).

At the Summer Solstice, mugwort was plaited into protective wreaths or belts and then burned at the end of the festivities. It is a great herb for all types of magical healing and protection, and can be used on its own or combined with vervain, a herb that enables the wearer to see into the future, befriend her worst enemy and be protected against all forms of enchantment.

Grape vines also protected against enchantment and could not only free anyone who had been bewitched but also punished the hexer. The way it worked was that lengths of vine were twisted together to make a switch which was then used to beat the victim's clothes. The blows were magically transferred to the person responsible for the psychic attack!

If we believe we are the victim of an erotic curse, which is a particularly unpleasant type of attack aimed at dragging the victim (usually female) to have sex with her attacker, then we should burn the leaves, blossoms or bark of a cherry tree. Although the cherry often features in love magic, in psychic self defence its main purpose is to free young girls from sexual enchantment.

The four-leafed clover was a popular remedy for dealing with bewitched animals and was either placed in the feed or hung up in the cowshed or stable. Sycamore was another good all-round protector. In Cornwall, people hung bunches of sycamore and hawthorn around doorways to ward off witches and demons, avert lightning strikes and prevent milk from going sour. In Germany, sycamore twigs were pinned on window and door frames on St John's Day/the Summer Solstice. Since sycamore is deciduous it may be a good idea to dry a few leaves to ensure we have an all-year-round supply.

The sycamore leaf's distinctive shape was often used symbolically. In some parts of Wales, women used the leaves as stencils on newly whitened kitchen floors while in the west of England, 'Revel Buns' were traditionally baked on Sycamore leaves at Easter time and other festivals. The leaf shape was even incorporated into loaf tins that were still being sold in the 1990's.[114] Since the symbol could not easily be seen at the base of the loaf, it

---

114 De Cleene and Lejeune (2003) Vol 1: 686

suggests its real function was magical rather than purely decorative.

Nailing a yew stick behind the door prevented evil from entering the home, and yew twigs were also placed in cellars, kitchens, living rooms and stables, often in the shape of a cross, which is not exclusively Christian and often appears in much earlier contexts. In Bavaria it was believed no evil magic could exist in the presence of yew; in the Scottish Hebrides, yew branches were placed amongst the thatch on roofs to protect against fire.

The connection between yew tree and fire is very old; in the Old English (Anglo-Saxon) Rune Poem, the yew is described as *'hyrde fyres'* which could mean either guardian against fire or even guardian of the fire, depending upon the translation used.[115] Yew is therefore a very useful plant for protecting against poltergeists who often use fire as part of their armoury of psychic phenomena.

After using plants for magical protection, remember to dispose of them carefully afterwards. The traditional method was to cast them into running water, although this may not always be practical and we may even be accused of littering! An alternative is to burn the plants and then bury the ashes in salt in the earth.

If digging a hole is out of the question it might be better to put the ashes into a paper bag with some salt and simply put that out with the household rubbish or green waste. The main thing is to send the plant – which has absorbed the energies of the psychic attack – as far away from us as possible.

Protective Stones and Crystals

These can be a useful protective measure, placed on or near exits, entrances and paths. Although nowadays most people think of magical stones as crystals, centuries ago they came from a variety of sources. The Swallow Stone, for example, or *piedra dela golondrina* was found in the stomach of the first cockerel to be born in the new year under a crescent moon.[116] There were always two Swallow Stones, one green and one white and they were wrapped

[115] Elliot (1957): 259

[116] Nunemaker (1932): 562

in deer or calf skin and hung around the neck on a red silk thread to cure enchantment.

Swallow stones were sometimes also known as eagle stones, clapper stones or *aetites* although they had nothing to do with birds and were just a hollow stone (often limonite) with a loose pebble or piece of debris inside that rattled. They were highly valued as protective amulets and often given very ornate settings of gold or silver.[117]

Fossils, especially ammonites, have been used protectively since prehistoric times, and may have taken their name from the North African ram-horned protective deity, Ammon, whose cult eventually spread to Egypt and parts of Greece. Centuries ago it was thought that ammonites were petrified serpents, turned to stone by Abbess Hilda of Whitby in the seventh century, hence their nickname, 'Whitby Snake Stones'. Some were even carved to give the fossil a snake-like head and eyes. The smallest ammonites are no larger than a thumbnail and could be worn as a pendant or carried in a pouch, while the larger ones were more likely to be incorporated into boundary walls and buildings.

Coral was considered protective, especially when inscribed with a magical motto such as *'Nomen noctilucae, hoc est Hecates signum aut Gurgonis personam'*.[118] Few of us would be able to afford a piece of coral large enough to accommodate such a long inscription, so the best alternative is to inscribe it either in the air above the coral, or one letter on top of the other, using the tip of a needle. Remember that an inscription does not actually need to be scratched *into* the coral, just lightly indicated; it's quite acceptable to visualise the whole thing from start to finish if we prefer.

The use of Mirrors in Psychic Self Defence

A strategically placed mirror is useful for driving back hexes. The magical thinking behind this is that since it can reflect something physically, it must also be able to reflect (and deflect) things

---

117 Urban Holmes (1934): 195

118 Ch VII *Lapidus Corallius from Orphei Lithica, Damigeron de Lapidibus,* 1881: 169

magically. Although mirrors can be very helpful, I have always been a little wary of them because it is so easy to get the angles wrong and have things bouncing off to unintended places. There is no point deflecting a hex from behind a door if we've placed the mirror at such an angle that it will ricochet into a child's bedroom!

It's important to ensure that any mirror used for psychic self defence is benign. Mirrors vary a great deal in their quality and temperament, and some are less trustworthy than others. Public mirrors, especially in changing rooms and public loos can be positively malevolent, while mirrors used in psychic self defence, for example, will have a completely different nature to those used in other types of magic. The test of a 'good' mirror is to touch the glass with our fingertip. Ideally, we should be able to touch the reflection with barely a gap between it and our finger. Poor quality glass, however, can show a surprisingly wide space between the reality and the reflection. I suspect it is this gap that allows other influences and energies to creep in, and this in turn undermines our intentions.

It can take years to truly train a mirror for magical purposes, and this is probably where the old belief that breaking a mirror causes seven years bad luck originated. It's not that breaking a mirror is unlucky as such, but it does force us to start from scratch with a new one!

I have always found the best way to tame a mirror is to breathe on it. Yes, it will mist up, but breathing on it allows us to impregnate it with our own *dynamis*. As we breathe on the mirror, visualise blowing away all negativity, cleansing the glass until nothing remains of its original nature. Then with the next breath mentally tell the mirror what it must do. Keep the instructions as simple as possible though, since mirrors can be such wayward things. It is better to state the blatantly obvious than hope for the best and expect the mirror to second guess our real intentions. A suitable list of instructions could include:

- *Now and always, reflect back to the sender anything sent to harm me or those I love*

- *Now and always, keep me and my family safe*
- *Now and always, keep those I love safe*
- *Now and always, keep this home safe and secure from harm*

We can also adapt the *'As this... so may'* or *'Just as... so may'* formulae for use with mirrors. So the first instruction above could be rewritten, *'As you reflect back images, so you must now and always reflect back anything sent to harm me or those I love.'*

Some recommend storing the mirror by wrapping it in a dark cloth when it is no longer needed, while others prefer to keep it in position as a protective defence. If we do leave the mirror up, please don't forget about it and assume that it's doing its job. Pay it some attention from time to time since it will have been exposed to a wide range of energies and will require extra care. Make sure it is regularly polished (dusty mirrors tend to trap a lot of negativity instead of reflecting it back) and charge it with our breath on a regular basis, at least for the first few years. Recharge whenever there is some expectation of psychic attack.

If we are experiencing an active psychic attack, wash the glass regularly (and carefully) with a weak solution of blessed, salt water. (For instructions how to make this, see Chapter Twelve). Wring out the cloth as much as possible however, so that the salt content and damp doesn't damage the glass or frame.

From a purely practical point of view don't forget that mirrors can reflect and intensify incoming sunlight; if they are poorly positioned they can - and do - cause fires. Also, if we place a mirror in or near a window that faces out onto the street, make sure it cannot dazzle local motorists.

We now have a very basic set of guidelines for dealing with psychic attacks:

- Get rid of anything connected with the attack, or the attacker

- Clean the most severely affected spaces - begin by physically cleaning and then magically cleanse them

- Make sure the attack cannot return by magically sealing doors, windows and other openings such as cat flaps and hearths

- If necessary, we can use protective stones, crystals and mirrors to keep the attack away from our personal space

Always ensure that the basic materials, e.g. salt, a bell, garlic, cleansing herbs, a basic incense mixture are to hand as soon as a psychic attack is suspected. We don't need to be paranoid, just prepared.

CHAPTER ELEVEN

Cutting the red cord between our third eye and our attacker. Dealing with other cords, especially those attached to the Solar Plexus. Dealing with psychic vampires, house brownies, fairies, ghosts and poltergeists.

Although psychic attacks are usually sent *to* the victim, sometimes we have little choice but to deal with our attacker in person. Some attackers, particularly those who launch intentional attacks, muscle in on our personal space in order to see the effect they are having. Others find it easier to drain our energy from close quarters. Either way, dealing with them can be both intimidating and exhausting.

Before we allow them to move in on us, we need to understand how psychic attackers operate and communicate with their victims. Proper communication of an attack requires not only that one person should convey something but that other should receive it. We all know people who talk *at* us rather than *to* us, but although we usually think of words as an essential part of all communication, it's possible to convey a great deal of information using just the eyes, body language and even telepathy.

Although some psychic attacks seem to happen very suddenly, with hindsight we often realise it was more gradual, but the early warning signs were missed. Luckily such signs are rarely unique to a single attack but are common to most. For example, we may notice someone trying to dominate us in some way. This is usually someone we know rather than a total stranger. At first their controlling behaviour may be subtle, such a minor irritation that we may even feel we are over-reacting. Gradually, however it intensifies, overwhelming us before we are even fully aware what's happening.

No matter how subtle our attacker thinks he is, there is always some sort of 'tell,' and once we know what sort of thing we're looking for it's easy to spot. Most people will have *some* eye contact during a face-to-face conversation, and indeed, we'd probably think it strange if they didn't. However psychic attackers tend to follow certain patterns depending on whether they are trying to get into our world in order to dominate us or trying to prevent us from getting into theirs and dominating them.

For example, they may close their eyes when speaking to us. Sometimes they disguise this by pretending to rub their eyes or removing their spectacles and pretending to clean them. Doctors and lawyers often use this technique as a way of putting their own point across without taking anyone else's into account!

At the opposite end of the scale is the attacker who stares so hard at us that we end up feeling like rabbits caught in car headlights. Both types are trying to dominate and make us obey their will rather than our own. We're not talking here about someone who has sore eyes or is painfully shy and cannot bear to look anyone in the face when they speak. We are talking about people who use certain techniques in order to make others agree to do, say or think what they are told, no matter how unreasonable this happens to be.

How do psychic attacks actually work? How does an attacker, standing just a foot or two away, manage to make someone obey him? Often he uses something called the 'third eye,' located just above the bridge of the nose in the middle of the forehead. There are a number of explanations for the third eye and what it does, but we don't need to be an expert in order to recognise (a) that it exists and (b) the part it can play in a psychic attack. Basically, the third eye is the source of our spiritual or inner vision. If someone uses it to create a link between himself and a third party, he is gaining some sort of control over the exchange of information between himself and that person.

Before we become too paranoid about this however, remember that controlling an exchange of information does not automatically mean someone is launching a psychic attack. There are many times when setting up such a link is perfectly acceptable and even beneficial.

For example, when we attend a lesson or lecture, it often helps to mentally set up some sort of link between us and the teacher to facilitate the sharing of information. This is fine because the teacher has set out to share information, but it only remains fine provided the information we access from her is that which she was going to share anyway. It does not entitle us to go digging around in someone's head without their permission for information they do *not* wish to share. That is when we begin straying into the territory of psychic attacks.

In this type of attack, all mental traffic between the attacker's third eye and ours is always strictly controlled to his advantage, meaning he can do whatever he wants, whenever he wants. We may not even have any idea that something is amiss until the attack is well under way. However, as with all aspects of psychic self defence, knowledge is power. Once we know what's happening, there are a number of effective techniques that can help stop it.

It often helps if we think of the link set up between the victim and the attacker's third eye as a tough cord, rather like a length of nylon rope. Those who can see psychic colours usually describe it as red. Start with a quick grounding exercise, (see Chapter Nine) to calm our nerves. We should do this as soon as we see the attacker approaching.

Next, visualise yanking the cord out of the attacker's third eye by its roots (but we must resist the temptation to pull it out of our own third eye, in case this causes a psychic injury). Now imagine grabbing hold of the red cord, twisting it around the palm of our hand for a better grip and pulling hard. Really hard. Once the attacker's end of the cord is free it might start to wither or even drop off straight away, but if it doesn't then just visualise chopping it up using visualised scissors or a knife. (There are instructions for visualising psychic weapons in Chapter Nine). We then cut the cord back until it is level with our own brow.

Although it isn't unpleasant to touch, many people don't feel comfortable catching hold of the red cord, even though the entire thing is visualised. Alternatively, use visualised scissors etc., to slash through the cord and simply break the connection. It's always a pleasant surprise how creative some people are with this work, visualising lawnmowers, golden sickles and even axes!

The attacker remains in control only for as long as this thick red cord remains intact. Once the connection is severed, the link is broken and he is left with nothing. If he tries setting up a fresh connection, sever it again. What we must *not* do however is to try and set up a fresh link from us to our attacker, although it is understandable to want to give them a taste of their own medicine. However, any link – no matter who has set it up – gives the attacker the opportunity to invade our space again. We just need to concentrate on removing the red cord and nothing more. We certainly don't want an all-out psychic war on our hands.

People sometimes condemn psychic self defence for being somehow unethical. They argue that severing red cords, etc. is excessively violent, and that psychic weapons are just as dangerous as real ones. This is true up to a point, although many people carry and use psychic weapons without even realising it, something that doesn't normally happen with a real weapon. Also, no matter how high our own ethical values happen to be, our attacker is unlikely to share them. Indeed, he may well be the sort of person who is quite happy to creep up and hit us on the head with a psychic truncheon!

We owe it to ourselves (and others) to stop psychic attacks. Deliberate attackers very rarely limit themselves to a single attack on a single victim; once they find they have a talent for hexing, they go out and actively seek new targets. If we let them get away with attacking us, then perhaps next time they will pick on someone more vulnerable, such a child or someone who is sick. It's easy to end up hating ourselves for not preventing such things but if we do, we put ourselves at risk of psychic self-harm, which can be every bit as damaging as physical self-harm.

Other Types of Cords

The red cord that links an attacker's third eye to his victim's is probably the most common type of connection, although there are others. Some attackers prefer to link to the *solar plexus,* one of the main nerve centres of the body located between the breastbone and the navel. This cord may be any colour and can be tricky to locate because there are often many cords in this area, most of them perfectly benign. It is important to avoid the temptation to simply slash through everything we find, since this could mean cutting links that tie us to people we love.

Since the attacker has attached the cord mentally, we need our own mental powers to visualise severing it. This isn't as difficult as it sounds. One of the best times to do this is at night, when the attacker expects us to be asleep. We begin by feeling for *all* the cords attached to our solar plexus. Cords used in an attack are usually thick and strong, but so are the cords of love - and we certainly don't want to destroy those. However, with genuine, loving ties we can always 'see' the person on the other end. Cords used in psychic attacks usually hide the person who has set up the connection.

Another thing to bear in mind is that benign cords should feel quite comfortable when we touch them, whereas chords used in psychic attacks often tingle or pulsate. Some people even find they make them feel physically sick. Once we find a cord we suspect is being used by our attacker, we need to follow it to where it joins our body and press gently with our fingertips. Because it was placed there without our consent, we should be able to feel a tender spot where it has been attached to us. Benign cords do not usually feel tender where they join our body.

The red cord that links the victim's third eye to the attacker is quite short because normally it is only set up when both are physically close to each other. However, any controlling cord attached to the solar plexus is usually very long because it allows the attacks to be controlled from a distance. Yanking it out is not an option because it would be like pulling on a thick length of elastic. The quickest and most effective option is to use our psychic sword or dagger to cut the line, but first we must visualise heating the blade in fire in order to cauterise the line and make it impossible for it to reattach itself.

To do this, visualise plunging our psychic sword or dagger into a flame until it glows with the heat. Then we cut the cord as close as we can to our own body, being careful not to cut any of the other cords nearby. Since this is a long cord it may well thrash about a bit and recoil, partly because it is under tension, and partly because its natural instinct is to try and reattach itself to us. This will be impossible since it has been cauterised with the hot blade, but it will try nonetheless. It might even try and wrap itself around our neck or wrist (particularly our sword arm) which is a very unpleasant sensation.

If this happens, we just need to keep our nerve, since once the cord is cut and cauterised it has no more power, no matter how unpleasant it feels. Its function was only ever to convey information to and from our attacker. Some people like to keep slashing at it as a precaution because it makes them feel they are doing something useful (I've done it myself) but it's not essential.

If our attacker is very persistent, he may try to attach another cord, but we will now be ready for it. Don't panic. All we need do is repeat the exercise above, checking for any new cords or tender points. If we find them, just cut them again and cauterise them. Very few attackers are that persistent and once we show our willingness to stand up and fight back, most will simply move on. Remember that launching an attack requires considerably more energy than psychic self defence; in other words, the attacker will tire before we do.

I'm sometimes asked whether it's possible to perform a cord cutting for someone else, such as a child or sick person. Although it *is* possible, there are a few pitfalls to beware. Chief among these is the risk of turning the whole thing into high drama. This only frightens the victim who already has quite enough to contend with. I would therefore recommend performing cord cutting exercise on behalf of someone else only when that person is asleep. The same advice goes for sealing another person's Aura. (See Chapter Nine)

Another question I am sometimes asked is whether we should first obtain permission before performing any magical act for someone else. Ideally, the answer would be yes. But we do not live in an ideal world and sometimes need to make swift decisions. For example, what if the victim is too young and does not understand what we intend to do? How can they consent to anything? What about a victim who is thoroughly under her attacker's thumb? Or one who is too ill to give consent?

I believe the only answer possible for this question is found in the 'As above, so below' approach.[119] In everyday life we perform

---

[119] This comes from the Emerald Tablet of Hermes Trismegistus. The text can be read online at: http://www.sacred-texts.com/alc/emerald.htm

many acts for people without asking their permission first. We open doors for them. We may buy a jumper we think they would like. We choose what to give them for their tea. If they are ill, we might take them breakfast in bed. Sometimes the recipients of our well-intentioned acts are delighted, sometimes they may be horrified - as anyone who has ever let me choose a jumper for them will attest! At the end of the day we can only do our best, guided by what we know about the other person. Personally, I would rather try and help than stand back and do nothing, but each of us must make our own decision about this.

One word of caution, however. It is important to be completely honest with ourselves and certain that we really are acting from motives of love, free from personal interest. For example, supposing we want to cut the cord that binds a teenage daughter to a boyfriend whom we consider unsuitable; we might even convince ourselves he poses a risk to her.

It is all too easy in this type of situation to convince ourselves we are acting in someone's best interests when in fact we are acting only for ourselves. Resist meddling in someone else's life unless certain that person is in danger or at risk. And even then, consider exactly what sort of danger justifies our intervention - physical danger? Moral or emotional? Mental? It's a difficult call and there are no easy answers. As adults we may face such choices from time to time. We simply need to do the best we can.

If we decide not to intervene but are still uneasy and feel we need to do something, then one possibility is to make a psychic shield for the person we wish to protect. It will need regular recharging; we must keep thinking of it and visualising it in the same way we would do for our own shield. This takes considerable effort especially if we are also trying to maintain our own psychic shield at the same time. This method is therefore unsuitable if we believe we are under psychic attack as well, since all it does is risk leaving both ourselves and the person we are trying to protect more vulnerable than before.

If we still want to create psychic armour to protect a third party, try adapting some of the methods outlined in Chapter Nine. In addition to visualising the size, shape, weight and design of the shield we are trying to create we must also visualise the person we are trying to protect. Bear in mind that it is *her* shield and not ours. In an emergency of course, if we don't have time to make a shield for her, we can mentally dash in with our own shield, but this is at best a temporary measure.

When we create a shield for someone else, we should imagine that person using it, holding it, lifting it to defend herself. It can also help to have a phrase or saying to set the shield in place whenever it is required, something like 'Guard *Name* now!'

Not everyone wants or needs us to do this sort of work for them, of course. Some enjoy doing it for themselves; children, for example, are especially good at visualisation. Teaching them to set up their own guardian, using a favourite doll or teddy to protect them, can be very effective and give them much needed confidence, as can teaching them a protective chant or spell.

The secret is to keep it simple, make it easy to memorise and set up a strong rhythm. When I was young, the old-fashioned '*From ghoulies and ghosties and long-leggedy beasties, good Lord deliver us,*' was still very popular. The important thing is that the spell must address whoever or whatever is frightening them; some children are quick to give the phenomena/entities that trouble them a name, in which case we use that name. If they don't have a name for it, then something generic such as Bogeyman, Ghostie, Black Dog, etc., will probably do. It doesn't have to be a precise name, but the child does need to feel comfortable using it.

Keep the chant brief and easy to remember; something like:

Go away, Ghostie, go away,
You're not welcome here today!
So go, go, Ghostie, go away!

Poltergeists, Ghosts, etc.

In the course of a lifetime we will probably encounter a wide range of paranormal phenomena including hauntings, ghosts, fairies, poltergeists and chthonic entities. Although not all of these will be true psychic attacks, sometimes it can be difficult to tell exactly where one ends and another begins.

Hauntings

Most hauntings are a type of imprint, a form of place memory. Lacking intelligence, they just re-run from time to time, like a loop of videotape. They probably keep running even when nobody is there to witness them. They may appear purely in visual form, or we may hear (and sometimes also smell them.) Usually we cannot touch them, however. This type of haunting features people, animals and occasionally objects such as weapons; it can also cause the background or setting to appear different. For example, sometimes people have reported seeing a room or landscape looking as it would have done many years ago.

Although we cannot be sure what causes a haunting, it's sometimes thought to be caused by a traumatic event such as a murder or suicide, although a large number seem to be mundane repeats of everyday activities. There is very little that needs to be done about this type of psychic activity, and since it possesses no intelligence or intent it cannot be classed as a psychic attack. It certainly will not harm anyone.

Ghosts

Ghosts are popularly defined as the spirit or imprint of someone who has died. Unlike a haunting (which replays the same event over and over), ghosts often seem to have intelligence and sometimes a purpose. They usually appear clothed as they were in life, and again may be seen, heard and occasionally even smelled. Tobacco, perfume and food cooking are the most commonly reported aromas, and these are very different from the smell of rotting flesh, sulphur and excrement usually associated with a psychic attack. Animals can also appear as ghosts; both human and animal ghosts are usually attached to places rather than people.

I have known a few occasions, however where animal spirits have attached themselves to and moved home with their owners. Generally this is something that has been agreed between the two parties. At some point, even perhaps without realising it, the former owner has invited their pet's spirit to travel with them.

Sometimes spirits, especially those of young children, can become attached to living pets and will apparently play with them. Child ghosts also become attached to objects such as toys and books, which they sometimes move during the night. Yet despite what we see in horror films, such spirits rarely have evil intent, although they can be mischievous. If their visits are only occasional, it is usually possible to tolerate them. This is a very typical example of such activity:

> *When I worked in a bookshop, I started to notice most mornings that there would be a few books on the floor even though I was certain they had all been put away on the shelves the night before. The building wasn't particularly old, probably dating from the 1960's. Several mediums all said that it was the spirit of a young girl who had lived on the site long ago before the present shop had even been built. She liked to visit from time to time, and was fascinated by all the books, even though she had never learned to read.*
>
> *In the end I used to leave a few picture books out for her, and sometimes a toy or two. Gradually the disturbances stopped and there were no more books thrown about the place overnight.*[120]

Some people insist that all ghosts should be banished or '*sent to the light*.' (The latter involves explaining that the ghost has died and doesn't belong here any longer.) Personally, I feel there is an unfortunate tendency to view all ghosts as restless spirits that need laying to rest.

However, this is not always the case. Often spirits return to visit places (and people) where they have been happy. In such circumstances there is no reason to suppose that they wish to be laid to rest and I feel it is rather arrogant to feel we must banish them. Surely we can allow them a little pleasure, even in spirit form? It's quite different of course, if a spirit starts to muscle in on our personal space, but usually there is plenty of room for compromise. Often the solution is simply kindness and understanding. Some child ghosts will even be pacified by the

[120] Author's personal notes

presence of a kitten or puppy to 'play' with. They seem to get bored in much the same way as real children do.

Also, we must consider whether the ghost is someone who was known to us in life and who may simply be returning to keep an eye on us. Such 'guardian ghosts' are attached to people rather than places and will appear no matter where we happen to be. Such appearances are usually benign psychic events and normally nothing needs to be done about them.

If they threaten us in any way however, then we are not dealing with a guardian type of ghost even if we knew them in life. Remember that spirits can be just as spiteful as their human counterpart used to be. That said, despite what we see in the movies, ghosts very rarely return with any malicious intent towards living. On the extremely rare occasions when the relationship becomes fraught we should simply start cleansing the home or space where they appear most often and tell them to leave. It's as simple as that; contrary to what some would have us believe, requiem masses rarely have much effect on someone who did not hold similar religious beliefs in their own lifetime.

Years ago, ghosts were often pacified with something called a 'husher.' A piece of shiny metal was placed in a box concealed in the room where the ghost was most active. The idea was that the ghost would happily occupy itself playing with the husher and become so engrossed in this that it forgot to frighten the living!

I've tried this out myself for a little girl whose home was haunted by a previous tenant. Since we didn't have a piece of shiny metal, we used dry leaves and wrote words such as 'Peace;' 'Home'; 'Happy' etc., on them in felt pen. (Biro has a tendency to break the leaves). Then we painted the leaves very roughly with PVA glue and sprinkled them with glitter. Finally, we put the lot into a small plastic box and closed the lid. She kept the box in her bedroom and, I'm happy to say, wasn't troubled by the ghost again.

Children seem to see ghosts more often than adults, although this ability tails off as we get older. We shouldn't panic if a child announces they have seen a ghost; most are quite harmless and many are simply the 'haunting' variety, without any intelligence or intention. If we are worried however, then regular cleansing, especially in the child's bedroom (or wherever the ghost frequents) can be helpful as can hanging protective talismans (Chapter Nineteen) and sealing the child's Aura when she is asleep (Chapter Nine).

Very occasionally, a spirit seems friendly towards a child but hostile towards adults. We get the feeling that we are no longer welcome in our own home. This is unacceptable and we do not have to put up with it. Always start as we mean to go on and do not allow it to intimidate us even if our first instinct is to get out of the room as quickly as possible.

We need to be kind but firm and tell them something like: *'Hello, I can't see or hear you, but I know you're there. I will help you if I can, but you must remember that this is my home. I have the right to be here.'* Finish with a simple blessing, such as, *'I wish you well, and may your god/gods/goddess bless you and keep you safe.'*

If the entire house feels hostile, we must cleanse it regularly (Chapters Nine, Ten and Twelve), break up negativity (Chapter Thirteen) and bless it (Chapter Fourteen). This helps clear the atmosphere, making it more pleasant for us and considerably less welcoming for the spirit. In particular, we should bless the home whenever we enter or leave. The old blessing, *'God bless all here,'* is simple and to the point, and can be adapted to make it more appropriate to our own beliefs. For example, we can substitute, *'Goddess bless all here,'* instead, or name the specific deity we wish to invoke.

Some places seem to attract more ghosts than others. In my home, there is a cold spot that marks a portal or gateway where various entities come and go. All that psychic activity was very disconcerting at first but eventually things calmed down to a point where everyone - and everything - managed to coexist quite happily.

Dealing with Ghosts and Spirit Entities

The basic methods for dealing with ghosts and spirit entities is much the same as for house brownies and chthonic entities: *talk to them.* It sounds ridiculously simple but taking the initiative allows us to wrest back control of the situation. Just say something like, '*Look, I know we are sharing the same space, but we have to establish some ground rules here. We can all co-exist, but I don't want you to frighten me or my family.*' Then we list some of the things that we feel are inappropriate.

It is important to always leave room for negotiation, even if we don't really feel like it. Also, never threaten unless we are certain we can carry through. Yes, if we're experienced in this sort of thing we can stand there and order the spirit to leave. And sometimes it will. But sometimes it may increase its activities just to show us who's the boss although if we're experienced and confident we should be able to handle this, too.

If we're beginners however, we should always start off by being firm but kind, and many experienced psychics prefer this approach anyway. Keep it simple and straightforward, something like, '*Now, with regard to switching the lights on and off, I want you to stop doing that. I don't know if it was you, or a different entity, but we're not prepared to put up with that. If it wasn't you, then please tell whoever was responsible to stop it...*'

If we suspect we are dealing with a discarnate or earth-bound spirit, another remedy is to encourage it to move on to the spirit world. Sometimes these spirits do not realise they have died, viewing the new occupiers of their former home as interlopers. In this type of situation, we should again sit down in an area where the spirit has been active and encourage it to move on to the spirit world. Explain firmly but kindly that it has died and no longer belongs here. Talk to it about what is going on in the world nowadays, encourage it to look out of the window and see how the area has changed, and above all encourage it to 'go towards the light', where it will once again find people it loved in life.

If the spirit is not earthbound but just returns occasionally for a visit, there is really no need to send it to the light or anywhere else for that matter. There may be many reasons why it is returning; possibly it is just revisiting a place where it was once happy or may even feel attracted in some way towards us and our family or flatmates.

We don't need to do anything unless we feel it is trying to intimidate us. If this happens, then we must take a firm line and make it clear we are not prepared to put up with this. Explain that it is welcome to return occasionally, but this is now our home and we intend to live here as we see fit.

Things may not settle down straight away and if that's the case we will need to talk to the entity several times, repeating our requests and keeping up with magically cleansing our home. In the ancient world, when people wished to make peace with a ghost, they shared a symbolic meal with it. Certain foods such as honey dissolved in milk, wine, water barley and olive oil were believed to be particularly acceptable, although there is no reason we cannot offer other types of food. We then invite the ghost to share the meal. If we don't feel comfortable eating with a ghost, we can leave the food as an offering instead, having first explained that afterwards it must not trouble us anymore and should cease its activities.

Before setting out the meal, it was traditional to make a doll of the same gender as the ghost. If the gender was unknown then people made two dolls, one male, the other female. These sat at the meal to represent the ghost, were treated like living beings and afterwards taken to a beautiful spot and left there.

This is a symbolic 'setting free' and not abandonment, so the words we use should reflect this. Before the meal, tell them what we are going to do, *'We will share this meal together and then I will set you free afterwards.'* When we are about to leave, say something like, *'I honour you with food and freedom. You are now free, may the gods bless you, keep you safe and may they lead you back to your family and those you love.'*

In the ancient world, people exorcised ghosts using a circular motion with their hands. This suggests that breaking up the atmosphere was an important part of the banishing process and works on the same principle as the exercises for breaking up negativity in Chapter Thirteen. We can adapt the exercise using a simple pole in a figure-of-eight pattern to break up negativity for dealing with ghosts.

If we are suddenly confronted by a ghost, try the ancient method of blowing on it, beginning at the feet, or the lowest part of the body that is visible, and moving upwards on a single breath before blowing as hard as possible directly into its face.[121] Since it requires more breath than most of us normally have, it is worth practising this, just in case we need it. This method can also be used for dealing with infestations of psychic animals and should reduce any paranormal activity to a reasonable level. However, if it persists or worsens then turn to Chapter Eighteen for more suggestions on banishing and exorcism.

Crisis and Point-of-Death Apparitions

Not all ghosts are people who have died. Very occasionally a person who is still living may appear to a third person, usually one of their next of kin. These are often known as 'Crisis' or 'Point-of-Death' apparitions although these two terms are not identical. A Point-of-Death apparition normally only appears once, when someone is hovering on the threshold of life and death or has just died suddenly. There is nothing we can or should try to do about it, other than thank it for thinking of us, and blessing it.

A crisis apparition is slightly different, and often manifests when someone is in danger and is trying to call for help. Usually (though not always) it will be someone known to us, but unlike a Point-of-Death apparition, crisis apparitions may appear several times. If we suspect we may have witnessed one of these phenomena, we should try and find out where the person is since they are probably in danger or distress.

Poltergeists

Most people seem to fear poltergeists above all other psychic phenomena. This is partly I suspect, because poltergeists tend to focus on a single person or place which makes their activities feel

[121] Lucian Philopseudes 11-3 c170s AD and the Lives of SS. Cyprian and Justina 3-9 c. Mid 4th century AD. Both Cited in Ogden, (2009) Extracts nos. 49 and 335 respectively.

unpleasantly personal. Also, they appear to possess enough intelligence to manifest as mischief and even malice. Yet many are not aggressive or threatening and although they can take some getting used to, some people have learned to co-exist with their resident poltergeist.

The word poltergeist literally means a noisy ghost, and certainly most poltergeists create a racket quite out of all proportion to the amount of actual damage they do. It might sound as though they've just smashed all the plates, yet on closer inspection most people find that none have even been chipped.

Thanks to numerous horror films, most of us think we know what a poltergeist attack would be like. However, very few are anything like as bizarre, terrifying or protracted as Hollywood portrays. Even films 'based on true stories' are usually so far removed from the truth as to be unrecognisable. Films are intended to be entertainment, so they must keep our interest and attention for at least ninety minutes, sometimes more. Real life is usually far less exciting, even with a poltergeist. If the disturbances only happen occasionally, it can be difficult to decide whether what is happening is part of a psychic attack or part of a poltergeist manifestation.

For example, just because lights switch themselves on and off does not *of itself* mean that we have a poltergeist. Objects can frequently move in haunted buildings; aural disturbances such as knocks and raps can occur as a warning of psychic attack; and while some will insist that sudden foul smells with no obvious physical cause are a sure sign of a poltergeist, they can also be a warning of an impending psychic attack.

The most common signs of a poltergeist attack are objects being thrown out of thin air and people being apparently manhandled and thrown about by some invisible force. However, it's quite easy to fling ourselves from one side of the sofa to another and claim we were thrown, making it impossible to prove either way.

It's often said we can recognise poltergeist activity when writing appears on walls, especially in empty rooms. Nowadays writing sometimes appears on computer screens too – a sign, if it were needed, that such things move with the times. Yet although the odd bit of writing may be disturbing, it is not 'proof' of a poltergeist. It may be some other type of entity trying to communicate. If unsuccessful, it becomes frustrated and then indulges in some poltergeist-like activities, rather like throwing a tantrum.

For example, imagine trying to communicate to someone who only speaks another language or who cannot hear us properly: we often end up shouting, waving our arms around – very similar, in fact, to the activities of some noisy spirits. Perhaps they just want to be heard! In the 1840's, two American sisters, Margaretta and Catherine Fox communicated with a spirit in their home by means of knocks and raps that spelled out messages. This eventually led to the foundation of the Spiritualist Church.

Of course, not all poltergeists wish to communicate. Unfortunately, some create a Catch-22 situation, terrifying their victim whose fear in turn feeds the poltergeist. The only way to handle this is to break the cycle or at least reduce it. This is why I always stress that no matter what paranormal phenomena are sent our way, we must remain calm. We need to practice the grounding and breathing exercises in Chapter Nine until they become second nature to us in order to steady our nerves.

Many years ago, poltergeists were often regarded as a form of demonic possession, (in some places they still are) although this theory is less popular nowadays. The influence of religion, which tended to see demons in everything, has declined, which is probably just as well, since people who jump to the conclusion that they must be dealing with devils and demons generate so much fear that the psychic activity quickly intensifies. In fact, as we shall see in Chapter Eighteen, situations that truly require exorcism (which literally draws an invading spirit out of a human body) are extremely few and far between and manifest differently from a poltergeist once we know what we are looking for.

There is some dispute about whether poltergeists attach to places or people. It seems more likely they attach to people, since many manifest suddenly, after a family has been living peacefully in the same house for many years. This suggests that something has changed in the household's dynamic or energies.

Ghosts and chthonic entities however, are different since they are either noticed upon moving into a new property or have been around ever since the occupiers can remember. Previous occupants may have had similar experiences too. This suggests they attach to a place rather than to a person and remain roughly the same no matter who happens to be living there. Ghosts that return to the same place tend to appear only at certain times of the year, on anniversaries of certain events or during specific moon-phases. Months, even years can pass without any activity at all. Hauntings also tend to favour anniversaries of specific events.

The main difference between a ghost and a haunting is that a haunting is virtually identical every time. Ghost that return simply to visit may appear in different parts of the home or behave in different ways although ghosts that are trapped as opposed to visiting tend to be more active and unpredictable in their appearances. People troubled by ghosts and chthonic entities however, usually notice that the first few months of moving into a new home tend to be the most active, as both sides try and adjust to each other's presence.

Dealing with Poltergeists (Part One)

Poltergeists feed off fear, rather like a bad actor playing to the gallery, but once the victim stops being intimidated, its power declines. We see a good example of this from 1845 in the Welsh town of Aberdovey, where a family's home had been troubled with noises for some time. Plates flew across the kitchen and landed on the table without breaking so that eventually (and desperate to get a good night's sleep), the family asked a friend's father to come and sit with them. He arrived, sat downstairs, opened his Bible and started to read. When the noises started up, he ignored them and eventually they stopped and never returned. Local people believed that the man had somehow exorcised them by reading his Bible, although he always insisted that he had simply been preparing a lesson for the local Sunday School.[122]

---

122 Evans (1892): 274

As with any other psychic phenomena that seem to have some sort of guiding intelligence behind them, it's always worth asking if the poltergeist needs any help. If they are only manifesting because they need human aid, and we cannot give it, then we must tell them to go and try someone else. We should never promise things we either cannot, or do not want to do.

There is no single explanation for why a poltergeist will suddenly make its presence known. Down the years people have attributed them to demons, the Devil, ghosts, the jealous dead and even children approaching puberty. Not knowing the cause makes it more difficult to decide the best way to deal with them.

Many people feel they should immediately call in their local priest to perform and exorcism or bless the house. Yet often this makes no difference at all and the poltergeist continues on his merry way. However, since one of our main concerns is to lower the level of fear, if we feel that calling in a local clergyman will put our minds at rest then by all means, we should do it.

Many people, especially those with strong Christian faith feel reassured by blessings and exorcisms. Remember though, that it's unlikely the local priest will rush around and perform an exorcism – this is a specialised field and he may have to refer the matter to a local bishop first who in turn may agree to call in a designated exorcist. Most priests are usually willing to perform a house blessing.

We really do not have to call in an expert, however. It's our home and the poltergeist is disrupting it. We have every right to ask it to leave, just as we would if a human visitor outstayed their welcome and started throwing breakfast cereal around the kitchen and juggling with the cutlery. If we don't have the authority to protect our family and tell the entity to leave, then who does?

We should begin by doing grounding exercises to steady ourselves, then speak to it firmly, stating that these disturbances must stop at once. Remember it is essential to remain calm even if the cushions start dancing round the room. Never show how irritated or afraid we feel. Portray outward calm, always. If anyone of a nervous disposition is present, it is better to ask them to leave. We don't need extra drama.

The poltergeist may well put on a show of defiance and increase its activity, but if we deny it all attention it will eventually fade and disappear. Most poltergeist activities only last a few months anyway, and it is very rare for full-blown attacks to continue much longer than that. Take heart from the fact that a large percentage of poltergeist phenomena are isolated one-off events.

Poltergeists are complex entities; often their energies seem to be entwined with those of living family members. It has been noticed that poltergeists often focus on homes where there are children approaching puberty, or where there is strong emotional or mental stress. Teenagers and young people can generate huge amounts of energy and some people suspect that poltergeist phenomena is due to a combination of raging hormones and teenage *angst*.

Certainly, many young people are fizzing with vitality, and just like some of the other phenomena we have looked at in this chapter, poltergeists both generate and drain energy. They are not really interested in the young person's character or personality at all, which is why poltergeists sometimes suddenly manifest at times of emotional crisis and mental anguish, both situations where our natural energies increase. It is thus quite possible that at least some of the phenomena emanate from people within the home, manifesting as a type of psychokinesis (i.e. when mental and emotional energies can move physical objects.)

Even if we believe there is a poltergeist targeting us or a member of our family, remember that nobody has deliberately caused the phenomena, nor have they somehow 'invited' the poltergeist into their life. The last thing anyone needs at a time like this is victim blaming and leaping to such conclusions only makes things worse. Remember - our home is *not* being invaded by demons, zombies and devils, but if we start believing it is, the fear thus generated will make the problems multiply.

Likewise, if anyone in the household is faking poltergeist phenomena in order to get attention (which has been known) then a calm, matter-of-fact reaction will encourage them to stop it. Inviting the neighbours around to witness a poltergeist showing off is asking for trouble. However, enlisting the help of a sensible friend to make *discreet* notes about what happens will help ensure we remain objective.

What we are looking for are patterns. Do certain phenomena only occur at certain times of the day, or moon-phases? Do they only occur when a certain person is absent/present? If there are any family pets then note their reactions too, in particular whether the poltergeist seems to be targeting or ignoring them.

If there are children or young adults in the home, try - without making too much fuss - to arrange for them to sleep overnight at the house of a friend or relative. Note whether the home remains quiet that night and if so, whether the phenomena followed the child to where they were staying.

It's important however, not to make the child feel the weight of our expectations. If we tell them, 'See if anything happens when you're staying at Aunt Jane's,' then we are planting the seed in their mind that something *should* happen when they stay at their aunt's – and happen it probably will!

Despite what people claim, it's quite difficult to prove whether a child is really the focus of a poltergeist. For example, if the child sleeps away from the home and the phenomena follow her there, then it is indeed more likely that it is the child who is being targeted. However, what if nothing happens, either in our home or wherever the child is staying that night? What does that prove? Absolutely nothing. It can be very frustrating.

Nowadays it is often recommended that a young person who seems to be the focus of poltergeist activities should visit a trained counsellor. The key word here is 'trained.' Very few counsellors believe in poltergeists, much less have any first-hand experience of them. A poorly trained counsellor may do more harm than good, so do be careful with this.

Dealing with Poltergeists (Part Two)

It is essential to remain calm and firm when dealing with a poltergeist. Remember that it has a certain amount of intelligence and will take advantage of our doubts and uncertainties if we let it. What we must do – over and over if necessary – is to explain that this is our home, our family and it is not welcome. Tell it to leave and cease its activities – and sound as though we mean it!

We should keep our statement brief and to the point and be prepared to repeat it while the poltergeist misbehaves. Do keep the theatricals to an absolute minimum. We are not part of the cast of *The Exorcist,* we are simply telling an unwanted visitor to leave. Just be firm and calm. We do not need to wave Bibles or crucifixes about. We say what we have to say and have done with it as soon as the poltergeist is quiet.

It's probably best to prepare what we are going to say in advance and mentally rehearse it, since the poltergeist may well start playing up while we are speaking or very soon afterwards. Although it can be frightening, it's mostly bravado. Despite what Hollywood sometimes claims, poltergeists rarely physically harm the people they torment. All we need is a simple statement, something like, *'We don't like your bad behaviour. You are not welcome here. You must leave now and never come back.'*

It also helps if we visualise our words filling the room or home with brilliant light while we speak. Some people like to visualise white light, others prefer silver, blue or gold. It doesn't really matter, just imagine it as a heavy shower of shining raindrops filling every room, creating an atmosphere of peace and love that will prove intolerable for any self-respecting poltergeist. It will also raise our home's energy levels, countering the poltergeist's chaos and fear with a shower of light and love. Best of all, it will make us feel we are doing something positive.

Even if the poltergeist does not disappear completely, we will have given it a warning. It now knows that *we* have power too and can make it feel uncomfortable and unwelcome. Also, because we draw our authority from a solid source i.e. the protection of our home and family/friends/loved ones, no entity will be able to weaken our resolve. We must keep countering its attacks as often as necessary. Eventually - provided we believe in what we're doing - we will wear it down.

Many people believe we should only use mainstream religious ritual in psychic self defence, such as calling in the local priest or minister, putting up religious pictures and wearing religious symbols.) In my experience, like many other methods of psychic self defence, these work best if we are *already* religious or spiritually inclined, but not if we are just going through the motions or paying lip-service. It must be genuine and sincere.

For many people, it's more effective to act with a sense of righteous anger, because we're protecting our home and family, rather than to pretend to a religious faith we do not actually possess. Also, if the poltergeist has been generated by the energies of someone - living or dead – who in life never had a religious or spiritual bone in their body, or was from a completely different spiritual tradition, then religion-based banishings are unlikely to succeed.

As a general rule, anything we do in psychic self defence must have meaning for *us*. We have to see the power behind any symbols we use, so if, for example, we use the five pointed pentagram, we need to see it as representing authority over the four physical elements, i.e. earth, air, fire and water, together with the fifth element of spirit. This endows us with authority over everything corporeal and ethereal that we may encounter, *but only provided we believe it*. Symbols act as a focus for our mental energies but are not imbued with magical power in their own right: this is something we must do for ourselves.

While the poltergeist's activities continue, remember to continue regularly cleansing the home in order to break up the tension, stress and negativity caused by the attack. Also don't forget other, practical precautions. For example, in our home we once experienced psychic activity that manifested as switching on the microwave (and even setting the timer!).

The first few times this happened I made a point of saying loudly, *'Thank you! But I don't need the microwave at the moment,'* and then switching it off. As a precaution however, we also disconnected the microwave from the electricity supply, just in case it was switched on when nobody was there and caused a fire! When dealing with a poltergeist, we are engaging with an entity that has a certain level of intelligence. It will exploit our weaknesses in any way it can.

Dealing with Chthonic Entities

'Chthonic entities' is a wide collective term that includes fairies, house brownies etc., that seem attach to a particular place. Other names we may come across include the Kobolds or Heinzelmännchen (in Germany); the Nisse (in Norway and Denmark) and the Tomte in Sweden. Generally speaking, a chthonic entity is attached to a particular place rather individuals or families and can be found as far afield as North America and Australia.

Their behaviour varies. Some are helpful and protect us from other entities. Others will drive us up the wall with their practical jokes that are often more spiteful than funny; in fairness however, although we may regard these as 'attacks' they are rarely motivated by malice. These entities often take things especially if they are bright and shiny, for example, small pieces of jewellery, keys, coins etc., and then bring it back later when we're no longer looking for it. If they become very mischievous or feel aggrieved, they will simply take things and not return them.

Obviously, part of the problem stems from the fact we are all occupying the same space with little understanding of what others need. To build a workable relationship there must be some mutual give and take. Years ago, people made food offerings, such as honey, cream or even mead. (In Wales however, the fairies were insulted if they were offered alcohol although this attitude might have owed more to the nineteenth century Welsh Temperance Movement than the wishes of the fairies themselves!)

Brownies and hobs enjoy some human contact and sharing one's home with them was generally considered lucky. As with the fairies, leaving a bowl of sweet milk or a small honey cake out for the House Brownie is a time-honoured way of showing appreciation.

Personally, I don't feel it's right to try and banish such entities unless their behaviour is making our lives intolerable. After all, they have as much right to be here as we do. Normally we can all co-exist peacefully with a little mutual respect, so it's important we don't become too angry with their antics, while at the same time we shouldn't be afraid to ask them for help. The Gentle Folk – or whatever name we choose to bestow on them – are surprisingly hi-tech at times, able to use computers, electrical equipment and even ATM machines! Remember to thank them if they have done something kind, no matter how small it is.

Of course, there may be times when their activities put us at some risk, for example, if they persistently hide our house keys, or play with our smoke alarms. Traditionally there are two options – flattery and coercion. Flattery is usually better, because we don't really want to lose our House Brownie, otherwise all our luck will leave too!

Of course, occasionally people are determined to bid farewell to their House Brownie, either because they feel it should be set free or because they really cannot bear living in close proximity to it anymore. Years ago, in Scotland and its borders, people would give a suit of clothes to their House Brownie in order to persuade it to go. In Lincolnshire however, the opposite held good, and leaving out a fine white linen smock ensured that the brownie would continue to help the farm and home throughout the coming year. Leaving them gifts of food also encouraged them to remain.

Of course, another method is to just sit and talk to them. We may not be able to see or hear them, although they can certainly see and hear us, so it's important to be sincere. We need to find somewhere where we can be undisturbed for a few minutes and speak to them using the same pitch and tone of voice as we would when speaking to a friend. Explain that we're sure they don't mean any harm, and are happy to share our space with them, but we really would be much happier if they stopped whatever activity is causing the problem.

Address them respectfully, perhaps even as *sigewif* which literally means the 'victory dames' a term normally reserved for the Valkyrie (although obviously we're *not* dealing with the Valkyrie here). Sometimes it is helpful to add that we haven't meant to offend them and would like to put things right. Perhaps leave them an offering that evening, again saying aloud that we want to be friends, that we understand that they like playing jokes, but that some of their tricks are causing us problems and we would really appreciate it if they stopped.

What we are trying to do is impress upon them that there is plenty of space for us all to co-exist peacefully. To keep things on an even keel, chat to them often and don't forget to thank them for any kindnesses. Once they are appreciated, House Brownies can be the most helpful of residents!

There is another type of chthonic entity which usually cannot be identified by a single name. This type is basically an earth spirit or entity, bound or trapped in a specific place, often connected with the element of water, particularly wells, springs and underground watercourses. These often act as a conduit for paranormal activity, thus becoming a magnet for any psychic phenomena or energies that happen to be nearby.

If it's any consolation, chthonic entities are tied to places and not people, which means that if we move to a new home it is unlikely to come with us. If they ever do move, it's usually to follow a source of water, either above or below ground. Very rarely do they travel far. Once they have been in existence for a while, they tend to be rather brittle and static anyway.

Chthonic entities often lurk in cellars, or anywhere they are unlikely to be disturbed which will include unused rooms, cupboards or even under the stairs. Occasionally they cluster in lofts, roof spaces and attic rooms. Although they can often be found in very old houses, the age of the house is not really all that relevant. I once knew someone who encountered a chthonic entity in a brand-new home. Upon investigation the site turned out to have an underground watercourse running beneath it, so it had probably been at the site for a long time.

Although they tend to be rather sluggish and produce a noticeably heavy and dark atmosphere, given time a chthonic entity can become extremely powerful. If our personal space is ever affected by one of these entities, we will notice a high level of very varied psychic disturbance, together with astronomical electricity bills. Batteries in torches and similar appliances will suddenly go dead. Because they are so dense and heavy, these entities need a constant source of energy and we also may notice 'cold spots' as they even siphon off the warmth from their surrounding atmosphere. Constantly hungry, they feed off people's energies too, and we often notice that those sharing their home with a chthonic entity suffer fatigue, low energy levels and persistent chronic health problems.

These entities also feed on other people's fears and emotions and we may notice a higher than normal level of arguments, petty squabbles, and even shared dreams (especially unpleasant ones). Animals are especially susceptible to the presence of chthonic entities. Often, they will react as though something is nearby that frightens or antagonises them even though we can't see what it is. Cats arch their backs, their tails standing up like a bottle brush, while dogs growl and the fur along their spine stands erect.

Much as we might like to ignore a chthonic entity and hope it will just leave us in peace, this is exactly what it wants. Left alone it will grow bigger, more demanding and start to attract similarly minded thought forms. Although a chthonic entity is *not* a thought form, the two often seem to go together. To counter it, do some thorough cleansing, (Chapters Ten and Twelve) paying particular attention to the methods for breaking up negativity in Chapter Thirteen. If we notice that the entity starts to drain us whenever we try to shift it, we will need to approach it bearing a psychic shield, and in more extreme cases, a psychic sword, to show we mean business. (Chapter Nine)

The best place to start is in those areas where the cold spots and unpleasant atmosphere are the most noticeable. Don't be surprised if it is necessary to repeat the exercises several times, since chthonic entities tend to be very hard to shift. If we feel it is damaging our own health or well-being, place purifying herbs or oils into our bath water and treat it as a ritual, cleansing bath. We should also use the exercises for sealing the Aura in Chapter Nine. Once we notice a real improvement in the atmosphere, we can perform a simple house blessing (see Chapter Fourteen). Never be tempted to perform a house blessing in lieu of proper cleansing however: blessing a chthonic entity is like putting a band-aid on a broken leg. It is simply not enough.

Chthonic entities usually focus on a single dwelling although occasionally we encounter unpleasant manifestations that appear to cover an entire area, usually connected by underground streams, or geological features. If such entities are infesting a whole area, we will usually hear rumours that our neighbours are experiencing similar phenomena, although some will be more willing to talk about this than others. Shared phenomena over several households almost always suggests a chthonic entity, sometimes combined with a thought form or two.

Obviously this wider-ranging entity will be more difficult to deal with unless those affected by it are willing to band together and work as a group. However, we can certainly keep cleansing our own space and get rid of our own share of the problem. It may not solve the problem for the area but it will at least reduce the difficulties in our own home. Sometimes we just must accept that is the best we are likely to achieve.

CHAPTER TWELVE

Creating our own rituals. Attacks and defences using the elements. Candles, incense, consecrating salt, using it with vinegar or blessed water. Making a simple herb brush.

At its simplest, a ritual is a statement of intention. We could say, *'I will cleanse this room,'* because that is what we intend doing at some point in the future. However, for our purposes it is better to say, *'I cleanse this room,'* since this is what we are doing now, in the present. To expand the ritual we can then add more words, hand gestures, candles or incense etc.

People sometimes feel uncomfortable with hand gestures, perhaps because we so rarely use them in everyday speech. However, there is no mystery about them, they simply reinforce our thoughts, will and intention. What matters is that the gesture should feel appropriate and meaningful to us. We should never let people tell us that moving our hand to the right instead of to the left will negate the entire ritual. It won't.

Some gestures are just common sense. To indicate 'stop' 'halt' or 'go back' (all useful in banishing and cleansing), raise the hand with the palm facing outwards. Remember that our intention (in this case 'stop' or 'go back') is the focal point of what we're doing, and the rest of the ritual should be built around this. To develop our ritual still further we can light candles or incense. For psychic self defence we can set out some consecrated salt at our shrine or working area but remember that it doesn't keep very well, so make a fresh batch when required. Consecrated salt is useful to throw at anything that suddenly tries to threaten us. (Instructions for making our own are given on page 230).

Some feel that rituals should only be conducted at a purpose-made altar. With psychic self defence however, we must take our ritual to wherever the threat is strongest. This could include the attic, cellar or even the bathroom. A small portable altar (on a tea tray for example) is practical for this, but not essential. Just be flexible and prepared to improvise. The secret of ritual is that in order to feel comfortable with it, that it should mean something to us, and that we believe in its power.

We can incorporate a number of other things into our rituals, too, such as incense, candles, blessed water, onions, garlic, kitchen herbs and bells. Even if we must purchase some of these, they are relatively inexpensive and easily available. (Small bells often turn up in charity shops!)

It is not necessary to spend a lot of money on this: even though we might prefer to use rock or sea salt from the local delicatessen, remember that ordinary table salt will do the job just as well, and a humble tea light is every bit as effective as an expensive scented candle. We can burn common kitchen herbs for incense, while blessed water is simply tap water that we bless for our own use.

As a guideline, remember that most attacks will use one or more of the four basic elements: water, fire, air and earth. Each has its own distinctive properties and these influence how the attack will manifest. Ether or spirit, sometimes called the 'fifth element' can control all the others, which is why visualisation skills are so important in psychic self defence. Strip away the candles, incense, etc., and what we are really doing is pitting our own mind and willpower against that of our attacker.

Mostly it comes down to common sense. For example, many attacks are sent via the medium of water, so I always advise anyone who feels under an active psychic attack to avoid going anywhere near the sea, lakes and rivers (and even bridges!). Likewise, if we feel the attack comes via the element of air, then avoid high mountains, cliffs and multi-storey car parks. If the attack emanates from the earth avoid tunnels and cellars. Needless to say, fire is something most people generally avoid anyway, but should one occur near Bonfire Night (November 5th) or any other fire festival, then stay away from the flames.

Remember too, that if an attack comes from outside our home, we must protect everyone and everything we care about which includes pets such as rabbits or chickens in outdoor hutches. It's easy to forget that they too can be caught in the fall-out of a psychic attack. Fortunately, it usually only takes a few extra moments to include them in our psychic defences, and we can always visualise extra protection such as walls or high barriers for them during the day or just before bedtime. Alternatively hang a protective talisman or plant on their runs and hutches etc.

Attacks Using the Element of Water

Since ancient times, water has been associated with magical and psychic attacks. One old tradition says that if we cross water in the dark, we should spit three times to protect ourselves against '*evil spirits and witches.*' In some countries, such as Greece, it's still considered lucky to spit on children. This may be a type of water offering, since dehydration is a common symptom in psychic attacks.

Water conducts psychic energies quickly and easily, and underground streams may sometimes bring an attack to our door before we're even aware anything is wrong. Theoretically, if we can change the direction of a flow of water which is conducting the attack, then we can physically turn the attack away from us. This is easier said than done however, unless we are willing and able to dig ditches and drainage channels. Even then, the local Council and the Water Board would almost certainly object if we did this on public land. It may therefore be better to concentrate on neutralising the attack instead.

One of the easiest methods of defusing attacks conveyed via the element of water is to add a small amount of salt to the water. This is easy if the water source is visible and accessible, but if it is several feet underground our best option is to bury the salt in the earth above wherever we suspect the water is flowing. Salt dissolves very easily in water and damp ground, so it will seep down into the flowing water and counteract the hex.

Some people make a great ritual out of this, others just bury the salt, say, '*That'll put a stop to your games,*' and have done with it. There are no hard and fast rules. Do whatever feels right. For example, we could say something like, '*With this salt I clear all ill wishing, all evil and all hexes that are carried here by water. I bless these waters, may they bring only good things to everything and everyone they touch.*' In this way not only are we neutralising the hex, we are also turning the water into a source of blessings.

Blessing Water

There is no real mystery about blessing water. People have been doing it for years, until organised religions took it over and claimed it for their own. All we need do is stretch out our hand, palm downwards above the surface of the water we are going to use and say, *'I bid you be blessed,'* or *'May this water bless and protect all it touches.'*

A small pinch of salt is traditional when blessing water although people have relied on other additions. I once knew a priest whose parishioners pestered him endlessly for holy water because they believed he somehow gave it the 'odour of sanctity.' Although he always protested this was simply due to storing the ready-blessed 'Holy Water' in empty bottles of mouthwash, the stories persisted for many years!

Attacks using the Element of Earth

These attacks not only include infestations of insects and animals, but also anything that manifests with the intention of being seen. Some are quite bizarre and do not seem to be based on real creatures at all. Thought form attacks (if we can actually see them) are a good example of attacks using the element of Earth and so is the Night Mare. One of the earliest warning signs of any attack using the element of Earth are infestations by a combination of spectral and real animals, birds and insects. Sometimes it's difficult to tell which are real and which have been magically summoned, since spectral animals often seem to attract their real-life counterparts.

Often the best defence to a really serious attack is a combination of magical and everyday methods (e.g. rat poison, fly spray). Unless the problem is *very* severe, use these moderately and always follow the instructions. A salt barrier (literally a trail or scattering of salt) is still one of the best methods I know to deter psychic infestations but if the attack is already under way, look at the suggestions in Chapter Fourteen.

Consecrating Salt

Salt has been used to purify and preserve for many centuries and we still sometimes throw salt over our shoulder to ward off evil. Salt is also useful to help keep anything out that wants to get in, giving us some useful breathing space so we can deal with what's already present before tackling the next stage of the attack.

Although we tend to think of salt as part of the element of earth, strictly speaking it is closer to the element of water, since it comes from the sea. Even rock salt does not come from rocks, but from salt deposits left by ancient seas. The salt mines in Cheshire, UK, for example, were created two hundred million years ago, when Britain was an inland sea surrounded by desert near the Equator.[123]

Salt is a good standby in an attack via any of the elements. It can be combined with water, sprinkled on fire (though it sometimes 'spits' and too much will extinguish the flame altogether) or even included (in tiny amounts) in incense ingredients. It can also be placed in small dishes to guard and protect any room that is troubled by psychic phenomena.

While water is often blessed before use (although it *can* be consecrated), salt and vinegar are usually consecrated. There is a small but important difference between blessing and consecration: a blessing wishes good things upon the recipient, but if we consecrate something it is empowered towards a specific use. For example, if we consecrate a particular knife for cutting herbs, then use it only for that purpose and not for cutting a birthday cake. In an emergency however, if we really must use it for another purpose then make sure it is properly cleansed afterwards, before reconsecrating or rededicating it.

To consecrate anything, we need to be clear what we want to achieve. Although many people still believe there must be special words and incantations for consecration, it's best to keep things as simple as possible. Remember that it's what goes on in the mind that brings power to an object or ritual. We can pronounce all the

---

[123] https://www.onlinerocksalt.co.uk/knowledge-base/salt-basics/what-is-rock-salt

wonderful magical spells in the world, but if our mind is drifting off somewhere else, wondering whether the kettle has boiled or the washing machine has finished its cycle, then it will be useless!

Now to practical matters. We are unlikely to need an entire packet of consecrated salt, so it's better to consecrate little and often as and when we need it. Pour a little into a small dish (even a spoonful in an empty egg cup will do) and stretch one hand over it with the palm facing downwards. As we have seen, it doesn't really matter what words we use – what's important is to state the purpose clearly, leaving no room for doubt. Any of the following should suit our purpose perfectly well:

- *'Salt, I consecrate you to cleanse this space/room/house* (or whatever seems appropriate) *and disperse all evil and negative energies.'*

Alternatives include:

- *'May this salt be sacred and blessed and may it protect…'* [here name whoever or whatever we feel needs protection].

- *'I consecrate this salt for the purpose of driving away all who wish me harm.'*

- *'I consecrate this salt, to cleanse this house/room/space, and free it from all baneful energies and influences.'*

- *'I consecrate this salt and make it sacred for the purposes of psychic self-defence.'*

If we prefer to invoke a deity, say something like , *'In the name of _____ I consecrate this salt for the purpose of banishing the entities/forces that threaten me and my family.'*
Or *'O _______* [name of deity] *consecrate this salt and empower it to do my bidding.'*

While we speak, visualise the salt cleansing the space leaving it fresh clean and wholesome again. It may sound simple, but that's basically all we need do.

The more effort we put into something, the more special it feels, so it becomes easier to visualise. Although it's not essential, I'm going to suggest some ways to enlarge this ritual of consecrating salt.

For example, we might decide to clear a space, visualise it being clean and then light a candle or tea light, or perhaps some incense before consecrating our salt. I often place my right hand, palm downwards, above the salt, sometimes moving the hand in a clockwise direction as I speak. The words can remain the same.

A wand can also be used to consecrate the salt. Simply tap the container of salt on the rim three times (or any multiple of three) after speaking the words consecration suggested on the previous page. Sometimes I tap the dish three times, give it a third of a turn clockwise, tap it three more times, and then give it another third of a turn clockwise and tap three times again. These actions help turn a simple procedure into a ritual while at the same time helping to focus and strengthen our intentions. This is where the real strength of all ritual lies, not in what we do or say, but in how we keep our minds focused on the task in hand.

It is important that we only perform ritual actions if we feel they have meaning for us. There is no point in following someone else's guidelines if we don't understand them. For example, at home I regularly light a tea light in front of a small ornament of a seated goddess. If I am consecrating salt, I generally do this in front of the statue and the lit candle because I find that the combination of light, deity and ritual helps me concentrate better on what I'm doing. By thinking about what I'm going to do, and observing the light, salt and statue as I'm working, I can keep my mind on my intention.

Don't worry about the colour of the candles, the type of incense, tools or robes we use. They don't matter as much as some would have us believe and are really only aids to the force of our will. That said, if these things are important to us, (and they often are, especially for beginners), then they *will* make a difference simply because getting them 'wrong' distracts and makes us doubt ourselves. They are not essential however, and I rarely use more than my bare hands, a few herbs and a plain tea light.

Once we have consecrated the salt, we can consecrate some ordinary brown vinegar. It's exactly the same procedure, with just a few changes to the words. Then mix the two together, and say something like, *'May this consecrated salt and this consecrated vinegar prove more powerful than the sum of its parts, and may it restore peace and happiness to my home and/or banish the entities/forces that threaten me and my family.'*

Leave the mixture on a shelf or somewhere it will not be disturbed for a few days, so it can absorb negative energies. Repeat as often as necessarily, but each time we're ready to dispose of the old mixture, we should make a point of thanking it. A simple, *'Thank you and bless you for keeping us safe,'* will do nicely. Then pour it into the earth, saying, *'Salt and vinegar return to the earth from whence you came, and be at peace with my blessings.'*

Another way to use salt is to scatter it as a protective barrier, for example, around our home, desk or car. We can consecrate it first if we prefer and this is one time when we shall need to consecrate larger amounts. Make sure there is enough to set up the entire barrier in a single attempt – we don't want to have to stop what we're doing to consecrate more salt and then pick up from where we left off!

Although the basic method of consecrating salt for a barrier remains the same, we can add an extra statement such as, *'May this salt be sacred and blessed. May no evil intention cross any line made with this salt.'* As we strew the salt, remember to make clear exactly what we require it to do, for example, *'Protect my home/car/desk; Those who wish me harm may not cross this barrier; may no evil intention cross this consecrated line of salt.'*

Then, taking the consecrated salt we walk the boundaries of our home/room/car or whatever needs protecting, sprinkling the salt as we go, saying *'Blessed be all those I love, blessed be this place. Let no evil cross this barrier of salt, as I will so must it be.'*

It helps if we get quite a good rhythm going with this, and really put some energy into it. While we scatter the salt we should visualise the attacker being driven back behind the line. Remember that whatever we do in the physical world affects the magical worlds that exist all around us – and vice versa.

I was once given some very wise magical advice: say what you want to do, say what you are doing and then finally, say what you have done. It might seem like overkill but it concentrates the mind wonderfully when casting spells.

If we don't have any salt then we can substitute either an incense stick or blessed water to create the barrier. We can consecrate the incense just as we did the salt, and then light it and carry it around the area that needs protecting, adapting the words given above, for example, *'Let no evil cross this barrier of sacred incense/blessed water,'* etc.

If we use blessed water, we can dip our fingers in it and flick them so that the droplets are scattered. However, this can be rather unpleasant on a freezing cold January day, so instead make a herb brush by dipping a sprig of any evergreen or aromatic plant into the water. Suitable protective plants include box, laurel, rosemary, lavender, mint or sage. Then we simply flick the sprig as we work so that the water spatters, and the droplets will perform the same function as the scattered salt. Obviously if using blessed water indoors, do take extra care anywhere near electrical equipment and sockets.

Please don't be put off doing this sort of work for yourself. It's not as difficult as it sounds but I know many people still feel they would be happier if someone else did it for them. However, defending ourselves and those we love is *our* job. Nobody else's, because no-one else will ever protect us as effectively as we can protect ourselves.

Plants can be used in various ways in psychic self defence. We can heat them in water (rather like making tea) or burn them as incense that can be used to deal with attacks via any of the elements. Other ways to use them include placing some sliced garlic or a halved onion in a dish in any room where there is psychic disturbance.

We can also use leeks or shallots cut into thin slices in the same way and some people swear by placing slices of lemon on the windowsill. I was always taught there should be enough sliced onions to cover a tea plate (alternatively try three cloves of garlic with the cut side uppermost.) Although some people might feel that garlic smells just as bad as anything sent in a psychic attack, it is a powerful, protective plant that can deal with a wide range of psychic phenomena and protect us while we sleep.

If we use sliced onions, garlic, etc., they must be changed every day while the attack is active. Ideally dispose of them by burning, although quite apart from the smell, very few houses still have open fires. An outdoor fire, perhaps in a small garden waste incinerator could be used instead. Alternatively, put the used plant matter into a plastic bag with some salt and tie the top of the bag or tape it down before disposing of it in the household refuse. It is important to remove it right away from us as soon as possible, so don't be tempted to compost any plants or vegetables used in psychic self defence!

Attacks by Air and Fire

Just as we saw how water and earth may often be linked in psychic attacks, so air and fire may be similarly associated. One of the first signs of an attack conveyed via the element of air is often a really revolting stench that resembles drains, rotting flesh or sewage. To combat these, we use the element of air in the form of incense.

This method has been used since ancient times, working on the principle that a strong foul smell should be replaced with a strong pleasant one. At one time, the early Church wanted to ban the use of incense because it was closely associated with pagan ceremonies. Eventually they relented and incorporated incense into Christian rituals where it has remained ever since.

There are several ways to burn incense. Joss sticks are ready-made, easily available and inexpensive. The only drawback is that the fragrance is pre-set and cannot be changed. Also they do not burn for long, although this can be an advantage if we are in a hurry. Contrary to what some people insist, there is no 'correct' incense for this type of work. We should be guided by our noses and choose something fairly pungent but pleasant!

One alternative to joss sticks is to burn incense on charcoal blocks. We can either mix our own incense or buy a ready prepared mixture. We can even burn dried herbs such as rosemary or sage from our kitchen spice rack.

To burn solid incense requires some sort of heatproof container since the charcoal (available as small, ready-made discs) will become very hot. It is slightly trickier to light solid charcoal than it is to light a joss stick. The safest method I have found is to grip the charcoal disc in a pair of kitchen tongs and hold it in a candle flame. It may spit and send a shower of hot sparks so be careful. When it gets hot, the black charcoal will start to glow red and when almost half the disc is glowing, place it in the heat proof container. We can then sprinkle dried herbs or small pieces of suitable plant matter onto the charcoal. Although white sage is very popular nowadays, I like to use rosemary, cedar woodchips, lavender, bay and juniper berries. We can also add some solid incense to the block. Frankincense and myrrh are both excellent for this, although benzoin is probably the cheapest.

When we become more accustomed to using this sort of incense it's quite easy to make our own mixtures, grinding up the resin, leaves, berries, bark etc., in a pestle and mortar, perhaps adding a tiny pinch of salt, wine or honey and sealing the mixture in a small, airtight jar. In the early days it's wise to experiment, adding ingredients to the charcoal block separately and seeing which ones are the most effective for our purpose.

Incense should be lit in the room where it will be used, since unless we manage to obtain a thurible, which is basically a container on a chain and designed to allow incense to be carried around, solid incense is better kept in one place. If several rooms need clearing then begin with the most severely affected first, and then deal with each one gradually in turn. Otherwise we might be better off carrying a joss stick instead. Bear in mind that the incense and charcoal produce gales of smoke, so it's not the sort of thing we can do without anyone else in the house noticing and it will almost certainly set off the smoke alarms.

While burning incense, we need to visualise the fragrant smoke driving back the psychic attack, cleansing and purifying everything. The following prompts, either said aloud or to ourselves, may be helpful:

- *'As this incense burns to ashes, so may all evil/harmful intentions also turn to ashes and be scattered on the four winds.'*

- *'May the smoke of this incense cleanse everything it touches, drive out all harmful intentions, repel psychic attacks and leave my home cleansed and me/my family/those I love free from harm, and free from the threat of all harm.'*

Incense can be burned both as a defence against an active attack and as a preventative against future ones. Use it in any room that is particularly troubled by the psychic attack and also, if possible, in the hallway, which often picks up a wide range of psychic influences from outside.

Incense is useful in magical cleansing since it reaches hard-to-get-at areas, and traditionally it was believed to act as a go-between for Mother Earth and the gods. Don't forget that when we burn incense, we are showing our attacker that we are willing and able to fight back. In psychic self defence where so much is concentrated on mental focus, this gives us a real advantage. We are no longer passive victims but can turn the situation around and wrest back control.

Using Candles

Psychic attacks often intensify as it grows dark, and winter attacks can be particularly trying since it grows dark so early! With the dark mornings and short hours of daylight, it's very easy to feel like a mole at that time of year. Lighting candles not only acts as a warm and welcoming focal point but also reminds us that the dark (whether it's the early evenings or the metaphorical darkness that accompanies a psychic attack) is only temporary.

Since candles bring light to dark places, they are useful wherever psychic attacks manifest as aural and visual disturbances and also if we have no idea who our attacker is. When using a single candle, try and envisage a small ritual because striking a match is so quick that it's all over and done with before we know it. For example, as we put the candle into its holder, we should explain what we intend to do; I have set out a rough guide as follows:

Begin by saying, *'As I light this candle, may its light drive back the power of those who wish me ill/harm.'* Then as we strike the match, say something like, *'This candle flame burns bright and clear against your darkness. You cannot pass. I send you back.'*

Next, as we hold the flame to the candle's wick, we should visualise it burning the attacker. Don't be afraid to make this vivid; some people visualise smoke, flames and even smell singed clothes!

One word of caution however: although we can burn a candle in any room wherever there is a need for protection, I would not recommend it in any place where a poltergeist is active since they seem particularly drawn to the element of fire and sometimes like to set fires of their own. They don't need any encouragement.

Fire can be very unpredictable which is why we must take basic safety precautions with it every single time. Although candle flames usually burn down without much fuss, as an element, fire can manifest as anything from a sudden, intense flash, to a more subtle, smouldering glow.

In psychic self defence, candles are useful because even a fairly small one takes several hours to burn down, thus helping to keep our intention focused during that period. Obviously, we will not be able to concentrate on our intention solidly for hours on end but every time we glance over at the candle flame it will remind us. Symbolically the burning flame keeps our magical intention alight and active even if our concentration wanders!

We can use many different types of candles, including tea lights and even candles for birthday cakes (which are particularly useful if we cannot spare the time to sit in the room for several hours.) Nor need our candles be any specific colour; although some people prefer black ones for banishing, they aren't essential and personally I find ordinary white household ones, along with tea lights and even birthday candles will do just as well.

That said, some people find that coloured candles help them visualise. For example, a blue candle might remind us of a great blue wave coming and washing away the attacker, while a pink candle might be a shaft of pink light that envelops the attacker in so much love than he/she is rendered powerless. A red candle left over from Christmas could be visualised as a great ring of fire that protects us from all harm.

These are only suggestions but whatever we use we must ensure it is positioned safely and never leave it unattended. There is no point in protecting ourselves against psychic attack only to go and burn our home down!

Using Bells and Sound

Bells have always been one of my favourite methods of magical cleansing. They are quick and simple to use especially if we have several rooms to cleanse because we can walk around while ringing them. It's a good method to use whenever the attack is generated using the element of air, especially against aural disturbances and foul smells.

In the ancient world, ghosts, spirits and demons were said to have an aversion to metal, especially iron and bronze (both of which make excellent bells). In fact, ringing bells in church before a service was originally intended as a protective measure and not just to urge the congregation to hurry up!

The simple rule of thumb when using bells for psychic self defence is that the smaller the bell, the more we need to ring it. However, a large bell can be very heavy, especially if we need to carry it around. Ideally whatever size we choose should have a pleasant sound, and the clapper should move freely inside so that it is easy to ring. A cracked bell doesn't ring, it just makes a flat, dull thud which is useless for magical cleansing. When we've finished ringing it, stretch out our hand afterwards and if we've done our work well, we should feel the air tingling, especially around our fingertips.

As with any sort of cleansing, when using a bell we must state our purpose either mentally or aloud, just as we did when sprinkling blessed water or salt.

- *As I ring this bell, I cleanse this room.*

- *As I ring this bell I send back all those that wish me/us harm. You are not welcome here, I drive you back.*

We can also adapt any of the other statements mentioned this chapter.

If we carry a bell around with us, then ring it at doors, hearths and windows – all places of coming and going - or at the four corners of a room, home or garden. Wherever the problem seems most noticeable, that's where we ring our bell. For example, if we notice a terrible smell in one room, we should ring the bell there; if the problem is our car then we first ring the bell as we walk around it and then ring it inside. Of course, this may be feasible if we have a driveway or garage but embarrassing if we're parked in a busy street. In this case it might be better to set up a discreet, protective circle of salt around the car. If the area is reasonably quiet, we can sit in the car with the doors closed and ring our bell (a small bell will be quite sufficient.)

Bells are one of the easiest methods of magical cleansing; the only drawback is that there is no way of hiding the noise, so if we share our home with others and don't want them to know what we're doing, we'll have to wait until they've gone out. (Wind chimes are not a substitute, because ringing a bell is a deliberate act with a specific *intention* and effort behind it, whereas wind chimes simply move and sound randomly in response to the breeze).

However, if matters are urgent and we cannot find a suitable bell, then a chiming clock that strikes the hours can be used instead. Unlike wind chimes, clocks can be set to chime at a precise time, which means we have some control over them. All we then need to do is ensure we are ready to perform the cleansing at the moment when the bell strikes. Simply state our intention to magically cleanse the room, for example, *'May these chimes strike against all those that wish me/us harm. I drive you back and cleanse this space/room/home.'* It requires close attention to the timing but can be very effective if done properly.

Another traditional method of driving out unpleasant energies is something called 'rough music' where we bang cooking tins, saucepans or even bottles with a wooden spoon to make a noise. Back in 1842, in Barmouth, North Wales, a house was plagued with a very noisy poltergeist. Witnesses reported that it sounded as though all the china was being smashed although there were never any breakages (which is often a sure sign that a poltergeist is responsible.) A local conjuror was called in but failed to stop it. (Conjuror used to be another term for exorcist. The idea of a conjuror being a stage magician only came much later.)

Eventually the family could stand it no longer and went to stay with relatives for some peace and quiet. The poltergeist seems to have accompanied them, for as soon as they arrived the noises started up again. The children however, refused to be intimidated, shouting that they would make as much noise as the spirit. They took sticks and started hammering the floors, doors, tables and tin kettles until the poltergeist was finally silenced. Afterwards they admitted they didn't feel as brave as they had pretended, but it did the trick; the family were never disturbed after that night and were able to return home next day.[124]

Although these events took place over a hundred and sixty years ago, the magical principles remain faultless. The poltergeist hadn't cracked so much as a plate, but its activities were harmful because it never allowed the family to rest. The children fought back using sound as a weapon against the 'noisy ghost.'

Just as sweet-smelling incense drives out foul smells that are part of psychic attack, so sound can be used very effectively against attacks that manifest using noise. The story from Barmouth also shows how determined we need to be; there can be no wishy-washy half measures. Psychic self defence can be quite strenuous and leave us feeling exhausted. As a general guide the following may be useful:

- For attacks using the element of Earth – i.e. those that can be seen - use salt, or tapping the ground with a pole (see Chapter Fourteen).

---

[124] Evans (1892): 275

- For attacks using the element of Air - foul smells and noises - use incense, bells, sound and candles. The latter brings light to dark shadowy places, which are after all, insubstantial, which is a typical attribute of Air.

- For attacks using the element of Water - especially if they affect our emotions - use blessed water and salt.

- For attacks using the element of Fire - those that are sudden and intense usually come under this element - use incense, and also blessed water and/or salt (because on a physical level both can extinguish fire). We can also use candles but should avoid these if dealing with a poltergeist.

We are also free to adapt any of the above to suit our own circumstances. Not everyone can use incense, landlords in particular don't take kindly to it and it will set off our smoke alarms. Also, not everyone likes using candles or feels safe around them. There is plenty to choose from so we shouldn't be afraid to experiment until we find something that works for us.

Problems while Cleansing

The solutions in this book may seem simple, but they are supported by sound magical principles and *will* work. It is true however, that occasionally we may encounter some resistance. Rest assured that this is rarely as dramatic as we see in Hollywood films, but it can still be unnerving, and in the early days, when we lack confidence, it can be very unsettling, unless we are prepared for it.

The most common problem we are likely to encounter is the feeling that something is trying to prevent us cleansing the space. For example, one day I was burning incense as part of a cleansing ritual only to find that the charcoal block I was using, which had been stored in an airtight container and was as dry as a biscuit, simply would not burn. It's easy to panic in a situation like this, imagining there is some demon with damp breath lurking in the corner. And of course, if we panic we'll start imagining all the wrong things. It's strange that even people who find it nearly impossible to visualise anything seem to have no problem imagining all sorts of devils and demons the moment things start going wrong!

If this happens, remember we must not to allow ourselves to be swayed from our purpose. We try another charcoal block, if we have one, and if we don't then we can burn a joss stick. If that doesn't work then just hold a piece of incense or sprig of dried rosemary in a candle flame using a pair of kitchen tongs, or pick up a bell and ring that instead. We can even copy the children in North Wales and bang a stick on the floor. The important thing is not to be intimidated. If one method doesn't work, we must keep trying alternatives until we find something that does.

I've even known the dense energies of a psychic attack to interfere when I was using a bell to clear a room. I'd used this bell many times before without any problems, only to find that suddenly it would not ring. Now bells are simple mechanisms and there is very little that can go wrong with them. Obviously if the bell is cracked, all we will hear is a dull thud. But when I tapped the bell with a spoon it rang true, and when I turned it upside down the clapper was still moving freely. Nevertheless, when I tried to ring it again, there was still no sound.

Using a vigorous combination of spoon, shaking the bell and pushing the clapper with my fingers I persisted. After a few more nerve-wracking minutes, the bell did begin to ring again and has never given me any problems since.

However, it taught me a valuable lesson: always persevere, no matter how much the odds seem stacked against us. Just be persistent and prepared to improvise if necessary. For example, just before the bell started ringing again, I'd made up my mind to go down to the kitchen to fetch a saucepan and a wooden spoon and if those hadn't worked, I planned to bang a shoe on the floor. To be good at psychic defence we need to think flexibly.

Of course, it is one thing to be prepared but quite another to dwell on potential problems too much because that inserts the seed of doubt in our minds, something that has a nasty habit of turning into a self-fulfilling prophecy. It is vital that we keep telling ourselves that we *can* defeat whatever is causing the problems. We are stronger, braver and more resourceful than our attacker.

I have every confidence in you. Have confidence in yourself.

CHAPTER THIRTEEN

Dealing with negativity; the difference between negativity and a psychic attack. Methods of banishing. Using a staff, pole of brush to break up persistent negativity.

The presence of negativity, no matter how unpleasant, does not always indicate a psychic attack. However, we cannot totally ignore it because it can have adverse effects on our emotional and physical wellbeing, damaging our Aura and making us vulnerable to all sorts of attacks but especially from thought forms.

The difference between negativity and a genuine psychic attack is basically a question of scale. A good comparison would be a crime such as shoplifting. It is wrong certainly, and it is illegal. But would we place it in the same category as armed robbery? Of course not. Yet although negativity may not start out as a very serious matter, it can act as a magnet for more of the same and eventually when it grows big - or bad - enough, these energies become very harmful indeed.

It is the same with many crimes: often the evil deeds that shock society to the core have been preceded by a catalogue of smaller acts, which if not criminal are certainly marked by the presence of sadism and/or spite. Obviously, not all petty criminals turn into evil monsters and in the same way, not every patch of negativity will turn into a psychic attack. Even so, if we deal with it swiftly and decisively, we shall be doing ourselves a favour.

Another problem with negativity is that it gets everywhere. Clean it up and it comes back again, turn our backs for a day and there it is. We cannot just banish negativity and have done with it once and for all; we must work at it on a regular basis. Even if we are not frequently dealing with negative people and situations, we should aim to psychically cleanse our homes, workspaces and even our modes of travel (bike, scooter, car, etc.) on average every 3 -6 months just as a preventative measure. If we use public transport, cleansing ourselves once a week may be necessary and always after any unpleasant incidents.

If we must deal with negativity on a near constant basis (at home, school or work, for example) then be prepared to cleanse regularly for some time, (i.e. months), before seeing results. Once the negativity has departed, it is a good precaution to continue cleansing once a month for a while to discourage its return.

The biggest problem with negativity is its sheer persistence. It seems to keep returning no matter what we do, and this is often because we cannot avoid contact with the people who are causing the problem in the first place. The perfect solution would be to cut all contact with them, or at least minimise it. However, if the negativity is caused by a close family member or work colleague, this may not be practical. All the same, we should try to drastically curtail contact with them so far as possible.

Understanding what such people do is half the battle. For example, some people constantly try to bait us, winding us up just to watch us go. We feel trapped in a vicious circle of provocation and reaction. The best response to this is what I call 'blanket politeness' where we simply smile but refuse to react. Note however, that blanket politeness is not the same as putting on a brave face while seething inwardly, because that does us no good at all. We need to really blank them out completely in order to prevent them pushing their own negative attitudes onto us.

It's surprising how quickly this method works to prevent any more negativity from entering the situation. Left unchecked, negativity feeds off ourselves and others, and can gather momentum very rapidly indeed. Once starved of attention however, it often withers away.

It's therefore very important to be able to recognise negativity. Some describe it as a feeling of heaviness in the atmosphere rather like a cake that hasn't cooked properly in the middle. Others describe the feeling as a slight shadowing of the light, a dark cloud or mist. I used to have an aunt with a particularly caustic tongue who carried her own little cloud of negativity around with her wherever she went, like a dark umbrella. I used to swear I could see her coming from a distance because whenever she was around it felt as though the sun had suddenly disappeared!

Once negativity is recognised, the next step is to isolate and break it up so that it can disperse by itself. Small pockets of negativity are everywhere and most do very little harm; it's when they cluster together into a great block that they cause problems. Even though such things may seem a million miles away from the evils of a psychic attack, if we don't deal with it promptly and effectively, negativity can swiftly change into or attract a full-blown psychic attack. It can also damage us so that we become less able to deal with other, unconnected attacks.

Other measures we can take include the basic cleansing methods in Chapters Ten and Twelve, and the preventative ones in Chapter Nineteen. It also helps to visualise a large psychic shield (see Chapter Nine) which we raise to protect ourselves whenever we feel a surge of negativity coming our way. For example, if someone who is regularly sarcastic and bullying makes an unpleasant remark, we just imagine raising our shield to block it. Done regularly this technique is extremely effective and the atmosphere soon improves.

Just as we should avoid contact with situations and people who bring negativity into our life or personal space, so we should be careful of contact with any items that such people have handled or worn. This is because - for better or worse - everything we touch is imbued with our own personal magnetism. Sometimes this bestows a blessing (which is the thinking behind holy relics), while at other times it can harm us. If ever we feel burdened with negativity from an unknown source, we should be careful what we bring into our home from the world outside.

The most vulnerable domestic spaces for attracting negativity are the hearth, table and bed. Traditionally the fireside and the table are places where people gather. They may bring negativity with them intentionally, in the form of a grudge or resentments, or they may bring it accidentally (something they have picked up along the way.)[125] Negativity can stick to us like chewing gum! When I was young, I was often told off for putting my shoes on the table to clean them. Even though I first spread newspapers on the

[125] Unfortunately, some bring negativity intentionally, too!

table, I was warned that shoes pick up negativity from out in the street – and newspapers aren't much better!

Beds also attract negativity, and since we are at our most vulnerable when sleeping, even low levels of negativity there can cause problems. Years ago, it was considered unlucky to place coats on a bed. In very cold weather however, people sometimes used a coat as an extra quilt (I've done it myself), but this was usually a last resort. Like shoes, coats are meant to be worn out of doors where they will pick up negativity quite easily. A coat worn to a workplace that is seething with negativity will bring some of it home with us, and if the coat is then placed on our bed this energy will rub off on it. Then we wonder why we've had a bad night's sleep, plagued by disturbing dreams.

Negativity isn't always easy to recognise and presents in many forms. For example, sometimes we encounter people who generate huge amounts of energy, affecting everyone around them. Tempers then become frayed, mood swings are extreme and nobody is happy. Of course, such people are not really generating huge amounts of energy at all; they are *draining* it from others. Often the culprits are teenagers whose behaviour is simply attributed to hormones. The parents may even be told, '*All teenagers are like that,*' which isn't strictly true although they may not realise what they're doing. However, elderly people can be just as negative and draining; negativity is no respecter of age.

Part of the problem with these energy drainers is that in the modern world we often spend a great deal of time shut away in hot and stuffy places. These become full of something called positive ions, small charged particles that exist all around us. Despite their name however, positive ions are not helpful, and can contribute to a wide range of symptoms including insomnia, irritability, tension, migraine, nausea, heart palpitations, fatigue and even some types of depression.

Teenagers often spend long periods in their bedrooms in this highly charged electro-climate, staring at their computer screens, phones or other electrical gadgets, all of which generate a high number of positive ions. Conversely, when we spend time outside amongst nature, we are surrounded by a high proportion of beneficial, negative ions.

Obviously in any home where there is a high level of unchecked positive ions the atmosphere will be adversely affected. For a teenager shut away in her room, there is the added problem that the negativity has nowhere to go because the bedroom door is usually closed. It therefore clusters in her room and will stick to her like glue. It's like a faulty pressure cooker waiting to explode.

If we are faced with a situation like this, begin with some thorough psychic cleansing not only in and around the room, but also any other areas of the home that seem affected. Use the techniques in Chapters Ten and Twelve for this. I would also recommend placing a clear quartz crystal or rose quartz near any electrical equipment, especially the computer. (There are more suggestions for using stones and crystals in Chapter Fourteen).

If this isn't practical, we can at least place a few crystals in other areas of the house to reduce any unpleasant effects there. Often the most unobtrusive method is to make a small windowsill display with a crystal, plant or vase of flowers, or even a photograph. Salt lamps, which are blocks of rock salt fitted with a light or even made into candle burners, are another possibility though if these are not switched on regularly, they tend to produce a lot of moisture.

A cheaper alternative is a small dish of consecrated salt. With both salt lamps and crystals, we can cleanse them regularly (visualising is the easiest method), while consecrated salt should be replaced daily for the first week. After that we can replace it weekly until things have settled down.

Ringing a bell (Chapter Twelve) is a particularly useful cleansing technique for dealing with other people's negativity since we can do it when the child is out at school or college and it leaves no traces. The sound helps break up any negativity, which may have already begun to fester.

At this point, we should think about the ethics of cleansing another person's room without their express permission. It's probably best viewed in much the same light as doing their washing or changing the bedclothes. We do these things because they're necessary although people may not have given their express permission on each occasion. Besides, it surely isn't unreasonable to protect ourselves against psychic attacks and negativity in our own home. It's just another type of housekeeping.

For the sake of general peace and harmony, psychic cleansing within the home is often best kept private and done when the person at the centre of it is out of the house. It is certainly more tactful than trying to explain to our teenage offspring that we are ringing bells to erase their anger and negativity! We shouldn't neglect cleansing our own bedrooms either, since some negativity will almost certainly have seeped in there and manifested as problems with sleeping.

Sometimes however, the person who is causing the problems remains stubbornly in the house so that we seem to be living in a constant state of confrontation. The answer then is to have our psychic shield at the ready and to practice careful breathing and grounding whenever this person is around (see Chapter Nine).

As we breathe out, imagine our breath dispersing her excess anger and challenging behaviour. Some people find it helps to imagine their breath changing negative emotions into something pleasant like helpfulness or even flowers or stars. However, being realistic, most of us in this situation are so frazzled that steady breathing is probably the best we'll manage, at least initially.

Whenever constant negativity is forced upon us, we must remind ourselves that we are in charge and fight back. Use protective plants such as strong-smelling herbs, roses, garlic, onions or lemons either in displays, as a decorative wreath to hang on a door or window, or grown as potted plants.

In spring and early summer, sprigs from the hawthorn and blackthorn bushes are very effective if brought indoors and placed in water. Traditionally hawthorn protects women and blackthorn protects men. (There are further ideas on using plants for protection in Chapter Twelve). Young hawthorn leaves are edible and were popular in spring years ago, providing a welcome addition to the diet at a time of year when other fresh foods were in short supply. When I was young, hawthorn was sometimes called 'bread and cheese' although to be honest I'm not sure it tasted like either! However, we can always incorporate one or two of its finely chopped young leaves in a salad in the hope that it will help calm everyone.

Placing a bay tree outside the front door is another method of encouraging harmony and peace in the home. A rose can be used in much the same way, either in a pot or planted in the ground. It's particularly useful if we feel that some of the problem is coming from outside the home. If we combine a rose and an archway, we are combining the protective power of the rose with the magical, curved shape of the arch. Cut roses, especially thorny ones, are useful because the negativity will become caught on the thorns. In winter, incorporate holly (another protective and prickly plant) into a decorative wreath for the door. There is more information on hoops and circles in Chapter Fourteen.

Another method is to make our own charcoal by burning some pieces of wood and when they are cool use them to draw protective signs and sigils. The best ready-prepared charcoal comes from the willow tree, which has an excellent reputation for magical protection. The symbols can be anything that seems right to us, such as enclosing the subject's initials within a protective pentagram or circle.

This type of work should be kept simple, and if the signs need to be concealed then remember that anything drawn in charcoal will be visible. Some people pull back the carpet and draw them on the floorboards beneath or draw them on a piece of paper that is then hidden. We can also incorporate protective sigils into any rituals to seal doors and windows with blessed water (see Chapter Ten).

Banishing Psychic Attacks and Negativity

As we have already seen, the main difference between psychic attacks and negativity is one of scale. Both are accompanied by a notable change in the atmosphere, and both can be dealt with using very similar techniques. I'm not convinced that we can really destroy negativity, although we can certainly break it down into more manageable chunks. One of the best methods is to break it up physically with a pole, besom or sweeping brush.

Of all the magical tools we can own, I feel a pole, staff or stick are the most useful. In the past, wooden rods were used for 'beating the bounds' and were also known as Rods of Life. It was believed that striking a person, animal, tree or the earth with one of these rods endowed it with fertility throughout the coming year.

The stick or pole doesn't have to be anything fancy, an old wooden mop handle will do, but it needs to be reasonably smooth without any jagged ends or splinters, since it's possible to 'hook' negativity, rather like catching a fish. A smooth pole will prevent this and it should be cleansed before use. To do this we should simply blow along it from top to bottom, visualising our breath blowing away any residual negativity. Try to complete the cleansing on a single breath.

Now, taking the pole in both hands, imagine that we've chalked the number eight on the floor. The number should be big enough to allow us to make wide sweeping movements. As a guide, I'm not very tall (5' 3"), so I tend to visualise a shape about a metre long from top to bottom.

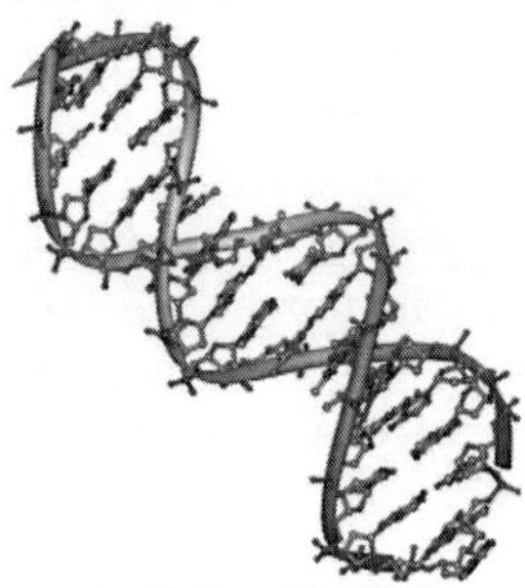

DNA Double Helix
Picture by Jerome Walker, Dennis Myts [Public domain]

The figure eight has an interesting shape, very similar to the double helix of DNA (*See image above*). It is also a fascinating number in its own right, being the first of the cubic numbers, i.e. 2 x 2 X 2 or 2^3. Both Aristotle and Pythagoras believed that the number two attained perfection in its third power as the number eight, and the early Christian church regarded the number as so significant that traditionally Christening fonts were octagonal in shape. In Buddhism, the Wheel is often shown with eight spokes, while the Lotus is shown with eight petals symbolising cosmic harmony. In Hinduism, the god Vishnu is shown with eight arms, while in Norse tradition the god Odin rode an eight-legged horse, Sleipnir.

Holding the pole as we would a sweeping brush, we keep moving over the outline of the figure eight, parallel to the ground. Use a sweeping motion and imagine breaking up the negativity. Try and keep the tip of the pole a few inches above the ground. If it starts to feel unusually heavy, that will be because some of the negativity has caught on it. If this happens, simply tap it firmly a few times on the floor and the negativity will fall away. Aim to do about five minutes vigorous 'sweeping' at a time - little and often is the most effective method. Remember that by breaking up negativity, we also weaken the effects of any psychic attack.

As we work, we should also concentrate on our breathing: breathe in normally through the nose and then exhale strongly through the mouth. We should visualise a long straight stream of breath, breaking up the dark patches of negativity around us so that they form into long, ribbon-like swirls. These will grow gradually smaller and fainter as we continue sweeping.

In those rare cases where negativity is so dense that even sweeping it away is difficult, tap the end of the pole on the ground instead. I find the best rhythm mimics a heartbeat. The tapping vibrations create a 'ripple' effect that breaks up the negativity so we can then sweep it away.

We can tap the figure-of-eight shape or use the wooden pole to walk the boundaries of our home, rooms, around the car, workplace, desk etc., tapping it on the ground every few steps, to break up any stubborn patches of negativity. Some people also vacuum afterwards as a way of removing all the physical debris although this isn't essential. If we choose to do this however, we should remember to empty the vacuum afterwards.

Apart from using a wooden pole, we can also use a sweeping brush or traditional besom (witch's broomstick). The besom's head, made from twigs, is great for sweeping leaves from the grass in autumn. To use it effectively however requires a slightly curved movement. This makes it excellent for breaking up negativity since we can use it to sweep in a circular motion and not just backwards and forwards like an ordinary sweeping brush. However, an ordinary sweeping brush with its simple straight to-and-fro motion is perfect whenever we want to visualise sweeping our attacker out of the front door!

If we lack a broom pole, witch's besom or suitable sweeping brush, one alternative is to use a large mixing spoon. With this method we must visualise stirring the air, using the figure-of-eight motion, like mixing a giant, cosmic cake. Again, what we are doing is breaking up the negativity that lingers in the air. (Slotted spoons are no use for this as the negativity just slips through the gaps).

Never be put off doing something because we don't have the 'right' tools – improvise instead. Even a clothes' brush will do if we have nothing else to hand, although it might take more effort. All we need to do is visualise vigorously brushing the atmosphere until it is clean.

Another method for dispersing negativity is to use our breath. We've already seen how we can use it with the pole, but it can also be used alone and is a useful technique when we need to act discreetly. Remember that our power lies in the out breath (as we exhale) because that comes from within us.

Take a deep breath in, and then as we breathe out, while keeping our head straight we should visualise blowing away all the negativity that surrounds us. Our airway and mouth should feel soft and relaxed throughout. I find it helpful to lightly tuck the tip of my tongue just behind my lower teeth, so it doesn't obstruct my breath. Don't forget to put some force behind the out breathe, to literally blow the negativity away.

Learning breath control is a useful skill not least because we can do it anywhere without being noticed. We can use our breathing to steady ourselves, to draw pleasant things towards us, and also to get rid of unpleasant ones. We can even use breathing exercises whenever we feel that negativity - our own or someone else's – is weighing us down or affecting our health. The exercises are also useful for dealing with night-time attacks since we can do them lying in bed.

In order to get the most out of breath control, begin by practicing the simple breathing exercises given in Chapter Nine.[126] Next, we need to strengthen the force of how we exhale. When we are starting out, stronger breathing is better with a shorter breath (in for five and out for five will probably suit most people) but we must force the breath out between pursed lips as hard as we can. I often used to practice increasing my breathing power by using a large candle, gradually moving it further away to see if I could still blow out or 'shake' the flame.

Whenever we need this technique, take a few deep breaths first to prepare, then breathe in for a count of five. Next, on a strong out-breath, visualise blowing the psychic attack or negativity as far away as possible. We only need to repeat this a few times (I usually do three, seven or nine breaths) otherwise it can make us feel dizzy. Wait and see whether the atmosphere improves before trying again.

One of the most important remedies against any type of psychic attack is a good night's sleep. Unfortunately, psychic attacks often target us at night, making sleep difficult if not impossible. We should cleanse our sleeping area first (see Chapter Nine for some suggestions) preferably using incense although cut garlic placed around the room is a good – if slightly pungent alternative.

It is not particularly pleasant (or safe) to sleep in an incense-filled room, particularly for someone with conditions such as asthma, and we mustn't put our health at risk. Use blessed water or consecrated salt and vinegar instead. Then make the sign of the pentagram above the bed. If there is some other symbol that has more meaning for us then we should use that instead. Aromatic and protective oils such as lavender can also be dabbed on pillows to ensure a combination of security and a good night's sleep.

---

[126] For a more in-depth discussion of how magic can use the breath, see my book, *Magic on the Breath* (2011) published by The Wolfenhowle Press.

Psychic attacks or excessive negativity often make us feel run down and too tired to even defend ourselves. This is when it really pays to draw up a list of things to do so we can tackle them little and often. This would be a typical plan:

1. *Every morning when we rise, look towards the dawn sky and take a few deep breaths. Imagine blowing away all the unpleasantness and stress on the out breaths, and visualise drawing in strength, courage and love on the inhaled breaths.*

2. *Repeat this at night when we look at the moon. While taking these deep breaths remember not to allow any thoughts of the attack or the causes of the negativity to intrude. This is not a time for reflection. Just empty the mind of everything other than blowing away unpleasantness and drawing in strength and love.*

3. *We should check each night and morning whether an attacker has implanted a 'cord' into our solar plexus. If so, then deal with it (see Chapter Eleven)*

4. *Psychically cleanse those areas most closely associated with the attack. For example, if most of the problems come at night, then concentrate on the bedroom. If the attacker lives with us then try to magically cleanse any area especially associated with them, such as their room (if we have access to it) or their chair. Obviously, this is best done when the person is not around.*

   In fact, unless someone else is actively helping us, it's better to do this sort of work when we're alone, anyway. This allows us to work at our own pace and we don't have to break our concentration in order to explain what we're doing to anyone else.

5. *We should take a little time each day to concentrate on building and using our psychic armour. If we find the visualisation difficult, print a picture of a suitable sword and shield from the internet or cut or photocopy something from a magazine. Keep them somewhere close and look at them often during the course of the day. Most importantly, try and visualise using the shield against attacks.*

6. *Whenever necessary, be prepared to use the exercise for cutting the red cord in Chapter Eleven.*

7. *At night, just before we go to sleep, we should seal our Aura (see Chapter Nine).*

None of this is intended to cause alarm or panic. Most of the things that go wrong in our lives have nothing whatsoever to do with psychic attacks or magical wars. They are due to the actions we (and others) take, our choices and our characters.

Don't become paranoid. Curses and the Evil Eye are not lurking behind every shadow. Yes, bad things can and do happen to everyone, but only a very few ever originate as psychic attacks. For example, ID theft may have happened because someone fitted a camera to an ATM machine or managed to discover our PIN number, not because our neighbour cast the Evil Eye on us.

Always take sensible practical precautions - even psychic self defence needs a little help sometimes!

CHAPTER FOURTEEN

Performing a house blessing. Other magical tools. Other defences including stones, magic charms and laughter. Mirrors. Magical reflection techniques. Returning a hex. Hoops and arches. Performing a House Blessing.

When we bless our surroundings, we create a safe haven, a refuge. This is useful whenever we feel the atmosphere at home or work is oppressive, or if we feel we are under psychic attack. Blessings can be performed either on our own or someone else's behalf, and although many feel they need a clergyman or minister to give a blessing, these are quite easy to write and perform for ourselves.

The best time to perform a house blessing is immediately after performing physical and magical cleansings. It therefore pays to prepare a little beforehand. Clean and tidy, and if possible, sweep or vacuum the floors and clean the windows since the everyday world reflects the magical world. If our home feels fresh and clean it is more likely to be *magically* fresh and clean too.

The next step is to light some pleasant, floral incense to set the mood for our blessing. This helps to lighten the mood; just as unpleasant smells announce the presence of a psychic attack, so a pleasant smell announces the presence of psychic self defence. As an alternative to incense we could use a floral oil in an oil burner or even a couple of scented candles.

Another method is to use rosewater (obtained from a supermarket, pharmacy or delicatessen) to cleanse and bless the home. Before use, we should bless it using the basic methods given in Chapter Twelve for blessed water. Then sprinkle it lightly around the home, using either our fingers or a herb brush, being careful to avoid delicate fabrics, furnishings or electrical equipment. It helps to focus our will and intention if we speak as we work at this. The words don't have to rhyme, they should just make it clear what the blessing is intended to do. The following would be quite adequate:

I cleanse this place/room/home
And make it bright and clean,
Free from all negativity and dark thoughts.

I bless this place/room/home
With the gifts of love, joy and harmony.
May it be a refuge and safe haven for all who live here.
In peace and love, blessed be.

Another method involves simply walking from room to room, saying, '*Blessed be,*' and then exhaling gently to carry our blessing to the four corners. Done with proper intent and concentration this will do the job. We may wish to make this type of blessing or ritual more elaborate but it's certainly not essential. Embellishments for such blessings might include carrying a candle from room to room or placing a lit candle in the room while we sprinkle some rosewater around. Then we could add to our wording, for example:

'May the flame of love burn bright in this home and bless this space.'

The magical thinking behind this is to link the physical flame with its symbolic representation. Obviously when we use candles we must avoid leaving them unattended and observe sensible safety precautions. Fire must always be handled with care.

Another embellishment involves mixing together any four protective herbs (tobacco was traditionally used in North America) in honour of the four compass directions. We then scatter the mixture around the boundaries of our home or garden, stopping four times in order to face each of the compass directions and say a prayer to the spirits or deities we associate with that direction.

Traditionally the compass points are governed thus:

- North governed by the spirits of Earth
- East governed by the spirits of Air
- West governed by the spirits of Water
- South governed by the spirits of Fire

We may need to be a little flexible with this. For example, if north faces a river or the sea, some people find it easier to make that direction represent the spirits of water. Don't be afraid to experiment and do whatever feels best. What matters most is the level of visualisation we can achieve, rather than precise compass directions. Also don't agonise about how to address the various spirits, remember they know who they are! If we simply invoke the '*Spirits of the North, Guardians of the earth*' etc., that will do perfectly well. So we could say something like:

Spirits of the North, Guardians of the earth,
I ask you to protect this gateway/entrance/exit/property/my home,
With all the power at your command.
Protect me and my family/and those I love,
And keep us safe from those who wish us harm.

We can similarly adapt the first line for each of the other elements.

Obviously, not everyone is lucky enough to live in a place where they can walk around the perimeter of their home. If we live in a terraced house or flat however, we can instead place the herbs at the exterior doors and windows. Again, check the compass directions and – if possible – face the appropriate direction when required. For example, if our doorway faces north, we address our initial invocation to the spirit guardians of the north. Then, while still standing on the same spot, turn to face the east, south and west in turn, reciting a suitable invocation for each.

We can also hang up a pentagram or any other symbol that feels appropriate or draw this in the air. When the blessing is completed, finish by sealing the doors, windows and hearth, as explained in Chapter Ten.

Other Magical Tools

One of the most useful tools in psychic self defence is a staff. This doesn't have to be anything fancy and at its simplest we can use a wooden pole from an ordinary sweeping brush. Sand it down (it will freshen up the colour and is a good way to magically cleanse it. In particular, ensure the cut end is filed or sanded smooth since rough edges will inadvertently trap energies. Apart from using it to break up negativity (see Chapter Thirteen) we can also use it to send our intentions along the ground. This is useful when we cannot – or do not wish to – get close to whatever is threatening us.

Begin with some grounding exercises (see Chapter Nine) and then start tapping the ground with the staff/pole to set up a strong, regular rhythm. I've always found the most adaptable rhythm echoes the beating of the human heart and if we want to attract something towards us, then concentrate on breathing in at the same time. However in psychic self defence, the emphasis is almost always on repelling things, so we need to concentrate on breathing out and literally blowing away whatever is troubling us.

Using a combination of a pole or stick and breathing can also be adapted for dealing with psychic infestations of animals and insects. These may manifest as groups of cats, flies, snakes, slugs or rats that may be noticed loitering near or even in the site of an attack. (The flies are usually bluebottles.)

Some will be part of the psychic attack, others will be real, attracted by the magical manifestations. The attacker uses the element of earth to direct these creatures, and while they may not physically harm us, they are very unsettling and in the case of flies and rodents can be unhealthy.

Since it is difficult to tell which creatures are real and which are magical, it's best to use a combination of physical repellents and psychic self defence. A good method is to tap the ground with the end of the staff or pole while concentrating on breathing (see Chapter Thirteen for examples and suggestions) and physically blowing the infestation away. We can also use the same method for dispersing chthonic entities or any hex conveyed via the element of earth (see Chapter Eleven).

Stones and Crystals

Many people like to use stones, particularly crystals, as part of their defence against psychic attack. Traditionally, these were either left plain or engraved with pictures of gods or inscriptions to enhance their power. If we use crystals to empower our defence, don't forget to regularly 'charge' or empower them; this is sometimes also referred to as 'magnetising.' Basically this entails channelling our will into the stone in order to empower it towards a specific purpose. The ritual can be as complicated as we wish, but at its simplest we are telling the object what we want it to do. We should give this some thought first, because it's important to be completely clear in our minds. Muddled instructions create to muddled results!

The following is a useful template that can be adapted to suit a variety of situations:

> *Crystal, I give you this sacred charge, to protect me/my family/my loved ones from all harm and/or maleficium. Use all your power, all your strength to this purpose and this alone. Do not rest, day or night, until this duty is properly fulfilled and I/my family etc. are safe.*

Of course, words mean nothing if we just recite them; we need to think as vividly as we can of setting the crystal on guard. Imagine it sitting on the windowsill (or wherever we choose to place it) and giving off showers of sparks to repel the attack. Psychic attacks often enter our homes via doors, windows, chimneys or other physical entrances, but can also invade our space via any or all of the following:

- Clothing or footwear
- Objects that are brought (even unknowingly) into the home, or even secreted there by an attacker. This includes hexes that have been sent through the post!
- The internet
- Direct contact with the attacker (although the victim is sometimes unaware of this)

If we suspect the hex has (or will) come into our home through a doorway etc., then place the crystal near that and regularly cleanse it using any of the methods in Chapters Ten and Twelve. If we suspect there is a hexed object in our home, then we must search until we find it. Once found, it should be ritually destroyed. (For suitable methods, see Chapter Fifteen).

Clear quartz is useful whenever we suspect the attack is being directed at us via the internet. It should be empowered and then placed close to the computer, laptop, phone etc. Although haematite is useful for dealing with internet attacks, it should be placed further away from the computer than quartz. Although haematite is not, strictly speaking, magnetic, many pieces contain enough magnetite to allow them to be attracted to an ordinary magnet and should be avoided where computers are concerned.[127]

Personally, I prefer to reserve haematite for dealing with attacks that involve the element of earth. It should be cleansed first and then placed in the areas most prone to psychic disturbances. If we're not sure where these are, or if everywhere seems equally affected, then begin by placing the stone near a door, window or hallway. That way, its natural properties will attract and divert the attack and prevent it entering on clothing, footwear etc. Remember to cleanse the stone every day, as this will help drain the attacker's power until we are sure all threat is past. Just rinse it briefly in running water - under the tap will do - while performing a cleansing ritual (see Chapters Ten and Twelve).[128]

Attacks conducted through direct contact with the victim (rather than simply on the victim's home or workplace) are best countered by carrying a cleansed, empowered crystal in one's pocket. An empowered piece of jewellery containing our chosen crystal is another possibility. Traditionally, the primary function of much early jewellery (and perfume for that matter) was protective rather than purely decorative. Diamonds were considered superb protectors, along with moonstones and selenite.

Turquoise, (especially the green variety which was more popular in ancient and medieval times than the blue) was regarded as an excellent amulet for seafarers and was believed to prevent them from drowning. Anyone who is under psychic attack and who cannot avoid travelling by or near water should consider

---

[127] https://geology.com/minerals/hematite.shtml

[128] Some people do not recommend immersing haematite (or other crystals) in water, but a quick wipe with a damp cloth will not harm it.

carrying turquoise for protection. The stone can also be used against attacks that use the element of water.

If we are under active attack, (or have good reason to believe that one is about to materialise any time soon), always take added care when negotiating any hazardous situations. Don't become paranoid but do avoid unnecessary risks. Most psychic attackers are bullies who don't play fair and will think nothing of attacking when we are at our weakest or most distracted.

Centuries ago, some of the most powerful protective stones were not what we could call crystals nowadays. The Swallow Stone, or *piedra dela golondrina*, was said to lie in the stomach of the first cockerel born in the New Year under a crescent moon. It was believed there were always two of these stones, one green and the other white, and they had to be used together.[129] Wrapped in deer or calf skin, they were worn around the neck on a red silk thread as a cure for enchantment and witchcraft.

The Eagle Stone, also known as *aetites* or clapper-stones, was a hollow stone that rattled because there was a tiny pebble or piece of debris inside. These were used to protect pregnant women and were considered so valuable that they were often ornately set in silver or gold.[130]

Laughter

I am a firm believer that laughter is one of our best defences against hexes.[131] I'm not entirely sure why they work, but experience has taught me time and again that they do. Perhaps it is because laughter lightens the spirit and seems to tighten up our Aura so that psychic attacks just roll away like water off a duck's back. When I was young and the atmosphere at home became too dark and grim, I used to resort to my trusty store of joke and limerick books. Nowadays of course there is far more choice - go and rent a

---

129 Nunemaker (1932): 562

130 Holmes (1934): 195

131 Dion Fortune also mentions the power of laughter to avert a psychic attack in her book *Psychic Self Defence*

really funny DVD and watch it, something that will make us laugh out loud; it's surprising how clear the air feels afterwards.

Laughter can also be useful when faced with someone who is either attacking us (or intending to.) Obviously, it isn't considered polite to laugh in someone's face, although I have known people who have done just that and swear it works:

> *Some time ago I was confronted by a man who regularly made unpleasant comments to my face, and also made derogatory remarks about me to other people. It really got to me. When I didn't have to see him it was great, but then I would have to and I would think, 'Oh no, here we go again.' And then I suddenly realised how stupid it all was, and how stupid he was and how he ought to get a life. And I started to laugh. And once I started, I just couldn't stop, in the end there were tears running down my face.*
>
> *His face was a picture – there he was, wanting to intimidate me again, and I was just standing there laughing at him. In the end he just walked away and that was the last I had contact with him. I think my laughter really did break his hexing.*[132]

Although not all of us can keep our nerve for such a direct confrontation, we should aim to keep any contact with such people as light as possible. We should smile, even though we probably don't feel like it, and make good use of our psychic shield to deflect any unpleasant intentions and prevent them from reaching us.

Have I failed?

We shouldn't be surprised - or disheartened - if we need to perform banishing or cleansing rituals more than once. Indeed, sometimes we must repeat them for several weeks. This doesn't mean that our first effort failed. Really determined attackers can sometimes be a bit like a dog with a bone, persistent even to the point of recklessness. This is partly due to the addictive nature of

---

[132]Author's personal notes.

hexing itself. They just can't leave it alone even when they must realise they aren't going to succeed.

Standing up for ourselves against a psychic attacker will *not* make things worse in the long term. Even if, as sometimes happens, the attack appears to intensify just after we begin to stand up for ourselves, we must not lose our nerve. Once attacked, we must either defend ourselves or submit. There is no middle way, no appeasement. So whatever method we chose, we must be determined. Even if initially the attack intensifies, rest assured that it *will* eventually slacken off.

All psychic self defence requires plenty of courage, persistence and a little know-how.

Magic Charms

A magic charm is only as strong as the person who uses it. If we are just paying lip service, repeating what we believe are '*magic words*' then be prepared for disappointment. The best charms are often those we create ourselves, because they are unique to us, and have real meaning for our present situation.

Writing our own charms is not difficult. We're not trying to write poetry, just a rhythmic chant, something with drive and energy. I once ran a spell writing workshop where we dealt briefly with writing a hex-busting charm, and one student came up with:

I block your path
You cannot pass
I'll drive your hex
Right up your arse

I have no doubt this would have worked too, because the wording, although a little crude, came right from the heart. I then helped her build this up into a small ritual by taking a broom pole and striking it on the ground as she spoke the final word of each line – the very last word was accompanied by a powerful upward thrust of the pole. It was not only very graphic but also very effective and did the trick. I think sometimes the charms we use need to employ this raw energy and even swear words where appropriate, simply because these add real force. However, what we say, and how we say it, must still come from the heart.

Magical reflection techniques

Some people worry about the ethics of returning a hex. I must stress that psychic attackers do not share other people's moral code. They rarely play by any rules, not even their own and because of this, I feel that having their own hex rebound upon them is a kind of rough justice. *'What goes around, comes around,'* is particularly satisfying in the realm of psychic attacks.

The best advice is to be guided by whatever seems reasonable to us *in real life.* For example, if we feel that we would never be justified in retaliating, no matter what the provocation, then concentrate instead on magical cleansing and protective measures. On the other hand, if we would feel justified in taking a swipe at someone who is physically attacking us or our family, then we should have no qualms about employing the magical equivalent.

There are a variety of methods for returning psychic attacks to their creators, usually involving reflective surfaces such as mirrors. Used with care, these can bounce a hex straight back to its creator. Used recklessly, however, they are often the cause of unintentional psychic attacks on people we don't even know.

The secret is in the positioning. If we use a single mirror it will bounce the attack in a single direction, and whatever it comes in contact will experience all the power of the original hex. If we place a number of small mirrors in a semi-circle, they will bounce the hex (or parts of it) in several directions at once, and although it may have a scattergun effect; anyone caught in the rebound will not experience the full force of the original attack.

Using a concave (i.e. magnifying) mirror takes an attack into an altogether different sphere; at its mildest it was intended to blind the victim and at its most intense to incinerate him![133] Due to its curved surface (which could send a hex almost anywhere), I would

---

[133] Voss 2006: 149

discourage anyone from using a magnifying mirror to deflect a hex. It is too unreliable.

The best method for using an ordinary mirror to deal with a psychic attack is to empower it specifically to disperse and disable the hex (this can be a specific hex or hexes in general). Whatever bounces off its surface, and wherever it goes, we don't need to worry because it's already been rendered harmless. Place the mirror near the main entrance of the home or workspace etc., where it can reflect anything unpleasant that tries to enter.

As always, cleanse the mirror first. One of the easiest methods is to blow on its surface, beginning in one corner and breathing diagonally across to the far side, visualising all negativity dispersing. Another method is to wipe it down with salt water and leave it to dry although this is only suitable if the salt water will not damage the frame. Make sure the cloth used for wiping is wrung out as dry as possible. Then hold one hand, palm facing downwards over the mirrored surface and say any (or all) of the following:

- *May this mirror reflect light and deflect darkness*

- *May this mirror break up hexes, shatter their power and turn them into showers of light*

- *May this mirror send all harmful energies and thoughts back only to their creator*

Returning a hex is particularly tempting when dealing with psychic vampires who can do us a great deal of harm if left unchecked. However, the single most important response is to simply break all contact. Not only should we avoid seeing them face-to-face but all contact (by letter, phone, email, and even via third parties) should be suspended.

It's amazing how many people are suddenly eager to involve themselves in our business once there's a psychic attack going on. They may seem to be doing us a favour by relaying the latest news to us, but actually – whether they realise it or not – they are working on the attacker's behalf, keeping the lines of communication open so that we are forced to deal with him, albeit indirectly.

Psychic attackers tend to be very good at persuading or coercing others to aid them. Often these third parties will try and present themselves as a friend, when in truth they are nothing of the sort. Either avoid contact with them too, or, if that's not practical, keep our psychic shield at the ready whenever they're around. Always remember whose side they are really on.

Sequins are another effective method of returning a hex, as are tiny mirrors sewn into clothing and bags (the sort we see in some Asian garments). These all have a protective function as well as a decorative one. One good method is to make a doll or poppet and decorate its clothing with a few sequins, the brighter and shinier the better. Then set it on guard, just as we did with the crystal, to protect us and our home.

Poppets and Dolls

Many people are rather fearful of poppets, although there is nothing intrinsically 'wicked' about them. As with all things magical, their only power is in the force of their creator's will although it's amazing how many people make these objects and are then afraid to get rid of them. There is no reason to fear getting rid of a doll that was created only to protect us.

If we wish to dispose of a poppet all we need to do is just tell it that it has done its job and now its work is over. Make a point of thanking it, treat it with respect and dismantle it. Some people bury the pieces or cast them into running water while others just burn them. The important thing is to then forget about the doll and move on. Nothing conjures up a self-hex more quickly than a misplaced sense of guilt.

If we have not yet made a defensive doll or poppet but are thinking of doing so, then set it up with a given 'cut-off' date. After that time we can dismantle and burn it without any further regrets. Remember, we can always create another.

With anything we have empowered, remember to treat it as sentient while it is active on our behalf. Even if all we say is a simple '*Thank you,*' or '*Keep up the good work,*' we are keeping the lines of communication open. And if we feel its work is done, and don't wish to think of it as sentient any longer, then we just thank it and ask it to '*Stand down,*' or '*Be at ease,*' until further notice. I strongly believe that many things we think of as inanimate objects do have intelligence and often all that is required to get them working on our behalf is a simple acknowledgement, a little gratitude.

Dishing out 'Magical Justice'

I am often asked whether it's acceptable to add a little something of our own to a hex before returning it to its creator. It would be easy to say no, never, but of course real life is often more complicated. There *are* some types of attack, for example on small children, the vulnerable, the sick or the elderly that really cannot be excused or condoned. If the attacker goes unpunished then others may be harmed in future. We can either hope that someone else deals with them or decide to be the instrument of punishing the attacker ourselves. It's up to us.

My advice is always not to do anything until the matter has been properly and thoroughly considered. If we do something rash, can we live with ourselves afterwards? Some people have no problems in this respect, others do. This book is only intended to show how to defend ourselves however, and not how to mete out magical revenge.

Hoops and Arches

Since ancient times people have recognized and used the protective power of circles, hoops and arches. Despite the best efforts of the medieval church to eradicate them, some of these traditions lingered well into the early twentieth century. People would pass sick children through clefts in trees, crawl through bramble hoops and under bushes (particularly thorny ones such as blackberries), and even through tunnels in the earth. Magically speaking, thorns were supposed to snag and catch any evil (including all forms of psychic attack) or sickness, while being in contact with the earth was thought to strengthen the patient.

Silence is often a very important part of these rituals, although occasionally we come across a spoken charm, such as:

In bramble, out cough,
Here I leave the whooping cough.[134]

This charm was common many years ago in Devon as a cure for whooping cough but could be easily adapted for dealing with psychic attacks too. In most areas the patient had to crawl from east to west, while in parts of Cornwall the crawling was performed nine times anticlockwise in a circle.

In Germany, a couple who believed their relationship was in trouble due to someone casting the Evil Eye upon them would sometimes crawl through or under a blackberry bush. Anyone who has ever come into close contact with blackberry thorns will know how painful they can be and appreciate the couple's determination.

A less painful alternative is to crawl through holed stones. Although large specimens are rare, they are found as far afield as Men-an-tol in Cornwall to sites in France, Ireland and even in the Far and Middle East. In Kintyre, in Scotland, people used holed stones in order to solemnise a wedding especially when a couple were eloping. All they had to do was clasp hands through the holed stone and they considered themselves legally married and therefore out of the reach of their pursuers.

In North America people would crawl under animals (especially donkeys), under tables, through the rungs of chairs and even ladders![135] In North Carolina, for example, people who thought they were bewitched were first passed through *all* the rungs of a ladder. This was done from the bottom to the top and then back down again which must have been very difficult for all but the very small or supremely agile. As if that wasn't enough,

---

[134] Hand (1968): 384

[135] *Ibid*: 398

they then had to pass through a horse collar – which was also a remedy against a wide range of enchantments, from being moonstruck after sleeping out under a full moon (in Russia) to being squeezed by trolls (in Denmark).

In Poland, up until the late nineteenth century, someone who was bewitched would be passed through the legs of the eldest woman in the family and then through a horse collar. Presumably the large collars used for shire horses were big enough to accommodate some adults!

Crawling through another person's legs seems to have been a common magical protective remedy. Pregnant women were often considered particularly vulnerable to enchantments that caused the birth of a sickly child or caused the mother to undergo a long and difficult delivery. One popular remedy was for the expectant mother to crawl through her husband's legs, while sickly children were encouraged to pass through their mother's legs. The latter suggests a magical re-enactment of the birth in order to recover the health and vitality that should accompany birth and life itself.

Of course, anyone who is ill or heavily pregnant will find crawling difficult and there are many accounts of people being pulled through an arch or hoop by friends and family as part of a magical healing ritual. Indeed, when we talk of a sick person 'pulling through' (i.e. recovering) this may be a distant memory of these ancient healing ceremonies.

Luckily for us, most magical practices can be adapted. We could use the protective properties of the willow to plait a willow hoop or even a bangle to be used as an amulet. This is not so far removed from the old practice of keeping a piece of bramble or a suitable branch from a healing tree to use as a portable healing hoop. In Germany willow hoops were used to cure fever. The hoop was placed over the patient's head and then drawn down to his feet. In Scotland, a 'girth of woodbine' – a hoop made from wild honeysuckle – was used in the same way to cure a wide variety of illnesses. Presumably this would have been useful if the patient was too sick to crawl by herself.

Rowan was also a popular plant for healing hoops, especially at Beltane (May 1st) and Samhain (November 1st). In the Scottish

Highlands, sheep and lambs were driven through these hoops to protect them through the coming year. An easier alternative was to make a loop of yarn, either a single thick thread or several thinner ones, and pass the bewitched person through that. Afterwards the thread was usually burned, although in southern Saxony the loop was preserved and reused.

Arches were thought to have similar healing powers to a hoop or circle, perhaps forming a magical gateway between health and sickness. Turf arches, where a trench is dug in the earth and turves piled over it to make an arch were very popular in some areas and were often made in graveyards. The thinking behind this was probably that leaving sickness in the ground would not harm the dead and would help the living. The patient was then dragged through before the arch was sealed up with thorns - magically preventing the sickness or hex from following the patient.

Healing arches and crawling trenches were also set up at forks in the road, crossroads, or any field or property boundaries (especially at sites where four properties came together.) These are all places associated with supernatural activity. Most traditions stipulated that the patient had to be passed through the arch or trench three times in complete silence, preferably before sunrise on a Thursday. In Northern Europe, Thursdays were sacred to Thor, in the classical world they were sacred to Zeus or Jupiter.

If the patient or victim was unable (or perhaps unwilling) to crawl through an arch in person, it was still possible to effect a cure by taking their clothing and drawing this through the loop of a church key. Anyone who has ever seen a large, old-fashioned church key will realise that these were quite capable of accommodating some fairly bulky garments! Given that such keys were usually made of iron, this suggests that at some time in the faraway past, iron hoops were also used for magical healing rituals.

Sometimes specific garments were empowered for psychic self defence. This method was used to protect young children who were often considered prime targets for bewitchment. In Scotland, concerned relatives took either the child's first shirt, or some of the clothing its mother wore during the birth, twist it into a loop and pass the child three times through this. With a little imagination, almost anything can and has been used to create a healing hoop or arch. Sometimes the child or their clothing was passed three times around a shepherd's crook – which is of course yet another curved shape. In Ireland, pregnant women deliberately pulled their clothes through holes in order to ensure an easy and safe delivery, which is an obvious form of sympathetic magic.

People sometimes carried a small healing hoop with them to deal with emergencies. I suspect that even rings worn on the fingers were used in this way, since wedding rings were thought to be very effective for divination by dowsing. I remember my mother threading hers on a strand of hair and using this to determine the sex of an unborn child.

Although my own family had no problems with removing their wedding rings for divination, many people when I was young believed that wedding rings should never be removed. I suspect this was either to discourage divination, or in order to concentrate the ring's power entirely on the wearer. If we wear a wedding ring, or any other ring with special meaning to us, remember that it is our own highly effective healing hoop, and should be treated with appropriate respect.

If all this sounds a little simplistic, that's true, it is, but do remember that anything will have power *if we truly believe in it.* The star-shaped badge that a sheriff wears, or the crescent moons incorporated into old horse brasses are just pieces of metal and not in themselves powerful. They only acquire power once the wearer (or in the case of a horse, its owner) actually believes in them. Then their protective powers are very effective indeed!

CHAPTER FIFTEEN

Disarming a hex written on a material substance such as paper or parchment. Dealing with hexes conveyed by dolls and tattoos, 'name claiming'. Other methods of conveying hexes

Just as not everything that glitters is gold so not everything that appears to be a gift is actually desirable. Sometimes people present their target with a gift as a way of enforcing a psychic connection. Almost any material is capable of being used in this way, including metals and crystals (just think of the alleged curse on the Hope Diamond!) Speaking from my own experience, the most powerful attacks come with leather, fur, wood – basically anything organic that has once been alive, because if it once had life it can be reanimated.

In one of my early encounters with a psychic attack I had to deal with one of these 'hex gifts.' I was about fifteen years old and after years of living in the same house there had been a sudden outbreak of very unpleasant psychic activity. What I didn't know at the time was that there was a full-blown magical feud going on between my mother and several of her relatives.

I was duly sent to search my home for anything made of leather or fur because these seem to hold hexes well. Sure enough, I eventually discovered that the culprit had left a rather pretty tribal art picture made of hide, fur and grasses, hidden between books on a shelf. It would probably have remained unnoticed for a long time if I hadn't had some idea what I was looking for.

Once found, the picture was ritually destroyed straight away. It is important to get rid of these things as soon as possible rather than leave them hanging around. Some people will claim that the dark of the moon is the best time for disposing of such items, but in my opinion, this is a counsel of perfection. No matter what the moon-phase happens to be, it's better to ritually destroy it sooner rather than later.

Sometimes these objects are hidden in our home, sometimes they will arrive, quite literally on our doorstep. (This usually happens when we have already sensed an attack is building up, which often happens in the week leading up to a full moon). There may be strange sounds, smells and phenomena around the home, or the air may be fairly crackling with energy. This latter isn't always a sure sign of a psychic attack however, sometimes the weather and even planetary alignments seems to affect us more strongly than others. Without becoming paranoid, in these circumstances, I would suggest keeping a lookout for anything out of the ordinary, such as a scrap of paper with scribbled markings on it that suddenly turns up out of the blue. It might even look as though a piece of rubbish has just blown in from the street.

Before throwing it away, first check and see whether 'the rubbish' is quite what it seems. Look for papers bearing marks or symbols. Often these are scribbled on the backs of innocuous things such as receipts or envelopes, and it's easy to miss them unless we know what we're looking for. Yes, they may well be harmless doodlings by next door's toddler that happen to have blown over the wall, but very occasionally they turn out to be a carefully planted hex. If we're not sure, *and if we feel that some sort of psychic attack is building up anyway,* treat it as a hex and dispose of it accordingly. Better safe than sorry.

Disarming a hex

Methods for conveying a hex vary. Some are hidden, and the victim only suspects their existence, while others are nailed on doors, left on doorsteps, or occasionally left in some place that the victim is known to pass, perhaps on her way to work. The intention of a visible hex is that the victim should be suitably intimidated and become anxious and jumpy. This will do much of the hexer's work without him needing to lift a finger. Another popular method of conveying a hex is to send it out in the post; it never fails to amaze me how many of these things must be whizzing around courtesy of the Royal Mail.

Of course, if we convey a hex in a physical form, whether by letter, doll etc., then we cannot later claim it was unintentional. The only exception is when the hex doesn't reach its intended target and harms someone else instead, but then it could be argued that it should never have been sent out in the first place. There are several reasons for writing down a hex. Firstly, the attacker can be more exact about what he intends. He can specify both the means and the outcome he desires. Secondly, by making sure the victim knows she is hexed, the attacker has a clear psychological advantage. Most victims are terrified, their imaginations running riot as they try to imagine what all the squiggly symbols threaten. (Actually, the attacker has given them an opportunity to destroy the hex and limit the harm it can cause, but too few victims do this.)

Sometimes a written hex is ambiguous; a piece of paper or leather bearing a few symbols could mean anything. I know a keen psychic attacker who sends out her hexes every year like clockwork using Christmas cards. At first sight these seem perfectly normal, but there is always something a bit 'off' in the wording inside the card. She sometimes uses a different alphabet to convey her message, which when decoded letter for letter is clearly a hex. For example:

Ικυρσειουαλλ

This uses Greek letters, but when examined more closely it breaks up into four sections: Ἰ κυρσε ιου αλλ, which by substituting the nearest English letters for the Greek ones reads 'I curse you all.' Not pleasant, but not really powerful either, and certainly not as powerful or awe-inspiring as the sender would have liked the victim to think! (It's not even Greek, just letter for letter substitution of Greek letters for English ones). Obviously not everything that looks like a hex really is one. Some are genuine while others just want to induce fear and have no more ability to convey a psychic attack than a pork pie!

One of the most unpleasant aspects of dealing with this type of hex is the difficulty of interpreting it. In this respect it is the opposite of a poison pen letter which always makes the writer's feelings crystal clear. Obviously if open threats are sent to us, we should keep the letter and envelope and show it to the police. But most psychic attackers are too subtle for this, so the best method of dealing with anything they send is to burn it and sprinkle a little salt on the fire to purify it. By putting salt on the fire we avoid sending the hex into the smoke and thence into the four corners of our home (or anywhere else for that matter.) Remember though that salt will sometimes 'spit' in the flames. Other things we can add to the fire include frankincense, sage and any other protective herbs, but not too much at a time!

As we watch the hex burn to ashes, keep repeating '*I disarm you, you are powerless,*' or something similar, over and over. Never leave a burning hex unattended; either the mischief will extend into the flames and set fire to something else, or the paper will simply refuse to burn. (The latter is surprisingly common in my experience!)

Once the hex has burned to a cinder, save and cover the ashes so they cannot blow back onto us, then mix them with some salt and take them away somewhere quiet to scatter them. A windy day is best because it will disperse them, although we can bury the ashes in salt or cast them into moving water if we prefer. What we must *not* do however, is flush the ashes down the sink, since the curved waste pipe will trap them there and ensure they remain in our home for weeks to come.

As we dispose of the ashes, keep repeating, '*Blessed be all those I love, blessed be this place,*' to ensure that any ill wishing still attached to the ashes will be properly dispersed. We can also adapt this method for ritually destroying any object that has been used to convey a hex. Again, the most effective methods are burning; casting it into water (particularly useful for anything that has had a ritual purpose) and burying it in salt.

The salt is important. We had a hexed knife in the house once when I was young. It had been found hidden up in a bedroom chimney on a ledge, and once it was found, some very unpleasant paranormal activity began to manifest in the home. Unlike a hex written on paper, something made of iron is more difficult to destroy, and we certainly cannot burn it, so one of my aunts volunteered to bury it in salt on some waste ground not far from where we lived. She also volunteered for me to go along with her and dig the hole.

'Don't forget the salt!' my mother called after us.

'Stop worrying!' said my aunt.

Anyway, off we went to the waste ground. Unfortunately, at that point my aunt realised she had not only forgotten the salt, but also the trowel. The ground was much too hard and dry to dig a hole using a stick or stone, so instead she just muttered a few words and threw the knife over a nearby wall and into some bushes.

'Don't tell your mother,' she warned, before we set off back towards home.

Well, the hex left the house, certainly, but it seemed to transfer its unpleasant energies to the place where she'd thrown it over the wall. We used to walk the family dogs past the area every day and noticed the change in atmosphere at once. It was like a malevolent blob lurking there. Even the dogs avoided it.

At this point, I wish I could say that my aunt went back, found the knife or cleansed the area and that all was well afterwards, but she didn't and it wasn't. All sorts of odd things started happening on that bit of waste ground, culminating in a suicide a few months later. The moral of this tale is that if we try to get rid of something that has been hexed, ensure it's done properly!

The atmosphere in any house that has held or received a hex will always lighten once the hex has been properly removed. If the atmosphere remains heavy even after the area has been magically cleansed, there is probably another hex hidden somewhere nearby. This may be deliberate; the first hex is relatively easy to find in order to divert attention from another, more powerful one.

Once we've disposed of a hex, we should also perform some magical cleansing in and around the home (or other spaces such as garage, shed, classroom or workplace) afterwards, since energies can occasionally linger even when the object that held the hex has gone. Remember to wash any clothes worn when we dealt with the hex, since these sometimes attract unpleasant influences; it helps to add a *small* pinch of salt to the washing water as a precaution. We must also remember to be good to ourselves. It's quite normal to feel tired and drained after dealing with a psychic attack.

Hexes Conveyed by Dolls

Sometimes psychic attackers use a doll to convey their hex, which is an old-fashioned but highly effective method practised over two thousand years ago in ancient Greece (and long before that, elsewhere). The doll (sometimes called a poppet) can be made of wood, bone, clay or wax and has usually been fashioned to resemble the victim in some way, like a rather cruel caricature.

Sometimes the attacker even 'names' the doll after the victim, writing the name on the torso using an alphabet such as Theban, Greek or Runic. If there is no visible name, then it may have been ritually named during its making. We should however be able to recognise who it represents since people who use dolls for hexing tend to pay great attention to detail. I've even heard of people giving them accessories such as umbrellas or handbags made to resemble those used by the intended victim.

Dolls may also incorporate something belonging to the victim, such as a scrap of clothing (even just a thread or two), some hair (just a few strands) or nail parings. In the case of a clay doll, these are often buried deep inside the clay and no longer visible. Some dolls are then drenched in excrement or urine.

If we believe we have been cursed using a doll, then our first task is to try and recover it. This is not as impossible as it sounds; some hexers are arrogant enough to place a poppet somewhere we can see it, hoping our own fears will work against us psychologically and enhance the hex. If we do find the doll, we will probably notice it has been damaged in some way. Magically speaking, damaging the doll helps activate and enact the curse, so the remedy is to repair it as quickly and completely as possible.

For example, if it has been pierced with a pin, then remove the pin and treat the hole where it pierced the doll as a wound. It is important to try and undo everything that has been done to the doll, and we should say what we are doing as we work. For example, if the doll is smeared in excrement, we should gently clean it up and say, *'I declare you,* [Name of doll or victim], *cleansed and pure. Nothing that has been done to you by others now harms you or* [Name] *in any way. Be safe, be well. Be clean. Be whole.'*

If a limb has been broken off the doll, make a new one out of balsa wood or clay, saying, *'I declare this limb of* [Name] *to be as good as new.* [Name], *be safe, be well.'* We can also anoint the doll with lavender oil, stick a Band Aid on it, and pronounce healing blessings such as, *'I free you of all the harm that has been done to you,* [Name] *I declare you are now healed and well.'* If the hands are bound then untie them, and state that the doll is no longer bound. *'Just as I free you from these ties, so I free you from all enchantment. I now declare you* [Name] *healed and free.'*

It's important while we work to keep repeating (mentally or aloud) that the hex is void, it has been disarmed, it cannot hurt us, our loved ones or anyone else. It has no power. This focuses our minds on what we're doing, preventing any stray energies still attached to the doll from harming us. Once we have finished undoing what has been done, wrap the doll in a clean white cloth and keep it where the attacker cannot get at it again. Then do some careful cleansing.

On a practical level, anything removed from the doll such as pins or nails should be burned, buried in salt or cast into running water. We could say something along the lines of, *'I free you from the hex that claimed you. I cleanse you of all ill will. Be clean. Be safe. Do no harm to anyone or anything.'*

Any cloths we use, for example to remove urine or faeces, must also be properly disposed of with a few words of purification. Dissolve some ordinary salt, as much as seems appropriate, into the water we used for washing the doll. When getting rid of the water afterwards remember to avoid the kitchen or bathroom sinks and instead pour it down an outside drain. If we must use an indoor sink, flush it well with plenty of boiling water afterwards and then a little more salt, just to be on the safe side. Some people like to use products for unblocking drains too, just to be on the safe side, but unless the situation is dire, there is really no need for this.

Once everything has been attended to, we should once more tell the doll that it is now free, it has been cleansed, healed and has no magical connection with us whatsoever. This is important because at some point we shall probably wish to dispose of the doll, and it needs to be quite empty of our personal magnetism for us to feel comfortable doing this.

When should we dispose of such a doll? In my opinion, the sooner the better, since once it is disarmed it serves no useful purpose. Certainly, we should not keep it once we feel the threat has gone. Bury it in salt, or burn it adding a pinch of salt to the flames, but please, get rid of it.

Usually, of course, we cannot get hold of the doll even if we suspect its existence. In this situation we need to set up several magical guardians around the home. These can be other dolls (I've even known people use teddy bears) and magically it makes good sense because we are using the *similia similibus curantur* or 'like cures like' approach. These guardians should be temporarily empowered to protect us, since we may not always want them on guard, and a teddy bear that has acted as a guardian bear for years on end doesn't always make the most pleasant thing to play with afterwards! Some become positively fierce.

All we need to do is simply take the doll (or teddy bear, etc.), blow gently from the top of its head down to the bottom of its feet (a very old method of exorcism) to purify it, and then say something like: *'I* [give our own name], *empower you* [Name of doll/teddy] *as my protector.*[136] *From today* [give date] *until…* [give our chosen date which should be about a week or month ahead] *you will stand guard for me. Prevent any harmful entities and energies from entering this place and watch over me and keep me safe.'*

Depending on where we intend keeping the doll, we may need to change the final sentence. For example, if we intend keeping the doll in the car, we may need to say something like: *'Prevent any harmful entities from entering this place, or from crossing my path, or from hurting me and my passengers when we are in the car or travelling or at any other time.'*

We should remember to acknowledge the new guardian whenever we pass it, as this keeps the link between us open and active. I also thank my guardians every day for a job well done. (There is information on creating guardians in Chapter Five).

---

[136] If it already has a name, all well and good, otherwise just say 'doll' or 'bear'

Hexes Inscribed on Metal

In the ancient Graeco-Roman world, hexes were often written on metal, especially lead, tin and pewter, which are all relatively soft and easy to write on with a pointed stylus. It is a long-lasting medium, (although does deteriorate) which probably explains why so many have survived from ancient times in places such as the Roman Baths at Bath. They are known as cursing tablets, *defixiones* (Latin) and *katadesmoi* (Greek).

Nowadays, few psychic attackers will go to the trouble of making a hex using this method, but some still do, and small offcuts of lead are easily available wherever roofing work is being done. Most hexes can be written on a piece of metal about the size of a credit card, making it easy to hide (usually in graves, springs or wells, or in the victim's workplace or home).

Essentially, *defixiones* seek to bind or restrain the victim in some way. The lettering may be jumbled or twisted in order create physical confusion and sometimes the metal is rolled up, pierced or twisted to cause the victim further pain. With this type of attack, the hexer often invokes ghosts or underworld powers to carry out the curse, but sometimes the curse tablet conveys the attacker's own mental energies without relying on any further help.

If we ever find ourselves the subject of a *defixio* and can lay our hands on it, there are several methods to neutralise it. Apart from burying in salt, it can also be melted in the heat of a blow torch, but if we choose this method then the area must be well ventilated since lead fumes are *extremely* toxic. We can also hammer the lead sheet quite flat so that all the writing is flattened or hammer our own blessing over the top in order to nullify the curse.

The important thing to remember when dealing with any cursing tablet is that whatever we do to it in a physical sense is repeated magically onto the curse itself. Thus if we melt the lead we say: *'Just as I am melting this lead, that it runs like water, so may the words of this curse run away and be rendered completely harmless.'*

If we decide to hammer out the letters, we could say: *'Just as I make these letters fade from view, so may the harmful intention of this spell fade away and be made harmless.'*

This 'Just as... So may...' method is an extremely ancient formula. It is very effective since it links the present physical situation with the desired future outcome and is particularly useful when we are trying to dismantle any type of psychic attack.

Hexes Conveyed via Tattoos.

Sometimes we find ourselves on the receiving end of a psychic attack and unable to break some of the links that bind us to our attacker. This is particularly true if we have a tattoo representing our attacker, or *vice versa.* And of course, although removing tattoos is possible, nobody needs our consent in order to have our name or image tattooed on *their* body.

Whether we are the person whose name is now blazoned across the biceps or bosom of someone we cannot bear to set eyes on, or whether we are carrying the name of someone we no longer care for on our skin - the problem is similar. What we want to do is neutralise its effect.

If we are the person whose name is tattooed on someone else's skin, we must prepare a ritual to break the tie between us and reclaim that name as ours alone as nobody has the right to control us through our name. For this exercise we will need a piece of string and a sharp knife or scissors. First rub the string against our skin (and the tattoo if possible) to magnetise it and then say the following:

My name upon your flesh is only ink,
It does not give you power o'er what I think
Or do, or say. I will not answer to your call,
Fiat (here cut the string) – *now I break this link*
And set you free; and set me free.

'*Fiat*' is an authoritative sanction from the Latin and literally means '*Let it be done.*' It is very useful in this type of magic. When our spell is finished, we can either burn the string or cast it into fast flowing water. Do not be tempted to throw it into the sea since we do not want to risk it returning to us on the tide!

If we are the one with a tattoo, and the former relationship has now become hostile, our skin may feel very uncomfortable. Some people recommend having the tattoo professionally removed but that isn't always practicable or necessary. Instead first try cleansing the tattoo in order to free it from any association with the person whose name we still bear.

Begin by washing the skin with salt water (about a teaspoonful of salt to a pint of water) or perform any of the cleansing rituals suggested in Chapter Twelve. We can also easily adapt the words of the ritual given above for dealing with someone who has a tattoo of our name. Again we need to cut the string (which represents the ties that used to bind we) this time saying something like:

Your name upon my flesh is only ink,
You have no power o'er what I think, nor I o'er you.
I will not answer to your call,
Fiat – Now I break this link
And set you free and set me free.

Sometimes people manage to cause problems with their *own* tattoos – a type of pictorial self-hex. It's becoming increasingly popular to have a 'psychic' tattoo, intended to bind some aspect of the owner's character that he finds difficult to control. Examples of this would be anger or jealousy. The person then has a tattoo designed to try and permanently control this trait.

All quite harmless, we might think. Unfortunately, people sometimes become convinced that their tattoo has somehow become unstable and that the violent aspect of their character is trying once again to break out and cause mayhem.

It goes without saying that much depends on the subject's own character. Are the original character traits still a problem? Were they *ever* really such a big problem? It's virtually impossible for any tattoo created under these hazy circumstances to be able to control its owner.

Most of the power we invest in anything – pictures, charms, amulets, comes from our own mind, so any remedy will likewise need to rely heavily upon the power of the mind in order to succeed. This means that the subject – the person with the tattoo –

is going to have to do much of the work for himself. No amount of tattoo ink will do any good without proper, sensible visualisation.

I certainly would not recommend scratching at the tattoo or cutting the skin. Apart from the fact that it is highly disfiguring, it may allow something else to literally get under our skin, with unknown consequences. Some people recommend reworking the original tattoo in order to 'set it free'. This is quite complicated and by no means a quick solution. Again, the subject is going to have to co-operate and not simply sit back expecting someone else to do all the work.

For a start, the subject should consider why he had the tattoo in the first place. For example, was he so jealous that he became unable to maintain a normal relationship? If so, why? What was his real fear? Loneliness? Insecurity? Only when the real source of the problem has been identified (and this could take some time) should a new tattoo be designed to cover the original and deal with the original character trait in a positive way.

Having a new tattoo is not an easy option since we need to find a sympathetic tattooist who understands the spiritual aspect of what we are trying to do and is willing work with us to produce a pleasing new image. An unpleasant looking design – no matter what the intention behind it – will always sit uneasily on our skin.

If we really cannot face – or afford – another tattoo, it's possible for the subject to do the same sort of work using the power of his own visualisation. This is just as effective and powerful but will require considerable effort over a long period of time. Begin by focussing on the original problem since it is part of us, who and what we are. However, whereas our character traits are hidden, the tattoo is visible. We shouldn't fear our inner self but learn to accept it, control it and work with it. Not all apparently negative traits are dangerous. Some can save our lives.

For example, stubbornness is often considered negative. Yet many of the people who survive shipwrecks, storms, accidents etc., do so because they are extremely stubborn and simply refuse to give up. Anger is another characteristic that is often viewed as totally negative. But sometimes anger can be positive; anger at unjust situations, for examples, often enables us to fight and obtain justice for ourselves or others.

Some people are very tense and anxious by the time they get around to doing something about a tattoo that is causing them problems. Remember however, that even though tattoos are permanent, spells are not. They can wear off, fade away, lose their power. If we have a tattoo that no longer has any meaning for us then we shouldn't worry too much about it. Once the meaning has faded, so will its power. Remember symbols are powerful only when they mean something to the people involved.

Disarming a Curse Stone

Most cursing stones are marked, often with a painted cross (although I have seen some that were stuck on with coloured insulating tape!) They are usually left out of doors (gardens are popular) and can easily be mistaken for a marker stone for a pet's grave. However, a curse stone has a distinctly unpleasant feel to it and should be dealt with appropriately. If the stone has insulating tape on it, simply remove and burn it, just as we would a hex written on paper. Afterwards cleanse the stones and bury them in the earth with some salt. Alternatively throw them into a fast running river or leave them on a beach *below* the high tide mark. The sea will wash them clean in time.

If the stone has been marked with felt tip pens or paint, it's more difficult to remove this but we should do our best. Afterwards bury the stones in salt somewhere they will not be disturbed for a very long time. Sometimes people like to plant a sapling to mark the spot, in the belief that something good will eventually come out of it. Personally, I would not plant anything that could disturb the ground. Just cleanse the stones, bury them and then forget about them. That advice holds good for dealing with all manner of hexes and psychic attacks. Once we have performed the appropriate rituals of psychic self defence, that's it. Stop worrying and get on with your life!

CHAPTER SIXTEEN

Dealing with night-time threats including the Mare. The basic methods. Erotic curses and their remedies.

Many people describe attacks by the Mare as the most frightening thing they have ever experienced. Unlike ordinary nightmares, the memory stays with the victim for days, sometimes weeks - and even years - afterwards. Because of this, it's important not to allow the attacker to see how he is affecting us, since our distress only strengthens his resolve. It is never wise, therefore, to tell the whole world and his dog that we're being attacked; we should only confide in people we know are trustworthy. If our attacker doesn't hear whether the Mare is even reaching us, he will doubt himself. Has he sent the Mare to the wrong place? Has he lost his power? Self-doubt is lethal for spell work, which requires calm, quiet confidence.

If the attacker knows he is frightening us however, he will redouble his efforts. When he sees no reaction from us, even though he may continue trying to summon the Mare (or other entity), his resolve will be considerably weakened. If he runs into the magical equivalent of a brick wall or must deal with our strong psychic defences, he will eventually believe his attacks are unsuccessful and abandon them. He may, of course try something else, but eventually he will get the message that we are no pushover and very few attackers want a prolonged struggle.

Always remember that no matter how terrifying a psychic attack may seem, *all* magic - stripped of its ceremony - is essentially about the will. A psychic attacker uses his will to harm his victim and in order to prevent the attack from reaching its target the victim must deflect, defuse or destroy the hex.

As we saw in Chapter Seven, not all night-time disturbances are true psychic attacks. Until we are certain what we are dealing with we should try and ensure a good night's sleep by all physical means possible. This means not eating too late in the evening and avoiding cheese and eggs whenever an attack seems imminent. When I was young, I was always warned against eating cheese before going to bed as it was thought to cause nightmares, and there seems to be some truth in this old tradition. Also avoid too much alcohol before bedtime and make sure the bedroom is neither too cold nor too warm. Psychic attacks, especially at night, can make us too frightened to go to sleep, but it is better to avoid sleeping tablets while attacks are active.

Anecdotal evidence suggests the Mare is more likely to attack people who are stressed and nervous just before retiring to bed, so try sprinkling lavender essential oil on pillows and bedding. It's not only soothing and cleansing but also aids sleep and helps repel unpleasant influences.

If the problems persist, we can next use magical cleansing to clear out any unpleasant influences that might bother us at night and if that doesn't do the trick, try other methods such as visualising psychic armour, sealing exits and entrances, placing garlic or consecrated salt and vinegar in the room etc. Although the smell of garlic in the bedroom can be off-putting, it is always a powerful protector against night-time psychic attacks. Slice the garlic cloves in half lengthwise, replacing them every morning while an attack is active. Sliced onions are another possibility, but not leeks since in Welsh folklore, leeks were said to 'produce terrible and fearful dreams.' [137]

Years ago, a popular remedy against the Mare was for the victim to urinate in a bottle and keep it under the bed. The attacker was then magically prevented from urinating until the bottle was removed.[138] The mere presence of such a bottle is a clear visual reminder that the victim is willing to fight back. It also shows how the action of one person (in this case the victim) can be projected onto another (in this case, the attacker). Just as the victim's urine is sealed in the bottle, so the attacker's urine is 'sealed' within the bladder. Traditionally, those who preferred brute force to magic preferred to swing a bottle (hopefully empty) at the Mare, although this ignores the fact that the victim always feels paralysed during an attack.

---

137 Bonser (1926): 360

138 Hufford (1982): 9

Not all folk remedies are helpful. For example, we would need to be very desperate indeed to consider sleeping with a board of nails strapped to our chest. Apart from damaging our mattress, bedding and anyone foolish enough to sleep beside us, a board of nails strapped to the chest would force us to sleep on our backs, which is the very position thought to encourage attacks by the Mare. (In fairness, however, attacks are also reported when people sleep on their stomachs or even in the foetal position.)

We should also think about how the attacker manages to reach us. As we saw in Chapter Fifteen, sometimes hexes are conveyed when the attacker has something belonging to the victim such as hair, nail parings, or even a treasured possession that bears our signature, for example, a book. We may have given this to him (think of sentimental items such as hair in a locket) or conversely, the attacker may have helped himself without our knowledge.

It's difficult to request the return of such items, and even if we do, our attacker will probably deny all knowledge of them. Sometimes of course, it works the other way and an attacker gives us something that conveys *his* magnetism (and therefore the attack) to us. It might be given openly, but more likely he will have hidden it somewhere without our knowledge. The best place to start looking is probably the bedroom but if we cannot find anything there, we will have to widen our search.

There is a long tradition that attacks by the Mare are connected to physical objects. In one old folk story, a farmer who suspected that his horses were being '*ridden by the Mare*' every night, noticed two sieves standing against the fence in the field where he kept his animals. Intrigued, he took the items home with him. Later that day, two women came to his farm asking for the return of their sieves, but the farmer refused until they promised never to bother his horses again.[139] Although I suspect this story has become somewhat garbled in the retelling, nevertheless it reminds us to be on the lookout for anything belonging to the attacker no matter how unlikely it seems. If we find anything, we should dispose of it immediately as suggested in Chapter Fifteen.

[139] Quoted in de Blécourt (2003): 237

Traditionally, one of the most popular herbal protections against the Mare was mistletoe. Unlike other plants used for Christmas and Yuletide decorations, which had to be burned as soon as the festivities were over, keeping mistletoe hanging up all year was supposed to bring protection and good luck. In Flanders and Holland, mistletoe was named *Maretak* and was believed to grow wherever the Mare or an elf had sat. In Germany, holding a sprig of mistletoe was said to bestow the power to see and talk to ghosts.

The interesting thing about mistletoe is that it works by drawing the Mare *away* from us. So don't be tempted to take a sprig of mistletoe to bed for protection and avoid hanging it anywhere near bedrooms, stables, cow sheds, rabbit hutches etc. Instead put it in some place where it will attract the Mare away from potential victims.

The peony was another old remedy for '*Those that are troubled in the night with the disease called the Night Mare... and... melancholicke dreames,*' according to Gerard's Herbal which was first published in the late sixteenth century. Depending on the time of year, placing a bunch of peony flowers in a vase in the bedroom, or even a dish containing some of the seeds was a good protective measure; people also carried pieces of the root or leaves as an amulet.

It can also be helpful to protect ourselves against the Night Mare by sealing our Aura before we go to sleep (see Chapter Nine). This is also sometimes referred to as the Openings of the Body ritual and helps repair damage from earlier psychic attacks, preventing our energies being further drained and weakened. Drawing or visualising a pentagram outside our bedroom door with the two points nearest our room, and the single point uppermost and pointing away is also effective.

Obviously just sketching a shape in the air does not imbue it with magical power. To do that we must really set our minds to it and imagine creating a fiery trail with every line we draw. This is not difficult, but if we still struggle, try repeating, *'With this line, I create the pentagram, driving back all evil and all who wish me harm.'* It doesn't matter whether this is said aloud, or silently: if we believe in what we're doing, it will work. If we simply stand there waving our arms around and feeling a bit silly, then it won't. It's up to us.

If we suspect the Mare (or any other type of psychic attack), is being invoked against us by someone we live with, just draw the pentagram with the single point facing inwards towards *their* bedroom. The single point will keep anything hostile at bay whereas the two points will protect anything that lies in front of them.

The most tactful time to do this is just after they've retired for the night (remembering to close our own bedroom door afterwards.) Being entirely visualised, there is nothing for anyone to find the following morning whereas using a real pentagram made of metal, wicker, wood, or even drawn on paper is fine if we are protecting ourselves but could take some explaining if the others find it.

In these situations, people often wonder about the ethical side of drawing pentagrams (or anything else for that matter), outside another person's door. Is it acceptable? Can it be justified? Do we need their permission? I always feel that when we are under attack we are entitled to defend ourselves.

Think of it as putting an extra lock on our door when there are burglars in our area. There is no law, written or otherwise, that demands we should first obtain anyone's permission to do this (unless it is someone else's door, of course.)

In much the same way, by sealing someone's door with the pentagram all we are doing is preventing our attacker's objectionable energies from reaching us (or anyone else.) If they weren't attacking us in the first place there would be no need to do anything. If we concentrate only on repelling a psychic attack, and don't attempt to add a counter-attack of our own, we are not crossing any ethical thresholds.

Another useful defensive method is to use a *psychic* sword to mark out a protective circle around our bed. We need to be organised beforehand however, since ideally we should not mark out the circle until we are ready to stay inside it for the next few hours. Some people claim we can cut magical doors in the circle if we need to get out again, but personally I would try and avoid doing so unless absolutely necessary. An unbroken circle is always stronger than a repaired one!

When attempting any magical ritual, work quickly and with intense purpose rather than allowing it drag on. (This is not the same as rushing through a ritual, since when we rush we often make mistakes and miss things we meant to include.) When about to mark out our protective circle, we take a few quick breaths to ground ourselves then begin to visualise tracing a circle right around our bed. We should try and hear the sword scraping on the floor as we work, but don't worry if our bed is right against the wall, since when we visualise something we can work through and even beyond a mere brick wall!

As we work, say aloud (or under our breath), *'With this sword I draw this circle to keep me safe from all harmful intention.'* This is very much the same formula we used earlier in this chapter to visualise drawing a pentagram. This magical technique is known as 'performative intention' since it indicates the precise enactment of our spell.[140] It turns up not only in magical rituals but also in mainstream religious ones. One of the best-known examples is found in the Christian wedding ceremony, with the famous phrase, *'With this ring, I thee wed.'*

We can perform a similar ritual by drawing a visualised pentagram in the air above the bed to banish any harmful intentions being sent our way. As with all defensive presentations of the pentagram, begin drawing it at the bottom left hand point. Although most magical visualisations only last for as long as we actively imagine them, the protection offered by a circle around the bed and the pentagram in the air will usually last most of the night.

Sleeping with a knife under the pillow was another popular magical remedy against night-time attacks and is clearly an example of 'as above so below' thinking. To be *physically* prepared for an attack, even though when it occurs the victim feels too paralysed to move a muscle, is also a way of being *magically* prepared.

---

[140] Mees (2009): 56

A less obvious precaution was to turn one's shoes before getting into bed in order to confuse the Night Mare who sometimes stepped into the victim's shoes and followed him to bed. Turning our shoes or arranging them '*coming and going*' i.e. with the heel of one shoe pointing in the direction of the toe of the other was thought to make this impossible. In Holland it was recommended to place one's clogs crosswise in front of the bed, while in other areas, placing the toes of shoes so that they pointed *away* from the bed was thought to convince the Night Mare that the wearer had got out of bed again. If so, the Night Mare must have been thoroughly stupid not to recognise that if the shoes were still near then so was the bed's occupant!

Shoes have been used for magical protection for many years. They were popular as ornaments, made into pin cushions, and even hung on the back of a cart or later, a car, when newlyweds left the church. I've also seen old shoes burned with salt on the open fire at home, as a protection against hexing. The fact that so many people still swear by using shoes to combat the Mare suggests it is worth trying. Remember that the ritual of doing something – *anything* – is very comforting; it helps us feel more confident and less stressed, which is sometimes all we need in order to prevent or deflect another attack.

People have also used prayers and religious medals to deter the Night Mare and these may be very effective for someone who is already in the habit of praying or invoking holy names. As with shoes, the combination of faith in a particular action and the comfort afforded by feeling that we are at least doing something to help ourselves can be a very powerful force in psychic self defence.

> *'I was only bothered with the Night Mare once. It was terrifying. Then my wife told me to keep a blessed medal under the pillow which I did (and still do to this day.) Since then it has never happened again.'*[141]

If this had simply been a case of sleep paralysis, caused by disturbance in the REM pattern of sleep then it could surely be

---

141 Author's personal notes

expected to recur, whether or not a holy medal was used. The fact that it did not suggests that either the amulet comforted its owner to the extent that he was no longer fearful and there were no more attacks, or that the amulet itself had the power to repel a psychic attack. Sometimes *how* something works is not as important as the fact that it *does* work.

My own feeling is that it is the victim's *belief* in the amulet that gives it its power. For example, sleeping with a blessed medal under the pillow has a better chance of being effective *if we already believe in its power.* Although in this case the victim's wife suggested the holy medal, it seems likely that the husband probably shared at least some of her beliefs.

If we prefer a non-religious charm (the best time to recite it is probably just before retiring for the night) then try this example from northern Britain, which dates from the fourteenth century:

Tha mon o' micht, he rade o' nicht,
Wi' neider swerd ne ferd ne licht.
He socht tha Mare, he fond tha Mare,
He bond that Mare wi' her ain hare,
Ond gared her swar by midder-micht
She wolde nae mair rid o'nicht
What aince he rade, thot mon o' micht.[142]

Recited aloud, the rhythmic power of the charm is still quite incredible! It uses a narrative introduction, a very old style of charm, that basically tells the tale of an earlier, successful, assault on the Mare. The magical thinking behind this is, '*Just as this has happened before... so may this happen again in order to help me.*' The charm increases the victim's confidence by showing that the Mare has been overcome in the past and therefore can be defeated again.

If we find the dialect a little difficult, try this version (although I think the original is far better!):

That man of mine, he rode the night,
With neither sword nor fire nor light,

142 Graves (1981): 26

He sought the Mare, he found the Mare,
He bound the Mare with her own hair,
And forced her swear by mother's might
She would no more ride out at night
What once he rode, that man of mine.

Holed stones were also known as hollow stones, holy stones and even Hog Stones, which is probably a corruption of 'hag,' (another name for The Mare), rather than any reference to a pig. They were highly valued as amulets in many European countries including the UK especially against the Night Mare. In Scotland they were known as Mare-Stanes, and one example that was exhibited in the nineteenth century had two human teeth inserted in natural holes in the stone which was believed to make it particularly powerful.

In Europe, however, such 'manufactured' stones were frowned upon and the most powerful ones were those that occurred naturally; best of all, they should be found without actively looking for them. These were very popular amulets in the North of England and could either be hung above the bed or worn around the neck. Their power is summed up in the old description of a sorcerer as someone who could:

Chase evil spirits away by dint
Of sickle, horse-shoe and hollow flint. [143]

To be most effective, the holed stone needed to be placed very close to the person or animal it was intended to protect, for example hung either on the bed or placed between the sheets. In Queen Elizabeth I's time people were instructed to, '*Take a Flynt Stone that hath a hole of hys owne kinds, and hang it ouer hym.*'[144] To protect animals, especially cows that were due to calve, the stones were placed in cow sheds and stables. Hanging a holed stone from the key of the stable door was said to deter the Hag from riding the horses kept there at night.

---

143 The Earl of Ducie (1888)
144 *ibid*

Although flint is widely available in many parts of Britain, in other countries different stones were used, suggesting that the stone's power is due to the presence of the hole, rather than the type of stone. The only stones to be avoided were agate, onyx and obsidian: traditionally the onyx harboured the Mare while in Iceland it was believed that obsidian and agate caused quarrels.

In many areas, holed stones were often boiled in water that was then given to animals that had been enchanted or overlooked. In Weymouth, Dorset, holed stones were tied inside the bows of fishing boats presumably for general protection, since there is no tradition that being at sea attracts visits by the Night Mare.[145] There is however a tradition from Somerset that boring a hole through objects made them 'safe' to throw overboard.

Just as puncturing or breaking an object physically causes it to sink, so magically it could ensure that the waters had accepted it.[146] This could also be the thinking behind many ancient ritual depositions uncovered from rivers, wells or streams which appear to have been broken before they being placed in the water.

We can adapt this magical principle whenever we need to dispose of objects that were used to convey hexes and/or the Mare: we simply break them and then place the pieces in deep or running water. Extend either both hands or our preferred hand over the object and say something like: *'Just as I break this* [Name the object] *... so I break any curse that has been laid upon it. Your power is exhausted. Be clean. Be pure. You can harm no-one.'* Here we can see how the *'Just as...so I'* links the physical act (in this case, breaking

---

145 Elworthy (1903): 20

146 We can see similarities here with the old Trial by Ordeal of 'swimming the witch'. Bound hand and foot and thrown into water, if she floated (which is after all, what anyone would hope to do) she was guilty, whereas if she sank, she was innocent. At first sight this seems to be a case of *'Damned if you do and drowned if you don't.'* However, looked at from a magical point of view, it could also be interpreted as the water accepting her, meaning that she was innocent. Of course, this was little comfort to the accused who almost always drowned.

the object) with the magical intention of breaking its power and rendering it safe.

Given that the Night Mare was sometimes attributed to the magical activities of dwarves and elves, it should be no surprise to learn that a holed stone also protects against 'Pharisees' – a term that had nothing to do with the Bible but was in fact an old word for fairies. It was believed that fairies would ride horses all night and leave them sweating and covered in foam,[147] a story with such strong similarities to tales of the Mare that the two traditions may have either become confused or share a common, ancient source. It is widely believed that anyone who looks through a holed stone or even a wreath of herbs (which is basically the same magical principle) will be able to see fairies.

Holed stones have other protective functions too. Hung up in trees they protect the garden, while behind the front door they protect the home. Placing them next to or near a horseshoe is believed to increase their power considerably. In Italy, holed stones are still hung up over shop doors, sometimes alongside a goat's horn or a horseshoe.[148]

Horseshoes have long been regarded as 'lucky' even though their original function was protective, and we often see them nailed up on doors and walls and even on church doors.[149] There is some argument about which way up they should hang, but I was always taught that the curve goes at the bottom with the two prongs at the top. That way their energy doesn't drain away. If we don't have a real horseshoe, then a picture can be substituted.

In spite of the protective properties of horseshoes, horses themselves seem to have been particularly susceptible to the Night Mare. Horrified owners would find them the next morning in their stables, exhausted, covered in foam, their manes tangled and knotted. Sometimes a horse's skull was placed above the stable door in order to protect against Night Mare attacks.

Preventative measures against an attack by the Night Mare are one thing, but what do we do when an attack is actually

---

147 Scott (1665): 51

148 Elworthy (1903): 18

149 Dyer (1892): 308

happening? For most people the answer is, very little, since the victim feels paralysed and unable to move or cry out. If possible, concentrate on moving just a single finger or toe; once we can do this, the rest of the body follows suit.

If someone sleeps beside us and knows what to expect, we can suggest in advance that they either touch us or say our name backwards which is believed to be more effective than saying our name the right way around. In the morning after an attack, cleanse the bed and bedroom and repeat any of the preventative measures suggested in this chapter.

The Mare can take a variety of forms, including cats, dogs, wolves and birds. However, one thing that intrigues me is that if the Night Mare really is 'all in the mind' as some people claim, we would expect our personal fears and phobias to play some part in the form it takes. However, some of the most widely feared creatures – snakes and spiders for example – rarely feature in reports of the Night Mare. It is true that a 'Spiderwight' is mentioned in an Anglo-Saxon charm in the Lacnunga, although the English translations range from 'a creature all swathed' to 'in spider form'. This may not refer to a real spider however, but to a spirit or creature that has shape-shifted into spider form. In various folk traditions dwarves are often connected with spiders, and in old Breton, Welsh and Cornish, the word *cor* can mean both a dwarf and a spider.[150]

In the Anglo-Saxon charm, the Spiderwight carries a bridle which he puts onto his victim in order to ride him, rather like the Mare, who will sometimes ride her victim around the countryside. There are similarities with an Icelandic folktale that describes how the Mare, '*...was busy fixing something in his mouth; he realized that it was a magic bridle... As soon as she bridled him, she led him out...got on his back, and rode away as hard as she could.*'[151] Usually the 'riding' is confined to the room where the attack takes place although sometimes the victim reports being ridden up into the air.

The Anglo-Saxon method for dealing with a Spiderwight required sufferers to take seven wafers (communion wafers are

---

[150] Gay (1988): 175

[151] Simpson (1972): 46

implied although there is nothing to stop us using ice-cream wafers and they will certainly be easier to obtain) and write the name of one of the Seven Sleepers of Ephesus on each.[152] Traditionally these names were: Maximianus, Malchus, Iohannes, Martimianus, Dionisius, Constantinus and Serafion although there are other versions. The names were usually invoked to cure violent or spasmodic illnesses, both adjectives that can apply to the effects of the Night Mare.

We can easily consecrate our wafers by adapting the techniques suggested for consecrating salt in Chapter Twelve. Before writing anything on them, we simply stretch out our hand (the right hand is traditional for blessing and consecration) and say something along the lines of: *'May these wafers be sacred and blessed and may they be empowered by the names that I shall write upon them. May they protect…*[and here name whoever or whatever needs protection] *from attacks by the Night Mare.'*

The simplest way of writing names on the wafers is to use a fine, dry paintbrush and some food colouring. Use this sparingly however, since otherwise it will 'bleed' into the wafer. Alternatively try scratching the names into the wafer using a sharp pin. Remember, nobody else needs to be able to read the words; we are constructing a charm, not doing calligraphy!

Next we need to sing the following charm :

Here he came in walking, in spider form;
He had his harness in his hand,
He said that you were his steed,
He put his traces on your neck:
Then they began to travel from the ground;
So soon they came from the ground;
Then their limbs began to cool.
Then came in walking the beast's sister;
She put an end to this then and swore oaths

---

152 The Seven Sleepers of Ephesus is a legend about seven young Christian men who were walled up alive by a pagan Roman Emperor, and then eventually discovered, still alive, some centuries later.

That this would never harm the sick one,
Nor that one who might find this charm
Or knows how to recite this charm.
Amen. So be it.[153]

Since the melody has not been handed down to us, we could sing it as a simple chant. We can also adapt well known melodies, but in this example, it's difficult to get the words to fit because the rhythm is so irregular. The charm must be sung first into the sufferer's left ear, then into his right, and finally over the top of his head. Traditionally a virgin then hung the wafers around the sufferer's neck (presumably first having threaded them onto a cord although the charm does not mention this) and left them there for three days.

Apart from dwarves, elves were also thought to cause the Night Mare and other unpleasant night-time apparitions. Remedies against 'the elf-kind and nocturnal goblins,' or 'frightful nocturnal goblins and terrible sights and dreams,' suggest a variety of ceremonies over herbs which are then thrown into running water. *The Old English Herbarium*[154] recommends betony (*Stachys officinalis*) which is also known as bishopswort, for shielding, '*against dreadful night-goers and against frightful visions and dreams.*'

An alternative is to wear the leaves of the plant about either carried in a pocket or shoe. However, since we remove our shoes to go to bed, and since most attacks by the Mare take place in bed, we could just place an additional fresh sprig of the herb under the pillow at night.

Remedies for Erotic Curses

Another type of attack that usually occurs at night is the enactment of an erotic curse. This is a very ancient spell, which usually manifests in one of two ways. Either it causes the victim to fall in love with (or at least consent to have sex with) the attacker. This is known as an attraction spell and its symptoms – which include

[153] Gay (1988)

[154] Pollington (2000): 281

insomnia and extreme restlessness – are relatively easy to spot. The second type of erotic curse will break up the victim's relationship with someone else and is known as a separation spell.

Erotic curses are enacted using either the attacker's magical will, or a created thought form which is sent to fetch the victim. The thought form may be male or female (but is usually male) and either entices or forces the victim to accompany him. There is no confusing these attacks with the Night Mare. Thought forms created for the purpose of enacting an erotic curse have one job and one only; to bring the victim to the attacker.

More than any other type of psychic attack, an erotic curse (whether to attract or separate) often makes use of a poppet/doll/*kolossoi* and the attacker will almost certainly have obtained some of the victim's hair, nails or clothing beforehand. The doll may be pierced with pins or nails and its hands may be bound. It can be very upsetting to find one of these, especially if we believe it is meant to represent us.

Luckily, they are not all that difficult to deal with (See Chapter Fifteen) although it is unusual to be able to get hold of a doll used to create a hex. Usually we just concentrate on cleansing ourselves, our homes and any other places we frequent, using any of the methods suggested in this second half of the book.

If we suspect a separation curse has been cast, then purification and cleansing is important in order to disperse the sour sense of hostility that will build up between us and our loved ones. Causing discord between victims and their family is a common method of initiating a psychic attack. It tends to occur when the attacker knows the victim well enough to understand exactly which buttons to press in order to get his intended results.

We must be on our guard while all this is going on. Have as little as possible to do with the attacker and also with anyone who could convey information to that person. Starved of regular reports on the attack-in-progress, many psychic attackers lose their way when unable to discover which aspects of their attack are causing the most distress. When they finally realise we are going to fight back, they often abandon the attack altogether.

As in all matters connected with psychic self defence: If we truly believe we can defend ourselves, we will.

If we doubt ourselves, we won't.

CHAPTER SEVENTEEN

When our own spells cause problems: a few hints for 'undoing' them.

Many people are horrified at the idea they can somehow hex themselves, but it *is* possible. Sometimes it is our own spells that have caused the problem, but often it is something in our character, which makes self-hexes both difficult to identify and even harder to accept. However with the right attitude they can be prevented from happening, and if they do occur, they can almost always be resolved.

Undoing our own Spells

Most people, if asked, will claim that they always cast a spell with the best of intentions. That's probably true. However, sometimes we are rushed, tired, or don't know all the facts before we start. Sometimes situations change quickly so that the spell we did is now inappropriate or worse, downright harmful. The question is – what can be done about it? Is it possible to undo a spell?

The short answer is yes – provided we can remember exactly what we did in the first place. Keeping a record of every spell we cast isn't always possible, I know, but it *is* good magical practice. Unfortunately, the type of spell that needs undoing later is usually cast in the heat of the moment, and detailed notes are rarely made. That is our first problem.

The second problem is the sort of people who cast the spells that later need undoing. For example, a few years ago, a neighbour asked me for advice. 'I don't know anything about magic,' she announced, (and sounded proud of the fact) 'but a few years ago I did this spell and now I want to undo it…'

I wish I had a pound for every time I've heard that! Even for an experienced spell-caster, undoing a spell is much more difficult than casting one in the first place. For a beginner, someone who doesn't know anything about magic, undoing such a spell can be almost impossible. This is because when we regularly cast spells, we usually work to a routine. Afterwards, using the routine as a template we can then undo the spell. The rash novice, however, takes no notice of what she is doing and rarely remembers anything about it. Her lack of any basic magical knowledge means she cannot even hazard an educated guess about what she did in the original spell and it is extremely difficult to undo something we cannot clearly remember.

So, if we find ourselves trying to help someone in this situation, they should begin by writing down as much as they *can* remember. Since spells vary so much, it's impossible to be more precise than this. If they remember using a spell in a book, then they must try and find the book again; if it's a spell they created for themselves, they must look for their draft or notes. If they still cannot find the original spell, it will have to be reconstructed from memory. This isn't ideal but it's better than nothing.

Deconstruction involves working line by line. Some people work the spell backwards, even to the extent of reciting the words in reverse order. I tend to avoid this because jumbling up words, (and in particular, reversing them) was traditionally used in hexes. Therefore, undoing a spell by reversing the words runs a very real risk of creating a full-blown hex – albeit unknowingly- as is undoing a spell by reversing words that one is not certain were actually used is taking an unnecessary risk.

The best method is to take each part of the spell and then literally undo it. One method is to work with pieces of knotted string for each section of the spell. Once we have reconstructed the original spell to the best of our ability, work out how many sections it has, and tie the same number of knots in a single length of string. (Do this without repeating the original spell because we don't want to set that in motion again.)

To undo the spell, go through the original and if it says something like, '*I bind* [Name] *to my will,*' silently take the string and undo the knot, while saying, '*I now release* [Name] *may she be unbound, may she be free.*' We continue in this way until all the knots are untied and (hopefully) the spell is reversed. The cord should then be cut and cast into running water (this has always been my favourite method, although we could burn or bury it in salt if we prefer.)

If a poppet or doll was used in the original spell and we still have this, then we can undo its making until it becomes nothing but its component parts, fabric, stuffing, clay, clothes peg or whatever we used. Any damage we did to the doll in the course of the original hex should also be ritually undone or repaired. For example, if we pierced its heart, then remove the pin (which will need to be properly disposed of) and repair the wound, even using a Band Aid or some ointment if necessary. If we cannot get hold of the original doll, we could create a new one, without any damage this time, naming it after the original subject, blessing it and setting it free. For example:

> *'I bless you* [Name] *and lift the spell I placed upon you* [if possible give the date or at least the year. But if we cannot remember do not guess!] *You are now free from enchantment, your free will is again your own.'*

In ancient Europe, whenever it was necessary to disenchant a poppet, people placed a dish of food before it and shared a meal together. Afterwards the poppet was taken somewhere remote (woodland was always preferred) and left there, but not before it was told that it was being set free. I would also recommend blessing both it and the original subject of the spell before leaving.

There are still a few hexers who use the old method of writing a curse on a piece of lead. This is then rolled up and sometimes pierced with a nail before being thrown into deep water such as a healing spring or well. Some were also buried in cemeteries, where it was believed the spirit of the deceased would assist with enforcing the curse.

Curse tablets were very popular in the ancient world, but then, as now, hexers sometimes thought better of it, or suffered an attack of remorse. An inscription from 4th century BC Pella, in Macedonia, suggests that one method of undoing a curse was to retrieve the tablet and read it aloud again.[155] Others claimed that simply retrieving the tablet would reverse the spell.[156] The *Greek Magical*

[155] Ogden (2009) :227
[156] *Ibid* : 221

Papyri recommended that anyone who created an erotic curse should make a point of noting where it was buried in case they later changed their minds![157] A word of caution however – never be tempted to reverse somebody else's lead cursing tablet that we encounter *by chance,* since they were often primed to lay a curse on those who found them!

If we still have any of the materials used in the original spell (such as cloth, hair, nail clippings etc.) we should use these, preferably burning them while saying something like: *'As I burn this cloth/hair/whatever so may the original spell I cast against* [Name] *be destroyed utterly and consumed in the ashes. May* [Name] *be free of my spell against her.'*

It is also important to burn all the notes etc that we made in respect of both the original spell and its reversal. Although normally I would say we need to keep records, this is one time when we really need to get rid of *everything,* cleansing it in the flames, scattering salt on the ashes and finally casting them into running water or burying them in salt, preferably far away from where we live. Again, keep repeating at each stage that the original spell is reversed and that the subject/victim is now free of it.

When we undo a spell, we must ensure that none of the original energies still cling to us. Although some people like to take a ritual bath before doing any spellwork, when reversing a spell it is better to do this afterwards, adapting the cleansing bath suggestions in Chapter Nine, and adding a simple blessing, this time for our own wellbeing: *'With this bath/shower I cleanse myself spiritually, physically, emotionally and psychically. As the waters drain away, so may all remnants of the spell I cast against* [Name]*now leave me.'*

We can also add some flower heads such as lavender (these need to be tied in muslin or cheesecloth to prevent them clogging the water outlet) or alternatively a drop of lavender oil or spoonful of salt.

If we prefer to take a shower instead of a bath, then visualise the water washing away the last remnants of the spell we originally cast and its reversal. See the energies in the mind's eye, how they drain away and leave us feeling cleansed and refreshed.

---

[157] Ogden (2009) :233 [PGM IV 2943-66]

Add a few drops of good quality lavender oil to some baby or olive oil and rub this sparingly into our skin later, when we've dried ourselves.

Once we have attended to everything, it is time to let it go. We made a magical mistake that we have now tried to rectify. Do not dwell on it however, otherwise the whole process could start up again. Sometimes learning to let go is one of the most important magical skills to be learned.

Hexing Ourselves

There are times (See Chapter Six) when we seem to hex ourselves. This is something that has been recognised since ancient times and may be one of the reasons why people were discouraged from looking at their reflections, either in mirrors (which were rare until relatively recently) or in still water. Usually however, when we hex ourselves this has nothing to do with our physical reflection and everything to do with our personal character.

For example, self-hexes often occur when we have raised energy levels by brooding on a slight (real or imagined) or have been under prolonged stress or anxiety. We may not have intended to raise energy, indeed in the normal course of our lives we may not even believe that it's possible... but nevertheless, that's what has happened.

The problem is that if we raise energy – whether this is for magic or any other purpose - we cannot just turn our back on it and expect it to meekly disappear by itself. It won't. It may pick up other, like-minded thoughts, or absorb some elemental essence, but the most likely thing that happens with surplus nervous and emotional energy is that it turns tail and begins to bother or even attack its creator.

If we suspect we may be hexing ourselves, then we should concentrate on thorough magical cleansing of our bodies, possessions and home. Cleansing is particularly important in cases of self-hexing, since we are both the giver and receiver of energy. For the hexer, self cleansing helps minimise any potential damage, while for the victim, self cleansing removes the polluting effects of the hex. Magical cleansing and purification are therefore essential to prevent any of the detritus from the attack returning to trouble us at some point in the future.

While purifying baths and showers can be very helpful, we should also make a point of sealing our Aura each night when we go to bed, at least until we feel things are improving (see Chapter Nine). We also need to work out what triggered the attack so we can then take steps to stop it. It is essential – as soon as possible – to dismiss any energy that may have accumulated before it can join up with any elemental essence and create a thought form. (Use the exercises for dispersing negativity in Chapter Thirteen for this.)

Sometimes people say that all we need to do is to 'think good thoughts' if we are under any sort of psychic attack. In my opinion this is not only over simplistic, it is impossible to maintain for any length of time and isn't very effective unless combined with other methods of psychic self defence. Also, it carries an element of implied victim blaming, as though the reason we are under psychic attack is because we were *not* thinking good thoughts.

Many of us know that the ancient Egyptians believed in something called *ma'at* (meaning balance, harmony etc.). However they also recognised *isfet* (meaning chaos) and everyone, from the Pharaoh and his vizier down to the humblest slave, had a part to play in maintaining a healthy balance of *ma'at* and *isfet.* People are sometimes surprised when I try and explain the importance of embracing and balancing our dark side and that actually not all the things we might consider 'dark' or 'negative' are bad for us. Controlled anger, for example, can be very useful, rather like the valve on a pressure cooker. Without it there is always going to be the risk of the whole thing exploding and blowing sky high.

The key thing here, of course, is control. If we let our emotions run wild, they are liable to cause all sorts of problems. Instead we must learn to accept, confront and control our destructive thoughts in order to prevent them attacking us or other people. Initially at least, it isn't easy. Some of these negative emotions seem to be so deeply suppressed they might as well be buried down a mineshaft. Often the most unpleasant and persistent self-hexes have their origins in our childhoods, so this can be a good place to start by thinking hard about those things that happened when we were young yet still cause us pain. If we carry them around with us long enough, they may end up attacking us.

As children we felt powerless in an adult world and it doesn't take much, even as adults, for these feelings to start pouring in again. Then we don't just feel anger at our current situation but all the suppressed rage from years ago also starts bubbling to the surface. Occasionally things that happen to our own children will renew these unpleasant memories. If we were bullied as children, for example, and then our own children have similar experiences, the second time round it is often worse because we still carry the emotional baggage from our own childhood. We must deal with our experiences once and for all so that we can move on.

But how? In my workshops I often found that when I encouraged people to put their original pain into words, they were surprised how raw it still was, how near to the surface. In fact, when they wrote down their feelings, these often sounded uncommonly like a hex! If we can take those feelings and diffuse them however, we set them free without the risk they will come back to attack us.

To do this we must first reach back in time and remember what it was like to be our younger selves. Remember also how it felt to be powerless; did the adults in our lives nurture or neglect us? Did they ridicule or protect us? Most important of all, how far are these childhood experiences still ruling – and maybe ruining – our lives?

Sometimes the cause of our problems lies in something we did (or failed to do) and the subsequent fear of discovery. This can be a powerful trigger for creating a self-hex because the victim feels like two people: one has the face we present to the world and how we wish to be seen, but the other fears what people would think of us if something we had done or said became widely known. Even if our problems were caused by being bullied, remember that the most timid victim can hate their tormentors with a passion, and it is this passion that, when turned inwards, helps to create the self-hex.

One useful remedy is to write down all the feelings connected with the original source of our pain. This may involve exploring just one event, or several. Initially we just write down how it made us feel at the time and how it makes us feel now. We shall call this the 'original hex.'

We keep this paper with us for a few days, ticking off all those feelings that were completely beyond our control *at the time they happened.* It's no use looking at it with the benefit of hindsight. We might do things differently now (and if so, that's a good sign) but we need to understand why we reacted as we did *at the time.* For example, sometimes we were young and powerless. Or ignorant of the true circumstances of a situation.

True choice only comes with power, something we usually lack when we are young. Sometimes there are other constraints; for example, we may have had to protect someone else, or the person who hurt us so badly had some sort of hold over us.

This exercise helps us tick off many of the feelings on our list. We may realise that guilt, for example, was something our tormentor laid at our door unjustly. Some people are very good at holding a grudge against us for something they did and not us. Or it may be that at the time we had to go to school and had no way of avoiding the class bully. It may even be that *we* were the class bully and have come to realise that what we did was wrong and have been deeply ashamed of it ever since.

Whatever it was, we must be honest with ourselves and try to come to terms with it. (It goes without saying that this work must be private, and not shared with others.) Then set about writing a brief spell to diffuse this. Some people claim they can do this for us, but the best results are obtained if we do it ourselves. If we can't think what to write, use the following as a template and make whatever alterations seem appropriate:

With this charm I break the chains
That have held me tight.

With this charm I set me free
And turn the dark to light.

I move on to a new place
Full of peace, free from the past.

May the circle turn around
And let the heartache rest at last.

We need to accept that we may never feel able to fully forgive whoever or whatever was the original cause of our problems, but we should certainly feel able to forgive ourselves. In dealing with a self-hex, learning to forgive ourselves is sometimes hardest task of all.

Once we have forgiven all that is possible in our hearts, we should burn the written charm in a candle flame. My favourite method is to set fire to the paper in an old cooking tray kept specially for such purposes. Sprinkle the flames with salt (too much will put the fire out) and pass a lighted incense stick over it.

When it is reduced to ashes, sprinkle a little water on them. In this way we will have used the four elements of fire, water, earth (in the form of salt) and air (incense). Finally, take the ashes outside and away from our home boundary and disperse them in the wind, running water or bury them in salt.

Next, we need to prepare a candle. This doesn't have to be anything fancy, an ordinary white household one or even a tea-light will do perfectly well. Take a drop of olive oil (or aromatherapy oil if preferred) and rub this along the length of the candle (obviously this isn't suitable for a tealight, but it can still be held in our hand) and recite once more the last four lines from the spell above:

I move on to a new place
Full of peace, free from the past,

May the circle turn around
And let the heartache rest at last.

Make sure the candle is allowed to burn right out, this will mean being able to work undisturbed for a few hours, since ideally we need to remain in the room with it until it dies. When it is finally burned out, we must tell ourselves – and mean it! – that all the pain and hurt has now gone and we are set free.

Yes, we may still experience the odd twinge from time to time, just as we sometimes do with an old scar or injury, but we must also keep repeating to ourselves that we are now healed.

Consign it to the past, and move on.

CHAPTER EIGHTEEN

What about exorcisms? Is there such a thing as demonic possession? When is an exorcism necessary?

Although we often hear of people and places being exorcised because they live in a haunted house, most hauntings are not psychic attacks, and do not normally require either banishing or exorcism. We share this planet of ours with many different species and most of the time we can co-exist with a wide variety of entities. If things become too difficult, the techniques of cleansing, purifying etc., in this book can all be used to reduce the effects of any haunting or interference. Diabolic infestation (which some claim can even extend to mattresses, furniture, dolls etc.) is normally just paranoia, but if something is really troubling us, we should carry out thorough cleansings and protective rituals because these will reassure us.

The only time we really should consider performing an exorcism is when we are certain that a person has been possessed by another entity. In ancient times this sometimes happened as a result of curses and certain types of magic, and many religions still teach this. However, most cases of possession are not due to devils, demons or playing with Tarot cards or a Ouija Board but are the result of a spirit/ghost becoming fixated on a living person.

The Common Signs of Possession?

Usually it is other people - family or friends - who notice something is amiss long before the victim is aware of it. Some of the most common signs of 'being possessed' are:

- Waking with unexplained bruises, welts or scratches, although this could also be a sign of an ordinary psychic attack so please don't overreact if this is all the evidence there is.

- Suddenly exhibiting great physical strength.

- Suddenly speaking or understanding languages that were previously unknown to the subject although this can sometimes be explained by past life memories. Also, some Christian denominations often claim to 'speak in tongues.'

Obviously, none of these symptoms are conclusive, so we must rely heavily on our own observations. A possessing entity may appear harmless at first but will soon start influencing the victim and imposing its own thoughts and emotions on her, causing tremendous distress not only to her but also her friends and family.

One of the most reliable indicators when someone is possessed is that they may behave strangely for no *apparent* reason. However, don't jump to conclusions; there may be many reasons for this, not least illness, disease or even severe stress. These things should all be thoroughly checked and eliminated first. What we are specifically looking for is evidence that someone or something else is behind the controls, but this is so subjective, it is impossible to draw up a list that will fit every case. For example, just because we may not approve of a son's or daughter's new partner does *not* mean they are in the grip of a demonic entity.

People have tried to categorise the different types of possession, giving each its own set of symptoms. They make for interesting (if unconvincing) reading so I shall list only two of the more common ones here:

- **Diabolic Possession** is sometimes thought to endow the victim with unexplained knowledge of occult matters, a fondness for blasphemy and an aversion to anything religious or sacred. However, this can also be explained by personal preference. Just because someone swears a lot, dislikes organised religion and has an interest in, say, the Tarot, does *not* automatically mean they are diabolically possessed.

- **Diabolic Oppression** is even more vague, being apparently present whenever we have problems with our job, marriage, relationships, feel depressed or fly into sudden rages. However, these are common problems that happen to most people at some time or another. They are *not* conclusive proof of demonic possession.

The main problem with people seeing the Devil lurking around every corner is that it creates a giant smokescreen of paranoia that disguises the real (though rare) cases of genuine possession. *Everybody* gets problems in their life from time to time, and if losing our temper has become a problem for us then we need to seek professional help, not exorcism!

Likewise, I have seen it claimed that people who are thinking of suicide and who are self-harming are suffering from Diabolic Obsession. ***This is totally untrue and very dangerous nonsense.*** People in this situation need urgent professional medical help from a doctor specialising in mental health, not an exorcist. Exorcism is never a substitute for proper medical help.

The practical aspects of exorcism are also full of misunderstandings and misrepresentations. Chief among these is that only a clergyman can carry out an exorcism. This is untrue and I hope to show in this chapter that we have as much chance of success as anyone else. Many people who claim to be exorcists only try to banish ghosts from people's homes, which is quite different from trying to force a possessing entity to leave someone's body!

Although I don't believe human beings own the psychic right-of-way over the entire world, we do have the right to possess our own bodies. A real possessing entity (and not just a bad temper or a vocabulary consisting mainly of swear words) *needs* to be banished. Any victim of a possessing entity has the unassailable right to control his, her or their own body, mind and soul. Before we start putting together a ritual of exorcism however, we should start by looking at its history and past uses.

In ancient times, supernatural powers were relatively easy to access. People approached their gods directly or consulted any number of priests, priestess, seers, mages, sorcerers or diviners. Admittedly, the state did not extend equal tolerance towards all these groups; in particular, magicians and astrologers were often persecuted and sometimes executed, especially in the Roman

Empire even before the advent of Christianity. There was certainly no tolerant 'anything goes' policy extended to one and all in ancient times. Astrologers for example, had to be very careful when casting a horoscope since attempting to predict when the Emperor would die incurred the death penalty!

Most of the time, however, the political state turned a blind eye to love spells, protective or healing magic. They even ignored judicial binding spells (which prevented an opponent in a legal trial from putting forward his case properly), unless they affected the wealthy elite or interfered with political life. With the coming of Christianity however, the early Church tried to discourage independent access to supernatural power which meant that all rituals, including exorcism, could only be performed by the Church unless one wanted to risk being accused of working with the Devil.

The Devil is essentially a Christian construct. Previously people had been aware of spirits (both good and bad) that occasionally seemed to move in and take over a living person. This wasn't always harmful; sometimes people were able to prophesy or even heal as a result. However, the early Church decided that such activities were dangerous and soon just about everything connected with spirits was classed as evil, and the most evil entity of all, according to the Church, was the Devil.

The Christian concept of an arch-fiend that exists only to make people do evil, was new. There were trickster deities in many pantheons, together with unpleasant demons, but the Devil was different and by the Middle Ages had become a horned, cloven-hoofed creature with a tail and a pitchfork. The Devil became a composite of many pagan deities from the former Roman Empire, for example Cernunnos and Pan had a combination of horns, hooves and tails, while others, such as Poseidon, carried a trident (which also became one of the Devil's attributes.) Possibly the early Church found these deities hard to eradicate and decided instead to morph them together into a single caricature of evil.

However, even demonising the old deities did not entirely solve the problem. It was all very well to frighten people by telling them the Devil lurked everywhere, waiting to pounce on the unwary, yet if the Church made him seem too powerful then he could appear to be God's equal, or worse, his superior.

Manipulating the Devil thus became a skilled balancing act, and the consequences are seen even today, when terrible acts such as the child abuse scandals in the Roman Catholic Church are still blamed on the Devil. Indeed, some senior clerics still make claims about the Devil stalking the corridors of power within the Vatican.[158]

If we are ever confronted with what appears to be a case of possession, we shouldn't jump to the conclusion that we must be dealing with the Devil. There are many other possibilities to consider, none of which can be reliably described as arch-fiends. Even the word demon did not originally have the evil connotations it has nowadays. In the ancient world a *daimon* was a minor or intermediate deity; while a *daemon* could be a good or evil spirit of a dead person.

Higher gods were sometimes referred to as *daimones,* while Socrates' *daimonion* was his own personal deity. The terms *daimonas* and *daimonizomai* however were both generally used to indicate that someone was being possessed.[159] Both Homer and Plato referred to demons while Plutarch wrote that, 'Certain tyrannical demons require for their enjoyment some soul still incarnate, being unable to satisfy their passions in any other way.'[160]

Of course, the next question to ask is: Why do such entities take an interest in some of us? Why possess one person and not another? The early and medieval Christian Church taught that certain sins automatically caused demonic possession, as did making a mistake or omitting words during baptism.

Another method of demons gaining entry was through the mouth which is why people say, *'Bless you!'* when someone

---

158 http://www.dailymail.co.uk/news/worldnews/article-1257119/Catholic-sex-abuse-scandals-evidence-Devil-Vatican-says-Popes-chief-exorcist.html

159 Luck (2006): 496

160 Wickland (2008): 6

sneezes. It was even believed that demons could lurk in food, hence the tradition of saying grace before and after meals. However, it's one thing to give thanks for having food on the table, but quite another to seriously believe that if we neglect to do so we will become possessed. Yet a nun was once believed to have become possessed simply by eating an unblessed lettuce![161]

If we suspect a case of possession, then we must establish who or what is doing the possessing. Often we cannot answer this until the exorcism has begun, because part of the ritual is about getting the entity to identify itself. Don't be surprised though, if the spirit simply identifies itself as 'Fred' or 'Susan' rather than giving the name of some infernal demon!

Most possessing entities are not 'evil spirits' sent by the Devil but discarnate spirits who do not realise they are dead. Sometimes, the possessing spirit has known the victim in life (they often seem to come back and attach themselves to relatives and friends) and occasionally the victim is living in the spirit's former home.

Other spirits simply want to remain in the familiar life they once enjoyed, attaching themselves to the living in order to do so. For example, spirits who in life were alcoholics or drug addicts will sometimes become parasites on the living in order to enjoy drink or drugs through their victims. They won't experience getting drunk in quite the same way they once did, but it will be close enough to satisfy them and prevent them wanting to move on.

The effects of such possession on the victim can be quite devastating, however. Even if he already has a fondness for drink or drugs, this will become considerably worse once a possessing entity becomes involved.

In a nutshell...

The most likely culprits in a case of possession are the discarnate souls of people who have died but who, for whatever reason, remain earthbound. Some spirits do so by choice while others

[161] Kallendorf (2005): 233

don't know they are dead, or don't understand they can move on to the spirit world or afterlife.

It's also important to understand that victims rarely invite possession although this remains a popular view in some quarters. Dabbling in the occult, Ouija boards, even Tarot cards, crystals and yoga have all been blamed for this in the past! It is simply not true that only wicked people (either individuals or whole communities) become possessed. This is victim blaming and should be avoided.

Often the nature of the possessing entity holds the key, and people who have been particularly controlling in this life remain so after death. They would therefore have no misgivings about taking over someone else's body; in some cases, they might even deliberately set out to cause trouble for their victims, by turning them into criminals and alcoholics.

In the ancient world, possession was often believed to be the result of hexes that attempted to raise and enrage demons before channelling the unpleasant results in the direction of the victim.[162] There is also anecdotal evidence that some people just seem to be in the wrong place at the wrong time, attracting the entity because of something in their character or Aura, which by its nature is magnetic anyway.[163]

Back in the 1920's, an American psychiatrist Dr Carl Wickland published a book entitled *Thirty Years Among the Dead.* In it, he explored a number of cases that had proved difficult to treat and came to the conclusion many of them were due to the presence of a possessing entity. He felt that sometimes such patients were best treated by exorcism.

Even now, there are still a small number in the psychiatric profession who believe that certain intractable types of mental illness, which do not respond well to conventional treatments may be due to possession.[164] According to Wickland, few possessing spirits were vengeful or evil; most were mischievous or didn't realise they were dead and needed to move on. He believed it was

---

[162] Luck (2006): 215

[163] Wickland (2008): 17

[164] Betty (2005)

possible for both possessing spirits (and their victims) to be initially unaware of what was happening.

This point of view is quite different from the official Catholic Church's, which often claimed that victims were somehow to blame for their own possession. Many clerics from the Middle Ages onwards were interested in necromancy, i.e. summoning the dead in the hope of finding out information concerning arcane knowledge or hidden treasure. This interest was not confined to medieval clergy (who were sometimes put on trial for invoking and summoning demons); my father's occult library contained many books that had come from a nineteenth century Catholic priest, defrocked for his occult interests and activities!

Some clergy trod a thin line between Christianity and the very things it condemned, which might explain why within a century or two, the blame for 'witchcraft' and 'Devil worship' was shifted onto ordinary people. It also sheds new light on why the witch finders (who were almost always clerics) asked the questions they did – I suspect they simply projected their own knowledge of necromancy onto others, classing it all as 'witchcraft.' The replies they received were always going to be unreliable, since under torture people will say anything.

Before long, the practice of exorcism became well established within both the Roman Catholic and Protestant Churches of Europe. Initially, the Roman Catholic Church had distinguished between two types of exorcism, routine (or virtual) and real.[165] Routine exorcism was performed as part of baptism and blessings in order to purify people, objects and animals before the ritual took place. It does not mean that any demons were actually present.

'Real' exorcism was reserved for people who showed the signs of possession by evil spirits or demons. These included strange, jerky, often involuntary movements, the ability to speak in tongues (although this was also thought to be a sign of divine favour) and the ability to unveil secrets. It was no wonder the line between sainthood and demonic possession was so narrow and could take

---

165 Russell (1996): 95

centuries to resolve: Joan of Arc for example, was burned as a witch in the fifteenth century, and not canonised until 1920!

Even though Martin Luther ridiculed exorcism and Calvin described it as 'papal magic,' exorcism remained in use by Puritans, Anglicans and Lutherans alike. In fact, some of the most famous witch trials, such as those in Salem, Massachusetts and the activities of the Witchfinder General, Mathew Hopkins, in Essex, England, took place in Protestant communities.

Dealing with Possessing Spirits

Dealing with a possessing entity is probably the one aspect of psychic self defence that most people prefer to avoid, fearing it will be completely beyond their control and should be handed over to the experts. But that begs the question - just who are these experts? Although nowadays many people still feel that only a priest can perform an exorcism, until as late as the early sixteenth century, exorcists in Catholic countries did not need to be priests. Instead many exorcists held 'minor orders' as lectors or porters and were never fully ordained.

In medieval universities, many students were automatically ordained into the minor orders, which meant they could perform exorcisms. Some undoubtedly were later ordained as priests and given a book of exorcisms at their ordination ceremony. Nowadays however, even if we contact the local vicar or priest, it doesn't mean they will automatically help us. Exorcists must be licensed by the local diocese, and the local Bishop is required to give his permission for an exorcism to go ahead.

The fact that demonic possession and exorcism occurs world-wide shows that the problem is not confined to any single religion or belief system. In places such as India, patients suspected of being possessed by a *bhut* (a ghost or earthbound spirit) are taken to the temple to be cured by the *baba*. A survey back in the 1970s at a healing centre in Pune, India,[166] discovered that it usually needed several sessions before patients were completely cured.

[166] Stanley (1988): 39

It's important to bear this in mind if we decide to tackle an exorcism, since it's unlikely to be a one-off thing and we may have to repeat the ritual several times. Don't be disheartened if this happens; it's quite normal. The idea (common in Denis Wheatley novels and certain television programmes and films) that we hold up a crucifix and the possessing spirit will promptly flee, bears little resemblance to reality.

What does an exorcism entail? Basically, we must persuade the possessing entity to listen and obey us. It's a good start if we can make it understand that it has died and persuade it to depart. This is really the sole purpose of almost all exorcisms. The religious belief of the victim (and the exorcist for that matter) isn't the issue. What the spirits respond to is the fact that someone has come to persuade, argue and, in extreme cases, to do battle with them. They often feel threatened by the exorcist whether it's a Catholic priest with holy water and a crucifix, an Indian *baba* with a tray of lights or a Taoist priest holding an ivory tablet.

How should we address a possessing entity? It's rather like trying to get someone's attention in a noisy room. We might literally have to shout, '*Listen to me*!' or something similar. Of course, we must sound as though we mean it. Spirits that are confused or convinced they are exactly where they ought to be can take some convincing.

It also helps if we can find out what the entity wants rather than immediately trying to banish it. Occasionally possessing entities seem to want the justice they were denied in life. However, we must be careful not to let them give us the run-around!

It's crucial therefore to know exactly what we are doing before we start, otherwise any possessing entity worth its salt will only defy and disobey us and often wreak havoc. First of all, we must note down exactly what we hope to achieve in the exorcism which should include some or all of the following:

- To determine that the subject is indeed possessed. This means we must to rule out other things first.

- To identify its causes – who or what is the possessing entity and what does it want?

- To heal the subject. Usually subjects feel much better once the possessing entity departs.

Always aim to work in a calm and peaceful atmosphere. Nowadays formal exorcisms conducted by the Catholic Church are usually rather secret affairs, but this wasn't always the case. Centuries ago, local people were encouraged to watch and even to jeer at and abuse the demon. In fact, things could become so rowdy that one fifteenth century exorcism manual sternly reminded the exorcist to control the crowds and prevent them laughing and roaming in and out of the church when the ceremony was being performed. Above all, on no account should they bring dogs into the church! Another reason why exorcisms were held in public was because they encouraged the bystanders to become Catholics. A successful 'show' could bring in several hundred new converts.

Personally, I think we should avoid both complete secrecy and an exorcism circus. The best thing is to have no more than a friend or two present, either to help in a practical sense or provide moral support. Don't allow anyone who is very emotional or fearful to be there, since entities are very good at feeding off such energies. What we need are sensible and calm helpers, those who are good in a crisis. We also do not want anyone barging in, saying, '*No, that's wrong, this is the right way to do it,*' and trying to take over! There should never be any doubt who is in charge.

Exorcists need to confront the possessing entity with something that symbolises authority within their own tradition. For example, a Protestant Christian might carry a Bible, a Catholic priest would have a crucifix and holy water, a Hindu *baba* would carry *arati* or tray of lights and a Taoist priest would carry an ivory tablet. By that yardstick, any pagan who attempts an exorcism could carry a pentacle, triskele, awen or other symbol that had meaning for them.

We are sometimes told that the symbol should also mean the same to the possessing entity. This might have worked centuries ago when most people in the west were nominally Christian, but nowadays this would hamstring exorcisms to the point where *nothing* would work. A symbol of authority is simply the equivalent of a sign saying, '*This person has the power and authority to perform this exorcism.*'

There is no right or wrong way to perform an exorcism. There are, however, better and worse methods. Remember that we will probably be dealing with someone who has once been alive, just like us. Talk to him firmly but politely, stressing that it does not belong here. Keep it simple. '*You are no longer living, you do not belong here. What do you want?*'

Only now, at the very beginning of the ritual do we ask what it wants. Thereafter there can be no negotiation. Remember that any spirit desperate for help will accept our offer readily. If it doesn't respond to our first approach, then any later requests for help are simply delaying tactics.

If the spirit wants something (occasionally they do) we should only agree to help providing it first leaves its victim. Never allow it to remain *in situ* while we go and do or get something for it. Some spirits – like some people – are liars. However, if we undertake to do something for the spirit, we must keep our end of the bargain. Spirits rarely appreciate broken promises.

If we feel we cannot promise, then we just say so and don't feel bad about it. We are perfectly within our rights to order it to leave without promising to do anything if its request is unreasonable. Remember, just because it claims to have suffered an injustice is no excuse for it to take over someone else's body!

Many spirits move on once they are ordered to do so, but if it refuses to leave, then we must abandon being reasonable, and treat it as we would an angry teenager. Remember that these entities only have the power if we allow them to hold it. While some entities are confused and frightened, others try to *cause* confusion and fear. The more we fear it, the more it will try and terrorise us. If we show we are shocked by its profanities for example, it will try even harder to shock us. So be calm, but firm. The spirit does not belong here and we must say so, over and over if necessary, using simple language that cannot be misunderstood:

'You cannot stay here. You are dead. You do not belong in [Name]'s *body, it is not yours. You must leave this person* [Name] *and move on to your proper place in the spirit world /Otherworld/Summerlands/light.'* (choose which term you prefer to use and stick to that throughout)

Luckily, many spirits will depart without too much fuss once they realise they are dead, although some will argue. They may claim that they are in their own body, but don't recognise us or anyone else in the room. This is a good time to use a mirror and show it that the body it is now occupying is not its own. Holding up mirrors and talking to unseen entities may seem laughably simple. Yet trying to communicate with discarnate souls is a very old technique. In Shakespeare's play, *Hamlet,* Marcellus says, '*Thou art a scholar, speak to it, Horatio*.' The idea of scholars – i.e. those who were well read in such matters – being able to speak to spirits is not some New Age waffle but deeply rooted in tradition.

It would be foolish and rash to attempt this sort of work expecting it to be plain sailing every time. Some entities will try to trick us, others will cry fake tears, some get nasty and still others – according to some accounts – can produce some very frightening phenomena, such as vomiting slime, pins or stones (collectively referred to as 'charms'.)

In the Valley of Tena in Northern Spain, a group of women who were exorcised between 1637 and 1642, vomited so many objects during exorcisms that their mouths bled.[167] Vomiting charms during exorcism seems to have continued right into the twenty-first century.[168] However, this is not common to all exorcisms nor does it occur in all traditions.

The victim may well start to struggle or swear; he may even attempt to hit us. This is where our calm friends can help us restrain him so that he cannot hurt us or himself. Do not, under any circumstances, get into a punch up. Instead repeat over and

---

167 Kallendorf (2005): 220

168 http://www.dailymail.co.uk/news/worldnews/article-1257119/Catholic-sex-abuse-scandals-evidence-Devil-Vatican-says-Popes-chief-exorcist.html

over that the possessing entity *must* leave. It does not belong here, and we will not allow it to remain. *'I have the authority to command you to go and leave* [Name] *in peace,'* is perfectly acceptable and simple, but we must always be prepared to answer the question, '*Who gives you such authority*?' without hesitation.

Although we can claim authority from whatever deity or power we wish, it's best to choose one that means something to us and isn't just a name we've picked out of the air. In the Bible (Acts 19.13-17) there is a story about Jewish exorcists who cast out spirits in the name of 'the Jesus whom Paul preaches' who were challenged (and attacked) by an angry demon. It is possible of course that this tale was told in order to encourage people to convert to Christianity, yet in the past, exorcists who were neither Jewish nor Christian would still claim authority from Solomon, Moses or Jesus because some ancient pagans recognised these as powerful *magical* figures, if not religious ones.

Despite what we see in horror films, exorcisms do not often turn violent. If we suspect this might happen, perhaps because of an obvious personality change in the victim, then do take sensible precautions beforehand. These include:

- Do not undertake an exorcism when we are alone with the victim if we suspect the possessing entity may become violent. Make sure there is always help at hand.

- Do not attempt an exorcism if we, or anyone helping us is unwell. It's better to wait.

- Make sure anyone helping us is properly briefed what to expect and discuss with them beforehand what to do in an emergency.

- Make sure there are plenty of pillows, cushions or quilts around the victim to minimise injury.

- Remove anything sharp or heavy that could cause injury.

Some exorcists try to attract the spirit in order to draw it out. A traditional method of doing this was to blow on the victim, beginning at the feet and moving upwards on a single breath until the exorcist reached the face.[169] The spirit was then forced out, usually through the mouth or nostrils and could be ordered to depart.

Another method was to place a strong-smelling herb such as marjoram beneath the victim's nose and ask him to sniff the fragrance. This was believed to 'arrest the demon' so that it could then be magically drawn out through the nostrils and again ordered to depart. There is nothing mysterious about this process - we do not need to physically grab hold of the demon; simply order it to depart.

Magical treatises from the Graeco-Roman world suggest that the traditional method of banishing ghosts (and remember that many possessing entities are the spirits of the dead rather than demons) involves making circular gestures with the hands. To me this sounds very like breaking up negativity using the figure of eight movement in Chapter Thirteen. The principle behind using circular movements and gestures is to break up the heavy atmosphere so that it can be dispersed more easily.

Many exorcisms are surprisingly quiet and low-key, but there is an unfortunate tendency to believe that if a spirit departs peacefully the exorcism somehow cannot have been 'real'. This isn't true; many spirits were reasonable people in life who simply became confused when they died and didn't understand where they were.

Once the spirit has left, it is appropriate to say some sort of prayer or blessing mark its passing, such as: *'May you go swiftly to the Summerlands/Otherworld/Spirit World, and may you find peace and happiness there.'*

The victim's Aura should then be sealed (see Chapter Nine) for further protection. This must not be done until we are certain the entity has departed however, since we really do not want to seal it in!

---

[169] Ogden (2009): 49, 329

It goes without saying that we should never attempt an exorcism unless we are determined that come what may, we will see it through. If we are confronted by pins or nails these should be treated in the same way as anything used to convey a hex. Collect the objects together during the exorcism and keep them safe. Afterwards cleanse them by passing each object through fire or incense, and then bury them, remembering to pour salt into the hole both beneath and above the object. Then fill in the hole, saying, *'You have no power, I command you to be at peace.'*

No one religion has a monopoly on casting out spirits and entities. In ancient times, the Egyptians, Jews[170] and Greeks[171] certainly performed exorcisms using a wide variety of techniques. Nowadays there are many methods available, from the gentle spiritual help offered by some Spiritualist churches, the ten-minute exorcisms in the Church of England,[172] to the more vigorous exorcisms which sometimes extend over several days, as seen in the Roman Catholic Church, India and the Far East.

Of course, it tends to be the really spectacular exorcisms that make it into print. If we just say, *'Please, leave this person alone. You are dead and you have to move on, so please stop being such a nuisance,'* and the entity leaves, it would hardly merit a single line in the local newspaper. If, however, the exorcism is accompanied by breaking windows, flying cushions, cursing, screaming and fighting, etc., this grabs people's attention and may be extensively reported.

There is a famous instance of an exorcism at a monastery near Shanghai, in the 1920's.[173] The exorcist was a Taoist abbot, who held an ivory tablet as a symbol of his authority, and repeatedly ordered two possessing entities to come out of a young farmer. Over a period of three days, the abbot invoked the spirits in the name of Shang Ti, the Taoists' Supreme God. During this

---

[170] Josephus *Antiquities* 8:5:2

[171] Apollonius of Tyana 3.38, 4.30

[172] Roffey (1994) http://www.independent.co.uk/life-style/firsthand-i-dont-spend-all-my-time-with-poltergeists-casting-out-demons-and-laying-ghosts-to-rest-is-routine-for-dominic-walker-church-of-england-vicar-and-exorcist-1445788.html

[173] Goullart (1961): 86

nightmarish confrontation, the victim's body swelled up and started voiding foul-smelling bodily fluids and excrement. Eventually the swelling subsided, only for the man to become so heavy, he broke the bed on which he lay. When eventually the spirits left him, the victim had no memory of anything that had happened during the exorcism.

Loss of memory after undergoing exorcism is quite common. In some Indian exorcisms when the possessing spirit or *bhut* becomes agitated or violent the victim will later claim to have felt nothing, since it is the *bhut* who is affected and not the patient. The usual explanation is that the victim is insensitive while the possessing entities are running amok.

The downside of this view is that it encourages over-zealous and irresponsible exorcists to inflict physical harm on the subject and claim that only the 'devils within' could feel the pain. This is patent nonsense and there have been a number of cases in several different countries (including the US quite recently) where patients have been beaten to death during an exorcism.

One cannot help wondering whether the role of exorcist attracts certain types of people because of the power it gives them and not because they genuinely want to help others. Remember that evil is always at its worst when it masquerades as good.

When we are putting together a rite of exorcism, (and we should always prepare thoroughly before attempting this ritual) we should remember how what we think of as a 'traditional' exorcism developed. Centuries ago, most Catholic priests had a classical education, as did all the contributors to the *Thesaurus Exorcismorum* which was one of the most famous texts ever written on exorcism, published in 1608 in Cologne. A few years later the book was rewritten and abridged, becoming part of the Catholic church's official exorcism handbook, the *Rituale Romanum* which is still used today.[174] The present rite of exorcism is known as *Of Exorcisms and Certain Supplications* (*De Exorcismis et Supplicationibus Quibusdam*).

---

174 Kallendorf (2005): 211

The service of exorcism usually begins with Biblical readings from Psalms, Revelation, and the Gospels. These are followed by a litany, a prayer, and then the actual exorcism. Curiously, instead of being deeply rooted in scripture, the rite of exorcism basically follows the pattern of a classical Greek or Roman court case, a *tribunal domini nostri*[175] where the offending entity (usually referred to as a demon) is put on trial and the exorcist acts as not as a priest but as a spiritual lawyer for the prosecution.

The exorcist begins by accusing the demon of committing the crime of 'possession,' and the demon – often speaking through the victim – usually claims that the victim was wicked and deserved it. The exorcist then calls upon the Virgin Mary and various saints to help defend the victim and prove him innocent. Obviously, the demon is not going to be allowed to win this case, and the exorcist uses a combination of commands and persuasion to induce it to leave. This method is very similar to that employed by pre-Christian *magi,* although they tended to regard commanding and coercing as a last resort for only the most extreme situations.

The Christian Church also borrowed in other ways from pagan exorcisms. We've already looked at blowing on the patient, starting at the toes and moving upwards on a single breath as a method of exorcism. This was later incorporated into early Christian christening ceremonies when even the oil used for anointing was first exorcised. Yet although there was some borrowing from pagan exorcisms, there were differences, too. Exorcisms carried out in ancient Greece and Rome usually followed the following pattern:

- The demon is ordered out. It may not obey at first.

- The demon is ordered out again, with all manner of threats. This time it does obey.

---

[175] *Ibid*: 214

- At some point during the exorcism, the exorcist adjures the demon in the name of any powerful sorcerer or religious figure, e.g. Solomon, Moses, Apollonius of Tyana or Jesus.

- The demon is forced to confess its name; to know the entity's name gives us the power to expel it.

- After the demon is expelled, it must give a physical token of its departure - either it makes itself visible as it departs, (usually in the form of a dark shadowy figure), or it is made to knock over an external object (often a jar or vase). These were usually placed some distance away from the patient.[176]

At the end of an exorcism, which may take anything from a few minutes to several days, the demon is found guilty, excommunicated and sentenced to thousands of years of punishment. Traditional Catholic exorcisms make no provision for failure, although it does happen. Other traditions may repeat the exorcism several times.

Exorcising Ghosts

Often people are called in to exorcise a troublesome ghost (rather than a possessing entity.) Personally, I think this is rarely necessary, but if it absolutely must be done, try the traditional method of offering milk, honey, blessed water, wine and olive oil. Some people also offer bread. The food was traditionally set out as a meal to be shared with the ghost on the understanding that it would then leave and not trouble anyone again.

If we know the identity of the ghost, then we can address it by name, explaining that we are going to share a meal together but afterwards it must leave. If we don't know the ghost's identity, we should create a doll or poppet in its approximate image and of the same gender as the ghost. If we are not even certain of this, perhaps

[176] Ogden (2009): 167

because we have only heard the ghost and never seen it, then create two dolls, one male and the other female just to be on the safe side! The doll(s) can then be a stand-in for the ghost and invited to the meal (rather like a doll's tea party!). Afterwards the doll should be taken to a pleasant spot such as woodland and left there. I would also give it a brief blessing, something like, *'Now I bless you and you are free. You cannot return to my home, but I wish you well.'*

When we return home, we should thoroughly cleanse the house magically with any of the methods suggested in Chapter Twelve.

If, for whatever reason – perhaps the ghost becomes more active during the banishing – we must resort to threats and coercion, then we must ensure we have a piece of iron, or length of chain to hand. Ghosts are traditionally weak before iron and bronze, while the chain symbolically represents our power to bind them.

If the spirit still refuses to leave or resists in any way, then we should threaten to bind it. Say something like: *'If you do not obey me, if you do not leave now, then I will bind you with this chain/iron.'* Don't be afraid to repeat it once or twice, but not endlessly; if necessary, go on to a performative intention such as *'With this iron/chain, I bind you to my will. Leave* [Name/place] *and never return.'*

What we do not want to do, obviously, is to bind the entity to *us*, otherwise we might have difficulty getting rid of it again. We simply need to bind it to our will (not our physical self) and force it to leave. Banishing is like training a puppy – a battle of wills.

If we have shared a meal with the ghost first, and it still shows no sign of leaving, do not be tempted to try and banish it immediately afterwards. This is because it is always better to perform magical exercises such as banishing on an empty stomach.[177] (Conversely, if we personally are under psychic attack then it is best to eat regularly.)

This puzzled me for many years, until eventually I realised that an empty stomach tends to heighten both concentration and sensation. This can be very helpful when we're the ones doing the magical work, but not so pleasant if we happen to be on the receiving end of someone else's magic!

---

177 Fortune (1970): 161

If we are going to try and rid someone of a possessing entity (it stands to reason that the victim cannot do this for himself) then we must be certain not only what we are doing, but why we are doing it. Does the person really want our help or does he simply want our attention? Do his family and friends feel it is a good idea? And if not, why not?

The most difficult challenge whenever people ask us for help to banish an entity is in understanding the personalities and characters of the people involved. Some need help and are grateful for advice, others will demand help yet make it impossible for us to do anything at all.

One of the most common problems arises when someone wants us to help 'a friend' who is apparently suffering very unpleasant attacks yet everything we suggest is dismissed as unreasonable, unworkable or against the friend's religion. In situations like this, just remember that if anyone refuses to help themselves or to be helped, there is very little we can do about it.

In psychic self defence, as in life, just do your best.

CHAPTER NINETEEN

Sensible precautions to deter and prevent psychic attacks. Why we feel more vulnerable at certain times of the year. Amulets and talismans. Defences against Internet attacks. Prevention is better than cure – sensible precautions, amulets and talismans

For thousands of years, people have recognised that when it comes to psychic self defence, prevention is better than cure. In fact, the ancient Latin saying, '*Si vis pacem, para bellum*' which means '*If you want peace, prepare for war*', can just as easily be applied to psychic attacks as to real battles. No single book on the topic of preventative psychic self defence will ever be exhaustive – it would require an entire library to even begin to do it justice. The suggestions in this chapter are just guidelines that can be easily adapted.

Since ancient times, names have been regarded as possessing great power. Even if our own name is relatively commonplace, nevertheless it defines us in a very precise way. In some societies, a dead person was never referred to by name after they died because it was believed that this would call up their spirit, which would be angry at being disturbed.

The ancient Egyptians, however, believed that speaking the deceased's name ensured they had an afterlife. If a Pharaoh later fell out of favour, perhaps because his dynasty was replaced by another, his name would be obliterated from all monuments and cartouches thus effectively denying him life after death. The Romans used *damnatio memoriae* which was similar; inscriptions and statues were removed or destroyed and occasionally even coins were re-minted.

If we are under psychic attack it is important to avoid mentioning our attacker by name. Instead, as far as possible, use the Egyptian method of referring to them as 'he/she/they-who-shall-not-be-named.' Another method is to use reflexive pronouns such as yourself; himself; herself; etc., instead of the attacker's name. These methods are surprisingly effective in keeping attacks at a distance.

Internet Attacks

The internet can be a powerful weapon and source of psychic attacks. This is a relatively new phenomenon and will become more of a problem as use of the internet becomes ever more widespread. Many of us have a computer in the home, often in the bedroom, while modern mobile phones have the capabilities of computers and people often take them to bed with them.

Normally the bedroom is an area where we should feel safe, yet the internet allows all sorts of information and images to come and go at will and it is relatively easy to manipulate it for sending out thought forms. When large groups of people become involved, for example on social networking sites, they can then empower the thought form with a strength it would never have gained years ago by ordinary, physical means.

If we feel there is a chance that we are being attacked via the internet it is vitally important to break all connections, just as we would in real life. We must not message the attacker or visit any websites where we are likely to encounter them, and we should update our privacy settings so that nobody knows when we are online.

From a practical point of view, we should always shut down or snooze our computer before going to bed otherwise the light from its screen makes our body think it needs to keep producing hormones instead of letting us get some much-needed sleep. For teenagers, who often use computers in their bedrooms, the problem of psychic attacks via the internet, combined with lack of good quality sleep can be particularly acute.

Mostly we should deal with an internet attack just as we would any other psychic attack, i.e. by cleansing, clearing and banishing. We can also set up an internet guardian which is an image we create or adapt, setting it up specifically to guard our computer. One of the easiest methods is to use it as a desktop image. Choose something we regard as a guardian, either animal or human; some people use images from the Tarot, others prefer a picture from a magazine. Name and view the image as our personal protector. We should spend time choosing and thinking about the guardian's personal qualities until we find one that feels right. We will also need to talk to it regularly and set it on guard both when using the internet and when we're away from the computer. Remember our guardian is there to protect, not counter-attack. All we want is peace and quiet, not an all-out magical cyber war.

Remember too, that computers and other electrical equipment dish out high levels of positive ions which need clearing from time to time. Leave a dish of consecrated salt (no water or vinegar) in the room where our computer is kept, changing it regularly: once a day if we are under active threat, otherwise once a week. The general cleansing exercises given elsewhere in this book can also be used.

Other Preventative Strategies

Sometimes we may not have proof that we are under psychic attack yet recognise that something doesn't feel right. We might pick up the sensation of a slight 'buzz' in the air. While I always caution against jumping to conclusions, if we have good reason to believe that a psychic attack is on its way (perhaps because we've recently received a hex or threat in the post), then it makes sense to take a few basic precautions.

With unintentional attacks, people who rage and seethe inwardly find that their feelings can be projected onto others who in turn act out that anger on the attacker's behalf. The result is that we may be psychically attacked by a total stranger. Although we can't do much about someone absorbing another person's anger, nor prevent someone hexing us; we can however ensure there is little for their anger to work on.

Whenever we suspect we are under attack, our first line of defence is cleansing. It is also an excellent preventative measure because it prevents negativity - which often attracts psychic attacks - from clustering. For best results try to follow a set pattern, for example:

- Physically clean and tidy

- Magically/psychically cleanse
- Disperse any negativity
- Bless the room/home/area

Doing things in this order prevents our attacker from re-entering our space.

If we feel that negativity has attached itself to us personally, then we need to seal our Aura and clear out any unwanted psychic cords. If the attack is active, we might need to do this every day for a while, then slacken off to once a week and then once a month. Eventually, once every few months will be adequate.

Something else we can do is to avoid wearing dirty clothes since these pick up a great deal of negativity. Wash clothes that are worn outdoors regularly, and also polish shoes, or at least clean them, because they've been out in the street and we do not know what psychic vibrations they will have picked up. In some societies people only wear slippers indoors, banishing their outdoor footwear to the hall or porch. This is becoming more popular in the UK nowadays.

We should also take extra care in any area of our home where we eat or prepare food, combining good hygiene with visualising the food, utensils and surfaces being magically cleansed. Centuries ago it was believed that demons could enter a person as he ate and as previously mentioned, this is probably where the tradition of saying grace before meals originated. Also, many religious dietary laws suggest that certain foods are unclean and will cause spiritual harm (rather than just a case of gastro-enteritis) if consumed. A protective wreath (see Chapter Ten) hung up in the kitchen and comprising of garlic and red ribbons is both attractive and very effective!

It goes without saying that we should always be careful about personal things we discard such as hair and nail clippings because in the wrong hands they can be used against us. Also remember to properly dispose of dressings, bandages and any personal clothing that has absorbed blood, semen, sweat etc. Years ago, people even used menstrual blood, ear wax and chamber lye (the thick brown deposit in unwashed chamber pots) for magical purposes!

We should never give hair as a keepsake unless we really trust the recipient. In the eighteenth and nineteenth centuries people made up the hair of their loved ones into jewellery such as brooches or pendants. Sometimes these were *memento mori*, reminders of people who had died, or keepsakes from people who were away for long periods at a time such as soldiers and sailors. I suspect these traditions were all echoes of earlier magic, knowledge of its true power by then forgotten.

Unfortunately, when such keepsakes are combined with strong emotions such as anger, envy or spite, they can become a potent means of psychic attack. In my own family, my mother kept lengths of hair from most of the female family members going back for generations, a sinister practice given that they all walked almost entirely on the dark side.

Even if we don't make a gift of our hair in a golden locket, someone can easily pluck a hair or two from our clothing and use it in a psychic attack. In the ancient *Greek Magical Papyri* there are many spells that use hair, nail clippings and even threads pulled from clothes. There is no need to be paranoid about this, but if we are forced to have close contact with someone who wishes us harm, we should brush our clothes carefully to ensure that no one can pick a hair from our back or shoulders, and keep our hair brushes and laundry in a safe place. Also we should be careful not to wear someone else's unwashed clothes, such as things we buy second hand; conversely, if we donate our own clothes or sell them on, these should also be washed first.

If we must deal with psychic vampires regularly, try and protect our solar plexus, which lies between the breast bone and the navel and is the site of many nerve endings in the body. Any sort of blow to this area - psychic or physical - can be excruciatingly painful.

The best way to protect our solar plexus is to spread out our fingers as though we are just resting them on our abdomen. This is fine when we are sitting down, but it does make us look rather anxious if we are standing up! Nevertheless, it's a very effective method of shielding ourselves from attack if we have not yet perfected a psychic shield.

We should also avoid slouching when sitting anywhere near a psychic vampire; instead keep our elbows tucked against our sides, and our knees and ankles together. This protects the genital area which was often targeted in psychic attacks in order to cause infertility and other reproductive and sexual problems.

Visibly protecting ourselves is very helpful if we are dealing with a deliberate attacker since it warns him that we know how to defend ourselves. If the attack is unintentional, then psychic protection will prevent them draining our energy.

On a practical level, we should do everything – no matter how small it seems – to stay fit and well, no matter what our current state of health happens to be. Drink plenty of water, since psychic attacks often dehydrate us, which is probably why a traditional protection against the Evil Eye is to spit on the victim; it's basically a way of replacing moisture. In India, kohl and kajal are worn not only to protect against the Evil Eye but also to prevent the wearer from hexing a third party.

Psychic attacks tend to be more common in the dark winter months, when our Aura is already weakened due to lack of sunlight (which is actually good for the Aura.) In the UK we rarely seem to get enough sunshine, and by the time spring comes around again, many people have low levels of Vitamin D, which is also known as the sunshine vitamin. This lack causes fatigue, aches and pains, so the addition of a psychic attack will drain us physically, emotionally and mentally even more; a course of Vitamin D can therefore be an excellent tonic for a range of psychic and physical problems.

Other practical measures we can take are to eat well, keep alcohol to a minimum and ensure we get a good night's sleep. It's also important to keep those places where we are at our most vulnerable, such as the bathroom and bedroom, as clean and tidy as possible. Wash bedclothes whenever we have experienced any sort of night-time attack in case anything lingers. If this isn't always practicable, for instance, in winter when it's difficult to dry bedding, don't despair. Simply spritz the bedclothes with a spray made of distilled water to which a few drops of good quality lavender essential oil have been added. Remember to spritz gently though; the purpose is to *cleanse* the bed, not drench it!

Psychic Attacks and the Seasons

People react differently to the strong energies generated as the seasons appear to change gear. Some become more aggressive while others become more sensitive. At the Equinoxes some people become very unsettled because the seasons seem to be 'rocking', as though they're teetering on the crest of a wave before toppling forwards. It's easy to mistake this sensation for the buzz we sometimes get just before a psychic attack and it's another good reason for keeping written notes that include time, date and moon-phase, whenever we feel we might be under attack.

When we live by the seasons, we become more sensitive to the sudden 'jolt' at the major astronomical points in the calendar, i.e. the Winter and Summer Solstices and the Spring and Autumn Equinoxes. The Solstices can be particularly challenging, especially if they happen to coincide with a full or dark moon. Subconsciously we seem to pick up on the combination of the solstice energy and the final quarter of the moon phase. When these two great energies collide it can be very unsettling. These are the most common combinations we may encounter:

- A full moon at the time of the summer solstice can produce so much energy that the air is fairly crackling!

- A dark moon on the summer solstice seems to attract hexing.

- A full moon at the winter equinox is normally benign and pleasant.

- A dark moon, or one in the final stages of waning at the winter equinox can drain our energies.

It's worth keeping notes about this, at least until we've discovered a pattern for ourselves. We may also notice strange phenomena around the festivals of Beltane and Samhain, i.e. the 1st May and the 1st November. This is because is the psychic veil thins out at this time of year (I like to think of it as Other Worlds touching ours).

As a result, we are more likely to notice the sort of phenomena usually associated with haunting: footsteps, shadowy figures and in our house, the clocks all go a bit mad! My home is usually very 'active' in a psychic sense all year round, but especially around the time of these festivals. Personally, I tend to just let it pass, knowing that it's a seasonal thing. If it really bothers us or if it persists, then carry out some simple cleansing rituals. There is no point trying to banish something caused by nature!

Amulets

Since ancient times, amulets have been one of the most popular defences against psychic attack. They come in all shapes, styles and sizes and are often confused with talismans, although sometimes the dividing line between them is very narrow. One definition is that an amulet prevents bad luck, whereas a talisman brings good luck. Also amulets (from the Latin *amuletum),* are usually worn, carried or possessed, suggesting the word originated from the Arabic *hamala* meaning 'to carry.' However, it may also come from the Greek word *apotelesma* which means the influence of heavenly bodies in the universe.

Whereas amulets are usually engraved on stone, metal or some other hard substance, talismen can also be inscribed on paper, parchment or even leather etc., under the appropriate astrological conditions with the intention of influencing a special event for the benefit of a single individual or group. If we look at some of the most common examples, examining their shape, meaning, the types of material used and even common inscriptions, we can see there are patterns that will enable anyone to find something appropriate for their own protection.

To understand how amulets work we need to understand the nature of the Evil Eye. Some societies believe it is hereditary, passing down the generations. It can also be involuntary, causing great distress to those afflicted with it. Another name for the Evil Eye is 'overlooking'; the 'first look' was considered the most dangerous, and some people were said to be able to kill trees with their first glance of the morning! An amulet therefore worked by distracting the hexer's attention so he forgot his original intention.

Some amulets, fashioned into the shape of an eye, were designed to convince the hexer that someone else with the Evil Eye was staring back at them. Such amulets are sometimes collectively referred to as 'eye idols' although a few have specific names, such as the ancient Egyptian Eye of Horus and the Eye of Ra.

In Syria, people used flat, round blue discs, about a centimetre across with an eye painted on it. These were pierced so they could be hung around the neck, especially to protect young children although they were used in many ways and sometimes even hung on trees. Whereas we use the term Blue-Eyed Boy to denote a favourite, in the late 19th century, Syrians believed anyone with blue eyes possessed the Evil Eye![178] In Turkey, large blue glass eyes are now popular in jewellery or as souvenirs although the original use of the Blue Eye was almost certainly protective.

Amulets that repel the Evil Eye are usually made into jewellery or key fobs, although they can turn up in unexpected places. I have seen a few on horse brasses, where the metal surrounds a central ceramic 'eye' disc. This is usually blue, but sometimes can be red or red and blue, both protective colours. In some Mediterranean countries eye amulets are painted onto fishing boats.

Many ancient amulets were sexual in appearance. The magical thinking behind this was that a phallus for example, would protect by distracting the Evil Eye. Sometimes the penis was displayed on its own, either erect or flaccid, but some examples show it with wings and even with an added bull's head, complete with horns. Phallic amulets, such as were found in excavations at Pompeii and Herculaneum, were still being used in Italy in the 19th century.

[178] Burne (1902): 202

In northern Europe, the rune sign Laguz ᛚ was popular because it was the first letter of the word *laukuz* which meant a leek, a contemporary euphemism for penis. This rune often appears in ancient inscriptions where its function is generally thought to have been protective. If we feel an affinity with northern traditions, then we can make a runic amulet by scratching or engraving Laguz onto any hard surface such as wood, bone, horn or metal. It can then be worn as a pendant on a leather cord or carried in the pocket.

The rune Tyr or Tiwaz ᛏ was another popular protective rune, often found on weapons. It is a useful amulet not only when we feel under psychic attack, but at any time when we feel the heaviness of other people's hostility weighing against us.

Amulets were often worn as jewellery, especially necklaces and pendants, and there is evidence in prehistoric graves and burials that fossils were also worn as amulets. However, even if we are taken unawares by the Evil Eye, we can always make an appropriate hand gesture against it. The most common are the *manofica* and the *mano cornuta*. Their distinctive shapes were also incorporated into amulets and worn in various countries around the Mediterranean. Since England and parts of Wales were part of the Roman Empire for several centuries, we must assume such gestures would have been known here too.

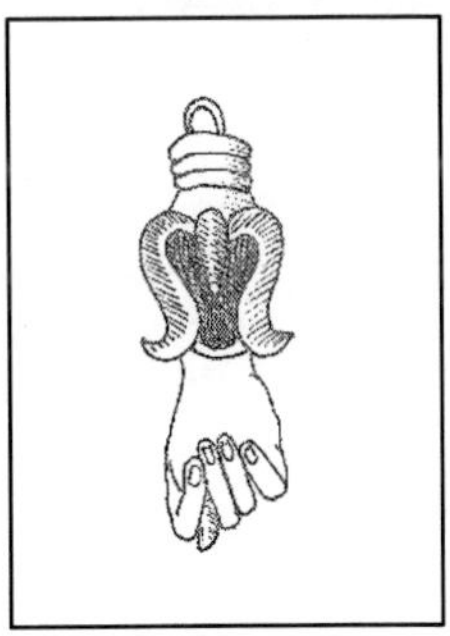

The hand gesture known as *manofica* (*See image on left*) is probably sexual in origin, with the hand made into a fist and the thumb poking out between the first and second fingers to represent the act of having sex.

Fica was not only the word for fig, a fruit associated with fertility and the female sexual organs but was also the Italian word for the vulva. Although it is often worn on its own, it is sometimes combined in amulets with an erect phallus and horns. (*See image above right*).

The horned hand amulet, or *mano cornuta* is known as early as Etruscan times and was traditionally supposed to repel the Evil Eye. However, I have also seen it used to cast the Evil Eye as well and perhaps originally represented invoking the power of the sacred bull. As an amulet it is usually worn around the neck as a pendant. Sometimes it is confused with deaf sign language for 'I love you.'

The difference between the two gestures is that for the *mano cornuta* the thumb is tucked in, lying on top of the second and third fingers, whereas in the sign, 'I love you' the thumb extends outwards.

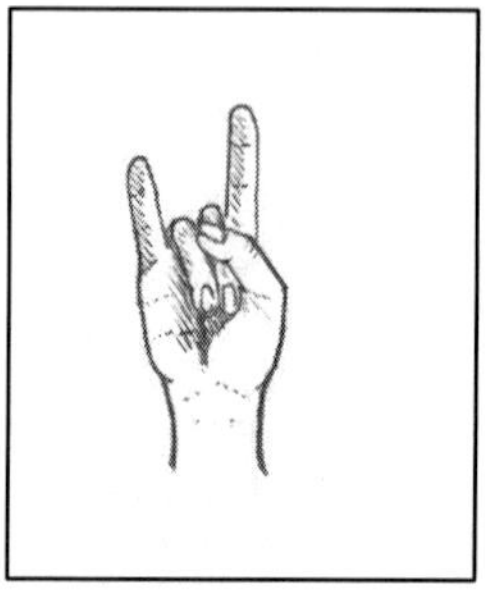

Mano cornuta

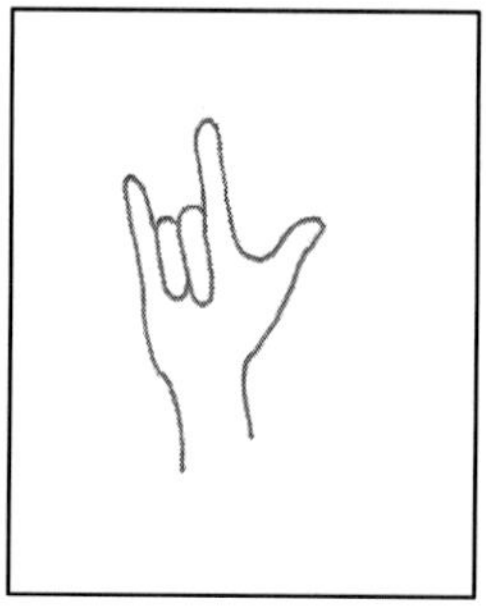

'I love you'

Amulets shaped like hands are also be combined with snakes and some show a hand grasping a serpent. Although serpents are often associated with Hecate, they were also closely associated with healing gods such as Asclepius, so possibly this type of amulet was also used to combat ill health, and not just protect against psychic attacks.

Some of the most popular horned amulets symbolised the horns of the crescent moon, sacred to the goddess Diana in Rome, Artemis in Greece, and Isis in Egypt. It was highly valued as an amulet in childbirth and may be associated with babies because the crescent moon is, quite literally, new born. Occasionally the crescent moon appears in the sky with the shadow of the full moon behind it; this is called '*the new moon in the old moon's arms.*' Its shape is also echoed in other protective symbols such as the horseshoe and the lunar crescents found on old horse brasses.

As jewellery, crescent and horn-shaped amulets are usually made into pendants of silver, coral, horn, pearl, shell, brass and even gold. Pendants were sometimes also made to resemble the full moon although these were usually worn as good luck charms whereas the crescent moon was worn for protection. Sometimes full moon pendants were decorated with a face, rather like the Man in the Moon.

Another popular horned amulet is the horseshoe. A real horseshoe was especially powerful since it was made of iron, a protective metal in its own right. Iron-bearing meteorites were regarded as a gift from the gods and were an important early source of iron. Modern horseshoes are made of steel, which contains iron.

In ancient times, horses were often dedicated to the moon and thought to be under its special protection since their hooves left crescent shaped footprints. Even a hair from a horse's tail was regarded as a powerful charm against the Evil Eye and as late as World War I, people would tie the hair of the white stallion into a reef knot around the little finger of a baby's left-hand (which was known as the 'heart finger'.)[179]

Horse brasses were originally intended to protect not only the horse but also the land and crops, both of which were valuable and therefore potential targets for *maleficium.* Although antique brasses can be expensive, modern replicas can be bought quite cheaply and often turn up in charity shops; they are still quite suitable as protective amulets.

Many of the most traditional horse brass designs: hearts, crescent moons, flowers etc., can serve as protective amulets, so can brass bells, which again can be bought quite cheaply in charity shops. Often old horse brasses had tiny bells attached to them; this is a tradition dating back to the chariot races in ancient Rome in order to protect both the horses and riders/drivers. A similar magical principle applies to cow bells and even church and chapel

---

179 Taylor (1933): 309

bells; all perform much the same sort of function, reflecting the old belief that demons and evil spirits fear the sound of metal.

Although polishing brass can be tedious (not to mention messy!) remember that horse brasses work better when highly polished since they were intended to catch the sun as the horse walked. One of the most effective brasses is a 'terret,' a small round brass disc worn on top of the horse's head. It swings back and forth as he walks and on sunny days flashed in the sunlight to dazzle the Evil Eye.

The most reflective surface of course, is a mirror although they were rare right up to the eighteenth century and were very much the preserve of the well-to-do. Yet over a relatively short period of time a whole range of superstitions grew up about them. When I was young, children were told not to look at themselves too long in the mirror in case the Devil looked back or looked over their shoulder. Another popular tradition was to turn a mirror to face the wall whenever someone had died in order to prevent their soul from being trapped and haunting the house.

I suspect these two traditions are linked to early beliefs that souls could separate from a living body and be viewed as a reflection. So long as the vessel containing the reflection, e.g. a bowl of water, mirror or piece of polished metal - remained intact, the soul was safe, but if it broke then death would follow. The real danger in looking at one's reflection therefore was not that one would encounter the Devil, but that the soul risked becoming trapped and unable to rejoin its body.

My own family, who pursued a tradition of hexing almost to the exclusion of everything else, took elaborate precautions with mirrors in order to minimise any fallout from their magical work. I counted the mirrors in the house once and as mentioned earlier in this book, there were over sixty. I couldn't move without glimpsing myself out of the corner of my eye. There I'd be, walking along the hall minding my own business, and suddenly I'd see the reflection of my back bounced off one of these mirrors. I didn't need eyes in the back of my head; the mirrors did that for me! Whenever I asked why there were so many, my mother would just say 'For dressmaking,' which didn't really explain very much, especially why some were placed in areas where I would have needed to be a contortionist to see my own reflection.

The real explanation of course was that the jumble of mirrors was intended to not only deflect incoming hexes from their targets but also confuse anyone attempting to track my family's own psychic attacks. In sending out a spell, the caster always sends something of her Self, which is why magic can weaken us. The hexer is therefore at her most vulnerable just after casting a spell, particularly if it rebounds quickly, as would have happened to any unsuspecting spell arriving at my mother's home. Likewise, by 'bouncing' a hex as part of the casting process, the hexer can confuse any victim trying to trace the source of an attack.

In psychic self defence, most mirrors reflect only in a single direction. A Witch Ball on the other hand, is spherical (like a giant Christmas tree decoration) and is useful for deflecting the Evil Eye when we don't know exactly where it's coming from. The earliest Witch Balls that have survived in the UK date from the early 19th century (although there are earlier examples from glass blowing centres such as Venice) and they were usually set up in the hallway or near the front door. These shiny globes come in various colours, but especially yellow and silver; some are up to twelve inches (thirty centimetres) in diameter. Although old Witch Balls are not suitable for outdoor use, modern shiny globes (sometimes called spirit balls) can be placed in the garden and serve the same magical purpose.

Some amulets are confined to local areas and families. Near Loch Rannoch in Scotland, people used pieces of silver (sometimes coins) to discover whether someone had been hexed. Local people would go out between sunset and dawn in order to draw water from a stream that crossed a public road on the route to the local cemetery.

The magical significance here was that the stream was regularly crossed by both the living and the dead. The water was collected in a jar, taken home and the piece of silver or magic stone was then added. Next the water was poured over the person or animal who was believed to be hexed, while saying '*In the name of the Father, Son and Holy Ghost*'. If the patient had indeed been 'overlooked' then the piece of silver would always remain stuck to the bottom of the jar. Some families owned magic stones which they used instead of a silver piece.[180]

Although plants make good protective amulets, once picked many wildflowers wilt and die quickly. One way around this problem is to make a copy of the plant in some long-lasting material such as metal. Pliny the Elder stated that the herb Rue (also known as the Herb of Grace) protected against various diseases, attacks on fertility and during childbirth. It was often made up into an amulet called a *cimaruta* which translates as Sprig of Rue and was a popular amulet to protect children. (*See image below left*). It has several branches with charms hanging from each, including the key, the crescent moon, a flower, a cock and a heart which symbolised *Diana Virgo*. Occasionally the symbol of the *manofica* is added too. The most powerful *cimaruta* amulets were made in silver, a metal sacred to the goddess Diana.

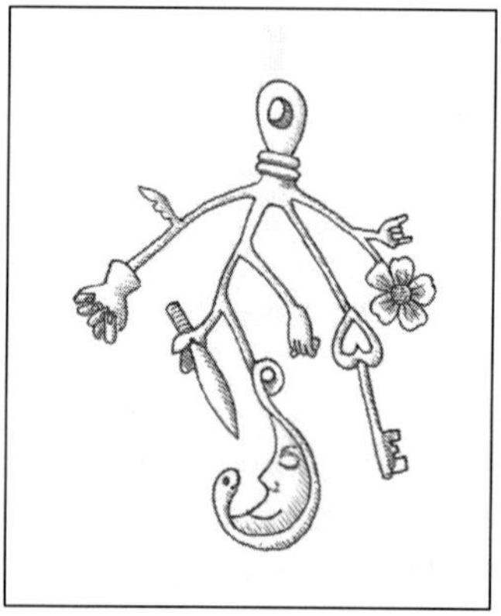

Although we associate the symbolism of keys with St Peter nowadays, in ancient times they were also associated with the goddess Diana and worn as protective amulets. This was because the goddess used keys to open the gates of the sky at dusk so that the moon could travel across the heavens before Diana locked the gates again at dawn.

Garlic is a powerful protective plant with long lasting corms although its pungent smell is unlikely to win it many friends outside the kitchen! With its bright, papery white skin it can be a very effective addition to a protective kitchen wreath.

Chillis are also protective and are unusual in that a copy made in other material, even plastic, is regarded as just as magically powerful as the vegetable itself. Its power lies in its horn shape and

---

180 Debenham (1897): 92

bright red colour. Other protective herbs that can be used in kitchen wreaths include bay, thyme, or rosemary. Finish the wreath by tying bows of red or blue ribbons. Alternatively, thread blue beads on red cords to produce a simple but effective amulet against the Evil Eye. In South America, red ribbons are a protective amulet in their own right, often tied around cribs, prams and cradles to keep the Evil Eye away from babies.

Perhaps one of the strangest (and most ancient) methods of magical protection is to pretend to change gender. This is usually done by dressing a potential victim in clothes of the opposite sex. For example, if a family has had all daughters and then at last a son, they might fear he would be targeted by the Evil Eye and would therefore dress him as a girl for the first few years of his life.

The magical thinking here was that if the daughters had survived infancy then perhaps it was their clothing that protected them. Although it is often claimed that the reasoning behind this was that it somehow tricked the Devil (who was said to have a fondness for small boys), girls were sometimes dressed as boys for much the same reason. In some countries, both young boys and girls were dressed up as Franciscan Friars to protect them from the Evil Eye during the first few years of childhood.

Crystals and Stones

The protective use of stones and gems or *lithotherapy* has always been particularly popular in Britain. Pliny the Elder[181] claimed that the Celtic provinces of Britain were knowledgeable about magic and it was they who taught the art to the Persians. Gems were used to gain favour, protected against fire and lightning, made people invisible, protected against poison and enabled the bearer to find treasure and love. Wherever it originated, *lithotherapy* was taken up and reinterpreted by Christian scholars during the Middle Ages and the Renaissance.

Crystals and various types of found objects can be used as amulets and were often incorporated into pieces of jewellery. The

181 Pliny the Elder, *Natural History* xxx.i

ancient Greek physician Dioscorides wrote a *Materia Medica* and Book V lists over 200 'stones' that were used for medicinal purposes. However, in ancient texts these names are sometimes misleading; for example, 'sapphire' often meant lapis lazuli.

Stones used in the pagan classical era remained in use well into the Middle Ages and even later. Inventories of jewels that belonged to rulers such as Charles V, a fourteenth century King of France, referred to ancient examples of engraved magical cameo and intaglio jewels. (Cameos are carved so that the subject is raised above the main surface, while intaglios are incised deep into the gem.)

The habit of engraving gemstones and jewellery continued well into the Christian era, and while some are obviously religious others are more ambiguous. One of the most popular inscriptions was AGLA, which is probably an acronym for the Hebrew *Atha Gebri Leilan Adonai* meaning '*Thou art mighty forever O Lord.*' A mediaeval Italian ring in the British Museum (number 866) incorporates the AGLA inscription thus:

+AGLA + AD///OS +VDROS + IDR¦OS + TEBAL + GVT +
G////////

while on the inside of the same ring the following is engraved:

TEBAL + GVT + GVTA//////

Sometimes pieces of jewellery are inscribed with AGLA on the one side and the words JASPAR, MELCHYSAR, BAPTIZAR on the other. These were traditionally thought to be the names of the three Magi or Kings who visited the infant Jesus although the Bible does not specifically name them. The names seem to have come from an Eastern Mithraic (i.e. pagan) tradition and are sometimes written as JASPER BALTAZAR ALTRAPA instead.

Another popular protective inscription that uses a form of these names is:

jasper • melchior • baltasar • in god is ar

The last word *ar* is generally taken to mean 'our trust'. Although I know some pagans find any reference to the Christian God very difficult to incorporate into their spirituality, if we look closely at the inscription, we will see that there is nothing here that directly links it to Christianity (or any other major religion).

The names do not appear in biblical texts and are only linked to the nativity story by legends. As for the line, *'in god is ar'* it is all lower case, whereas Christians always wrote God with a capital letter. The god in question could therefore easily be the god worshipped by the Three Kings – i.e. an Eastern deity, such as Mithras. And as I mentioned earlier, engraved pagan jewels were still being used well into the Christian era. This may even be an attempt to disguise a magical inscription as an acceptably pious sentiment. It's surprising how often these ambiguities occur!

For example in her book *Magical Jewels,* the author Joan Evans[182] mentions an Elizabethan jadeite pendant inscribed 'THE RIGHT ELATROP.' At first sight this is meaningless, although apparently it was supposed to mean, '*the speciall stone to staunche blooding & good against poyson.*'

Look a little closer, however, and bearing in mind that the Elizabethans (and their predecessors) were very fond of puzzles. 'The Right' may simply mean to read from right to left, instead of the usual left to right. Try it. That strange word 'Elatrop' now becomes 'Portale' meaning a doorway or entrance. Possibly the stone gave the wearer access to magical practices.

There are a number of ancient magical words that could be incorporated into any modern amulet. For example, in his famous treatise on hermetic and talismanic magic, the ancient author Kyranides stressed the mystical powers of the peacock's cry, written as Φ, AIΩ and also by the letters MAMENAKAA.[183]

Nowadays we usually think of the word *abracadabra* as something that belongs in children's fairy tales. It is a pity it has become so debased, since for thousands of years it was used to protect against sickness caused by magic, and was usually written

---

[182] Evans (2004): 175

[183] *Ibid:* 19

in an inverted triangle, beginning with *abracadabra* and with each successive line reducing, letter by letter to a single 'A'.

Although coral is often worn as jewellery, it is not a proper gemstone. Possibly because of its beautiful red colour, it was believed to protect against the Evil Eye, poison, lightning, defeat in battle and especially against spells intended to cause infertility. One of the most popular inscriptions was:

nomen noctilucae, hoc est Hecates signum aut Gurgonis personam[184]

Since this seems rather a lot to write on a piece of coral, I suspect the words were inscribed in the air above the stone using a fingertip. Another method might be to lightly draw the letters slightly above the surface of the coral, one above the other, without actually leaving a mark. This would enable quite long and complex dedications to be written on relatively small gemstones. The inscription would also be invisible.

Coral was also used in amulets to protect babies and was often hung on their cots. Old-fashioned teethers and rattles were sometimes made of coral and included metal bells. Shaking them in front of the infant was believed to distract the hexer so that any ill wishing would be harmlessly deflected. Adults also hung coral on their bed when they believed they were under psychic attack at night. Pieces of coral placed in a garden were believed to protect plants, especially vines since they could be badly damaged by storms.

Although the original use of most jewellery and gemstones was almost certainly protective (the same is true of perfume), some of the most powerful stones were not in fact gems at all but 'found' objects such as the Toad Stone or Crapaudine Stone. Shakespeare refers to it in his play, *As You Like it,* (Act 2, Scene I) '*...Which like the toad, ugly and venomous, wears yet a precious jewel in his head.*'

The earth toad or *saccos* was believed to have poisonous breath, but was also said to a carry magic stone in the marrow of its head.

---

[184] *Ibid:* 22

An ancient Alexandrian magical treatise promised: '*The earth toad... whose breath is poisonous, has a stone in the marrow of its head. If you take it when the moon is waning... you will have a powerful amulet.*'[185]

When I was young, we had a toad in our greenhouse and one of my uncles was so convinced that this creature had a magic stone in its head, he actually stole it while we were on holiday! Luckily for the toad, my uncle was kind-hearted and didn't kill it in order to acquire the toad stone. Instead he kept it in his own greenhouse believing it would bring him luck and help his tomatoes grow better. Actually, not all Toad Stones actually came from toads; sometimes a tooth from the palate of a freshwater fish would be substituted instead.

Like toads, serpents were also thought to carry a stone in their heads. The Snake Stone or *piedra dela sirpiente* was probably a type of serpentine, usually deep red in colour. What marked it out was the presence of a white spot that was said to grow larger and shine as the stone was heated. If it was placed next to a lamp that had recently been snuffed out but whose wick was still glowing, it was believed that the Snake Stone would relight it. In ancient Egypt, serpentine was a popular stone for scarab amulets.

Most of the magical stones named after animals and birds had no connection with the creatures. For example, the Eagle Stone or *aetites* was probably a piece of limonite with a loose pebble or piece of debris inside that rattled. These were sometimes also called Clapper Stones and although they were very plain, were so highly prized that they were often given ornate and expensive settings. They were considered particularly useful in protecting fertility and women in childbirth.

One stone that did come from an animal was the Swallow Stone or *piedra dela golondrina* which was removed from the stomach of the first cock born in the new year under a crescent moon. It was believed there would always be two stones, one white, the other green, and together they protected against witchcraft and hexing. To obtain the maximum benefit they had to be worn together in a

[185] Evans (2004): 19

bag of deer or calf skin and hung around the neck on a red silk thread.[186]

Pearls formed inside an oyster were traditionally worn both as aphrodisiacs and amulets to protect the wearer's health and safety when travelling and for general protection against the Evil Eye. In some countries they were even believed to protect divers against shark attacks! Like seashells, they were associated with female sexuality and fertility and were often worn as jewellery, especially when set in silver.

Amber is another popular defence against psychic attacks and the Evil Eye. If we rub a piece of amber on our hair or body we can 'charge' or magnetise it so it will pick up tiny pieces of tissue paper. Magically this makes it useful for attracting beneficial energies whenever we feel under threat.

Ammonites come in all shapes and sizes; some are small enough to be made up into pendants while others reach over two feet (sixty centimetres) in diameter. At one time they were believed to be fossilised snakes – another name for them was Adder Stones – and were sometimes carved with a snake's head at the widest, outer end in order to emphasise this. As an amulet, the ammonite brought general prosperity and protected its owner against night attacks and illnesses caused by hexing.

When I was young, I remember a large fossilised ammonite in a farm wall, some miles from where I lived. The farmer was always being offered money to part with it, but he refused, believing it brought good luck and prosperity to him, his family and his farm.

Of the more traditional precious stones, the diamond, clear, sparkling and incredibly hard, was considered impervious to all types of psychic attack, but particularly those caused by demons and the Nightmare. Christian treatises of the late Middle Ages and the Renaissance all regarded the diamond as a superb amulet. It later became a popular choice for engagement rings because it was believed to make a marriage happy, to protect it from ill wishing, and if things did go wrong it would bring about a reconciliation

---

[186] Holmes (1934): 562

between husband and wife. It was also said to protect against delusions, dreams and all kinds of madness. [187]

Men wore diamonds sometimes in order to be protected from poison, a very real threat to the rich and powerful even in Renaissance times, and also to protect him from the consequences of his own bad temper. Christian clerics recommended wearing them because they believed that diamonds, '*destroyeth lechery*'!

As we have already seen, sapphire was sometimes confused with lapis lazuli. Nowadays it is quite easy to identify gemstones by using chemical tests, but centuries ago accurate identification of gemstones was difficult. Sapphire was regarded as a very powerful amulet; it was approved by the Church who taught that Jesus called it holy, precious and described it as the '*geme of gemes*' although there is absolutely no Biblical basis for this belief.

At one time, all Bishops wore sapphire rings to symbolise heaven. Like the diamond, sapphires protected the wearer against poison and psychic attack, and promoted chastity. It could even break a prisoner's chains and set him free. Lapis lazuli, sometimes known as the Night Stone or the Stone of Truth was another popular choice for amulets that protected against charms intended to cause impotence and infertility.

The bright green emerald was worn to quell storms, ensure that one's lover remained faithful and repel all types of psychic attack. It also protected travellers and warded off snakes. Yet the Christian Church often associated it (along with the colour green in general) with the Devil. In Islamic countries, the emerald was highly prized and sometimes engraved with phrases from the Koran.

Chrysolite, another green stone, could repel all types of evil and psychic attacks, especially anything involving demons. It was also valued for conferring intelligence, competence and contentment and said to be particularly powerful when worn as a single bead on a silken thread. Topaz protected against illnesses caused by psychic attacks, although Christian clerics also recommended it for keeping '*a man from sinne & chaste*'.

---

187 Evans and Serjeantson (1933): 119ff

Amethysts were used for general protection (especially for sailors and drunkards!) and for dealing with attacks by animals, both real and psychic. The humble agate was always regarded as a powerful protector against the Night Mare, all types of night attacks and the Evil Eye. It was sometimes called the Fire Stone, or the Stone of the Wanderer since it protects travellers. According to the Romans, the most effective way to use agate as an amulet was to wear it in a ring.

Moonstone was both carried as an amulet and incorporated into apotropaic jewellery. It was especially popular with travellers because it ensured that the skies remained bright and clear so they could find their way by moonlight. Because of its association with the moon it was also effective in protecting against problems caused by menstruation, a characteristic it shared with the garnet. Garnets also preserved and protected fertility.

Many hexes in the ancient world were intended to prevent a couple from having children, which is why there are so many magical traditions associated with conception, pregnancy and childbirth. The name garnet probably derives from the Latin *granatum* which means pomegranate, a fruit that symbolised fertility. In Christian iconography, the Virgin Mary is often shown holding a pomegranate to symbolise fruitfulness. Garnets also prevent and protect against psychic attacks, especially the Night Mare.

Cornelian (sometimes also called carnelian) is another reddish coloured stone that was often carved into heart shaped amulets in Egypt. Its name comes from the Latin word for heart, *cor.* Like the emerald, in parts of the Middle East, cornelians were made into amulets inscribed with words from the Koran.

In ancient Egypt, the bloodstone with its tiny dark red flecks, was known as the Blood of Isis and was a popular amulet for women. In ancient Rome however, it was popular with men, especially gladiators and soldiers carried who bloodstones because they believed it prevented them from shedding blood if wounded. Since small spots of blood occasionally herald the presence of a psychic attack, we could place a small bloodstone in any area where these 'spots' appear, as a protective and preventative measure.

Lodestone was very much a physician's amulet, popular from the fifteenth century onwards. Its natural magnetic properties help it attract good health and beneficial influences. It could also attract iron, which was a powerful amuletic metal in its own right.

Tiger's Eye is a highly patterned stone that catches the light as its wearer moves. This makes it not only ideal for distracting the Evil Eye, but, since it is a beautiful and very attractive stone, it has always been popular for jewellery.

Sometimes a stone's magical properties are viewed differently with the passage of time. The brilliant green malachite for example, was a popular amulet for infants and usually hung above cradles where - like the Tiger's Eye - its swirling patterns distracted and repelled the Evil Eye. In the ancient world, particularly Egypt, malachite symbolised growth, regeneration, good health and eternal life. In some countries it was ground down to make eyeshadow which, like kohl and kajal, protected the wearer. By the Middle Ages however, malachite (along with anything else that was green) was believed to *attract* the Evil Eye. The same thing happened to onyx. Once a popular stone for amulets, by the Middle Ages it was claimed that anyone rash enough to wear onyx risked being assaulted by Demons and the Night Mare!

Topaz was always associated with sun deities such as Ra and Jupiter, probably because of its warm, glowing colour. The Roman Emperor Hadrian wore a talismanic ring set with a Topaz inscribed with the words :

NATURA DEFICIT FORTUNA MUTATUR DEUS OMNIA CERNIT

This roughly translates as, *'Nature decays, fortune changes, a god watches everything.'* In the Middle Ages, amulets against the Evil Eye often comprised a gold bracelet set with a topaz that had to be worn on the left arm.

The Ruby was regarded as one of the greatest of all gemstones and was especially popular during the Middle Ages and the

Renaissance. As an amulet it protected both humans and animals against poison, lightning, storms and any sort of curse or hex.

Clear crystal or quartz originally protected against hexes and the Evil Eye although by the Middle Ages it was said to restore virtue. Rose quartz was regarded as particularly effective against erotic curses, charms to cause infertility and can also help block the overwhelming sensation of sadness and despair that often accompanies a psychic attack.

My own childhood memories of quartz are that it has an innately magical quality. I remember when I was young, finding lots of small pieces of it in an old quarry, which I brought home and proceeded to play with in my garden. I left them outside and that night was a full moon; my mother called me to look out of the window and everything was shimmering as the quartz sparkled in the moonlight.

In Victorian times, jewellery made of jet was very popular and was made into mourning jewellery. Jet was also popular in the Middle Ages, when it was known as Black Amber and made into amulets to protect against witchcraft, demons, demonic possession and attacks by the Night Mare. In ancient times, jet from Whitby in England was considered so magically powerful that it was exported to Mesopotamia. Another black stone, obsidian, is often made into scrying mirrors and balls. It has the useful magical property of being able to absorb negative energy, making it an excellent amulet, especially against psychic vampires.

Protective Symbols

There are many symbols we can use for protection, incorporating them into our own home-made amulets. For example, we could use the cross, (which is not exclusively Christian as it pre-dates Christianity by centuries), the triskele, triquetra, pentacle, Three Hares, and a variety of Celtic patterns. To get the most from these, we must choose a symbol that has meaning for *us*.

For example, I once went through a period of using the triquetra and the triskele because to me they symbolised three specific people whom I wished to protect. Each arm of the figure therefore had a very precise meaning for me and it was a very suitable symbol to use at that time.

The six-pointed star within a circle, sometimes called the Seal of Solomon is another well-known amulet. Although often called the Star of David it is not a uniquely Jewish symbol and is found as far afield as India. The symbolism of the points varies according to tradition: in Christianity the three sides of the upper triangle represent the Father, Son and Holy Spirit, while in ancient Egypt they symbolised Osiris, Isis and Horus.

It's also important to remember that sometimes symbolic meanings change. For example, the swastika was once a popular good luck symbol in many different countries but nowadays, because of its association with Hitler and the Nazis, most people would hesitate to use it. Indeed, in some countries the swastika is banned (although in India it remains popular). Whether a few decades of being associated with evil can really wipe out millennia of being used for good is debatable, but the fact remains that it is now a very ambiguous symbol indeed and if we feel uneasy using something, then the chances are it will not work for us.

In ancient Egypt, many deities were portrayed carrying an ankh, which had strong religious and magical associations. It was also sometimes used to protect and enhance fertility or as a magical key. As Christianity replaced the ancient Egyptian religion, the ankh was adopted by the Coptic Christian Church as a specifically Egyptian type of cross, the *crux ansata.*

The scarab was one of the most popular ancient Egyptian amulets, often buried with the dead to ensure they enjoyed an afterlife. Although we think of them as primarily Egyptian, scarabs have been found in places as diverse as Syria and Spain suggesting they were highly valued and widely traded. They could be made of almost any material, including gold and silver, but were most commonly made of steatite (also known as soapstone).

Nowadays the fish amulet is usually regarded as a uniquely Christian symbol, and in early times it was used as a secret sign of recognition among Christians. It was also an acronym, since the Greek name for a fish was *ichthys,* each letter standing for: Ἰησοῦς

Χριστός, Θεοῦ Υἱός, Σωτήρ (*Iēsous Christos, Theou Yios, Sōtēr*) meaning 'Jesus Christ son of God Saviour.'

However, just like the cross, the fish symbol was much older than Christianity, and had already been widely adopted as a symbol of life and immortality by nearly all the religions in the Graeco-Roman world, including Judaism.[188] The ancient Mesopotamian god, Ea, god of water and wisdom was represented by a symbol made up of an ibex and a fish. In India, the fish symbolised the first incarnation of the god Vishnu, while the Buddhists believed it was one of their eight auspicious symbols. The Roman poet Ovid described how Venus once transformed herself into a fish, which thereafter were held sacred to her.

The shape of the fish symbol may have originally represented either the vulva or the womb. For pagans, a fish amulet could symbolise and honour various great mother goddesses. In fact, the tradition of eating fish on a Friday may have come about because the name for Friday in most European languages derives from the names of love and fertility goddesses including Freya, Frigg, Venus (the Latin for Friday is *dies Veneris*) and Aphrodite (the ancient Greek for Friday was *hemera Aphrodite.)* It's interesting that Friday is the only day of the week named after a female deity.

Snakes have been used as protective amulets in many countries for thousands of years. I can remember the first time my father showed me a thin and papery snakeskin in a ditch at the edge of a field. It seems as amazing now as it did then to think that a creature could just grow a new skin and discard the old. No wonder people believed snakes could rejuvenate themselves and must therefore hold the secret of eternal life!

In the Graeco-Roman world, the serpent became the symbol of the god of medicine, Asclepius. Even today the caduceus, a staff with wings and a snake (sometimes two) is the symbol of the British Medical Association. In the Old Testament however, the serpent was a symbol of evil, featuring in the story of Adam and Eve in the Garden of Eden and this theme was enthusiastically condemned by Christianity. Snake amulets are good all-round

---

[188] Fingesten (1963): 394

protectors, and especially useful if we believe our health is suffering as a result of psychic attack.

Years ago, many people swore by the power of a lucky rabbit's foot or a lucky grouse claw. Like the fish symbol, rabbits represented fertility. I remember the first time I was sent to buy a rabbit from the butcher, being asked whether I would like the 'Lucky Foot'; he was quite offended when I refused. Nowadays the only rabbit's foot amulets we are likely to come across are in antique shops where they sometimes turn up set in silver.

In Wales, it was traditional to brush the foreheads of new born babies with a rabbit's foot. This was a type of baptism that offered the child a long and lucky life, and afterwards the rabbit's foot was placed in the baby's cradle or hung above it. Once a rabbit's foot was adopted as a chosen amulet it was important to look after it properly since losing it was considered very unlucky.

Usually the Lucky Foot was carried rather than worn, while smaller amulets such as teeth and claws were usually worn either as pendants or brooches. The magical thinking was that these carried some of the animal's power, strength, fertility or even cunning to the wearer. These are all characteristics that can strengthen us against a psychic attack. The most powerful tooth and claw amulets are undoubtedly real ones; however, they are sometimes crafted in precious metals such as gold and silver.

When I was young, I remember my mother and aunts wearing brooches made of grouse claws set with amber and topaz (both powerful stones in psychic self defence.) These brooches were jealously guarded and nobody else was allowed to handle them.

Many of us might not think of the wishbone as an amulet even though they 'pull the wishbone' for good luck at the end of the meal where poultry has been eaten especially at Christmas or Yule. It's probably where the saying '*Lucky Break*' originates.

Although usually regarded as just a bit of fun, the more serious minded would not pull the wishbone straight after the meal but would keep it for a few days so that it could dry out; this made it brittle and therefore easier to break. However sometimes people kept a wishbone and hung it up with the two arms facing upwards, very much like the horseshoe and other horned amulets. Rings are sometimes shaped like wishbones and these are thought to bring the wearer good luck and protection.

In many countries around the Mediterranean, figures of owls are sometimes used as amulets. In ancient Greece, the bird was sacred to Athena, goddess of wisdom, and often appeared on Athenian coins. In ancient Rome however, the owl was regarded as a bird of ill omen and by Christian times was associated with witchcraft and the Devil. As an amulet, the owl symbolises watchfulness and knowledge. Unlike other birds, it hunts in darkness, making it a useful protector when we are under attack but do not know the identity of the culprit.

Frog amulets were popular in ancient Egypt and were usually made of gold, blue faience or steatite. Their main function was to protect against magically induced impotence or fertility problems. In Roman times, frog amulets protected the house and its occupants, and were closely associated with the goddess Venus because it was thought that frogs – like the goddess – were born out of foam.

Some Romans wore frog amulets to protect themselves against erotic curses that tried to steal their lovers away. Frogs were also associated with the Roman goddess Diana and depicted in amulets alongside a crescent moon. This association may be due to the fact that Diana was not only a lunar goddess but also presided over pools, streams and water.

In Christian times, the frog was sometimes said to represent resurrection because of the way it transforms first from the frog spawn and then from the tadpole. During the Middle Ages a frog's dried-up body was sometimes worn in a small silk bag around the neck as a protection against fits.

Spiders were also used in many forms of magical healing and the wearing of spider amulets, either shown alone or on their web was believed to protect against any curses that targeted wealth or possessions. This may be connected to the idea that a small spider – the so-called money spider – brings wealth, a belief widespread from England as far as Polynesia and the United States.

By Shakespeare's time however, most people believed that all spiders were venomous which may be why they are still so feared.

Even so, it was said to be unlucky to kill them, since this would bring bad luck and bad weather and there was a saying when I was young, '*If you wish to live and thrive, let the spider run alive.*' A spider on its web - either real or as an amulet - can 'trap' psychic attacks sent in the form of terrifying dreams. It works on very much the same principle as a Native American dream catcher.

Protective Plants

In the ancient world, vervain was considered a supremely magical herb. The Druids insisted that whenever it was dug up, it was a piece of honeycomb should be placed on the spot to atone for taking it. Its protective powers were widespread and well known. In France and Greece it was considered a holy herb, in Wales it was known as Devil's Bane while the Romans believed it protected against the Evil Eye.

Mistletoe has always been famed as a protective plant. Unlike other Christmas plants such as holly and ivy, mistletoe was not taken down at Twelfth Night but was left up in order to make use of its protective powers all year long, especially for homes and stables. People would dry and save its berries and leaves for years, keeping them in a specially made box (rather like a snuff box) in their pockets. However, if Mistletoe was used against the Night Mare it was important to place the plant *away* from whatever needed protecting.

The four-leafed clover has always been a popular plant amulet and was highly prized when I was young. My friends and I would spend ages looking for them, and when found we preserved them by placing between the pages of a book, which was also thought to preserve the luck and protection they brought. Often confused with clover, the shamrock is another powerful protective plant. Although usually associated with Ireland, it was also known in ancient India and its name may derive from the Arabic word *shamrakh*, an emblem of the triple lunar goddess of the pre-Islamic Arabs. Among the Celts it was thought that the three leaves represented the triple mother goddesses which may explain why St Patrick Christianised it by using it to teach about the Trinity.

Alternatively, we can rely on the power of the written word as an amulet in its own right. The *Ephesia Grammata* (also known as The Ephesian Letters) were six words that were often used in the magic of the Graeco-Roman world. These are usually written as follows:

- *Askion* (darkness)
- *Kataskion* (light)
- *Lix* (also light)
- *Tetrax* (year)
- *Damnameneus* (sun – although he may also have been one of the helpers of Hephaistos, the Greek blacksmith deity)
- *Aisia* (true voice). The first and last words are sometimes written as *Askion* and *Aision* respectively

They can also be written thus:

ΑΣΚΙΟΝ ΚΑΤΑΣΚΙΟΝ ΛΙΞ ΤΕΤΡΑΞ ΔΑΜΝΑΜΕΝΕΥΣ ΑΙΣΙΟΝ (or **ΑΙΣΙΑ)**

The Ephesian letters were always written in the same order, before being sewn into small bags that people wore or carried for protection and good luck. They were also sometimes used in curses.

Corn Dollies make good protective items for the home and were made from lengths of straw taken from the last sheaf of the harvest which was believed to contain the Corn Spirit. To ensure a good crop the following year, farmers made a small mother goddess figure out of the final sheaf, brought it into their homes and looked after it till the following spring.

By now we are in possession of a wide selection of the techniques needed to prevent and stop a psychic attack. Remember though that knowing is not the same as doing. We can have all the occult knowledge in the world yet go to pieces when a real psychic attack comes our way. Conversely, we can have only the most basic knowledge and yet stand up to some of the very worst attacks.

Years ago, I remember my mother-in-law banishing a psychic attack that had been sent by a particularly spiteful member of my family. Although not a witch by any means, my mother-in-law was brought up in a generation that understood about the Evil Eye and knew exactly what to do. She just rolled up her sleeves, cast salt on the open fire in the living room, along with an old shoe and some very impressive mutterings.

The terrible atmosphere evaporated at once. All was calm again. The attacker, realising that she could not intimidate her, became considerably more respectful after that.

My mother-in-law, bless her, took it all in her stride. *'It's simple,'* she said, *'You just have to know what to do, do it, and get on with things afterwards.'* If ever the art of psychic self defence needed a practical motto, then I think that's it.

Know. Do. And get on with things afterwards.

Bibliography

Classical texts referred to in this book:

Aeschylus The Choephori
Apuleius *The Golden Ass*
Herodotus *The Histories*
Horace *Epistles*
Josephus *Antiquities*
Pliny the Elder *Natural History, Volume 7*
Paracelsus *Supreme Mysteries*
Orphei Lithica accedit Damigeron de Lapidibus recensuit, Eugenius Abel (1881) Berolini, S. Calvary et socios

Newspapers and Magazines

Annual Register, [25 January 1791]

Athenian Oracle [1728], p292-3.

Brighton and Hove Gazette [20 December 1958]

Brighton and Hove Herald [20 December 1958]

Evening News [18 December 1958];

Life Magazine [10th February 1941]

The Lincoln and Hull Chronicle [4 May 1810]

Journals:

Adler, S. R., (1991) Sudden Unexpected Nocturnal Death Syndrome among Hmong Immigrants: Examining the Role of the

"Nightmare," *The Journal of American Folklore,* Vol. 104, No. 411 (Winter), pp. 54-71

Anonymous, (1884) The Folk-Lore of Drayton. Part III. Witchcraft and Other Things Preternatural-Astrology, &c. (Continued), *The Folk-Lore Journal,* Vol. 2, No. 12 (Dec.), pp. 357-369

Anonymous, (1909) A Modern Instance of Evil-Eye, *The Celtic Review,* Vol. 5, No. 20 (Apr.), pp. 343-344

Anonymous, (1949) Poltergeist, *Western Folklore,* Vol. 8, No. 4 (Oct.), p. 377

Barber, P., (1987) Forensic Pathology and the European Vampire, *Journal of Folklore Research,* Vol. 24, No. 1 (Jan. - Apr.), pp. 1-32

Berry, V., (1968) Neapolitan Charms against the Evil Eye, *Folklore,* Vol. 79, No. 4 (Winter), pp. 250-256

Betty, S., (2005) The Growing Evidence for "Demonic Possession": what should psychiatry's response be? *Journal of Religion and Health,* Vol. 44, No. 1 (Spring), pp. 13-30

Bonner, C., (1946) Magical Amulets, *The Harvard Theological Review,* Vol. 39, No. 1 (Jan.), pp. 25-54

Bonser, W., (1926) Magical Practices against Elves, *Folklore,* Vol. 37, No. 4 (Dec. 31), pp. 350-363

Bower, B., (2005) Night of the Crusher, *Science News,* Vol. 168, No. 2 (Jul. 9), pp. 27-29

Brown, N. O., (1973) XV. Kal. Mart. (February 15). Lupercalia, *New Literary History,* Vol. 4, No. 3, Ideology and Literature (Spring, 1973), pp. 541- 556

Burne, C. S., (1902) Charm against the Evil Eye, *Folklore,* Vol. 13, No. 2 (Jun. 24, 1902), p. 202

Crooke, W., (1913) Simulated Change of Sex to Baffle the Evil Eye, *Folklore,* Vol. 24, No. 3 (Sep.), p. 385

Davies, O., (2003) The Nightmare Experience, Sleep Paralysis, and Witchcraft Accusations, *Folklore,* Vol. 114, No. 2 (Aug.), pp. 181-203

Debenham, M. H., (1897) Charm for the Evil Eye, *Folklore,* Vol. 8, No. 1 (Mar.) p. 92

De Blécourt, W., (2003) Bedding the Nightmare: Somatic Experience and Narrative Meaning in Dutch and Flemish Legend Texts, *Folklore,* Vol. 114, No. 2 (Aug.), pp. 227-245

Dölger, F. J., (1929) Der Stempel mit dem Pentagram und ΥΓΕΙΑ im historischen Museum zu Basel kein heidnischer oder christlicher Weihbrotstempel sondern der Stempel eines antiken Arztes, *Antike und Christentum, Kultur- und religionsgschichtliche Studien,* 1:51-53

Ducie, The Earl of, (1888) Exhibition of Three "Mare-Stanes," or "Hag-Stones," *The Journal of the Anthropological Institute of Great Britain and Ireland,* Vol. 17, pp. 134-137

Durham, M.E., (1933) Whence Comes the Dread of Ghosts and Evil Spirits? *Folklore,* Vol. 44, No. 2 (Jun.), pp. 151-175

Elliott, R.W.V., (1957) Runes, Yews, and Magic, *Speculum,* vol. 32, pp. 250 ff.

Ellis, B., (1993) The Highgate Cemetery Vampire Hunt: The Anglo-American Connection in Satanic Cult Lore, *Folklore,* Vol. 104, No. 1/2, pp. 13-39

Elworthy, F.T., (1903) On Perforated Stone Amulets, *Man,* Vol. 3 (1903), pp. 17-20

Evans, G., (1892) Exorcism in Wales, *Folklore,* Vol. 3, No. 2 (Jun.) pp. 274-277

Faraone, C. A., (1993) The Wheel, the Whip and Other Implements of Torture: Erotic Magic in Pindar's Pythian 4.213 -19, *The Classical Journal,* Vol. 89, No. 1 (Oct. - Nov.) pp. 1-19

Faraone, C.A., (1996) Taking the "Nestor's Cup Inscription" Seriously: Erotic Magic and Conditional Curses in the Earliest Inscribed Hexameters, *Classical Antiquity,* Vol. 15, No. 1 (Apr.) pp. 77-112

Fingesten, P., (1963) The Six-Fold Law of Symbolism, *The Journal of Aesthetics and Art Criticism,* Vol. 21, No. 4 (Summer) pp. 387- 397

Gay, D.E., (1988) Anglo-Saxon Metrical Charm 3 against a Dwarf: A Charm against Witch-Riding?, *Folklore,* Vol. 99, No. 2, pp. 174-177

Greehy, J.J., (1978) Theology Forum: The Cursing Psalms, *The Furrow,* Vol. 29, No. 3 (Mar.) pp. 170-174

Hand, W.D., (1968) 'Passing Through': Folk Medical Magic and Symbolism, *Proceedings of the American Philosophical Society,* Vol. 112, No. 6 (Dec. 9) pp. 379-402

Hansen, A.J.D., (1977) Shakespeare and the Lore of Precious Stones, *College Literature,* Vol. 4, No. 3, Shakespeare Issue (Fall) pp. 210-219

Hocart, A.M., (1938) The Mechanism of the Evil Eye, *Folklore,* Vol. 49, No. 2 (Jun.) pp. 156-157

Holmes, U. T., (1934) Mediaeval Gem Stones, *Speculum,* Vol. 9, No. 2, (Apr.) pp. 195-204

Jentoft-Nilsen, M., (1980) A Lead Curse Tablet, *The J. Paul Getty Museum Journal,* Vol. 8, pp. 199-201

Jones, E., (1974) [1932] Beliefs concerning the nightmare, in *Psycho-myth, psycho-history,* in E. Jones, 110-13, New York, Hillstone

Kallendorf, H., (2005) The Rhetoric of Exorcism, *Rhetorica,* Vol. 23, No. 3 (Summer) pp. 209-237

Kittredge, G.L., (1885) Arm-Pitting among the Greeks, *The American Journal of Philology,* Vol. 6, No. 2, pp. 151-169

Lawson, J.C., (1926) ΠΕΡΙ ΑΛΙΒΑΝΤΩΝ. Part I, *The Classical Review,* Vol. 40, No. 2 (May), pp. 52-58

MacKenzie, D.A., (1922) Colour Symbolism, *Folklore,* Vol. 33, No. 2 (Jun. 30) pp. 136-169

Myres, J.L., (1905) The Evil Eye and the Camera, *Man,* Vol. 5, p. 12

Nunemaker, H.J., (1932) An Additional Chapter on Magic in Mediaeval Spanish Literature, *Speculum,* Vol. 7, No. 4, (Oct.) pp. 556-564

Oates, C., (2003) Cheese Gives You Nightmares: Old Hags and Heartburn, *Folklore,* Vol. 114, No. 2 (Aug.), pp. 205-225

Puhvel, M., (1965) The Legend of the Devil-Haunted Card Players in Northern Europe *Folklore,* Vol. 76, No. 1 (Spring) pp. 33-38

Scott, C.P., (1895) The Devil and His Imps: An Etymological Inquisition, *Transactions of the American Philological Association* (1869-1896), Vol. 26, pp. 79-146

Senn, H., (1982) Romanian Werewolves: Seasons, Ritual, Cycles, *Folklore,* Vol. 93, No. 2, pp. 206-215

Spier, J., (1993) Medieval Byzantine Magical Amulets and Their Tradition, *Journal of the Warburg and Courtauld Institutes,* Vol. 56, pp. 25-62

Spoer, A.M., (1926) Simulated Change of Sex to Baffle the Evil Eye, *Folklore,* Vol. 37, No. 3 (Sep. 30), p. 304

Stetson, G.R., (1896) The Animistic Vampire in New England, *American Anthropologist,* Vol. 9, No. 1 (Jan.), pp. 1-13

Stewart, C., (2002) Erotic Dreams and Nightmares from Antiquity to the Present, *The Journal of the Royal Anthropological Institute,* Vol. 8, No. 2 (Jun.), pp. 279 -309

Taylor, M.P., (1933) Evil Eye, *Folklore,* Vol. 44, No. 3 (Sep.), pp. 308-309

Tobin, J. J., Friedman, J., (1983) Spirits, Shamans, and Nightmare Death: Survivor Stress in a Hmong Refugee, *American Journal of Orthopsychiatry* 53 :439-448.

Wiseman, T.P., (1995) The God of the Lupercal, *The Journal of Roman Studies,* Vol. 85, pp. 1-22

BOOKS

Baring-Gould, S., *The Book of Werewolves,* Causeway Books, New York reprint edition, 1973

Bond, J., *An Essay on the Incubus, or Night Mare,* D. Wilson and T. Durham, London, 1753

Briggs, K.M., (1978) *The Vanishing People: a study of traditional fairy beliefs,* London, B T Batsford Ltd.

Briggs, R., (1998) *Witches and Neighbours,* Penguin Books

Davies, O. (1999) *A People Bewitched: Witchcraft and Magic in Nineteenth-Century Somerset*, Bruton: private printing

De Cleene, M; Lejeune, M. C., (2003) *Compendium of Symbolic and Ritual Plants in Europe,* Ghent, Man and Culture Publishers, Vols 1 and 2

Devereux, P., (1990) *Places of Power: Secret Energies at Ancient Sites: A Guide to Observed or Measured Phenomena: Secret Energies at Ancient Sites - A Guide to Observed or Measured Phenomena,* Blandford Press

Dyer, T., (1892) *Church-Lore gleanings,* London, A.D.Innes & Co. can also be read online at:
http://www.archive.org/stream/churchloregleani00dyerrich/churchloregleani00dyerrich_djvu.txt

Evans, J., (2004 edition) *Magical Jewels of the Middle Ages and the Renaissance Particularly in England,* Kessinger Publishing Company

Evans, J., Serjeantson, M., (1933) *English Medieval Lapidaries,* London: Oxford

Evans-Wentz, W.Y. (2004 edition) *Fairy Faith in Celtic Countries,* New Page Books

Ewen, C. L'Estrange (1933) *Witchcraft and Demonianism,* London: Heath Cranton

Fortune, D., (1970) *Psychic Self Defence,* The Aquarian Press

Graves, R., (1981) *The White Goddess,* London, Faber and Faber

Howie, M. O., (1989) *The Cat in Magic Mythology and Religion,* London, Rider and Company

Hufford, D.J., (1982) *The Terror that comes in the night: an experience centred study of supernatural assault traditions,* Philadelphia, University of Pennsylvania Press

Kiessling, N., (1977) *The Incubus in English Literature: Provenance and Progeny,* Washington State University Press

King James VI (Scotland) I (England), (1591) *Daemonologie,* Edinburgh

Levi, E., (1976 edition) *Transcendental Magic: its doctrine and ritual,* Mokelumne Hill

Luck, G., (2006 second edition) *Arcana Mundi,* The Johns Hopkins University Press

Lupton, T., (1579) *Thomas Lupton's A Thousand Notable things of Sunday sortes,* London, John Charlewood

Mees, B., (2009) *Celtic Curses,* Boydell Press

Ogden, D., (2009) *Magic, Witchcraft and ghosts in the Greek and Roman World,* Oxford University Press

Oldridge, D., (2000) *The Devil in Early Modern England,* Stroud: Sutton Publishing

Organista, P.B., Chun, K., Marin, G., (Eds), (1978) *Readings in Ethnic Psychology,* Routledge

Pollington, S., (2000) *Leechcraft: Early English Charms, Plantlore and Healing,* Anglo Saxon Books

Ritson, Joseph, (1831) *Fairy Tales,* London

Ross, C., (1995) *Satanic Ritual Abuse,* University of Toronto Press

Russell, L. M., (1996) *Dictionary of Feminist Theologies,* Lewisville, Kentucky Westminster John Knox Press

Scot, R., (1972 reprint of 1665 edition) *Discoverie of Witchcraft,* Dover Publications

Seligman, K., (1997) *The history of Magic: a Catalogue of Sorcery, Witchcraft and the Occult,* QPBC

Simpson, J., (1979) *Icelandic Folktales and Legends,* Berkeley

Stanley, J., (1988), Gods, Ghosts, and Possession. In Zelliot, E. Berntsen, M. (eds), *The Experience of Hinduism: Essays on Religion in Maharashtra,* Albany: SUNY Press, pp 26-59

Turner, S., (1840) *The History of the Anglo Saxons,* Volume 1, Paris, Baudry's European Library

Voss, A., (2006) *Marsilio Ficino,* Berkeley, North Atlantic Books

Wickland, C.A., (2008 edition) *Thirty Years Among the Dead,* Mokelumne Hill

Websites and Online Texts

Voltaire, *The Works of Voltaire, Vol. VII (Philosophical Dictionary Part 5)* [1764 can be read online at the online Library of Liberty: http://oll.libertyfund.org/index.php?option=com_staticxt&staticfile=show.php%3Ftitle=1660&layout=html (accessed April 2019)

http://www.abc.net.au/science/news/health/HealthRepublish_535895.htm

http://www.ama.com.au/node/5233, accessed 25th June 2010

http://www.bbc.co.uk/nature/species/European_Hare

http://www.dailymail.co.uk/news/worldnews/article-1257119/Catholic-sex-abuse-scandals-evidence-Devil-Vatican-says-Popes-chief-exorcist.html

http://www.independent.co.uk/life-style/firsthand-i-dont-spend-all-my-time-with-poltergeists-casting-out-demons-and-laying-ghosts-to-rest-is-routine-for-dominic-walker-church-of-england-vicar-and-exorcist-1445788.html

http://www.denniswheatley.info/denniswheatley.htm

http://www.sacred-texts.com/alc/emerald.htm for the online text of the Emerald Tablet of Hermes Trismegistus

http://www.sacred-texts.com/goth/vc/vc00.htm for the online text of Psychic Vampire Codex, a Manual of Magick and Energy Work by Michael A Belanger (2000) Sanguinarium Press

https://www.onlinerocksalt.co.uk/knowledge-base/salt-basics/what-is-rock-salt

https://geology.com/minerals/hematite.shtml

INDEX